Fascism and Democracy
in the Human Mind

Fascism and Democracy in the Human Mind

A Bridge between Mind and Society

I. W. Charny

University of Nebraska Press
Lincoln and London

Sources of previously published materials are credited
in the acknowledgments section, which constitutes
an extension of the copyright page. Typeset in Adobe
Minion by Kim Essman. Book design by R. Eckersley.
Printed and bound by Thomson-Shore, Inc.
⊗
Library of Congress Cataloging-in-Publication Data
Charny, Israel W.
Fascism and democracy in the human mind : a bridge
between mind and society / I. W. Charny.   p. cm.
Includes bibliographical references and index.
ISBN-13: 978-0-8032-1550-4 (hardcover: alk. paper)
ISBN-10: 0-8032-1550-9 (hardcover : alk. paper)
1. Fascism – Psychological aspects. 2. Democracy –
Psychological aspects. 3. Social psychology.
I. Title.
JC481.C465 2006 150.19'8—DC22
2005029660

To:
Judy (Always and Forever!)
and
Zachary
Yuval
Tal
Ori
Roni
Tamar
and all the dear ones who will come after them

Contents

Preface

The values we are seeking to define and perpetuate are values of democracy, freedom, and respect for the law and human life.—New York's Mayor Rudolph Giuliani, speaking after the terrorist destruction of New York's World Trade Center Twin Towers and part of the Pentagon, on September 11, 2001

This book is a statement of hope for a democratic way of life, beginning in our minds and extending to our relationships and to our societies.

It is also a sane radical statement about how people get crazy and upset and lose relationships in everyday life, and how people destroy life in societies, in both cases deriving from similar faulty fascist-type thinking.

This fresh message of a bridge between mind and society renews an earlier century's excitement and hope for understanding the human mind more than ever before and also for gaining some greater mastery over fascism and totalitarianism in the traditions of earlier works such as by Erich Fromm, Hannah Arendt, and Rollo May.

For people from all walks of life who care about democracy, and for mental health professionals and others who continue to have high hopes for psychotherapy, it introduces a novel conception of mental illness – and health – and a new direction for treatment. A fuller detailed technical presentation of diagnosis and therapy will be presented in a forthcoming book, *Fascist mind versus democratic mind in treatment of emotional disorders, breakdowns in relationships, and disorders of evil.*

For sociology, political science, and international relations audiences, the book offers a probing of the nature and manifestations of societal evil through the prism of the mind of the perpetrators – and the widespread potential for evil in so many of us in our human species.

For religious, spiritual, and philosophy audiences, it builds a renewed call to the sacredness of life, which is coupled with practical techniques for real-life implementation of this philosophy of life in one's own daily way of being and dialogues with one's family and other people in one's work life, community, and society.

It is very exciting to me to see whether I can make this exercise work. If I succeed, it will mean that I will have contributed a new bridge between concepts of phenomena of fascism and totalitarianism in society and the oppression and destruction that these same ways of using mind wreak on the life process inside of us as individual human beings.

Beyond actual treatment of mental conditions and relationship problems, and long before we get to the massive tragedies of societal terrorism and genocide, this book is about the everyday opportunities for life that we enjoy and the ways in which we can use our minds to live out better the gift of our life opportunities.

I believe that civilization on earth is moving rapidly toward a definitive crossroad at which humankind may rise to a stature never before reached of declaring genocidal murder of all sorts as evil and illegal. I believe humankind may rise to the challenge of setting up an effective international machinery for stopping terrorism, massacres, ethnic cleansing, and genocide and for prosecuting perpetrators of these horrible crimes under earthwide laws. Otherwise our human species could be heading toward destroying itself. For all the brilliant fragment of history we have enjoyed in the ineffable mystery of the creation of life, in the infinity of the galaxies in which we in our civilization are only a very tiny speck, life apparently will not miss us; it is we who will miss our lives.

Altogether, this is a book for people who love, treasure, and honor life for themselves, their loved ones, their people, and all peoples. It is a book for those whose commonsense understanding is that life should be made to be as safe, healthy, productive, and spiritually meaningful as possible for everyone on this planet.

This book is not for obsessively fiddle-faddle intellectuals who are unable to use commonsense understanding that the lives of all people are sacred and instead get hung up on endless definitional battles in their respective professions as to which mass murders are and are not to be condemned in human history.

The book is certainly not for explicit fascists, terrorists, or any people who commit serious harm to the lives of other human beings, nor is it for people who approve of or condone those who bring wanton death to others – even in the names of democracy or liberty, or say for purposes of medical research (see the infamous Tuskegee study of syphilis in the United States, or Japanese and Nazi medical experiments in the 1930s and 1940s).

Nor is this book for apologists for totalitarianism, such as those who would explain and condone a given totalitarian ideology because it arises, to some extent, in response to real social, economic, or political injustices.

Finally, this book will not be enjoyed by people who cannot bear taking a critical look at themselves to see the ways in which they, and indeed each of us, is engaging in at least some fascist ways of thinking and relating to other human beings.

The Case Histories in This Book

Throughout the book there are psychotherapy case histories and vignettes marked by 🍂 before the case, and the case description is set off in an extract in italics. Clinical illustrations or illustrations of emotional experiences and states that are not descriptions of specific treatment cases may also be set off as extracts in italics but are not preceded by 🍂.

Needless to say, there is no identifying information about the people in these cases.

The clinical illustrations presented have been purposely chosen also to include cases where the treatment was not helpful, or worse, had a bad outcome. I have always felt uncomfortable with as well as critical of a kind of hucksterism in many mental health books that present only testimonials to successes in psychotherapy. It ain't so – no matter what wonderful technique of therapy is used, and no matter how capable the therapist. I love psychotherapy and rejoice in the fact that we therapists help many, many people, but it is far from a cure-all, and there are regrettably many poor outcomes. Certainly this book, which is about not pandering to certainties and not suppressing disagreeable information, needs to project relatively authentic pictures of people and the outcomes of therapy. Besides, failed cases of therapy, like many of the mistakes we make in our own lives and the failures we all rack up, also are opportunities for much constructive learning.

Here is a first case history:

❧ *He is a tough teenager, bright, good looking, wiry, and strong, who continuously seeks to dominate his family and environment. There is a rumbling, threatening intensity to him as he bears down ominously on others with his requests, plans, and demands. Periodically he zeroes in on some demand and builds it into his current cause for an all-out war. On at least one such occasion, he drove himself into such a frenzy of conviction in his anger over not getting what he wanted from his parents that he lost control of himself and threatened quite seriously to commit suicide.*

He argues relentlessly and brilliantly with his therapist: "Let's say there are all these people who are against bin Laden, but do you agree that there are also people who are for him?" The therapist agrees.

The teenage boy continues: "Well, if these two people come to you as a therapist, are you going to try to convince them that they are wrong and that they should oppose bin Laden? No! You can't convince them what to believe in. You are only supposed to help them to do what they want to do."

He continues: "So what is it you want to make me believe and do? I don't want to come to see you. I don't want to be your clone where you say that therapy was successful only after I become a carbon copy of you."

The therapist replies: "I don't agree with you. The bin Laden supporter is wrong – and it's not maybe that he's wrong, but definitely so. The reason the bin Laden supporter is definitely wrong is that bin Laden is against innocent human life, and that's the one thing that is always wrong. Science, medicine, psychology, all learning, all business, for that matter all sports too are activities for living people to make life better. People who want to kill off life are criminals; they are crazy, bad, evil, whatever you want to call them that makes it clear that they are like a cancer you want to stop whenever possible."

The therapist then adds: "And the reason you are here is that along with being a hell of an interesting guy, and inside of you really a very sweet guy, the way you live is to push everybody around to get your way. You stop at nothing in your use of the power of your personality to get your way, you terrorize and drive people crazy with the pressures you put on them if they turn down what you want in any way, and you are scaring and exhausting the people who live with you. Your way is wrong, and that's why you are here for therapy.

"What do you say, Do you want to be like that?"

The youngster answers, "No!"

The therapist replies, "That's why I believe in you."

Acknowledgments

I want to thank very much the following colleagues for their warm support, encouragement, and various assistance:

DOUGLAS SPRENKLE, my colleague psychologist–family therapist and friend of many years, whose clinical and spiritual thinking about human beings and their intimate relationships has always spoken to me of a thoughtful, deep, and kind person and practitioner. I recognize Doug as a profound and authentic thinker, and had no question that if he disagreed with me or was critical of my thinking or writing, he would say so – and I in turn would listen respectfully.

HENRY THERIAULT, I dare to say wishfully my colleague philosopher (I was a philosophy minor in college!) and younger friend of recent years, whom I meet periodically in contexts of genocide studies, including our shared concerns with denials of known genocides such as denials of the Armenian Genocide.

ERIC MARKUSEN, in some ways my colleague in sociology (I was also a sociology minor in college!), and also my colleague in social work (after my having worked in social work settings including university schools of social work for many years), but most certainly one of my longest-term colleagues in genocide studies, including his serving as a member of the team of Associate Editors of the *Encyclopedia of genocide* that I edited. I also owe Eric a further thanks in that, notwithstanding his amazing schedule of professional travel far and wide across the globe and his responsibilities as research director of a pioneering Center for Holocaust and Genocide Studies in Oslo, he volunteered to help me with a page-by-page editing of an earlier draft of the manuscript.

ROBERT HITCHCOCK, a principled scholar devoted to human rights and the right to live of all peoples. I can't get together enough credentials to be a colleague with him in his being an anthropologist beyond the fact that all our social sciences are intrinsically close to one another. But in his case too, I can identify warmly with Bob as a colleague in our both also being genocide scholars (I remain forever grateful to him for an excellent conference on genocide studies he organized at the University of Nebraska in 1996).

To MARC I. SHERMAN, my close friend at home in Israel and assistant director of the Institute on the Holocaust and Genocide in Jerusalem and director of its Bibliographic and Information Services, I have many warm thanks for excellent bibliographic consultation, preparation of the index, and so much other meaningful assistance and encouragement in preparation of the manuscript.

Finally, with a special warmth, I also want to express my deepest appreciation to my capable secretary and office manager of many, many years, PAULINE COOPER, who helps me not only with her production skills, but as a very fine, thoughtful, crystal-clear and straightforward critic.

I also want to express my sincere appreciation to the following individuals and organizations for the permission they gave to quote from their publications:

The excerpts from Bridget Murray's *APA Monitor* article, "Teaching today's pupils to think more critically: Psychologists' techniques inspire students to look for a deeper understanding of the material they study" (March 1997, p. 51) was adapted for reprinting with the permission of the American Psychological Association. Copyright © 1997 by the American Psychological Association. Adapted with permission.

The Association for Humanistic Psychology gave permission to reprint the excerpt from John Rowan's article "Heresy hunting in the AHP" in the *AHP Newsletter* (April 1980), pp. 4–7.

Carmel Tapping, author, and Hugh and Maureen Crago, editors, gave permission to reprint excerpts from Tapping's review of Leonard K. Szmczak's 1996 Cuckoo forever more in the *Australia-New Zealand Journal of Family Therapy* (1996) 17(4), p. 240

Professor Henry Huttenbach, editor, *Genocide Forum*, gave permission to reprint an excerpt reprinted from an article written by him in 2000: Genocide and utopia: The quest for the perfect society. *Genocide Forum*, 8(4), 3–4.

Geoffrey Cowley and *Newsweek* magazine gave permission to reprint an excerpt from an article by him in 1997: Cowley, Geoffrey (1997). Viruses of the mind: How odd ideas survive, April 21.

The *New York Times* gave permission to reprint excerpts from an article written by Bob Herbert in 2002: In a culture of violence, every citizen suffers. *International Herald Tribune*, October 30, with attribution to original printing in the *New York Times*.

The Nuclear Age Peace Foundation gave permission to reprint excerpts from a booklet by Carl Sagan (1994). Nuclear war: The perspective of a planetary astronomer in the *Waging Peace Series* of the Nuclear Age Peace Foundation (Booklet 36).

Vivian M. Rosenberg, author, and Arthur B. Shostak, editor, gave permission to reprint excerpts from Rosenberg's "Utopian thought: Between dreams and disasters" in *Utopian thinking in sociology: Creating the good society (Syllabi and other instructional materials)* (pp. 8–12), Washington DC: American Sociological Association, 2001.

Doron Rosenblum gave permission to reprint an excerpt from his article "Who's sorry now? A scenario," which appeared in the *Haaretz English Edition*, July 1, 2002.

Donna Britt and the *Washington Post* Writers Group gave permission to reprint an excerpt from an article written by her in 1998: Britt, Donna (1998). "Young Monsters R Us," March 27. Reprinted as Britt, Donna (1998). "Want to raise kids from hell? Here's a how-to-primer." *International Herald Tribune*, April 1.

Parts of this book were previously published in *Back to basics: The Congress Papers of the Fifth International Congress of the F. M. Alexander Technique*, edited by Shmuel Nelken (Jerusalem: Shmuel Nelken, 1990), pp. 85–100.

Fascism and Democracy
in the Human Mind

Introduction

A New Bridge between Mind and Society

An Introductory Description of Fascism and Democracy in the Human Mind

Many years ago I decided in my role as a psychologist and psychotherapist that I would try to contribute my understanding of how our human mind works to the vital study of the Holocaust and genocide; that is, to see what psychology can contribute to our understanding of how everyday, ostensibly ordinary human beings turn into the rotten destroyers that many of us become. Now, after many years also as a genocide scholar, I am returning to my ongoing home field of psychology in the hope of contributing new understanding about the workings of the human mind based on what I have learned about our species from the study of genocide.

The larger theoretical frame and goal of this work is to explore the building of a new bridge in social science theory between concepts of collective structure and functioning in society and a theoretical model of the functioning of the individual mind.

Over the years I have come to the conclusion that our human mind, brilliant as it is, is so poorly evolved – such an early "software" version from the "manufacturer" – that it is basically organized around what I am calling a software program of *paradigms of fascist thinking*. Or, continuing in modern computer talk, that the "default" with which we go into the world – until some of us learn better and upgrade our software – causes us to think along the lines of a fascistlike absolutism: certainty, suppression of contrary information, and the exercise of violence toward those who differ or disagree with us, and even toward those parts of our own selves that do not conform to the rules we have made for ourselves.

In this book we are looking at two major ways of organizing our minds. I call the one a paradigm of a FASCIST MIND and the other a paradigm of a DEMOCRATIC MIND. Each of these ways of organizing our minds may be said to contain a large number of software programs for different areas of experience characterized by guiding principles we characterize as fascist characteristics of mind versus democratic characteristics of mind.

What Does the Study of Genocide Teach Us about Fascism and Democracy in the Human Mind?

I propose that the paradigms of FASCIST MIND and DEMOCRATIC MIND are not only political constructions but that the same kinds of psychological organizational structures that characterize fascism or totalitarianism in society – which lead to grave suffering, a breakdown of a decent society, and finally to widespread destruction of human life – are also at work in the construction of psychological or mental and relationship disorders of doing harm to oneself and disorders of doing harm to others. Here too fascist-type thinking leads to grave suffering, breakdowns of the normal organizational ego of individuals and their relationship systems, and to a shutting off of the opportunities for life. Just as democratic organization is the only hope-alternative to fascism in society, so too the workings of "democracy in the mind" present the healthy alternative for individuals managing their minds and their intimate relationships in mentally healthy ways.

Fascist programs tell you what to do with certainty, without questioning or alternative frames of reference; they punish you for not obeying; they instill in you a sense of superiority toward all those you consider inferior because they don't know or observe the one and only correct way to do things. They open the door to violence and then to denials of the very violence they have you wreak on anyone who doesn't obey, including yourself. FASCIST MIND compels the person, couple, or family to conform and obey the totalistic dictates of its ideology. Any deviation is treated as deserving of retaliatory punishment by unforgiving symptoms in the functioning of the self or of the interpersonal system. Such fascist paradigms will be seen at the center of many psychological problems, such as the inner rules that dictate major eating disorders; instances of self-hypnotic suicide processes; hedonistic insistence on "must have" pleasures such as continuous extramarital relationships; runaway escalating processes of hurt and revenge that culminate in marital separation and divorce; patterns of chronic anger and nastiness; flights from yielding to dependency or tenderness; obsessive-compulsive symptoms; chronic panic or anxiety reactions; or psychosomatic illnesses, including some unconscious decisions to die where the inner paradigmatic language is, "You are unable to perform as demanded, therefore you shall suffer as follows for your failure."

In contrast, the software of DEMOCRATIC MIND invites responsibility for choosing one's direction in life with an awareness that there are multiple possible directions from which to choose. It supports questioning and the testing of behaviors so to speak scientifically against their outcomes, accompanied by a readiness to change ideas as new information comes in. In the process, it encourages experiences of anxiety and humility, abhors superiority, and strives for a basic equality with other people even when one is in a leadership role. DEMOCRATIC MIND rejoices in one's existence and claims the inherent right to self-defense against dangers and extremes. But, along with protecting one's own life, it is always committed to deep respect for the rights of others to live and to rejoice in the quality of their lives.

Democratic thinking leaves one more uncertain and more aware of one's incompleteness and inability to solve all problems. It is anxiety provoking because it is known that one must often integrate contradictory ideas into a single policy and choose between imperfect possibilities. But because democratic thinking is sworn to protect the integrity of life and one's continuous opportunities to choose between competing ideas, it is ultimately safe for human life and generates a joy in being alive to choose and do.

DEMOCRATIC MIND software carefully enjoins violence as anti-sacred; but if one does end up nonetheless doing some kind of harm to others, it calls for acknowledging and accepting responsibility for having done this harm and ceasing to do it.

3

Although fascist thinking creates a certainty, and hence a sense of safety, security, and pleasure in having all loose ends tied down, slowly but surely its relentless quest for power and certainty destroys everything (life) that stands in its way, and eventually its own life as well. Fascism in the mind or in society is a nightmare of hell.

I prefer the democratic way.

In this vein, I view psychotherapy as an alternative "democratic mind-set" in which various aspects of humanness are encountered, processed, and integrated with one another to create a healthier flowing process that includes contradiction, complexity, and acceptance of natural ambivalences within one's mind and in intimate family relationships.

The Significance of a Bridge between Mind and Society

If the application of a paradigm of fascist thinking to explanations of everyday behaviors and human relationships holds up satisfactorily to the rigors of intellectual clarification and the scrutiny of clinical observations, we will have succeeded in bringing together in a new way two worlds that hitherto have largely remained split apart from each other: the realm of phenomena of the human mind and intimate relationships, and the realm of the social and political. If this thesis is true, then it opens an extraordinarily important door and builds an intellectual bridge between the study of mind and society.

These are, admittedly, the heady words of a large challenge, and I confess to a sense of wonderment. If successful, this theoretical bridge will strengthen the philosophic underpinnings for education for democracy on all levels of society. If successful, this application of societal-process concepts to the mental functioning of individuals will create a new, I believe deeply exciting, bridge between understanding the dynamics of repression and democratic freedom at the collective level of society, and the dynamics of repression and democratic freedom at the molecular level of individual mind.

It is deeply meaningful to me to dare hope for a breakthrough linkage in conceptualizing the conditions for fascist destruction and democratic health in both society and mind, thus taking us important steps forward toward a unity-of-science model of psychological process. From the point of view of a philosophy of science that posits a greater value or strength to models that are successfully applicable at different levels of experience, successfully applying concepts of fascism and democracy simultaneously to society and mind will strengthen the meaningfulness of the paradigmatic concepts at each of these levels and may shine persuasive new light on the importance of overcoming fascism with democratic processes in all human affairs.

Finally, I am also moved by the thought of making a possibly meaningful contribution to psychotherapeutic practice that can have practical consequences for increased prevention of psychopathology and for enriching peoples' everyday experiencing, thereby enabling them to lead healthier lives. I hope we can demonstrate that the same fascist thinking that destroys societies lies at the root of the ways in which people drive themselves to personal despair and dysfunction and also to damaging and destroying their primary intimate relationships.

In the long run, for me as a lifelong researcher of the destruction of masses of human lives in genocide, the fascist-democratic metaphor is part of a still larger paradigm humanity must develop that will provide a convincing psychoethical underpinning for the sanctity or right to protection of all human life against destruction.

If fascism on the societal level refers to the pursuit of certainty and absolutism; a totalistic definition of truths; escape from anxiety, complexity, and humility; demands for obedience, conformity, and oppression of contradictory information; posturing in claims of superiority accompanied by prejudice and intolerance for others; excessive power strivings and domination of others; violence and retaliation against dissent; and denial of doing harm to others, it is suggested that fascism on the level of managing one's own mind or one's personal relationships is also constructed of various of the same dynamics and principles. When people demand of themselves a given way of life – purity of thoughts, or clear-cut success, or expect-insist in a relationship (say with their children, that they be loving, honorable, and respectful) – and when the outcome that must be achieved is not, all manner of crushing mental health or relationship consequences ensue. *Life has failed the person, the person has failed life*. And in the fascist paradigm, there may follow renewed efforts at regaining absolute control, or remonstration, punishment, and rage – turned against the self, the other, or both.

The Epistemology of This Work

The fascist paradigm constitutes a mindset that is intrinsically available to all of us in the nature of the human mind. It is based on earlier or more childish forms of thinking, where right and wrong and truth and falsehood are neatly divided from each other. It is based on the mind's need for logic and consistency. It is also based on peoples' weakness in needing so much to be part of a confirmed social consensus or "to be in the right" – even when one has to decide in favor of a position that runs contrary to one's own senses and logic. An example is the classic Asch study in which actual participants agree to call the shorter of two lines longer, after they are set up by stooges in a group situation, all of whom say that the shorter line is the longer one![1]

I suggest that, ultimately, the fascist mindset thrives on our powerful anxieties of incompleteness, fears of not becoming what we can be, and dread of our mortality and limitations. We make certain that our way of life is the one and only right way in an effort to spare ontological dread of anxiety, limitation, and knowledge of one's finality.[2]

In contrast to a fascist or totalitarian mindset, a democratic paradigm of mind calls for, first of all, free speech or inner acceptance of the many different voices in one's own mind, including the lustful and the aggressive voices in us, and then follows up with a method of responsible "checks and balances" for processing emotions and thoughts toward ethical and realistic choices for how best to achieve one's real goals and to improve one's relationships with others. A democratic model of mind is an alternative to rigid, totalistic ways of demanding of oneself and one's environment obedience to absolute demands. Just as democratic organization is the only hope-alternative to fascism in society, so too a model of DEMOCRATIC MIND is the alternative to dark currents within a human being's inner self and interpersonal relationships. Thus the democratic use of mind accepts and even savors hostile impulses and fantasies toward

6

other people but does not succumb to acting out these impulses in actual violence. Democracy of the mind includes the freedom to experience anger, rage, and wishes of violence with full self-acceptance and even pleasure as a natural right of healthy personalities and as a first line of natural strength for self-defense to be mobilized and organized against emotional threats and attacks. The democratic mind treats impulses as mind desires, which are different from action plans. It processes impulses acceptingly along with an ability to make ethical and realistic differentiations between what we feel like doing or wish to imagine happening and what we shall actually do in our real-life behavior.

> *Want to kill so-and-so? Of course.*
> *The sonofabitch has been causing me endless grief*
> *(at home)(at work)(wherever).*
> *Go and kill so-and-so for real? Most certainly not!*

A democratic mindset not only protects one from doing coercive and violent harm to others, it also induces confidence and relaxation in oneself. The tolerant cathartic allowance of emotions and thoughts that well up in the heart releases people from many possible emotionally entrapped spaces, while the balanced interplay of emotions and thoughts allows each sphere of mind experience to correct and modify one another, so that one can head out to sound "policy" applications in how one conducts oneself in egalitarian, noncoercive relationships with other people.

DEMOCRATIC MIND rejoices in one's own existence and claims inherent rights for self defense against dangers and extremes but is always committed to deep respect for the rights of others to live and to rejoice in their lives along with our own.

In one's participation in the larger community, DEMOCRATIC MIND stands up for political democracy and tolerance of diversity and stands against totalitarianism and any use of violence except in self-defense.

It is my hope that this book will be in the tradition of pacesetting works like those of Erich Fromm on the escape from freedom and the capacity of the human mind for good and evil, Hannah Arendt on totalitarianism and the banality of evil, and Rollo May on the constructive meaning of anxiety along with the destructiveness of malignant power, all of which inspired me deeply years ago. [3] For me this work represents a continuation of the Jewish ethical traditions of respect for all human life, as well as my lifelong conviction and dream that science – in this case the psychological science of mind – has much to contribute to a more ethical way of life for human beings. I pray that this book will make a notable contribution to more peaceful minds both in the daily lives of individuals and in society.

On Straight Talk and Sense versus
Double Talk and Nonsense

I would like to reach those parts of the mind, even in intellectuals, that often are given over to serious falsehoods, such as reversing facts so that black and white (for example, victimizers and victims) are white and black; fact twisting; open deception and the fabrication of lies and untruths; the confusion of "some" and "all"; *post hoc* fallacious reasoning (if some Jews survived the Holocaust, then the Nazis did not intend to kill all Jews); obsessive defining, which kills the ability to see the essential larger picture; camouflaging; splitting off details from a larger pattern of information; distorting and implanting false counter-information and disinformation; cynical, self-serving, grandiose claiming of knowledge; competitive, rivalrous power seeking; saying anything that will advance one's status and seeking prominence or notoriety regardless of the consequences for truth and integrity; displaying obtuse, hard-to-understand, intellectual constructions in a manner that causes the subject matter to fade into obscurity; putting up smokescreens of sincerity and justice-seeking while intending to cover up unfairness, hate, celebrations of violence, dehumanization, and prejudice; self-serving realpolitiking; and for me (an incurable idealistic dreamer, says my wife lovingly), the ultimate betrayal of all knowledge – using one's knowledge and scientific skills to support totalitarian policies and megamilitary or destructive terrorist projects. [4]

Daily, callous murderous acts of terrorism spread across the planet. (No, for all that it is most personal for me, the Israeli-Palestinian conflict is not the "mother of all conflicts" in the world, and sometimes I even dare fantasize that by a strange quirk of history, peace will come to Israel and Palestine long before the broad panorama of conflicts between fundamentalist Muslims and other totalitarian governments and the West will be resolved.) I simply cannot stand it when intellectuals, sanctimoniously, can't call terrorism the pure evil that it is, or when they explain the legitimate political issues to which terrorists are responding as if these in any way justify murder of civilians.

At times it seems that an ethical malaise, or an inability to call things straight, threatens wide parts of our intellectual university. The new "postmodernism" that, while tapping a basic truth that much of any person's or culture's thinking is constructed through one's specific traditions of values and perceptual paradigms, has in too many cases declared all truth, facts, and values null and void. Again a totality is constructed out of a point of wisdom. One indeed should scrutinize all thinking and proposed conclusions for their sources of meaning and how and by whom they have been constructed, but one cannot live life as if there are no discernible facts. For example, the difference between whether a person is alive or dead is hardly a construction of reality, and whether a person was or was not put to death by a fascist killer is a too-real fact. There is a wonderful statement attributed to Galileo after his recantation in 1638:

> Having been admonished by the Holy Office entirely to abandon the false opinion that the Sun was the center of the universe and immovable, and that the Earth was not the center of the same and that it moved . . . I have been suspected of heresy, that is, of having held and believed that the Sun is the center of the universe and immovable, and that the Earth is not the center of the same, and that it does move. . . . I abjure with a sincere heart and unfeigned faith, I curse and detest the same errors and heresies, and generally all and every error and sect contrary to the Holy Catholic Church.
>
> *E pur si muove!* (But it does move!)[5]

Distinguished social psychologist M. Brewster Smith wrote about postmodernism in psychology:

The postmodern stance is one of radical relativism, rejecting the claims of science to a privileged perspective, rejecting the conception of truth as an approachable ideal . . . I am alarmed by the extent to which just such an extreme version of antiscientific relativism is gaining prominence at the margins of mainstream psychology.[6]

Another writer has linked postmodernism with self-deception:

At every level, the new orthodoxy is characterized by self-deception. It is aggressively egalitarian in theory but exists largely in the ivory tower. It claims political awareness but completely lacks political realism. It claims to have escaped from a "discourse" that traps the rest of us in traditional thought, yet nothing is more rigid and limiting than its own self-invented discourse.[7]

In short, I would like to find a way to decontaminate the fascist use of mind and succeed in influencing scholars to be committed to truth, respect for all life, and the protection of all human life.

PART ONE

The Choice between Fascism and Democracy in Everyday Life in the Individual Mind, the Family, and Society

CHAPTER ONE

What Is the Original "Mind Software" We Humans Receive at the "Factory"?

Fascism:

Fascis bundle. A governmental system . . . permitting no opposition or criticism.—*The American College Dictionary*, Random House, 1960

A system of government characterized by rigid one-body dictatorship, forcible suppression of opposition, private economic enterprise under centralized government control, belligerent nationalism, racism, and militarism, etc.—*Webster's New York Dictionary*, 1970

A political philosophy that exalts nation and often race above the individual and that stands for a centralized autocratic government headed by a dictatorial leader . . . and forcible suppression of opposition. —*Webster's New Collegiate Dictionary*, 1985

The Fascist Paradigm

By fascism, I mean a philosophy of totalities and perfection and a way of thinking in certainties and absolutes, powerful intolerance for any differences of ideas, demands for conformity to the certainties and often a cultivation of mindlessness or no thinking or questioning; taking a position of superiority over others who do not believe or cannot qualify for full membership in the fraternity of believers, and the cultivation of cults of power even among the believers; a readiness, in fact often a love for doing violence and harm to all who are defined as nonbelievers or enemies of the certainty; and in the end denials of having done any harm to life – one's own or others.

In this work, we look at fascism and democracy in society and at what I propose as corresponding programs or formats – "software packages" in the mind if you will – and how they define the experiences and behaviors of the individual as well as our interpersonal behavior styles and patterns in intimate relationships of marriage and family.

If this attempt to see FASCIST MIND and DEMOCRATIC MIND similarly at work in both societal and in individual and small-scale relationships is successful, we will have created a new, and I believe exciting and long-sought-for, bridge between mind and society.

In the course of presenting this material in many conversations, seminars, and professional meetings, I was told by a number of colleagues, especially younger ones for whom World War II, Hitler, and Nazism are "history," that to them fascism meant Mussolini's Italy and Hitler's Germany, or "political philosophies of the extreme right," but not, as I intend it, a generic term for a totalitarian ideology. When I asked these colleagues what other key word they might recommend I use in the title, some said instinctively "totalitarianism," and some said "fundamentalism," but then the overwhelming majority replied that I should use "fascism" after all. When I asked why, they said that, compared to other words, the word fascism retains a quality of the terror that the totalitarian state inspires, and that it is the word that will best convey the linkage and continuity between dreaded political-societal states and the dreaded conditions in the human mind that I intend to develop in this work. However, they also recommended that I make it entirely clear that I am referring to the generic phenomenon of any totalitarian or dictatorial orientation, without differentiating between the political right and left, which I am very glad to do.[1]

The Software of Our Mind

It is not common for us to think about ourselves as having chosen programs of thinking for our minds, what I am calling the "software of our mind." It seems to most of us that our minds are, first of all, just there as they have been given to us, at whatever quality level we were assigned by the "factory."

Most people have at least a dim sense that their minds are also being acted on and shaped by various environmental forces and societal identities, but these too seem for the most part familiar and the way life *must* be, because that's the way life *is* for us, through our parents, schools, churches, communities, society, governments, and so on.

As we get older, there also are many people who do begin to develop an intriguing sense of some relativity. We become aware, for example, that words are pronounced differently in different parts of our own country, or that customs of relating between people vary intriguingly between different regions of our own country (the nonverbal sign for hitchhiking in one place can be the insulting finger of another region!), let alone that people from entirely different countries and cultures really have considerably different conceptions of how life is to be led. For those who think further, it becomes clear that the "mind functions" and "organizing concepts" we take as a given really are a set of ideas and programs – a software program – much of which was transmitted to us by formative influences in our lives. *Our mind programs are not an immutable reality.*

How far and how deeply this learning goes varies enormously for different people. Some people are so touched intellectually and spiritually by the discovery that they set out to examine other kinds of programs for living. They attend other kinds of churches, literally and figuratively, including undergoing psychoanalysis or other forms of psychotherapy; study oriental philosophy and practices such as yoga or Zen; or they experiment with alternative social-political beliefs such as socialist and communist philosophies of the distribution of assets and resources. Much of humanity's literature, in effect, is a recording of endless possibilities of exploration and discovery of new modes of thinking and experiencing. There is a huge range of different ways of conceiving reality and of designing one's maps of the world that are available to any human being who will set out on a journey from the givens to which he or she was exposed in their original environments.

In the course of a profound spiritual experience, be it in psychotherapy, in response to a medical crisis, in the course of a religious process, or in response to a profound personal philosophical reorganization experience, a person can decide many things: to love more, to be more self-assertive, to allow for more anger in one's heart as a healthy release of responsive emotions to people and events who have been destructive, to reduce one's anger and hate and be more tolerant, to learn more about a subject, to practice a skill to a desired level, to care more for a given child, to let a child go more to his or her own destiny rather than keeping the child tied to oneself, to be kinder and more charitable to people in need, to develop into stronger and more capable leaders, to be more loyal associates and followers of one's leaders, and endless other choices for the software programs for our mind.

Final Solutions and Their Consequences

FASCIST MIND provides final solutions to life's anxieties. It prescribes a total solution to the problem(s) that people are facing and delivers the prescriptions with absolute certainty in their perfection and correctness.[2]

Generally, a fascist paradigm also invests the delivery of the solution with ritualistic meaning, fervor, and urgency, so that fulfilling the pre-scribed solution also takes on a kind of religious pageantry of having been loyal and dutiful, and makes one deserving of being rewarded.

Fascist ways of thinking demand absolute obedience and conformity to dictates; there is no pluralism and no choice. The right and correct way having been stated, it is an unquestioned responsibility to heed the fascist mandate in all respects and details. Fascist thinking also measures the effectiveness of fulfillment of the solution by an extreme and total standard.

By definition, these total, certain, priestly, and final solutions are supe-rior to anything that anyone else could possibly propose, so that identi-fication with such solutions in turn characterizes and endows those who accept the ultimate truth with qualities that make them superior to other people, and these others of course become inferior people, who do not see the way it is and must be.

As a fundamental part of its construction, the fascist paradigm also calls for the destruction or removal of inferior objects or sources and structures that contribute to the disgraceful and despised conditions of what is defined as inferior. Even if the fascist solution does not call di-rectly for destruction of whomever, the systemic consequences of taking a demanded solution all the way and imposing it on a field of events regardless of the contradictions or resistances encountered is likely to lead to violent actions and policies on behalf of the unquestioned truth and the greater good that it guarantees.[3]

In this book I propose to show how the fascist paradigm is a model for attempting to solve existential anxieties that trouble all human beings,[4] and that this paradigm is expressed not only in the familiar phenomena of fascism on a group-societal level but also in the construction of a variety of psychological dysfunctions or psychopathological conditions in the individual as well as family dysfunctions or disturbances.

The consequences of fascism on a societal level are sadly known to us from many frequent manifestations in history in life-shattering and destroying processes: wars of expansion in the name of one's ideology and glorified identity as the "intended" rulers of who-knows-how-much-of-the-world, the turning of the egalitarian sentiments of the French Revolution into a framework for an orgiastic bloodbath, the capping of the communist ethic in the USSR by the brutal murder of millions of people who were believed to stand in the way of the new justice, and of course in the height of cruel persecution and factory-systems of murder in the Holocaust.[5] *Washington Post* columnist, Richard Leiby observed:

> Tally the tens of millions of victims of Mao, Stalin and Hitler – ranked by some historians in that descending order on the scale of all-time evil – and you are left to wonder whether civilization has progressed at all since AD 1000, except in terms of its technologically advanced killing capacity.[6]

In our times, societal fascism appears in new forms of increasingly destructive international terrorism which, combined with certain traditional ethnic-religious identity strivings for power, carries with it the possibilities of major war for much of civilization.

Societal fascism is also known to us in smaller-scale patterns of oppression of freedom in the persecution of dissidents and nonbelievers, including throwbacks to a prehistory of civilization in primitive fundamentalist movements such as, for example, the Taliban in Afghanistan who blasted a monumental 2,000-year-old sculpture of Buddha out of existence because it was for them an "idol,"[7] and for years provided a safe haven for Osama bin Laden to hatch his ominous attacks against the

Western world, including the terrifying attacks against the World Trade Center in New York and the Pentagon in Washington DC on September 11, 2001.

After so many horrendous examples of death to so many people, it can sound trivial, but it is nonetheless relevant to note that fascism on a societal level is often also a "killjoy" that suppresses various levels of joy and pleasure in life along with, and as an extension of, the stringent rules it makes for peoples' minds. Writing ironically about "looking for a good time" in fundamentalist Teheran back at the height of Khomeini absolutism, *Wall Street Journal* correspondent Geraldine Brooks quoted Ayatollah Khomeini saying in 1979, "There is no fun in Islam."[8]

Societal fascism is abhorrent to many of us because on the surface fascism exacts a toll of human rights and human life. It is clear that this paradigm, or way of organizing human experience, brings cruel consequences for so many people in a society. However, it is not generally recognized that the same fascist paradigm is hard at work in the creation of any number of solutions, codes, and formulae that produce individual and family psychopathology or psychiatric or emotional disturbances.

In one of his earliest essays, Robert Jay Lifton described the damage to all human potential wrought by what he called "the psychology of totalism":

> Ideological totalism does great violence to the human potential: it evokes destructive emotions, produces intellectual and psychological constrictions, and deprives men of all that is most subtle and imaginative – under the false promise of eliminating these very imperfections and ambivalences which help to define the human condition. This combination of personal closure, self-destructiveness, and hostility toward outsiders leads to the dangerous group excesses so characteristic of psychological totalism in any form.[9]

The thesis that the fascist thinking familiar to us on a societal level is hard at work in the creation of individual and family emotional and mental disturbances opens an extraordinarily important door and intellectual bridge between the study of mind and society. The prevailing conception of mental health scholars and practitioners, including those who care very much about societal and political injustice and oppression, is that the knowledge we have been gaining about mind is certainly related to societal phenomena, but at best is far removed, based on analogies, and generally yields no more than metaphoric reminders of parallel phenomena that correspond somehow familiarly to organizational structures in society.

What I am now proposing is that there is a single sociobiological pattern of organizing thoughts, emotions, and experience that is a common source of many disorders of the individual psyche and also interactional disturbances in the interpersonal relationships of family units and at the same time serves as the conceptual and ideological base from which totalitarian forms of society develop and to which they appeal – inevitably gaining broad support in every society.

For those who accept the tenet of philosophy of science that, ultimately, there is a broadly unified pattern of organization of reality that applies to and encompasses different levels of existence – from subatomic particles to cell structure to whole organisms to social aggregates – the laying of new conceptual bridges between mind and society is meaningful and satisfying.

Similarly, for those of us who are concerned with fighting the age-old mass appeal of fascism everywhere, any contribution to greater understanding of man's horrible affinities for certainty, conformity, superiority, and violence will be helpful and welcome.

For students of psychopathology and psychotherapy, the conception that many states of emotional problems are conditions of "fascism in the mind" will suggest new ways of treatment that are "antifascist" in their nature. For those clinicians who love and find meaning in working with patients but also have wanted so much to be connected to "real-life" battles against the many ugly faces of totalitarianism that actually destroy human lives in the larger society, it will be satisfying to think of clinical work too as a battle against the fascist paradigm. This model also gives us a framework in which to explore further interconnections and possibilities of mutual enlightenment and facilitation between mental health and social and political issues.

Disconnection and Escape from Complexity,
Uncertainty, Anxiety, and Humility

Experienced mental health clinicians understand that the invoking of totality, certainty, and superiority means that a person is fleeing experiences of complexity, uncertainty, and anxiety. FASCIST MIND is, inherently, a crystallization of psychological defenses against fearful contradictions, tensions, and anxiety. It is another sense of what Erich Fromm called an "escape from freedom" in that a major price as well as privilege of real freedom is engagement of the limits and uncertainties of human security and knowledge. [10]

Societal organization around fascist ideas of totality and superiority are escapes from experiences of insecurity and anxiety on the scale of collective mass behavior. The political structures and processes invoked by fascist states become realities that capture and even hypnotize excitement and loyalty. Subterranean existential anxieties are banished by an orgy and pageantry of "perfect answers" to life's problems. There is ample evidence that in a fascist society both the leaders and the ardent adherents are immersed in feelings of megalomania, omnipotence, superiority, invincibility, and invulnerability.

> A nation seldom really finds out anything about Fascism until Fascism is in the saddle. Before that time the people see flags and colored shirts and storm troops and lusty scrambles with political enemies. What is behind all that is a myth. . . . The real features of the structure behind those tactical attitudes and temporary appearances are shrouded in mystic darkness. That makes the idol attractive. It is glittering and plastic, though apparently firm – and it is expedient. It is perfect for the leitmotif of Fascist policy: first power, then program. [11]

There develops in effect a collective madness of a false security and certainty. Fascist societies are collective escapes from being in our human condition, which by nature involves pain, loss, existential anxiety, awareness of vulnerability, and a spiritual pain of awe and reverence about both our finiteness and the infinite mystery of nature and life – of which we are such tiny parts.

In psychiatry's concern with the dramatic aspects of the manifest symptoms mental patients display (they *are* interesting!), and the management problems these symptoms create for the patient and for others whose lives are impacted by their distress and behavior, the patient's inner anxieties are often forgotten. Yet even in an age where psychopharmaceutical agents are used widely to overcome psychiatric symptoms as rapidly as possible, our best understanding of mental symptoms should remain that what the patients frequently are attempting to do through their symptoms is to flee their existential anxieties about life and death. The escapes that patients create through their mental illnesses, however discomforting, are intended in nature to hold back their suffering aspects of much more real anxieties. Were they able to say, "I'm scared," "I'm unsure," "I don't know what to do in my life," "I'm confused about my emotions toward so and so," and other such statements in which one accepts and engages one's vulnerability, they would likely be moving toward greater emotional health.

What I will be attempting to show is that in many cases of mental disturbances, fascist-type mind processes are attempts to substitute certainty for perplexity, power for vulnerability, and superiority for humility, just as fascist governments do in societies; the ultimate result in both cases is disastrous because the fascist program is an escape from our finest human potential. Erich Fromm wrote:

> The quest for certainty blocks the search for meaning. Uncertainty is the very condition to impel man to unfold his powers.[12]

Writing about anthropologist Gregory Bateson's ideas about power, Paul Dell looked at Bateson's analyses of why overincreasing one's power makes a person weaker and not stronger. He quoted Bateson thus:

> The metaphor of power derived from physics or engineering suggests that more power will always be more powerful. But this is an anti-biological, anti-ecological view of the matter – an untrue view.[13]

Why does Bateson criticize the engineering concept that more power will always be more powerful? Dell explains Bateson as saying that power beyond a needed level, rapidly destroys the flexibility, potentiality, and complexity of the ecosystem. Before there was a rich, multifaceted complexity; now, over time, the system collapses to its lowest common denominator (if not into death itself). This is true whether we are speaking of constantly injecting drugs or alcohol into the body, steadily injecting pollution into the environment, or expending constant effort to control one's marital relationship. Each of these do violence to the system in question. [14]

The Original Mind "Software"
We Humans Receive at the "Factory"

The Authoritarian Personality

Years ago, in the tragic wake of the indescribable hell that fascism wrought on millions of people in World War II, an effort that excited many social scientists was made to identify a basic fascist or "authoritarian person- ality," thus to arrive at an interface between a pathological personality structure in the individual and the pathological structure of societies. [15] However, despite an outpouring of somewhat suggestive research, the once-hopeful linkage fell by the wayside as it became increasingly clear that most people who engage in fascist acts are not organized in their overall personality structure as authoritarian personalities. [16]

FASCIST MIND software is, in fact, rooted in the earliest linguistic- cognitive possibilities in the mind of the young child who naturally ap- proaches life and reality in absolute and dualistic terms; for example, correct versus incorrect, success versus failure, and truth versus false- hood. The child's knowledge of certainty is further rooted in its attri- bution of perfection and omniscience first to its parents and then to its teachers. For many years, this dependent way of knowing about reality is further reinforced by a vast network of societal sanctions of approval and disapproval that encourage conformity to prescribed norms. Many of society's most significant institutions such as the church and other ideological institutions teach, without hesitation, indisputable answers to life's dilemmas and demand unquestioning obedience from those who seek the rewards that are the solace of the faithful.

Henry Louis Mencken wrote in 1919 ruefully: "The public . . . demands certainties; it must be told definitely and a bit raucously that this is true and this is false." Mencken knew enough to add, "But there are no certainties." Benito Mussolini, a real-life practicing dictator, wrote in the 1930s: "The Truth Apparent, apparent to everyone's eyes who are not blinded by dogmatism, is that men are perhaps weary of liberty. They have had surfeit of it. Liberty is no longer the virgin, chaste and severe, to be fought for . . . we have buried the putrid corpse of liberty . . . the Italian people are a race of sheep."

Religious philosopher Rheinold Niebuhr was especially concerned with the misdirection of religious thought into absolutes. Intellectual historian Arthur Schlesinger Jr. pointed out:

> Niebuhr was a relativist not because he disbelieved in the absolute, but precisely because he believed . . . nothing was more dangerous . . . than for frail and erring humans to forget the inevitable "contradiction between divine and human purposes." "Religion," wrote Niebuhr," is so frequently a source of confusion in political life, and so frequently dangerous to democracy, precisely because it introduces absolutes into the realm of relative values." He particularly detested "the fanaticism of all good men, who do not know that they are not as good as they esteem themselves," and he warned against "the depth of evil to which individuals and communities may sink . . . when they try to play the role of God to history."[17]

Ironically, some of the people who do learn to differentiate themselves from cults of certainty and totality are precisely those who suffered the insults of particularly unhappy childhoods. Insufficiently protected and poorly loved in their childhoods, they came to see and know the errors and lies of their parents, teachers, and society, and somehow they drew on a courage to be better people. Having gained clear knowledge of untruth and uncertainty, they embarked on new explorations of reality and a quest for a nontotalitarian epistemology for themselves.

However, a great many other people (including many who also were hurt in their childhood and don't recover) do seek guarantees of protection against trauma by adopting a certainty in their definition of their way of life. It is probably the majority of people who are afraid of the ambiguities and tensions of adult life. Rather than face risks of being broken by anxiety, they indeed "escape from freedom" (see reference to Fromm earlier) and flee into forms of certainty and totality.

The educational systems of most societies fail at every level of the teaching process to teach the processes and methods of staying in touch with the real truths of human experience. These processes include: tolerance of ambiguity; relativity of perception and knowledge; multicausality and multilevel reality; the legitimacy and necessity of alternative and even contradictory models of information and interpretation; the alternation of different explanations under varying conditions; dialectical processes, where conflicting ideas are taken as a sign of vibrancy and intellectual integrity leading the way to new creative integrations and syntheses of knowledge; humility in learning; the dignity of seeking knowledge without necessarily insisting on immediate or total solutions to problems; identification with knowledge-seeking and science-building as standing above and beyond personal needs for achievement, ambitions, or the politics of competitiveness; and reverence and joy at being alive as enabling one to explore and discover more of the mysteries of the universe.

Greenwald's Remarkable Concept of a "Totalitarian Ego"

As usual, the conception I am advancing here is not entirely new or unique. The overall notion that mind is lawfully organized along certain lines of structure and dynamic principles is, of course, a cornerstone of many psychologists, as well as linguists (for example, Noam Chomsky[18]), as well as philosophers. It is in effect the underlying principle of all of epistemology. The specific notion that the human mind is capable of becoming locked into rigidities has been observed by many psychological clinicians for many years, whether in studies of the breakdown of logic in mental illness, loss of plasticity and responsiveness to stimulation and information in brain damage, or rigidity and stereotypes in prejudicial and totalitarian thinking. But the proposal that mind, to begin with, normally tends to function primitively in rigid, locked-in patterns has not been advanced very often. In other words, rigidities are viewed in most cases as phenomena bespeaking pathological breakdowns of normal functioning, and the implication is that normal mind functioning is inherently flexible and nonrigid.

One important exception to the conception that mind is inherently flexible and is subject to rigidities only in pathological circumstances will be found in Anthony Greenwald's striking conception of "the totalitarian ego."[19] According to Greenwald, the human mind is inherently limited to being involved with its own needfulness more than with objective reality and is prepared to utilize *totalitarian* means to serve its means. Totalitarian in this case refers to control of information so as not to allow information that is contradictory and upsetting to the mind to be admitted into awareness. Writing in the prestigious flagship journal of the American Psychological Association, the *American Psychologist*, Greenwald proposed:

> Ego, or self, is an organization of knowledge that is characterized by cognitive biases that are analogous to totalitarian information-control strategies.[20]

Mind, according to Greenwald, necessarily attempts to create and maintain "a rosy picture" of the world and to shunt off distressing information and even to fabricate and revise information about reality in order to protect its interests.

> Ego's cognitive biases are egocentricity (self as the focus of knowledge), "benefactance" (perception of responsibility for desired, but not undesired outcomes), and cognitive conservatism (resistance to cognitive change).[21]

Kahneman's Pessimism about Human Decision Making

Another important student of human thinking who observes that our thinking is too often very wrong is psychologist Daniel Kahneman, who was awarded a Nobel Prize in Economics for work on how people make decisions. He too has come to a pessimistic conclusion about human thinking and decision making. He observes that people are involved in their own mind constructions at the expense of and in disregard of reality. They make up stories. They make even important strategic decisions based on their own stories. They believe they have much more to do with causing and shaping reality than they do. Moreover, so much of what people think is determined by what's in it for them rather than considerations of justice and ethics.

Here are some of Kahneman's observations:

Beliefs in events that didn't happen. Kahneman studies stories people construct about events that didn't happen, which he calls "counterfactuals," and concludes, "People hang on to their beliefs. When people are wrong, these beliefs help them to feel they were almost right.

"*Why do people take risks?* Many times because people *don't know* they are taking risks. There is delusional thinking.

"*People think they are right.* They think the arbiter will see they are right. . . . If there had been a Japanese general in WWII who had doubts about the future, he probably would have been shot or committed *harakiri* because he was disloyal to his nation.

"*People think their skills control events.* The truth is there is uncertainty about everything we do, and it turns everything we do into . . . an uncertainty . . . about which we can only have probabilities, but people and leaders create a striking confidence in their decision making despite poor outcomes.

"*Values.* People tend to think in terms of what they gain and what they give up and not values."

Overall, Kahneman expresses increasing disappointment and pessimism about human thinking.[22]

Further Observations about the Limitations of Human Thinking

In my point of view the healthy mind is an evolving instrument that includes serious original and continuing tendencies to blindness, distortion of reality, and insistence on its own a priori assumptions, but if and as mind grows, it learns to overcome these tendencies and employs other mechanisms that also await in our structural potential, namely an ability to think in contrasts and contradictions, and to bear and even enjoy discomforts of not knowing and not fabricating simplistic and overperfect solutions to complex problems and dilemmas.

The highly unusual *Encyclopedia of world problems and human potential* describes as one of the most limiting aspects of human civilization to date the prevalence of a style of competition of ideas in which,

> The survival of any integrative answer must be bought at the price of the elimination of all competitors. . . . This mind-set also fails to recognize the positive significance of a continuing disruptive emergence of new "alternative" answers. . . . Collective ability to respond to the crises has been effectively paralyzed. . . . An acceptable criterion is maintenance of the status quo provided it lends itself to being described as innovation. Significant social innovation is seldom sought, however eloquently it is advocated.

The editors of the encyclopedia propose as an alternative, which has rarely been used,

> to design a framework to internalize or embody discord, contradiction and logical continuity, even to demonstrate the negative consequences and limitations of blind consequences and [the] creative opportunity of judicious action in the light of destructive values.[23]

I couldn't agree more. The healthier human mind learns to tolerate and enjoy its internal processing, including contradictions, tugs of war between opposite emotions and points of view, serious doubts, and uncomfortable flows of anxiety. The entire process, which I envision as a kind of parliamentary democracy of the mind, is given its home respectfully and even lovingly. It is, moreover, constantly aided by and tested against the best empirical and scientific information available on issues under consideration.

This process of arriving at choices and decisions is very different from adopting absolute certainties as solutions.

It is not hard to understand that a FASCIST MIND way of organizing our experiences is the natural or default mode of response that is rooted deep within the first levels of our original human structure, beginning at birth. All we need to do is look at human babies. Whatever they feel is total.

There are no gradations – they feel pleasured, comforted, and safe; or they feel uncomfortable, pain, and distress. For many years after infancy, we continue to experience many moments of our lives in a totalistic way. Slowly but surely we all proudly develop varying capacities to grade and pace our emotional responses in different areas of our lives. Almost all (but even in this respect not all of us!) become toilet trained (thus, there is a reported 1% of the otherwise competent young male adults who remain enuretic). Far fewer of us, though most of us, learn to defer expression of many of our emotions, which we record and file inside without necessarily externalizing them and expressing them overtly to our surroundings.

Sadly, many of us fail to mature in our ability not to think in extremes. Overall, human society has not evolved toward teaching more extensive democratic thinking, and most of us continue to think of many issues in polarized terms: good and bad, right and wrong, spiritual and carnal, holy and unholy. Not being trained to think more in terms of processes, we can't help but think in extremes. We love to be crazy in love with a person, purpose, faith, sport team, nationality, anything; the total feeling of unity with our beloved is a beguiling state of safety and joy. Conversely, we have many moments of discomfort because something or other in our lives is out of place, be it even the triviality of a missing object; because there is a mess in the order of things in our lives or even of information; because discrepancies result in our experience of life being different from what we expected it to be; or because we have clashes of contradictions in our emotions toward whomever and whatever. Hundreds of our daily actions can be seen as efforts to correct contradiction and disorder. On the surface, the resolution of contradictions is not a bad move to make for more effective reorganization and recommitment. But insofar as a compulsion for order and totality takes over and seeks relentlessly to do away with every ambivalence and complexity within sight in order to create a single, unified monolithic experience, we can become slavish and rigid and then also nasty toward someone (it can be toward our own selves or others) in our insistence on a given order of things.

There are many moments well into adult life when our insides yearn for cognitive wholeness, a sense of unity, and a fusion with a state of total comfort and bliss. Many of us remain vulnerable to temptation by fascist philosophies of certainties, and in effect become practicing totalitarians. This happens in our political thinking. It also happens in other aspects of our lives, such as in inflexible insistences on certain types of relationships, and we are then at a total loss when other persons in our lives (such as a spouse or child) elect to feel and behave differently. If we are practitioners of a helping profession, many of us elect to offer only a single inflexible method of treatment or helping in a naive and stubborn belief that one treatment method is correct for all conditions, and we end up at a total loss when a patient or client really needs a different type of help.

On a political level, insistence on a given way of life and a supremacy of whichever group of people over another people results in horrors such as Nazism, Communism, Khmer Rougism, Talibanism, and an endless list of small and large national, regional, and international political movements that bring death through wars, terrorism, and genocide to the millions whom the powerful define as standing in their way.

I propose that this same kind of thinking is also at the heart of many highly personal problems and bouts with mental distress in the course of our everyday lives. What emerges from so many observations of the weaknesses in human thinking is that the original and quite natural source of the totalitarian thinking is the mind program we get at "the factory" when we are born. We have a gift of potential great brilliance for many thinking functions, but we also have a babyish and self-centered starting or default position, and this default seems to remain the operating program for many of us, especially in emotional matters, both in personal relationships and in highly valued ideological belief systems.

The Fascist Principle Also Applies to Too Much of a Good Thing

A value adopted in a fascist or overcertain way by an individual mind or societal group need not be a "bad" value. On the contrary. On the societal level it can be values of liberty and freedom adopted with ruthless certainty, or values of equality, economic justice, the betterment of the race, and such. On the individual level, the values can be a pursuit of fairness, purity, or the wonders of love, love, and more love.

The following case is an example of a fine, attractive man who all his life wanted only to be successfully in love and to lead a truly loving life with a beautiful woman. In childhood his mother was "always angry" at him and forever regarded him as a "bad boy." Wounded to the quick, he escaped into the world in search of a loving woman. Now see what happens to him when he and his lovers then take the idea of loving to its totality. Time after time, after enjoying the bliss and ecstasy of total fusion, he and his woman encounter one or another variation of inevitable separateness and distance from each other, which destroys them. Unknowingly, they are unable to contain any experiences of *disunion* along with their wonderful union.

The fact that in this case the repeated error is one of overdoing something quite wonderful – love! – is a very good illustration of the built-in hazards of totality and certainty. Further, in this case because we see three repeated variations on the same problem recurring to our hero and his mates, analyzing the process is easier. This is a man who must love; he is good at it and creates worlds of ecstasy with his lovers; and therein is his and their downfall when they cannot maintain perfection. Total relentless hurt replaces total relentless love; and a vengeful (though also confused and regretful) breakdown of the relationship follows.

In his mid-20s, as he was completing his graduate studies, and after having experienced a fulsome array of dates, affairs, and exploratory experiences of connection with a reasonable variety of women, he found himself very attracted to and progressively in love with one young woman in particular. In the background, unconsciously and quite normally, was a sense of the emerging timeliness of selecting a mate and settling down. The young couple's love quite properly took on all the marks of a steady relationship that could lead to marriage. However, a year into the relationship, the girl informed our hero one day that she was sorry but she did not feel that she was growing deeply enough in love with him, and she thought they ought to break up. Since neither he nor she had any real sense of how ambivalence and indecision can be natural parts of being in love that need to be experienced and worked through – for them you either were totally committed or you were not – they broke up immediately.

Our young hero now suffered all the appropriate pangs of hurt and loss as presumably did his girlfriend, for within a couple of months she recontacted him and asked that they come together again, which they did. You would think that now they would be even happier – which is what happens to many young couples who have to go through some episode of separating before reuniting more solidly. In the following year they were again going steady, and according to our hero during this time his girlfriend certainly fell more and more in love with him. Great? Not at all. Telling the story many years later, he explains how her growing love did not touch him. Throughout the ostensibly wonderful year of reunion, when he had enjoyed everything he had ever dreamt about, he continued unknowingly to nurture a fierce anger and need for revenge for his girlfriend's earlier dumping of him. For him the breakup at her initiative had been an abandonment of him. Period. He could not entertain the idea that lovers can come together, break up, and reunite again in a process of exploration, loss, and reaffirmation of choice. Toward the end of the second year in which they were going together, with every expectation that they were heading toward marriage, the girl proposed that she move in to his apartment. At this point, he told her, triumphantly, as she had once told him, "No!" So sweet was his revenge!

∽

Our hero's story continues. A few months later he discovers another beautiful damsel – after all he has reached an age of wanting to be in love and marry, and he is a good lover. He and his new girlfriend also fall head over heels in love. It is bliss and joy. And this time he and his girlfriend do move in together. Their union is perfection. In fact, a half-year later they marry. Mazel tov! Off they go on a honeymoon trip for several weeks far overseas, during which their love and passion and pure joy continue to know no limits. However, for the perfectly good reason that our hero now has an emerging career in a scientific field, he naively arranges to stay on overseas for all of one additional week without his bride to meet some professional people in his field. They arrange for her to return to their home.

When the husband returns a week later, *"something had changed drastically, and I never found out what it was."* From that time on, his wife who used to be drenched in sexual wetness even at the very beginning of their contact with each other (long before they would make it to the bedroom) now turned literally and uncompromisingly totally dry. Weeks and months followed where she failed to recover any ability to lubricate at all. They consulted medical help. They consulted psychological help. They consulted sex therapy help. They used KY lubricant and tried to make the best of attempting some recovery of their Paradise Lost. Nothing helped. Both of them had a deep sense that their love candle had been blown out and could never be relit. In their disappointment they decided to divorce because they had failed each other, and indeed they parted with deep sorrow, the embers of their once great love still glowing dimly in their hearts. To this day, as our hero reconstructed the stories of his lost loves in therapy, he had no idea what happened.

The mesmerized therapist who heard this tale of lost great loves now proposed to him, "I wonder if what happened is that your staying abroad for the week while your loving wife had to return to your home on her own punctured her sense of total love with you. Apparently she suffered from a concept of total love and being inseparable, like you do, or maybe even more than you. She had no idea how to repair her lost fusion with you; and you in turn had no idea how to help her recover.

"You believe only in total love. With your preceding girlfriend, it was you who was unable to recover from the hurt after she had once left you, even though she came back to you even more strongly. In this second chapter with your wife, I think she did a total turnoff from the total love you had – even though her heart and yours continued to love each other. You both lost something so beautiful unnecessarily, as apparently you and your first girlfriend had too."

∽

The story is still not done. After the above failed love, our hero continues his life and meets and marries still another woman. It is with her that he has now come to the therapy that is the source of the information being described here. What is their problem? They too love each other so very much, and there are moments in couple sessions in the current therapy when my office is virtually lit up by the glory of their heartfelt attraction as well as respect for each other. But they get into the blackest, most desperate and most vicious fights. When do these fights occur most frequently? The answer quite obviously is whenever there is a sense of a threat of separation.

The most pressing problem for them is his business trips. Since he knows she suffers when he travels, he has cut his trips to a reasonable minimum in this day of international commerce; in fact, he often makes his trips incredibly short despite the long intercontinental distances involved; but she is still inconsolable. How come? On her part, she has her story of an army-brat childhood and a major deficit in her bonding with her mother. In so many ways she is a wonderful, charming, creative, and generous person, but she often loses control of her emotions and sometimes of her behaviors (she has been known to toss quite a few things) whenever she can "prove" to herself that she has been abandoned.

◌

A concluding note on who this hero is who takes revenge on women who leave him or chooses women who suffer the pits of hell no less deeply than he after any separation from him?

Our hero is a self-made man who left home at age 13 and made himself into a highly creative scientist and entrepreneur. Why such an early departure from home? Consciously he doesn't really know, just as later he has no idea of how revengefully furious he becomes at women when they give him less than total love. The story he tells of his childhood is of a home in which his father was away for work all week long and only returned on weekends, while his mother who was his mainstay in the home never made him feel warm, connected, or quiet. As noted earlier, she was always angry with him and had him pigeon-holed as her bad boy. In his childhood he was loyal to her because she was his mother, and he felt safe because he was in familiar surroundings at home. But something he couldn't define simply didn't exist for him there, and when he became a young adolescent he left home to search the world for a more pure love.

As we have seen, our capable hero did find plenty of love, but it didn't help him have any idea what to do when the totality of a love had to revolve and go through a phase of incompleteness and separation.

◌

A side clinical note to those interested in such matters: This man always had a very active libidinal lustful temperament, and so all through his adolescent years he masturbated actively and repeatedly, but at no point

33

does he recall having any image whatsoever of any love object appearing in his fantasies when he masturbated. It was all clockwork-orange mechanical masturbation to climax. I don't recall ever meeting someone in my practice with such a total absence of any image of a desired woman over so many years of active masturbation.

Superstition, Beliefs in Magic, and All Sorts of Other Nonsense Abound in the Human Mind

There are many other irrational thinking phenomena, including gullibility, superstition, and belief in magic.[24] For one example, it has been shown that when a person is offered a detailed description of their personality on the basis of whatever – it can be a purported result of psychological testing that was never really done of them, or the chart of an astrologist or a numerologist – no less than a majority of people tend to see the description as accurate, and then they also adopt a belief in the method that generated the "accurate" report. Needless to say, if the personality description is a positive one, acceptance and belief in the description grow even stronger.

It is also commonly observed that when two separate events occur in an apparent sequence or contiguity, the time connection between the events can bring about unwarranted beliefs that the events are causally related, and the result can well be that people repeat one of the behaviors in the belief that it will likely bring about the other. The behavioral psychologist B. F. Skinner demonstrated experimentally that pigeons connect between random movements they exercise at the time when food appears and the "belief" that it was the movements that brought about the delivery of the food, and therefore continue to repeat the same movements over and over again. As the pigeon continues the now believed-in ritual and food pellets continue to arrive, the pigeon's belief deepens. Skinner saw in this experimental paradigm a dramatic representation of how fads and false beliefs develop.

False beliefs also rest on the regrettable tendency of people to accept any statement by known authorities. Rumors, current fads, and widespread myths always have the ears of the majority of virtually any population

– you name it, the Earth is flat, masturbation is sinful and weakens the body, cohorting with ethnic or religious strangers is a betrayal of your own people and gods, and so forth, and the belief is all the stronger when it is put forth by a recognized leader, for example, a religious leader.[25]

Susan Sontag also points out that anything that wears recognizable honored symbols gets to be believed in very readily and widely.

> There is a general fantasy about uniforms. They suggest community, order, identity (through ranks, badges, medals, things which declare who the wearer is and what he has done: his worth is recognized), competence, legitimate authority, the legitimate exercise of violence.[26]

Terrible phenomena of contagion and exaggeration of false beliefs are widespread in human experience. In other words, the defects present in the "software" of the individual's mind are put into play and then amplified and reinforced when shared with other people; there follows a variety of additional psychological mechanisms of needs for confirmation by others, conformity, and group intoxication superimposed on one's thinking. Thus, Aaron Lynch, an engineering physicist, has described "thought contagion," or how ridiculous ideas are spread in a sense as "mind viruses" much like diseases.

> By Lynch's account, the fate of a thought contagion depends on several factors, including how fast it spreads, how much fervor it inspires, how long each host stays infected and how much resistance it encounters in the population. Mainstream ideas can survive a lack of fervor, he says, because they meet little resistance. But unorthodox belief systems have to adapt to hostile conditions. One common strategy is to deem the outside world hopelessly corrupt and withdraw from its influence. Another is to declare that heaven is reserved for believers.[27]

The author of the article describing thought contagion comments further on one bizarre case of a cult whose members committed suicide together:

> It all seems perfectly ludicrous: 39 people don their new sneakers, pack their flight bags and poison themselves in the solemn belief that a passing UFO will whisk them off to wonderland. The rest of us have

more sense than that, right? Actually, most of us harbor beliefs for which hard evidence is lacking. In fact, our firmest convictions are often the hardest to justify rationally. As one analyst puts it, "Beliefs that survive aren't necessarily true, rules that survive aren't necessarily fair and rituals that survive aren't necessarily necessary."[28]

Another aspect of the weakness of our human minds is the ease with which so many human beings justify being cruel to themselves and to others. At this point I am not referring to the facts of our more-than-regrettable human cruelty and violence as such, which also are a major aspect of FASCIST MIND that is looked at extensively in this book, but the ease with which the human mind explains and justifies the cruelty as legitimate, and the perpetrator even denies being the agent of what he is in fact doing. Philip Zimbardo was the psychologist responsible for the Stanford University "prison experiment" where students were divided into prisoners and jailers in a simulation of a prison; the jailers acted so cruelly that the experiment had to be stopped. Zimbardo has written:

> What was the most surprising about the outcome of this simulated prison experience was the ease with which sadistic behavior could be elicited from quite normal young men, and the contagious spread of emotional pathology among those carefully selected precisely for their emotional stability. . . . Perhaps even more astonishing to us was the permeability of the boundaries between reality and delusion, between self-identity and situational role. What began as a simple academic exercise gradually became a force of monstrous proportion.[29]

Another psychologist writing in the *American Psychologist* has concluded: "It is evident . . . that nonrational thinking is highly prevalent and that even when people know their thinking is irrational, they often find it more compelling than their rational reasoning."[30] In short, the potential for being caught up in plain outrageous nonsense is pandemic and endemic in the mind of the human species at this time.

Thou Shalts and Thou Shalt Nots in Mental Health
Therapy – All Proposed to Be Scientific Truths

Even doctor of philosophy and medicine degrees too often are admission tickets to one or another club of certainty, including in the mental health disciplines. In many professional settings, cynical patronizing glances will be the lot of those who fail to avow loyalty to a single identifiable school of thought and instead weak-mindedly fall prey to the uncertainties of eclecticism. Woe be unto a heretic of the psychoanalytic paradigm in Freud-land; scorn will be the fate of the infidel who fails to perceive the systemic greatness of the new family therapy epistemology in family therapy centers and institutes that have adopted systemic thinking as the new reigning principle; and so on.

There is no end to the certainties promulgated by the "greats" in the world of mental health, where we would have expected and hoped for better. So many ostensibly educated professionals in the mental health field celebrate certainty by adopting, seemingly without embarrassment or strain, a complete identification with whichever given "school of therapy," in relation to which all other ways of treating patients are treated disdainfully as wrong, or as lesser mediocre choices (for example, the typical disdainful language is to consider the other therapy superficial or short-lasting).

Here are some classic rules of their days, some of which are still hanging on today in various pockets of political loyalists in the mental health world even as each generation of professionals continues to produce its new overcertainties and cults. The rules that follow are purposely set in contrasting pairs, each polarized certainty obviously contradicted by its partner. All of the following principles have been widely honored and celebrated at one time or another.

1a. Thou shalt not see members of any family together in family therapy because psychotherapy addresses only the private experience of each individual.[31]

1b. Thou shalt not see any member of a family in individual sessions, because the only meaningful therapy is systemic reorganization of the family unit as a whole.[32]

∾

2a. Thou shalt explore the childhood roots of all adult emotional problems as well as the manifestations of these problems in the transference to the therapist in every case.[33]

2b. Therapy must focus exclusively on the here and now, the past is irrelevant and misleading.[34]

∾

3a. Patients must be led to powerful affective releases of the cries and screams of hurt, yearning, mourning and rage that are pent up in them.[35]

3b. Patients should be given clear cognitive maps or behavioral training to guide them, and rarely an opportunity for expression of their emotions.[36]

Superiority, Power, Violence and Retaliation against Dissent

If one possesses the one and only truth; if one knows indisputably that the solution to life's problems requires total commitment to a single correct way of seeing and doing things and is prepared to make a total effort to achieve and ensure that outcome, then clearly one has been chosen to be superior to the large number of people who do not know the truth or do not have the wherewithal to execute without reservation the policies that are required by this knowledge.

So even if a quest for superiority and a delusion of grandeur were not original characteristics of the motivations of the person who adopts a fascist paradigm, it follows from the nature of identifying with any totality and certainty that one becomes superior to the masses of unknowing people who have not been selected to be bearers of the Truth.

It also follows that the carriers of the Truth must pay serious attention to the dangers issuing from those who do not understand and refuse to appreciate the wonders of the truth, those who are skeptics and nonbelievers, and most of all those who reveal themselves to be "radicals," "terrorists," and "counterrevolutionaries" who reject the redemption that is now possible. These opponents of truth must be neutralized at all costs, whatever the tension, unpleasantness, or even moral dilemmas that accompany removing them from the scene. Eliminating whose who stand in the way of crucial progress is defined not as what is generally meant by "destruction"; as Robert Jay Lifton taught us in his brilliant study of the Nazi doctors, it is redefined to be more in the nature of "healing" than "killing"; it is celebrated as "serving the greater need with the greater good" rather than a ruthless removal of one's opposition and enemies.[37] The removal of barriers to progress is a noble and enlightened act, even of sacrifice of oneself, for one's people and one's era, to do onerous tasks that must be done in the interest of a better destiny.

In writing about the perpetrators of the Holocaust, historian George Kren observed:

> There is something very strange and odd in the fact that almost all of the perpetrators of what arguably is the most radical horror of this century, while awaiting execution, argued, with obvious sincerity, that they had done no wrong. A recurring theme found in all the trial records of individuals who had participated in mass killing is the indignant surprise they express that anyone should blame them for their actions, since they were only doing their duty.[38]
>
> The commitment to ideals and the ability for transcendence, rather than simple selfishness, are made to account for most of the horrors of human history.
>
> The Nazi image of racial beauty and purity is at the root of the Holocaust. It is difficult to accept the proposition that much of human destructiveness has its roots in utopian visions, in the desire to transform the world as it is into a better, purer or even more beautiful world.[39]

Note that an actual interest in destroying other people and devotion to such destruction – features certainly associated with many instances of fascism in the world – is not necessarily present in the motivations of all people who adopt a fascist paradigm or mindset. The readiness to destroy others who are not-believers more often derives from the basic emphasis on totality and certainty, which in turn seduces and impels devotees to adopt policies that will protect their special view of ultimate knowledge and truth. Destructive acts are given euphemistic meanings from the outset, and the agony and suffering of the victims are redefined as necessary results of noble acts of leadership and service to one's beloved true faith.[40]

As referred to earlier, Robert Jay Lifton identified a "healing-killing paradox" in his study of Nazi medical personnel who variously assisted and commanded aspects of the vicious extermination of Jews and others – killing in the name of healing.[41]

Erich Fromm wrote about how intentions to create and further life are paradoxically at work in much evil/destructiveness. Many calculated justifications of destructiveness are seen as noble; in some cases, evildoers sincerely believe themselves and intend consciously to be doing good:

> All human passions, both the "good" and the "evil," can be understood only as a person's attempt to make sense of his life. . . . Even though the life-furthering passions are conducive to a greater sense of strength, joy, integration, and vitality than destructiveness and cruelty, the latter are as much an answer to the problem of human existence as the former. Even the most sadistic and destructive man is human, as human as the saint. . . . Destructiveness and cruelty . . . express *life turning against itself in the striving to make sense of it.*[42]

It also needs to be emphasized very strongly that striving for superiority over others and a readiness to destroy people who stand in the way are also prime attractions for many people to join fascist groups. Fascist groups recruit new believers and adherents who organize their emotional lives around hate and avowed intentions to discriminate against and brutalize and murder chosen target groups. After all, our world is also full of human beings who have adopted as a way of life the elimination of the rights and lives of others. For these people, a need to do harm and destroy others often precedes the adoption of whatever ideology the fascist group they will join offers. These are the ugly brutalizing hooligans and toughs, and the sadistic leaders in any given culture and era who are delighted to identify with and adopt whichever fascist paradigm history brings their way so long as they can justify their need for violence. Fascist groups are good homes for such people. However, the point that is most often not recognized is that a quest for superiority and the intention to eliminate people who are targeted as confirmed enemies also can derive intrinsically from the original acceptance of certainty and totality, so that even decent people, whose conscious philosophy and intentions are to respect life and not to harm others, often adopt vicious postures of superiority and engage in terrible acts of destruction toward others in the name of certainty.

This conception helps us understand many aspects of the Holocaust and other genocides in which we were stunned to learn that the torturers and killers were not only psychopathic and criminal bastards, and uneducated and loveless goons, but also included the best and greatest minds and personalities from every conceivable walk of life, education, religion, medicine, business, and so on, and also people whose personal and family lives were blessed with meaningful and essentially caring relationships. Tragically, we have learned that overall the "normal" and "ordinary" people were represented in huge numbers among the perpetrators of the Holocaust.[43]

Societal-Level Fascist Ideas in Mental Health Circles

Fascist thinking on a societal level is hardly foreign to mental health professionals, some of whom have adopted the most racist and totalitarian ideas of their eras and societies. To this day, many if not most mental health professionals do not know or have not faced the significance of the fact that the first mass extermination program in Nazi Germany was the euthanasia program for mental patients and mental defectives.[44] The designers of this program were distinguished mental health professionals, including titled holders of chairs in psychiatry at Germany's best universities. Frederic Wertham tells how one of these doctors was especially known in his time for his involvement with and kindness to patients.[45] The motivation for this extraordinary treatment of troubled people does not seem to have been based on sadistic motivations, but rather to represent another case of "going all the way" with an idea to its "ultimate solution."

Although the marvelous checks-and-balances of democracy protected against the same heinous development taking place in the United States, it is significant to note that there was also a powerful movement on behalf of eugenic solutions to society's ills in the United States that resulted in legislation to sterilize the mentally retarded in a number of states. This movement numbered among its supporters and promulgators some of the most distinguished names in American psychological professions including Truman Lee Kelley, William McDougall, Adolf Meyer, Lewis M. Terman, Edward Thorndike, Robert S. Woodward, and Robert M. Yerkes. These distinguished fathers of our psychological and mental health professions gave their names to public campaigns that called for the most serious measures against populations of the "inferior" in a language that can hardly be discriminated from the language of Nazi ideologues!

> The time seems ripe for a strong public movement to stem the tide of threatened racial degeneracy following in the wake of the War [World War I]. America in particular needs to protect herself against indiscriminate immigration of criminal degenerates and race suicide. . . . Eugenics stands against the forces which work for racial deterioration, and for progressive improvement in vigor, intelligence, and moral fiber of the human race. It represents the highest form of patriotism and humanitarianism, while at the same time it offers immediate advantages to ourselves and to our children. By eugenic measures, for instance, our burden of taxes can be reduced by decreasing the number of degenerates, delinquents and defectives supported in public institutions; such measures will also increase safeguards against our persons and our property. Eugenic Committee of the United States of America, 1924.[46]

An excellent and sadly shattering example of the way the mind of a devoted humanistic psychologist can move along the same track of the fascist paradigm to a point where he calls for execution [*sic!*] of the nonbelievers – in this case, nonbelievers in humanism! – is found in the posthumously published writings of no less than Abraham Maslow, recognized and beloved as the founder of modern humanistic psychology! The same Maslow who conceptualized the unfolding development of the mind and personality of a person as the highest state of human development, and who attributed to the "self-actualized" person an ethical and empathic orientation toward other human beings and the society in which he lives, was revealed after his death to be a highly self-involved, bitter loner filled with contempt and rage at the many people who did not appreciate him or his ideas, and who dared to conceive on a broader community level the identification and execution of those who opposed proposed humanistic policies for the betterment of society.

The following are shocking, almost unbelievable excerpts from Maslow's posthumously published writings:

> Humanistic psychology absolutely *needs* a doctrine of an elite, degrees of humanness, health and sickness, winners and losers, aggridants (whether by heredity or by learning), good specimens, no equal votes, non-equal weighting. The taste or judgment of one superior can and should outweigh 1000 or a million blind ones.[47]

> The Third-Force philosophy is antideath-wish, anti-exploiting of others, antistunting or crippling, antivalue-destroying, antibaby-crippling and diminishing; anti-unrealism = antifake. . . . We keep alive many of the people whom nature left to itself would kill off. So we are hurting the human gene pool, which must be deteriorating. We can certainly continue to do this, to be compassionate with anyone living, but this right to reproduce might very well be limited. In the immediate future – within the next century – we must anyway cut back the population of the world. The right to reproduce must surely become rather a privilege which is socially controlled and socially granted. . . . One could speculate that the worsening gene pool is partly responsible for the large number of naysayers, death-wishers and born losers and schlemiels.[48]

> I find myself secretly entertaining all sorts of "cold-blooded" possibilities . . . drug users are performing a kind of biologically unselfish act, a sort of noblesse oblige for the good of the species and voluntarily killing themselves "for the good of the gene pool." . . . Sooner or later, after the catastrophes force us to pace the overpopulation, we'll stop with all the crap about more food, or better strains of rice (which just produce more people). How can we give up on humanitarianism? But how can we not permit voluntary (or maybe involuntary) euthanasia

and suicide? One day we'll have to talk about the exposure or killing of monster-babies, or even of healthy *surplus* babies.[49]

As with some, nothing will work ultimately but shooting.[50]

These are terrifying statements from anyone, let alone a great psychologist, especially one who is recognized as one of the fathers of "humanistic psychology." Maslow's fascist intolerance of lesser beings and his readiness to call for real murderous actions on behalf of a super race of humanists is a powerful warning to all of us to look for the corresponding readiness in us, and to overcome such readiness with what we will be describing as a democratic mindset.

In a review of Maslow's diaries in *Contemporary Psychology*, Elizabeth Leonie Simpson wrote:

The petty, the trivial, the authoritarian, sexist elitist is exposed interacting with the prophet, the seeker, and the striver. He knew himself to be extraordinary – one self-actualizer among cohorts who were similar to the few just men of the Jewish tradition who live among lesser people and for whose sake God allows the world to continue to exist. . . . Liberalism had failed the superior being. He trusted himself more than others and, holding power, he would have exercised it absolutely, abandoning Fifth Amendment protection against such disruptive forces as civil disobedients, convicted criminals, and unemployed "loafers." . . . The ideal "B [Being] person" could choose to execute for good reasons and retaliate for evil with equal evil. He would do "whatever" the other felt free to do, readily converting the Golden Rule into "Do unto others what you believe they would do unto you."[51]

Retaliation against Dissent within One's Individual's Mind

It is hard to think of retaliation against dissent as an operation that also takes place within an individual's own mind. We understand easily what it means to try to suppress someone else from bringing up information that is contradictory to our beliefs or desires, but it takes some mental will to understand what it means to suppress in one's own mind dissent with oneself. And yet experiences of questioning, differences of opinion,

44

and strong objections to one's own self really are everyday occurrences in the minds of all of us.

Here are examples of healthy dissent in our minds:

• We are about to conform to demands to perform a certain task that has been laid on us by a parent, an employer, or a school system, and part of us protests strongly that we don't really want to do this task.

• We are on the verge of marrying someone, and a strong part of our inner minds tells us not to because the outcome will be sad and perhaps even disastrous.

• We set for ourselves a goal of being the super-most-successful stock salesman of the year in a highly competitive firm, but another part of us tells us that we would be much better off doing modestly well in our work and devoting ourselves at the same time to becoming more all-around sports-minded and relationship-nourishing people.

Awareness and struggle with alternative choices, questioning of a position on which one is about to embark, and the discovery of totally contradictory wishes, desires, and judgments inside of ourselves is not at all unfamiliar to a great many of us.

A continuous dialogue takes place in the mind functions of the human being. Insofar as a person does not listen within his or her self, but goes about life without an inner zest for tasting and tracking the life one is leading and unaware of unconscious inner experiencing, the voices of dissent can be silenced, and human experience can be turned into a gray, flat, and shallow routine of doing whatever one is told, beholden and expected to do. That is apparently what happens when the personality empties out under conditions of loss of self, such as in certain mental illnesses, or whenever a person "gives up." This is also the situation present when a person has not developed a real self but is, in effect, defined by the predominant forces directing him or her. Amazingly, some such people "look" perfectly well developed, and for whatever period of time in their lives appear to function well, but in time their lack of spine and spunk, and the truth of their living on a borrowed identity as it were, surface in telltale weaknesses of the functioning of their body or spirit.

FASCIST MIND dictates that there will be no dissent. One will observe the rules. One will fulfill the commands, demands, or wishes imposed by whomever – one's parent, the church, an academic institution, an employer, a social system, one's government. The individual defines for himself or herself the correct goals, and any dissenting thoughts or desires are treated as disloyalty, sabotage, and treason. The dissenting thoughts are to be suppressed. Moreover, due punishment is also to be inflicted on oneself for allowing and harboring any such thoughts.

• I wanted to kiss someone I shouldn't, and now I feel dirty and bad.

• I got angry with someone at whom I don't dare harbor anger, and my head is splitting.

• I am about to go off on a life career that is unacceptable to my family, and I take to bed in a state of overwhelming fatigue and perhaps breakdown.

In other words, there is a part of our individual mind that is exercising power and backing it with violent retaliation against our self if and when we don't obey the required correct and perfect goal or final solution.

In family life, the time-honored version of a fascist demand that there be no dissent is most familiar in the classic picture of the authoritarian patriarchal family. In this traditional family, father knows best, his authority is unquestioned, there is genuine fear of him, and everyone pretty much tows the line, at least visibly. Disobedience, indeed disrespect and even expressions of nonconformity and dissent, are understood to be invitations to punishment. In more severe cultures, there are physical punishments, most commonly beatings. In cultures that are more protective of the physical welfare of children, there are a wide variety of punishments such as the removing of privileges, and in any case there is stern disapproval and nonacceptance of the erring person in the family.

Less recognized alongside the patriarchal father is the often no-less-powerful matron, who rules many a family with the iron hand of her maternal power. Adorned perhaps by a sweeter, higher-pitched female voice, and even by a beguiling alternation between severity and a grace of female and mothering kindnesses, the matriarch nonetheless can be a supreme ruler who insists on obeisance and obedience without qualification.

In contemporary Western society, much of the overuse of power has shifted from traditional male dominance to new forms of female dominance. Beginning with the structural fact that there is a precipitous increase in the number of children who are being brought up by mothers living without husband-fathers, the expansion of the power of females also includes changes in the status of men and women in intact families that still have a father and mother working together. In the shift of power, fathers are many more times adjuncts who accompany the managerial centrality of their wives. In an amazing number of young couples, there is diminishing to nonexistent sexuality dictated by women's decisions to escape or stop the sexual activity.[52] Many if not most decisions to divorce in the Western world are now dictated by women in a complete turnabout from the opposite phenomenon not that many years ago when it was the men who took the lead in electing most divorces. In many Western families today, men have lost a sense of security about themselves as leaders let alone as equals to their wives, even as so many women have gotten seduced, as men did for centuries before them, to the narcotic joys of ever-expanding overuse of power over the others in their families.

Oppressive demands for towing the line in family life can be disguised in many ways, so much so that there may be times when one would almost welcome old fashioned archetypal forms of more brutal patriarchs or matriarchs because at least they have the advantage of making the use of power so apparent that it is clear to family members what their choices are. Much more insidious demands for total acquiescence and obedience in family life can be masked in styles of relationship and "political" styles that are seemingly more laid back and apparently permissive and leave decision making to the other, when in truth all parties to the communication system know that there is an absolute demand for certain behavior.[53] For example, the demands can be backed with a punishment system that is guilt inducing rather than with direct sanctions and retaliations. For example, *You'll kill me if you leave home; don't leave me alone with your father*, might be a the mother's message to a child who then remains devotedly at home. The child becomes a young adult who fails to develop skills for independence and intimate relationships and does not move on normally in his or her life, whether in work or love or both, because of a childishness and immaturity that result from not having struck out on one's own. Or the demands for obedience can be a function of bribery through excessively indulgent comforts and pleasures or even actual funds that are given to seal the deal of maintaining total control over the other. Strange as it seems, the damages that result from the more openly totalitarian styles of family life, however severe they are, may be more remediable than the damages that result from the more disguised, insidious, and seductive ways of invading the interior of another person's personality, identity, and capacity for independence.

He had never married and continued to live at home with his mother even as he approached his fortieth birthday. He was gainfully employed and carried himself with a degree of dignity as a person who was providing for himself economically, but in his social development there was something basically off that common sense simply made you understand was the result of his being a mama's boy who continued to live under her protecting and managerial eye. At one point he became so depressed that his doctor arranged for him to be in a psychiatric hospital for treatment. There they realized that the depression was a statement of the dulling of this man's energies and joy about himself because he was so locked and in truth dependent on his mother. The hospital responsibly saw to it that the hospitalization was brief and sent the man home with a recommendation for family therapy with his mother.

However, there was altogether only one session of said family therapy. A charming and at the same time obviously powerful personality, the mother seated herself authoritatively in the room as if bristling against the therapist for being an interloper in the world in which she ruled. Her son looked sheepish, yet with courage he dared to speak to his mother of his dreams of leaving home and being a more independent person. The ostensible text of mother's responses was perfectly kosher: "If you want to go and live on your own, you certainly should do so," she said in an acceptable way, but her narrowed eyes and intensity simultaneously betrayed her emotional message, which was something like, "Over my dead body."

A day later, the mother telephoned the therapist, it seemed with barely disguised triumph in her voice, to report that her son had suffered a heart attack that very same night following the first family therapy session in which he had asked for a greater independence. Obviously he was going to stay home for a long time. She indeed had won over his "dead body."

Psychotherapy as Antifascism

An emotionally whole personality weaves a path between a variety of dialectical contradictions: freedom to be oneself and responsibility to others, self-assertiveness versus yielding to dependency and intimacy with others, emotions of love and hate, tenderness and toughness, respect and criticalness, structures of order versus disorder, behavior sequences of progression and regression, cycles of activity and rest, and so on.[54]

What happens in dysfunctional or psychopathological conditions is that the wheel of life's contradictions is stopped, and emphasis is put on a single way of being that is seemingly guaranteed to protect one from all pain or loss. Wherever one looks in the psychopathologies, one sees that the patient has brought to a consummate and stubborn standstill healthy dynamic processes that normally involve an interplay, flux, and creative tension between opposing poles of experience.[55] In normal experience and growth, there is a continuous cycling of pain and uncertainty; there are periodic "downers" over what Judith Viorst has called the "necessary losses of life,"[56] or the more than enough cruel blows of fortune that have to be absorbed, bowed to, mourned, and overcome throughout life; and there is shame as we are periodically thrust up against our limitations and errors.[57] However, the fascist paradigm says that there can be no surrender to any such weakness, no acknowledgment of shame, no mourning of loss, no vulnerability, and never failure. (Mitscherlich and Mitscherlich applied this concept to the German society as a whole, suggesting that it was a society that had suffered an inability to acknowledge shame and regret [from the defeat in World War I] and that this was a major psychological or psychosocietal cause of the German people's making of the Holocaust.)[58] The fascist system of certainty is virtually guaranteed to work at least in the short term.

The experience of certainty is so beguiling that the fact that the real outcome of the policy may turn out to be failure and loss often doesn't change the policy (see Albert Ellis's major contributions to cognitive corrections of overcertainty).[59] For the committed political fascist, such as a Nazi or Communist, even after the war is over and lost, the defeated person may remain largely comforted by and still enamored with the unquestioned certainty and proud identification with their inviolate solution to life's tensions and problems for which they fought. And although at first there is a strain in using such language for psychopathological and relationship disorders, much the same is true of the individual who has gone overboard on a personal plan of emotional safety such as being a loner, or being suspiciously controlling of people, and who then loses out on successful relationships, such as losing a job or losing a marriage partner, but refuses or is unable to recognize the error of the mind program that has brought about the breakdown and loss to his or her life.

The pleasant and surprising thought that follows from the above understanding of fascist thinking is that many psychotherapies can be thought of as essentially antifascist. In effect, patients in therapy are being taught not to go crazy by staying rigidly stuck with a single idea, not to identify their existence with the fulfillment of any single idea, and not to remain rigidly committed to a program for living when life experience shows that it doesn't work and is getting them into trouble.

Psychotherapy is a series of *re*-searching, *re*-labeling, and eye-*re*-opening interventions intended to help pull despairing and bitter people out of the holes they have dug for themselves, such as mourning that cannot be ended; yearning that cannot be fulfilled; efforts at achievement and perfection that cannot be realized; beliefs in the necessity of being loved that cannot be fulfilled; locked-in hatreds that consume the hater; unrelenting guilt over the destiny of others; power-seeking at the expense of others; hedonistic, anxiety-avoidant insistence on feeling good; pacts to "insure" one is never alone; and so on of countless ideas about what one must be, should be, or should have done and should have been, which sap the spirit and personality with a single-minded solution to life that does not hold up.

*Paradoxical Interventions as Antifascist
Tools That Renew the Dialectical Process*

Very interestingly, in recent years there has been considerable excitement at the discovery of a relatively new range of powerful therapeutic tools of paradoxical interventions. Paradoxical interventions in effect call for, anticipate, even train for and convey an expectation of an intensification of symptoms as a paradoxical strategy for bringing about precisely the opposite or a reduction of symptoms. Interventions include relabeling and reframing; repetition and exaggeration of symptoms even to points of absurdity; challenge and escalation of crisis, even predictions of loss and failure, including the use of harsh truth about a person's dire future as a way of evoking untapped, latent potential and unused motivation to effect a better outcome than otherwise would have occurred without the confrontation with the likely dire future.[60]

To the anorectic youngster who is not eating enough to keep life and limb together, the paradoxical injunction may be that he or she is quite right about not having to eat, and certainly not in response to parental demands to eat; the impotent man and the wife complaining about his impotence are advised that they need not try so hard to have sex, and certainly he should not attempt sex out of obligation to his partner when he really does not want to have sex; the indifferent mate is advised to stay away from home because there is no point in trying for a closer and warmer relationship with the spouse; and so on of injunctions to continue, accelerate, honor, accept, and know that there is no way out of continuing whatever one's worse symptoms are. The result seems to be, often enough, especially for those who have been called "noncompliant" or "oppositional" patients, a rush of energy or reconsideration of the previously locked-in, inaccessible choice – to eat rather than not to eat, to try rather than not to try, to be rather than not to be.[61]

A variety of theoretical explanations have been advanced to account for the intriguing power of such interventions, which often seem to have the potential for being able to turn around especially obstinate situations to renew change and growth.

Learning theorists have referred to the known principle of satiation of a behavior. When any behavior is repeated over and over again, an inhibitory effect results from the frequent repetition, the behavior loses its "attractiveness" or "taste" and the frequency of its occurrence drops. Gestalt theory has led to the intriguing suggestion that the changing of a familiar context or set, which is what the paradox does by shaking up the blind, stubborn repetition of an ongoing pattern, frees the human mind from the blind grip of repetition and the compulsion to return to the familiar. Others such as Gerald Weeks have argued that the basic power of the paradox is that it poses dialectically an antithesis to the rigid thesis with which the person has become totally stuck, and thereby dislodges the symptom-producing pattern of behavior.[62] The paradox does not provide an alternative or correct solution to the dilemmas the patient is facing, but rather by "forcing" the patient off his or her stuck position, the paradox renews the dialectical process that is based on the experience of and reconciliation of opposites.[63]

Paradox renews possibility. It renews the possibility of seeing a situation that has been deeply problematic in an entirely new way. Lankton & Lankton suggest as follows:

> Perhaps the ultimate value in paradox rests in the understanding that ideas have cycles of existence. . . . What we *think* and *believe* now is cycled and in some way each seemingly polarized part allows for the existence of its opposite.[64]

Interestingly, in relation to earlier remarks about the tendencies to rigidity and dogmatism in the scholarship and professional practice of psychotherapy, there are scholars who credit the study of paradoxical techniques in therapy also with contributing to the profession of psychotherapy itself a new maturity:

> Seeing double or multiple meanings where singularities had previously resided . . . Psychotherapy's current concern with paradox and contradiction suggests a reorganization at a higher stage of understanding. . . . Rather than perpetuating the view that only one theory can be correct, a dialectical outlook would promote the view that each theory is "true," that is, reflects a valid explanation ventured from a particular level of observation. Moreover, the contradiction among the theories would themselves be valued . . . intertheory contradictions also signal the potential for new understanding emerging from their synthesis.[65]

Clearly, the present book is dedicated to our learning more and more how to turn our minds toward the software of DEMOCRATIC MIND in the service of the fullest opportunity for life, for ourselves and others.

CHAPTER TWO

The Choice between Fascist Mind and Democratic Mind

What Chance Do We Have of Changing Our "Fascist Minds" to "Democratic Minds"?

Human minds are wired in certain ways at the "factory," where we are all so to speak manufactured, so that all human beings have the same basic mind software program. However, although we all received the same basic computers at the "factory," it does not mean that all of us end up using our minds in the same ways in the course of our lives.

First, the incredible original software we are issued gives us a wide range of choices of the directories and subdirectories we are going to organize ; before long each mind computer develops its own character based on the kinds of categories of information and experiences created and organized on that computer within its original operating system. If, for example, one creates a major directory that is devoted to the quality of good human relationships, and another major directory to ethics or the moral meanings of the positions one takes in life, the person who is using this mind program will develop very differently from another person who has not organized much information on either of these categories or subjects.

Second, throughout life there are many opportunities for introducing new software programs to one's mind computer. Before long each mind computer develops its own character further depending on the kinds of software it installs. If, for example, one has been given to high emotionalism, undue anger, and vengefulness, there are many software programs, ranging from selecting a religious belief (for example, Christianity, Islam, or any of the thousands of bona fide religions in our world civilizations);

philosophical beliefs (for example, Zen Buddhism or the philosophy of Friends [Quakers]), to modern-day psychotherapies of all sorts, to plain old changes of heart and resolutions to be different, which can lead a person who chooses to do so to become far more emotionally mature, self-controlled, understanding, and gracious. These are software changes. There are many instances where people who have been given to criminality, or to brutality and violence, report a heartfelt transformation in themselves as a result of the inspiration and help of any of the religions or other modes of personal change. Thus, a man who has been given to beating his wife, who truly decides to give up violence and adopt a consistently nonviolent, respectful way for processing differences with his wife, will have achieved a software change. The possibilities are endless. They involve concrete small applications of mind to highly specific tasks, as well as choices of larger frameworks of styles of thinking, feeling, choosing, and doing.

FASCIST MIND is a software program, as it were, that seeks solutions to existential anxieties by adopting a specific definitional system, with definite and certain meanings, without any doubt, hesitation, ambivalence, room for contradiction and discrepancy, and without machinery for change in response to the realities of experience. The FASCIST MIND program lays down clearly who one is to be, how one is to function, what one is to do, where one is to function, and even why one is to be what he is to be.

Thus, a software program we can call "I must suceed" defines a powerful series of emotional responses and behavioral strategies that color much of a human being's life, who must then rise in the morning to a breathless, intense pursuit of success and avoidance of losses and failures at all costs. In some cultural modes, for example the Chinese or Japanese, failures will define a necessity of self-punishment, even suicide, because of the enormous shame of having failed to operate according to one's required software program. In other cultures, the failure will trigger a further software of despair and depression. For example, the culture of traditional Jewish life imposes heavy burdens of another kind of shame on those who do not produce the required outcomes, and there may follow considerable and even serious psychosomatic disturbances in expression of that shame.

❧ A decent young man worked hard as a laborer for a large company, and because of his earnestness and reliability rose in the ranks to become a supervisor and manager of the work force. He was delighted and proud of his success and status and, of course, continued to give his best. When it came to managing and coordinating the work schedules he was excellent; however, when it came to giving leadership to his workers he showed a subtle weakness of a lack of power and self-assurance that opened the door to doubt in his capability. After a few years in the job, at a time of economic reorganization, he was removed from his post.

The shame of his loss now paralyzed him. Since there were sufficient other sources of income for him and his family, he now began to live a secretive life, staying at home but telling neighbors and even his children that he worked at sales from home, and was unable to take any steps to look for work.

"What would you do if the funds you are all living on dried up?" asked the therapist.

"Oh, I would certainly go to work as a laborer or as a security guard because we would need my income, but I would have to work far from our home community. I would be too ashamed for people to see me."

Another example of a software program might be named the "Parent who demands the child function for the parent."

❧ One young adult who had twice attempted suicide over the course of her adolescent years introduced herself to her new therapist by explaining that she was a prisoner of her mother's demands of her to live for mother and not for herself.

The damages that can be imposed on the functioning of children and later on adults who continue to be influenced by demands in their childhood that they function for their parents can attach to virtually each and every function of the human mind.

• *Learn for me* can become transformed into learning problems.

• *Eat for me* can turn up in disorders of eating.

• *Perform athletic feats for me* can easily surface in forms of inhibition and breakdown even in an outstandingly talented athlete.

• *Be happy for me* is a classic invitation to undue rumination, self-doubt, and depression.

Software programs that obligate a person to perform for another are not necessarily restricted to parent-child relationships but occur between contemporaries as well, certainly between husbands and wives. The message, Do sex for me, is one of the prime sources of drooping, wilting, sexual dysfunctions and failures of pleasure.

Men who are burdened by a message that they need to work and earn "for" their mate often are unbearably overburdened, harassed, and ultimately even unsuccessful because of the burden imposed on them. In my clinical work, I believe I have seen a high rate of bankruptcies in the cases of men who did not know how to function for themselves.

෴ *There it was, that subtle drooping of his shoulders and the untimely half-closing of his eyes as he told how no matter how well he succeeded – as a consultant to megacompanies and governments – he never succeeded in winning his wife's interest in him and pride in his success.*

"I don't think I ever will gain her respect," this super-successful businessman said wearily. Interestingly, as a child, his academic successes were always under the eagle-eyed tutelage and critical supervision of his also very bright mother.

"Now as a successful adult and parent, who so to speak wears the pants between you and your mother today?" asked the therapist not referring to the man's actual mother, who had already died, but to the image of his mother inside his heart. "She does, definitely," he answered in a flash.

First Fascism Is Thrilling

FASCIST MIND software demands that a person create and live in a world prescribed, defined, and ordained by immutable authority to require a given style, philosophy, purpose, or code of behavior. While the purpose demanded may in its own right be a perfectly lovely and desirable goal, the fact that it is set as a demand for obeisance to authority and the fact that it is almost always cast in totalistic terms without margin for alternatives, let alone errors and shortcomings, removes a sense of choice or responsibility from the person's mind, which has been ordered to adopt such a software. Psychologist Peter Nathan observes:

> The leader is a superman. He knows. He acts. His is the power and the glory. And we, poor mortals, have but to praise, admire, work and obey. The ways of the leader are not to be understood by us; they are beyond mere reason or logic. He knows . . . What is to happen, is announced . . . no explanation, no reason. . . . There is no talk of committees, conferences, sitting down and working out the problem together, it is announced – what is to be done.[1]

> That one is someone, an historical entity, a part of a great movement, living dramatically amidst mighty events – this is drummed in continuously, subtly, blaringly by the propaganda machine. The speeches, uniforms, symbols (fasces and swastika), the marching, the dramatic policy of foreign subjugation, all this is used to rub in the feeling that one is an important participator in stirring times, when history is being made. The little man is encouraged to play an historical part.[2]

Beloved English psychoanalyst (and former pediatrician) Donald Winnicott also struggled with the successes and omnipresence of fascist societies. A scholar of Winnicott's work summarized his "simple but stimulating" thinking thus:

> Identification with authority . . . is unhealthy, immature, because it is not an identification with authority that arises out of self-disclosure. . . . This is a prosociety tendency that is anti-individual. People who develop in this way can be called "hidden antisocials."
>
> . . . Throughout human history, totalitarian societies have occurred far more frequently than democratic ones. The common ideological thread linking many of these societies was their search, not for *self-disclosure* in Winnicott's terms, but for a *new man* with new values, new morality, and new ideas about the future society and nation. Identification with this "new world," and its representation in a specific leader, provides an extraordinary possibility for escape from both old inner conflicts and dissatisfaction with the outer world. Aggressive drives

find a target in external enemies, thereby allowing for continued positive relations within groups. At the same time a totalitarian society is anti-individual, allowing only such behaviors which celebrate the "new man" as the "new society" or "new God."[3]

DEMOCRATIC MIND software is different at the outset. In many ways it is less attractive at first because it involves acceptance of considerable uncertainty, instability, discomfort, unknowingness, and vulnerability. A person who adopts DEMOCRATIC MIND software accepts in no small part the truths of being ultimately alone, and of being vulnerable throughout one's life, to being humanly incomplete and subject to many weaknesses in oneself. DEMOCRATIC MIND accepts an intrinsic degree of pain and anxiety regarding its positions and about our basic human condition. DEMOCRATIC MIND seeks connection and cooperation with others to share efforts to achieve shared goals, at times also in mutual support of one another's pursuits of respectively different goals. For example, an ecumenical cooperation of different religious faiths conveys that each remains devoted to its own fulfillment and even competition against one another for expansion, but not on the basis of blind obedience and conformity to its prescribed way of living as the only truth in the world.

We are all familiar with the concepts of fascism and democracy on the level of society. Based on the experience and information we have accumulated about fascist and democratic societies, we can see that the fascist process is especially thrilling at first. It offers certainty, clarity, order, and organization. Fascism captivates a mass audience in its pageantry, ceremony, atmosphere of heroism, idealism, and martial pomp. It is an excitement of conspiracy, revolution, and triumph, and the intoxication of organizing and consolidating power. It is the promise of redemption from ambiguity and inconclusiveness, the end of problems, and the blessings of certainty and absolute truth.[4] Fascism is also an adventure to be enjoyed as a part of an excited and exciting group and mass movement totally committed to a single purpose: We become Us versus Them, and the devotees of a higher Superior cause versus the lower Inferior cause of the others.

FASCIST MIND software is similarly thrilling at first also in the individual mind or in family life. Everything is clear, ordered, and organized. One knows one's direction in life. One knows how one's family life is organized. There is little tension of open choices or dilemmas. It is well known that people who have made a decision to commit suicide can become very quiet, relaxed, and even happier for a relatively long time before their suicide act, because they now have a clear and final purpose in mind to which they are unambiguously committed. It is also well known that families who remove conflict from the agendas of their experiences with one another can appear for a long period of time as infinitely happier. They ostensibly excel in their functioning until a later day of reckoning when such a conflict-avoidant way of family functioning, termed pseudomutuality, leads to devastating consequences of dysfunctions, including the serious and worst of major psychosomatic illnesses, manifest psychiatric madness, and unexpected dramatic separations and divorces of people who were least expected to break up.[5] In marriage, a husband and wife can agree, happily and without conflict, on a way of life of egalitarian promiscuity in an "open marriage." The decision and the excitement of fun sexual encounters will generally create an initial excitement of triumph over all the doubt and anxiety, or perhaps the boredom that troubled the couple before they came to their decision, even though over the longer haul this way of marital life generally leads to disasters for the marriage.[6] Any way of life that is organized at first with the power of certainty is likely to give a clear sense of direction, superiority, and rightness that seduces people away from considering the possibility that the choice may prove not to be the wisest one, or may be appropriate only for a limited period of time, or that it is basically in error – after all, we human beings make many mistakes in judgment at every level of personal life and in the organization of our communities and society.

The FASCIST MIND program tolerates no deviation. On the level of society, it is a tragic matter of the historical record how deviants are enemies silenced by fascist regimes. They are punished, tortured, excluded, and ultimately executed. The various ss- and KGB-type secret police tolerate no heretics. In Germany, even an alternative fascist police force to the ss, the sa, were literally executed en masse in the early days of Hitler's regime. Deadly purges of whoever were identified as potential sources of unreliability were characteristic of the Stalinist regime, the Chinese Maoist regime, and many other totalitarian regimes around the world. The victims of these totalitarian regimes mounted rapidly into the tens and hundreds and thousands of thousands. Human life is cheaply disposable in totalitarian regimes. The blood of victims flows like a powerful river, and no voice is raised in opposition in a fascist society.

Stunning as it may be to think of correspondent processes on the level of individual mind and in the small interactions of family life, the FASCIST MIND software similarly tolerates no deviation, weakening of the faith, or insults to its certainty on its lesser levels as well. If, for example, one is beholden always to honor one's father and mother, any experience of anger, certainly of hate, and also archetypal symbolizations (such as in dreams) of anger and hate in wishes that harm or death befall one's parent, are treated as cardinal sins of the mind and trigger demonstrable punishment of the mind to oneself. How many people have fallen ill to mental or physical expressions of self-punishment because they entertained rageful impulses toward a parent against whom they felt they were not allowed to harbor such feelings? Similarly, a failure to perform as required "for" whoever, say a parent or others in one's family as a whole, can mean punishment For example, a child who is duty bound to do well in college for one's parent, or a wife who must perform sexually for her husband. Those who violate the orders are subject to inner mind Gestapo-like punishments that can bring them experiences of deep shame, humiliation, guilt, depression, self-abnegation, and worse.

A young promising psychiatrist who was already in charge of a prestigious acute inpatient ward at a U.S. government psychiatric hospital, and who was clearly considered an up-and-coming future leader of the hospital staff, failed his advanced psychiatric board examination. The failure was catastrophic for him. He went into a near-psychotic breakdown and had to be psychiatrically hospitalized. In his mind he had failed the imperative dictated by himself that he must never fail, and the breakdown was the punishment he prescribed for himself – notwithstanding the fact that it certainly complicated his career further.

There Comes a Day When Fascism Is No Longer Thrilling

Inevitably there comes a day when fascism loses its allure. The pageantry, martial pomp, and slogans of heroism and idealism are still there, but they no longer lift the soul. A heavy air of destruction and impending doom begins to fill the air. Fascism is revealed for the oppressive way of life that it is. Life has become despairing and dangerous. Every day is filled progressively with fear and terror as the web of evil spreads over the breadth of human experience. People die. Others disappear. Others are broken. Many others wait in dread for what fate holds in store for them.

Characteristically, fascism brings about the progressive destruction of everything living in its path. Thus, life in Hitler's Germany moved from the heraldic triumph of a new era of German power and glory to the creation of a living morgue, not only for the millions of wretched Jews, but also for Gypsies and Slavs and many occupied peoples throughout Europe as the evil face of German Nazi politics revealed itself to be a satanic murderer of all peoples, including good German citizens, mocking every aspect of human values of decency and dignity. Eventually the German people ended up not only spiritually corrupted by the evil they did to others, but they also suffered losses of their own lives to their own regime, let alone to the reconquering hands of the occupied peoples and Western Allies who fought back.[7]

Similarly, along the great expanse of Russia, Stalinism accounted for the deaths of three times as many as Hitler had "achieved" on the western side of Europe. R. J. Rummel of the University of Hawai'i has estimated that 54 million Soviet people died at the hands of the Stalinist regime.[8] Life turned grim, perilous, and lacked the simplest vestiges of security for tens of millions more. The Soviet Union was ruled by the caprices of the powerful, and they too were ruled by the still more powerful who reigned above them, until one reached the ultimate level of Stalin who in turn regularly disposed of an untold number of the very chosen in whom he had vested the satanic powers to dispose of others. In the West there were countless true believers in the glory of the new egalitarian communism who for years refused to see the destruction being wreaked by their new god, until they had no choice but to face the facts that their beloved communism was a totalitarian ideology that inherently generated murders of millions.

Farther east, in mysterious China, the communist revolution proceeded apace to create a make-believe utopia of equality of the peoples, but before long was transformed into a bizarre culture that demanded total obeisance to the current ideas and the current leading personalities in whom power had been vested. In Mao Tse-tung's program of the Great Leap Forward, bizarre management policies led to the starvation of many tens of millions.[9] Millions of others were driven by loyalty purges during the Cultural Revolution into imprisonment, disenfranchisement, and poverty, because in some way they did not adhere to the prescribed standards for political and cultural loyalty to the ruling regime and were judged as deserving of disqualification by those who had the power to decide who was loyal and who deserved punishment. Rummel estimates that the Chinese communists killed 35 million of their own people in approximately 40 years from 1947 on.[10]

In exotic Cambodia, another bizarre variant of the process erupted as the Khmer Rouge declared an agrarian revolution and swept into power ostensibly to bring a new level of shared justice to all. In celebrating their conquest of the capital city of Phnom Penh, their very first step was to evacuate the city forcibly, on instant notice, with no exceptions![11] Sick people on surgical beds, old people unable to walk, nursing babies and mothers, everyone was forced into an evacuation march out of the city. Naturally, under these circumstances, tens of thousands died. Trapped, hungry, and ill, the population was then shunted into new agricultural settings, and now there began a witch hunt that culminated in a way of life that became known as the "killing fields." Who were the enemies? In this case, they were not members of another race, nor devotees of another religion, nor nationals of another country, nor adherents of another political philosophy. They were fellow Cambodians who, somehow, in the amazing trance of power, were identified by the look in their eyes (no less than the glasses that some wore that frequently were taken to mark them as dangerous intellectuals), or the sway of their bodies, or the words they dared speak, as irascible, obstinate opponents of the new enlightened way of life, and therefore were to be executed. One-third of the population of Cambodia (one to three million) were exterminated by their fellow Cambodians. (Cambodia has probably given us the definitive and ultimate proof that when human beings need to go on mass killing sprees, they can invent without any difficulty definitions of who are their hateful enemies who deserve to die!)[12]

The stories on the societal level are endless. As this book was being written, Western news reporters told of some anonymous Iraqi citizens daring to describe their lives under then still-ruling Saddam Hussein as pure hell. This was the fearful Saddam who years earlier had celebrated his rise to power by convening a meeting of his party's leadership, in the course of which he read out the names of those who had been identified as traitors; he had them taken out of the hall and immediately executed. In the 1980s he was reported to have been addressing the Iraqi parliament when he saw one delegate pass a note to another, and Saddam reacted by drawing his pistol and shooting both of them dead on the spot. Only a pure idiot could ever imagine that a fascist or totalitarian way of life will bring anything but increasing waves of enormous destruction of life to everyone in the reach of the fascist bullies.

Tragically, destruction and death ultimately are the prime achievement of the fascist software at every level of organization – in society or in the mind. Examples of fascist programs that were intended to solve all anxiety in an individual's life experience – but end in tragedy and irreparable loss of potential, and sometimes even life itself – include the bizarre regimes of eating regulations that characterize anorexia. Anorectics embark on a path to slimness and attractiveness, but slowly and surely their regimen grows to imprison and oppress them to the point where they lose all resilience and the option of choice. Similarly, individuals who seek a perfect love, or who insist only on fair and just relationships, often are shattered by the loss of a relationship, or by the injustice of the unfair and inhuman damages done to them. It is not only the loss of the lover as such, agonizing as that loss is for any sensitive person, nor is it the particular injustice done to one as such – whether economic exploitation or betrayal, or a damaging act of physical abuse; it is the overriding fact that one can be left abandoned and alone by a loved one or dealt with deeply unjustly, which shatters a person's confidence in themselves and in life. Many cases of psychiatric and also major medical illnesses present as responses to the disbelief, hopelessness, and loss of will to fight and live of people who have been rejected or hurt unjustly.

Teenagers seem to be outstanding recruits for minifascist programs. Tragically, for adolescents one favorite mind program is the formulation of a plan to solve their problems in living by committing suicide. There are countries and times where suicide is the leading cause of death in the age range of teenagers. What joy this solution brings the adolescent mind – so much so that there are times when one finds that the commitment to the plan overwhelms the original reasons for having the feelings of wanting to end one's life and formulate the plan to begin with.[13] The commitment to an adventure of eternal wholeness, totality, and absoluteness becomes the end all and be all. The teenager can nurse the suicide plan over weeks and months, savoring it, relishing the detailed preparation, and then, unfortunately, it is as if the teenager is committed to fulfilling the plan that he or she has made, as if the teenager is literally obligated to an inner fascist master to end their life even though by now the original reason for doing so may have weakened and might even no longer exist.

Much of contemporary psychiatry will reject the next possibility I lay out, which is that in a noteworthy number of cases of actual madness, what has happened is that a person has first chosen a way of life that was intended to solve their anxieties, and then this mind program takes over – as fascism intrinsically does. The chosen way of life then so dominates their existence, and pushes them to a kind of nonexistence of their real self, that we see them becoming psychiatrically mad and disabled. We do not realize they are in a state that is the result of the very wrong choice of mind software or way of life at an earlier point, rather than an illness that has descended from some biological or physiological source or more simply from a psychological pattern of being rejected, hurt, or abused. Traditional psychiatry has been antagonistic or at the very least wary of concepts of choice of mental illnesses by patients themselves.

• A young person who has not been particularly well loved and who is not well anchored inwardly may engage in a search of profound religious philosophies from the Orient, dabble in their wise and abstruse wisdoms, and then become slavishly committed to that religious way of life to a point of stopping to deal with the prosaic everyday realities of life. At a certain point their failure to cope with reality will lead to their being deemed psychiatrically psychotic or mad.

• Another person can dabble in an artistry of ideas and images intended to touch creatively on other ranges of human experience, say alternative mood states of relaxation and inspiration, but then become so addicted and enslaved by these experiences that the mind states are transformed into hallucinatory or delusional departures from accepted reality as if they are the true existence in which the person lives. Too-total adoption of the alternative artistic mind software leads here to madness.

Certainty brings downfall also on the choices of ways of life in marriage and family. The example of "open marriages" was mentioned briefly earlier. "Enough of your Victorian, middle-class possessive garbage," will say any number of freedom-seeking and fun-loving people in any generation. "We will make our primary love relationships, including our marriages, open to fully consensual freedom for sexual pleasure. Yeah, no more guilt. We will both enjoy free sex, which we will not conceal from each other." Yet before long, most of these marriages dissolve under the pressure of the request turned demand for absolute pleasure and an absence of tension, because it is precisely the capacity to process tension constructively together, within a framework of a commitment to making each other secure in a basic deep belongingness, that gives couples a chance to achieve enduring happiness in marriage. Note that the sense of safety and security derives more from a continuous choice and affirmation of exclusive commitment to each other than from bowing to a rule against infidelity – a rule that plain people, and preachers too, the world over delight in breaking. Requirements of fidelity and requirements of open marriages, surprisingly, are framed in a similar mind software in which obligation supersedes choice, and in both cases seeks an absence of frustration or tension. In contrast, a democratic mind software yields and even welcomes the waves and rounds of tension and conflict as inherent to the process of intimacy, and the couple is committed to processing their upset and differences toward renewed discovery of each other and deepened recommitment to each other. Over the years, such marriages grow in the security they offer, and the fires of sexuality in these marriages grow stronger with age.

Any frozen, unchanging, and ritualistic relationship seems to smack people in their faces before long. Thus, there are many marriages that look good and stable by virtue of the clear role differentiation between a more powerful spouse and the more submissive one. Yet heaven help the proud owners of these perfect solutions, as erosion of spirit manifests itself slowly but surely in reduced vitality and depression, certainly in the submissive spouse, for there is no possibility of sufficient spirit when one is cast in a permanently submissive role. The dominant spouses may also grow fat with power and increasingly ugly in their triumph as they preside over the downfall of their spouse, and perhaps a widening circle of those who are touched by the destructiveness of their excessive power, such as children who cannot marry or even children who give up the zest for their own lives and leave this world prematurely by suicide.

There is also a FASCIST MIND software that rules out the possibilities of joy and pleasure in this world. "Be grim and serious and devoted," is the order in this software program. So long as problem, tension, and limitation are at the center of one's dialogue with life, and one conceives of one's life more as suffering than pleasure, all is paradoxically well; but if, God forbid, there is danger of a serious improvement in one's status and life might become happy and joyful, all hell breaks loose. When joy rears its beautiful head, serious punishment must be meted out. In psychotherapy, these are the types of patients characterized by Wilhelm Reich long ago as prone to "negative therapeutic reactions," namely, that even as therapy progresses remarkably well and appears to be moving toward an imminent success, something terrible happens and there is an unexpected and quite dramatic breakdown in the patient that often proves irremediable and uncorrectable.[14] In the language of the metaphoric conception we are proposing, the secret police authorities of the FASCIST MIND respond with all their power to maintain control over the would-be escapee to a freedom that cannot be tolerated.

A similar program can be acted out toward another family member with an added dimension of tragedy, such as when a parent prevents a child from realizing his or her potential. The parent becomes committed to a FASCIST MIND program that says the chosen child has been selected to represent for them a punished object and cannot be allowed to achieve successfully or to be happy.

A ten-year-old boy achieved notoriety as a delinquent in his school and neighborhood, and was referred to a full-time school program for severely disturbed children.

In the program, he fought to maintain his superiority as a controlling, combative person; serious incidents occurred in which he pulled a knife on other children and on a teacher. Yet, perhaps to his own surprise, as the months went by, the youngster began to find himself intrigued and then drawn into a relationship with the psychologist-therapist who worked with him long hours day after day. There came a point when he yielded to the connection-socialization of the relationship with his therapist and began to show that he wanted to start living a life in which he could win the pleasure and respect of his therapist and other adults.

At this point, the boy's mother took ill. She called from her hospital bed to ask the boy's therapist to come see her, where an amazing conversation then took place:

The mother said: "I want you to stop changing my son. He is no longer my boy. If you don't stop changing him, I will die."

The alarmed therapist checked with the mother's physicians in the hospital. They said she was suffering an intestinal disorder that was not at all life threatening, nor was it potentially serious, and they expected it would soon respond to treatment.

Yet the mother died two weeks later.

A mature professional woman who had struggled for many years to overcome her mother's dictatorial control and fierceness found herself seriously upset in anticipation of a presentation of her work at a conference.

Free-associating, she remembered her mother's response to a charming musical performance by a grandson's fiancée. Sitting in the audience, the old lady had become enraged and spiteful. How venomous the old lady was even against the productivity and creativity of the young woman who was removed from her by several generations. Further free associations led to memories of how terrified she was of school as a child, and even earlier simply to expressing herself.

"But if I told my mother I was frightened or tense about school, she would encourage me. What a disguise she had! She was wanting me to do poorly, but if I was weak and suffering she would help me. No matter I became so upset about performing."

❧ An attractive professional couple adopted a little boy who had been taken from his disturbed parents at an early age. He had been difficult to manage in several foster families, and before long he became progressively unbehaved, negativistic, and stubborn in his new adoptive family setting. On the surface, the child was proving once again to be an obstinate, tantrum-raising youngster who was very problematic for his new family of mother, father, and four siblings, most of whom appeared to have been living reasonably good lives before his arrival into the family. Nonetheless, it was also true that underneath the overall picture of a decent and loving family, one of the four children was given to sudden and unexplained shrill tantrums that the parents had not succeeded in bringing under control. Beneath the picture of heartwarming devotion of the parents to each other, there also was a quality of fearful submissiveness by the husband to the dominating dictates of his wife. Moreover, a key historical truth was that as a child, the mother had suffered repeatedly being thrown out of her own home. She remembered scenes of her mother removing her physically from the house, and how as a young child she even needed to find alternative shelter for a night or several nights. Her mother would then suffer her return to the house only once again to exclude her some months later. Amazingly, the adoptive mother was adamantly unable to describe any of the emotions that had beset her during these experiences as a child, nor would she tolerate any discussion whatsoever of what might have been going on in her mother's heart toward her.

In the attempt at family therapy with the newly adopted child, the adoptive mother proved to be a relentless cataloguer of everything bad the child ever did. The therapist asked her to reframe her ways of describing the behaviors so that her descriptions of the boy's bad behaviors would be case-specific and informative but would not characterize him as a person *doomed to be bad and not leave room for hope and an expectation of change for the better in the future.*

"Please tell the boy you're disappointed, and you can say you're angry, but also put a lot of emphasis on the fact that you expect him to behave well and describe to him how he will look behaving as a good boy," the therapist explained.

But the mother would have none of descriptions of good alternatives. She was a prosecuting attorney, recounting the growing history of the boy's accumulated felonies. No matter how the therapist sought to retrain her, the adoptive mother grew more surly and aggressive; she insisted all the more on being an inquisitorial cataloguer who reveled at length in tales of the child's ill-doing and went on endlessly about her despair of the child. Slowly but surely she turned her bitterness against the therapy and against the therapist as well. Eventually, the husband joined the wife in complaints about the therapy not doing enough for the child, and also in angry dissatisfaction at the therapist for not stopping his wife's increasing bitterness at the therapy.

The unsuccessful therapy was terminated, and the adoption was essentially neutralized, with the child slated to be returned to an institution for delinquents.

Can Fascist Mind Software Be Changed?

The choice of DEMOCRATIC MIND software is a choice of being open to and indeed relishing criticism, correction, and advice; appreciating and respecting differences of points of view; and happily reviewing one's own ideas for possibilities of revision.

One reader of this manuscript reacted critically with the question, "Who really relishes criticism?" I was sure she meant it. Like many people, this capable person had been taught to use her talents successfully and "show well," and being criticized meant she had failed in the contest, and all that was left for her was to lick her wounds of shame. No wonder she was nervous at work and tired from it, even though she was very competent.

But I really mean it that one can or should train oneself to seek, appreciate, and enjoy criticism as an absolutely necessary part of the creative process and as a welcome quality-control device for monitoring one's performances. This does not mean accepting all criticism, and it does not mean agreeing to be lambasted by rude, nasty, and unfair critics – although listening even to them gives us another kind of sounding board against which to evaluate ourselves, and can also lead us to some improvements in presenting our offerings. Taking criticism means being happy to learn and improve onself in response to feedback based on our own thoughtful evaluation of what has been said.

Uncomfortable as it may be, DEMOCRATIC MIND even welcomes waves of anxiety and uncertainty as signals of process, like moving on the waves of the sea or through the turbulence of the air as we fly through the complex spaces of life. DEMOCRATIC MIND appreciates plays of oppositeness, and that there is room for simultaneously antagonistic emotions – such as to be both kind and accepting as well as firm and demanding of oneself and of others, or to both love and hate parts of oneself and others. The packaging of contradictions is committed to furthering a more decent life for oneself and others in which different sides of emotions check and balance one another. What one does, thinks, and feels are tested honestly against the real-life consequences of one's behavior. The mind is put to work as a kind of science laboratory to which the data of one's experience are brought for analysis and feedback. The guiding question is, "Am I serving the joyful opportunity of life and doing well by myself and others?"

DEMOCRATIC MIND software also does the best to fulfill life opportunities for oneself and one's loved ones in marriage and the family. Just as a democratic way of life in society is the best antidote known in human political thought against violence and destruction on a broad scale, so a democratic healthy self-correcting way of mind better protects people in intimate relationships against destructiveness.

DEMOCRATIC MIND reacts to the inevitable disappointments and problems in marriages and family lives with efforts at wisdom and constructivity. Instead of a raging hurt and need for revenge at being done in by a loved one, say, one strives for a combination of healthy hurt, anger, self-assertion, as well as understanding and such forgiveness as is possible for the humanness of the person who hurt us. It is the appropriate use of all the emotions, sequentially and authentically, that leads to the greater possibilities of recovery for the hurt person and if possible for the relationship. The effort is to achieve constructive problem solving. Real effort is put into fulfilling the original hopes and prayers for decent and rewarding marriages and family lives both in sickness and in health.

Our human condition is complex to say the least.

All of us get stuck at times on some kind of rigid unproductive thinking that characterizes what we are calling the fascist paradigm. The crucial question is whether human beings can make changes in long-established mind programs. The same question can be rephrased in relation to the psychological counseling of our age: Is psychotherapy effective?

I will be saying much more about the capacity for changing one's mind programs in psychotherapy, for that is the mode of change and learning to which I am especially devoted and in which I am most experienced. I feel I saved my own life through a never-forgotten therapy, and I am forever grateful. But I want it to be clear that I respect and treasure the multiplicity of paths to emotional and moral growth that are available to us, including profound spiritual and religious experiences, philosophical and other wisdom, the gifts of being helped in meaningful friendships and inspirational relationships, such as the acceptance of a calling to help people or society. But as I said, I will happily relate in particular to the world of possibilities for a more DEMOCRATIC MIND that opens up in psychotherapy.

Beginning with my own experience as a patient in psychoanalytic psychotherapy so many years ago, my conviction is that profound and deep changes can be made by many people who work hard at overcoming their problems with their "computer programs." I have been deeply appreciative for the help I received in my own treatment, including all the changes made at that time in the course of the therapy, and then also for all the tools that I was given to work with for making further major changes on my own.

When I continue with my experiences as a long-time psychotherapist, I continue in my conviction that psychotherapy can help many people, though certainly not all, to rise to the awesome challenges of one's human condition and existence. Obviously not everyone who comes to me for therapy has been helped (a point that, unlike common practice in many mental health books, I insist on illustrating throughout the book by providing any number of case illustrations where the therapy outcome was not good).[15] There are also any number of people who I thought for some time were being helped but who proved unable to gain from the therapy experience – for whatever reasons and whoever's "fault." The therapist has to bear a significant degree of responsibility for the outcome. I accept the fact that in each case that fails, I, the therapist, must search my mind and heart for the errors I may have made and which of my shortcomings may have contributed to the poor outcome of the treatment. At the same time, I know that treatment outcomes for better and for worse are also a function of the patient's role in determining their destiny. Patients who are genuinely out to win and get well will take everything useful from their therapist to help achieve the best result possible. People who are resolutely out to hurt themselves often will succeed in "proving" their therapy and therapist are worthless. (One of the major tasks of therapy in the latter case is to attempt to motivate the patient to change his or her inner desire to get well, so that the proper diagnosis of the patient's real motivation and the skillfulness of the therapist's efforts to remotivate the patient are important contributions of the therapist to the result of the case.)

    When I was about two years into my own psychoanalysis, I had the funny experience of receiving a new patient who told me that he had recently seen "a terrible therapist" who did not help him at all.

    "What was the matter?" I asked.

    "He is a cruel person, mean and unforgiving. I felt like he just wanted to make me feel worse."

    "Who was the therapist?" I inquired.

    The answer was that it was my very own psychoanalyst, a man whom I had come to trust – and later would come to love for my entire life – as a fine and caring person.

    P.S. I too was unable to help the patient in question.

My answer to the question of whether or not human beings can move from aspects of FASCIST MIND software to DEMOCRATIC MIND software is a resounding yes.

These examples come to mind:

• *The name of her computer program, so to speak, could very well be "I am a little girl." This was her chronic way of being in the world, although she was already in college. She spoke in a soft babyish way and kept her face smoothly angelic and innocent. Socially and sexually too, she had kept herself virginally innocent, and was afraid of social interactions with young men or women that invited any kind of spontaneity. Overall, she was the perfect little girl – except that she suffered terrible feelings of inadequacy.*

By helping herself stay "little," she had become relatively safe from the invasiveness of her mother who, from early in her daughter's life, had made continuous demands on her to serve her and comfort her. In effect, the daughter was commanded to be a mothering figure to her parent rather than mother caring for her daughter's development and happiness. Mother would also turn regularly and viciously on her daughter and berate her in brusque and insulting terms for failing her. Little wonder that her pretty daughter, who very much wanted to help mother as much as she could but could never satisfy mother's demands, seized on a personal program of remaining adorably childlike. Her mind was full of expressions of weakness, not only because she was deeply wounded by mother's attacks but also because this way she had so much less that could be "taken away" by mother's vicious attacks. The anthem of her helplessness was, "I am so little and frail, have mercy on me, do not hurt me."

The daughter's therapy was a difficult one. Periods of progress were inevitably followed by renewed "failures," which the young woman would present resignedly-triumphantly to her therapist. As things went from bad to worse, therapy built to a point of explicit choice: should she give up and resign herself to long-term and chronic weakness, including accepting psychiatric medication, because she would always be frail and emotionally limited? The therapy was now directed at a decisive moment of choice in the young woman's life, and excitingly, she made a courageous decision to transform herself into a stronger more adult person rather than adopt a life mode as a chronically weak person.

In the months following, she emerged a progressively more beauti-ful young woman. Her childlike voice deepened, and her beautiful body stretched into a new adult height as opposed to her earlier crunched up doll-like posture. She made resolutions to change many of her behaviors: to start to drive long distances she had never dared to drive before; to stay alone in her house, which she had feared to do for years; to end the long period of failure to have full intercourse with her boyfriend (for many months the immature couple had reported – entirely sincerely – that they could not find her vaginal opening!); and to speak more forcefully, yet also kindly, to her mother.

The changes she made were not aimed at relief of specific symptoms but expressed a change in her basic mind program that now was beginning to read, "I am a lovable, attractive woman."

No matter how many years I practice psychotherapy, I am in awe of the process and especially of the choices people make. There are dozens of intriguing techniques in therapy for helping people with major symptom complexes, including reeducation with respect to domestic violence, desensitization of phobias, strengthening the assertiveness of people who are too deferring, warming the heart of a person in a meaningful relationship with the therapist as a springboard for improving relationships with other people in their lives, and many more. But the part that fascinates me the most is the "secret" process in which the counselee or patient moves toward a basic spiritual decision of whether or not to undertake major changes in their basic mind programs.

The ultimate choices are expressed in moments of affirmation and resolution along profound lines. Watching people move toward their decisions is fascinating. Characteristically, as they approach their decision, there is a serious heightening of tension and frequently severe nerve-racking emotional crises for the patient, who suffers deeply and cannot help but fear she or he is getting worse. I am especially intrigued that such increased tension and anxiety are especially true of people who are on their way to a life-enhancing decision to give up their longstanding old ill-advised way of life. It is also fascinating to me that on the verge of imminent change for the better, many people look terrible physically –

74

as if all their makeup has been taken off and they are down to the naked bone. Small wonder, for they are on the edge of affirming the choice of a new path in life, and giving up the persona they have put on for years.

I never know for sure what decision the patient is going to make. It is as if there were a struggle of the gods inside the human being. I play my role in supporting the process, standing firm in the face of the regression and the terror as the decision approaches, extending hope, and praying for the spiritual capacity and courage of the patient to make the decision to grow rather than to stay ill, defeated, and abused. At the heights of these crises, I often lay out the full lines of the existential choice that is brewing, as I did with the young woman I described above when I proposed to her the possibility of her surrendering to a reality of being a lifelong weak person, including the possibility of taking the assistance of medication.

When the patient does make a decision to undertake a more wholesome way of life, the therapy room – and the experience of being with the patient – becomes a joyous place reminiscent of many other beautiful occasions in life, such as celebrating births, weddings, or important achievements. The affirmation of life elected by the patient is truly an occasion for celebration.

The following is a summary statement by a nice 32-year-old man after about a year of psychotherapy to which he had come "because something major is missing from my life."

I am a nice guy who goes along with whatever it is that my wife or other people like my bosses dish up, and I will always find the silver lining in a situation. But concealed in my admirable drive to be a positive person is a frightening degree of surrender to nonsatisfaction and nonsuccess. For example, more often than not my wife is unable to join me in sexual activity. We are a young couple, but this happens almost all of the time and can last for weeks at a time. When she says she can't have sex with me, I show her understanding. When my bosses fail to advance me to a position that I have been waiting for and feel I deserve, I accept their decision without a lot of resistance. I consider myself a very capable person who is headed for leadership roles in a number of areas of my life, and I do not like to see myself already falling into the beginnings of being a nonsexual and a nonachieving man.

"It all is sadly so familiar to me. My father is a person who to this very day is always trying to achieve but never will – I remember feeling sorry for him, as a kind of shadow of himself, for so many years since I was a little boy. My mother is even worse, broken, depressed and unfulfilled. They hold on together with some real caring for each other, I guess, but mainly in a pathos of accompanying one another in their mutual suffering that they cannot achieve what they wanted. They swallow the anger they have at each other for their repeated failures and their inability to create a climate of winning more. Their lives at home are chronically tired, as if they have succumbed to a perpetual mediocrity and humiliation in life."

In his therapy, the son of these loser parents decides to change: He decides to act more assertively and to insist on more of what he wants. With his wife he insists – artfully and charmingly – on having and developing their sexuality, notwithstanding her strong reluctance. In his work situation he insists on a raise – and gets it. He also develops new entrepreneurial business possibilities and begins undertaking independent financial investments and initiatives. His basic style in life becomes one of facing his failures and challenging himself to achieve whenever he faces challenges.

Again, regrettably, let it be very clear that in all psychotherapy practices there are many who do not change their mind programs successfully. It is part of every professional's experience to carry sadness, regret, and intense professional self-questioning in response to every patient failure.

But I am happy to report that, in my judgment, a majority of people who enter into serious psychotherapies, and certainly those whose emotional development already puts them into a position of being capable of making choices that they wish to be healthier and stronger, do achieve major changes for the better.

The capacity to change from FASCIST MIND software to DEMOCRATIC MIND software includes serious and critical clinical situations such as when patients successfully decide to

• stop being psychotic and make themselves rational
• stop being violent toward a loved one

76

• stop being depressed, and instead live in appreciation and wonder at the joy that is possible in life

• overcome a blockage and inability to learn and go on successfully to use one's mind and learn, including completing formal educational and training programs that were previously dropped

• stop being an angry, account-accumulating misanthrope, and become a loving person

• enjoy, frolic, and be libidinal

It can go both ways. The process of psychotherapy leads patients toward their definitive choice. Along the way, there will be initial and smaller choices that contribute in their own right and set the stage for the likelihood of a good outcome when the big crunch comes. But I have seen it go both ways. Sometimes there are painful failures, for months or even years, because the patient is too disabled and too much a captive of an inner psychology of weakness, loss, and incompetence until, finally, there comes a moment of inspiration and they rise to the challenge. Other times there are patients who seemingly go roaring toward lapping up the assistance of therapy only to come to a resounding halt even in view of the possible finish line – metaphorically something like the plight of Moses who sees the Promised Land but can never enter it.

He made the decision to stop being crazy. Previously he had been in mental hospitals five separate times. He had convinced everyone that he would never be well, but now he realized he was throwing away his dignity and that he did have a better choice. He resolved to put in a regular day's work and to stop talking crazy.

Over the following years, long after the therapy was concluded, he continued to work productively and to date has not played the role of a crazy. He never made it socially to the point of being able to have a steady girlfriend and marry, but he does manage a successful network of simple social relationships in his community, succeeds in working gainfully and in gaining the respect of his peers as a reliable working person, and has never been rehospitalized.

He decided not to go on in treatment after learning from the therapist that he would be expected to keep his posture up (instead of slumping);

go back to a coed gym group from which he fled because of the difficulty he had controlling his attraction to one of the woman participants; begin working at a regular income-producing job; and move away from his mother's house. It is not only that these are very hard tasks for him; one can argue that he is not ready for them but will need psychotherapy to get ready. It is also that all of these tasks and the basic idea of trying to become a self-sufficient person are unwelcome to him. Secretly he enjoys his life as a troubled and marginal figure. With his mother's complicity, he builds a schedule of intense activity in a distance-learning college and in physical exercise groups and pretends he is busy and normally productive like other people, while both he and his mother evade the facts that he is a 30-year-old man living with his mother, unable to develop social relationships and unable to work. He realizes the therapist will be working to change his babyish ways of thinking and of indulging himself like a combination child and teenager (and that the therapist will also hold him to giving up his beloved periodic public tantrums). Although at first he hailed the therapy as different from what he experienced in the past because of its emphasis on defining the goals of his life and in expecting a more grownup way of speaking of himself, he now announced he would not continue because it was "too hard."

Mother did not object to his decision.

CHAPTER THREE

The Fascist Believer

Totality, Overcertainty, and Suppression of Information

The concepts of FASCIST MIND versus DEMOCRATIC MIND refer to the mindsets, or "software," a person adopts as the prevailing organizing programs for the use of his or her mind in various aspects of life. These are the ways in which we frame, define, interpret, and organize our life experiences. These mindsets are programs that contain definitions of our values and goals as well as choices of the means we will use to achieve our goals. The mindsets are also templates for understanding what is happening to ourselves. For example, most people like to succeed, such as in winning a game or prevailing in a competitive situation in business, yet there are also large numbers of people who are driven by their inner mind program to fear success and prefer failure. If success comes their way, it can make them feel terrible and act terribly. The clinical literature traces many cases of inadvertent as well as planned suicides precisely to a person having fallen "victim" to successes they could not bear. So a good deal of life, though not all of it, lies in the beholder or in the mindset defining the meaning of events in our lives.[1]

The characterizations of FASCIST MIND and DEMOCRATIC MIND that follow are not intended to create pictures of absolute types or robotlike creatures, one purely fascist and the other purely democratic. People are highly variable configurations who combine both fascist and democratic characteristics in different areas of their lives. The descriptions given are an attempt to extract and highlight major characteristics of each type of organization of mind. When it comes to characterizing specific individuals, most descriptions will include component processes drawn from both lists of organizing processes.[2]

The value of the structural analysis is in providing a way for seeing which parts of a human being are characteristic of the rigid totalitarian thinking that we describe in the FASCIST MIND, and which parts are characteristic of a more flexible and life-protecting style of thinking that we describe as characteristic of a DEMOCRATIC MIND. I suggest that we can understand a variety of traditional psychiatric disturbances as well as relationship disorders as deriving from clusters of characteristics of the FASCIST MIND, and that ideally, the most desirable therapy or correction for any number of psychiatric disorders and relationship disorders is to teach and invite the development of more democratic mind processes in people. While this concept may be somewhat unclear and less concrete and definable than a prescription for a given medication to be taken x number of times a day, I suggest that this thinking is more optimistic, wholesome, and more respectful of the potential of many human beings to become emotionally healthier than many of the pills that address only the physiological sides of mind function, and do not seek to change the mind programs through which people define their goals and ways of living and the meanings of their experiences.

The following table summarizes the characteristics of FASCIST MIND versus DEMOCRATIC MIND. We shall look at each of seven characteristics as they are paired in dialectical contrasts in each of the two mindsets.

Totality, Overcertainty, and Suppression of Information

The first cluster of FASCIST MIND thinking we will consider involves totalistic thinking, certainty, and suppression of all contrary information. FASCIST MIND chooses total and final solutions that are "guaranteed" to bring heaven and perfection to earth for the true believers and loyal adherents of the fascist belief system. Uncertainty, ambiguity, complexity, alternative solutions, or multiple frames of reference are not acceptable. In each case, we will attempt to see how the former types of thinking, which are so familiar to us on a societal level, also appear in the working of individuals' minds and in the framing of intimate relationships, and here too instead of producing a paradise bring with them burdens of psychological disturbance and disintegration.

Table 1. Characteristics of FASCIST MIND versus DEMOCRATIC MIND

	FASCIST MIND	DEMOCRATIC MIND
1	Totality, final solutions, perfection	Processing and containing contradiction, diversity, and complexity
2	Overcertainty, absolutism, and magical thinking	Acceptance of uncertainty, process, possibility, creative tension, and anxiety
3	Censorship and suppression of information	Openmindedness to information, questioning, and use of scientific-like empiricism
4	Obedience, conformity, intolerance of dissent	Freedom, respect for dissent, and responsibility to make choices
5	Superiority, excessive power seeking, and prejudice	Basic equality and respect, sharing power with checks and balances against excessive power
6	Violence against self and/or against others, cruelty, sacrifice, and destruction of life	Nonviolence, conflict resolution, aggression for self-defense and seeking peace, kindness, belief in humanity, and goodness of life
7	Denials of doing harm to self and others	Acceptance of responsibility for doing harm to self and others

1. Totality, Final Solutions, Perfection	versus	Processing and Containing Contradiction, Diversity, and Complexity

Fascist societies know where they are going. They have an ironclad program – whether for national or economic growth, expansion of their boundaries, suppression of alien ethnic or religious groups, inculcation of a glorious era of their indigenous language or other aspects of their culture, development of a new kind of classless society, or what have you.

This is what Benito Mussolini is quoted as saying in the *Encyclopedia italiana*:

> Fascism affirms the state as the true reality of the individual. It is for the only freedom which can seriously be considered – the freedom of the state, and of the individual within the state – because, for the Fascist, everything is in the state, and outside of the state nothing legal or spiritual can exist, or still less be of value. In this sense Fascism is totalitarian, and the Fascist state is unity and synthesis of all values and gives to the whole life of the people its meaning, development, and forcefulness.[3]

Psychoanalyst Christopher Bollas analyzes the creation of the fascist totality thus:

> Something almost banal in its ordinariness – namely, our cohering of life into ideology or theories – is the seed of the Fascist state of mind when such ideology must (for whatever reason) become total.
>
> To achieve such totality, the mind (or group) can entertain no doubt. Doubt, uncertainty, self-interrogation are equivalent to weakness and must be expelled from the mind to maintain ideological certainty.[4]

Similarly, the FASCIST MIND process knows exactly what it seeks, be it to gain the absolute love of such and such specific person or of all people; to rise in a given system such as one's work to whatever designated rank; insistence on an absence of pain, or on self-indulgence and on only having pleasure; on "not being hassled" by emotional stresses or demands in intimate relationships; in short, whatever major theme is chosen by the person as the certain way they need to organize their life experience.

He was strange, with an air of brilliance and confidence about him, but also a foreboding grimness, and somehow even something frightening as if he might turn harmful and cruel if he didn't have his way. His wife in turn was angelically beautiful, demure, and sweet. But she was also seemingly hesitant and confused; she projected an air of chronic dependency on stronger people in her life, originally her parents, and now of course on him.

They had it all put together ideally, he claimed, or at least they would have it all if only she trusted him fully and respected him much more unquestioningly and followed his wise lead in all matters, certainly in their business but also in their family relationships and in bringing up their child. But her mistrust of him was so great she even stooped to the lowest of the low and accused him of having sexual relations with her sister! What a lie! In a burst of rage, he turned the whole house upside down. He would have nothing to do with such ridiculous accusations. The fact that her sister, who is the one who had admitted to the sex with him, continued to insist it was true, and the fact that their parents also believed the sister's admission, were all nonsense. In fact, he claimed it was he who knew a lot about her mother's and father's sexual betrayals over the years that he would yet reveal. In the meantime, he wanted never to see any of them again, and he forbade her to be in touch with her family.

The attempt at couple therapy failed (with at least four known therapists).

In contrast, DEMOCRATIC MIND calls for a processing and organization of contradiction and complexity. On the societal level, the trap of absolute solutions is eschewed as much as possible, and the major goals that are adopted are constantly re-reviewed and scrutinized for their effectiveness. There is understanding that a goal or solution often can prove to have been erroneous, even at costs of tens of millions of dollars. For example, a country's major change of a water system that was intended to solve a flooding condition may prove to have such a deleterious effect on the ecology of a region that it has to be reversed at considerable expense after the incorrectness of the original solution is recognized. In democratic societies the process of defining solutions involves a good deal of discussion, clarification, testing, and revision based on the results of observation, tests, and much deliberation. There is often a high level of controversy between the experts, as well as between the choices proposed by the experts and the choices acceptable to various segments of the people in the society with their respective interests. And notwithstanding the best efforts, it is still understood that huge mistakes can be made that will have to be corrected, or that new developments can change the rightness of a decision, or that new knowledge can result in a different conclusion.

Similarly, the mind of an individual that works in a more democratic way is committed to processing a variety of thoughts and experiences, including contradictory experiences, knowing that they are all parts of a single puzzle. Often ways need to be found not only to alternate between different parts of a solution but also to experience them simultaneously and to create a coordinating mechanism for allowing the different thoughts to take place at the same time even in their contradictions. For example, one can experience love for a child because he or she is so adorable and because one is committed to protecting the child, and at the very same time can experience anger and even rage at that same child for certain characteristics, say of opposition, surliness, or negativism. Being partial to one set of feelings does not mean having to cast away the other kinds of feelings. The contrasting emotions do not even have to be separated in time and space, even though at any given moment one aspect of feeling is going to be the predominant one. In the fully flowing and functioning mind, there is a possibility of accepting the continuity and interplay of all feelings simultaneously, up to and including a point of enjoying a symphonic energy that grows out of allowing contradictory feelings to flow unashamedly at the same time.[5]

Having contradictory feelings too much for one's comfort, or remaining overly ambivalent to a point where one cannot choose and act on a basic policy position, or becoming ruminatory or obsessive with alternating feelings also are not healthy uses of one's mind. The goal is to be in touch with one's contradictory streams of feelings and to be able to contain them in an overall position that has resonance and clarity. Thus, as to the universal truths of angry and hating feelings toward loved ones – such as a spouse and also our children, and they toward us – the hoped-for goal is to love the other very much, while being able at the same time to contain (meaning include and encompass comfortably) angry feelings as they arise within our overall love.

In an article written collaboratively by a Chinese and an American scholar on ways of reasoning about contradictions, it is pointed out that,

84

Life is full of contradictions. Even in science, the concept of a complex system reflects the reality of the world we are living in, a reality that is multilayered, unpredictable, and contradictory. . . .

The Western tradition of counterargument construction seems likely to result in more specific hypotheses and consequently more solutions that naive dialecticism could. Its emphasis on noncontradiction may also enable people to reason rationally to reject false statements (even ones they may like) and accept true statements (even ones they may not like). . . .

A dialectical approach may enable people to tolerate and even appreciate contradiction, consequently maintaining a view of the big picture. On the other hand, the dialectical approach may be accompanied by a tendency to accept too much at face value, failing to generate counterarguments for a statement and trying to reconcile opposing views, even when one viewpoint is inferior in terms of the evidence supporting it.

The authors conclude, in what seems to me to be also a delicious intellectual sense of humor:

The dialectical response to the linear question of which is the better way of thinking is "it depends." The logical ways of dealing with contradiction may be optimal for scientific exploration and the search for facts because of their aggressive, linear, and argumentative style. On the other hand, dialectical reasoning may be preferable for negotiating intelligently in complex social interactions. Therefore, ideal thought tendencies might be a combination of both – the synthesis, in effect, of Eastern and Western ways of thinking.[6]

Struggling with complexity, different ideas, and differences of opinion seems to be healthy and enriching both on the level of decision making by leaders of society and in the workings of the individual mind. The authors previously cited point out that much research has shown that the quality of decision making in Western societies is enhanced by argument, debate, and conflict. Two other researchers of what they call intriguing "mindfulness" note that the process of seeking to draw out distinctions and contradictions on the individual mind level generates

(1) a greater sensitivity to one's environment, (2) more openness to new information, (3) the creation of new categories for structuring perception, and (4) enhanced awareness of multiple perspectives in problem solving. The subjective "feel" of mindfulness is that of a heightened state of involvement and wakefulness or being in the present.[7]

It has to be clear that the DEMOCRATIC MIND process does not make a (fascist-like) fetish of ambiguity, uncertainty, contradiction, or complexity, and certainly not of confusion, indecision, and failure to act on life's challenges. A fogged-out false-to-life nirvana of being "laid back," "cool," or indifferent to life is not what democratic mindfulness seeks or allows. There is no less alertness, responsibility, and organization of self to act in DEMOCRATIC MIND, but it is based on more analysis of and acceptance of the many sides of issues and solutions and a constant linking of decisions and choices to the best empirical information available. DEMOCRATIC MIND takes the best constructive action possible to enhance life for oneself and others. It does not serve certainties blindly, and it does not sink into confusion and passivity.

| 2. Overcertainty, Absolutism, and Magical Thinking | versus | Acceptance of Uncertainty, Process, Possibility, Creative Tension, and Anxiety |

It is not that human beings do not need goals to guide their organization of themselves and their lives, but a rigid adoption of any given idea or program or mindset becomes a trap that imprisons a person and in effect creates a torture chamber and jail.

On a societal level, many countries and peoples have thrived on images and plans for the triumph of a new era, say America's New Deal, or the Jewish people's adoption of Zionism; but insofar as the societal goal is translated into and expressed in authoritarian repressive police-state measures, such as Stalin's Great Purge, Mao's Great Leap Forward and his Cultural Revolution, or even the guillotine-avid French revolution in the name of liberté, égalité and fraternité, even millions – in some of the above cases even tens of millions – of human beings can lose their lives. Progress may demand conviction, dedication, and sacrifice, but it is far kinder than what is achieved by zealots proclaiming overcertainties and enforcing their absolute beliefs ruthlessly. Christopher Bollas describes the role of certainty in fascist thought as follows:

> The core element in the Fascist state of mind (in the individual or the group) is the presence of an ideology that maintains its certainty through the operation of specific mental mechanisms aimed at eliminating all opposition. But the presence of ideology (either political, theological, or psychological) is hardly unusual; indeed it is quite ordinary. The core of the Fascist state of mind – its substructure, let us say – is the ordinary presence of ideology, or what we might call belief or conviction."[8]

On the level of mind, countless human beings have adopted personal mental programs with absolutism and overcertainty. Among these are requirements of success and the treatment of failure as an unbearable catastrophe, perhaps even as a virtually life-destroying experience; insistence on achievement of a certain level of status, acclaim, or power; insistence on having a totally clean mind and a heart free of any hints of whatever is defined as sinful, bad, or evil; overdevotion of oneself to a given aspect of life, however valuable and beautiful it may be in its own right, for example the very widespread problem of overdevotion to work at the expense of relationships as well as at the expense of relaxation and expression of other aspects of one's mind and creativity ("all work and no play makes Jack a dull boy"); and endless other possibilities of the selection of any one aspect of life and its disproportionate expression at the expense of other parts of the spectrum of human experience. It is hardly fun to live as a rigid, driven, slavish person.

Knowledge that derives from a quest for certainties and absolutes is, of course, rigidly inflexible. Either an idea or a way of life must meet the prescribed standard, or it is a serious violation of the required injunction and rule. Psychiatric conditions also thrive on a substrate of restricting oneself to absolute goals. Exaggerated certainty and absoluteness in the selection and definition of one's experiences acts as something of a psychological disease-breeding culture. It breeds pangs of debilitating anxiety over failure to achieve the absolute goal; it breeds energy-sapping depression and psychiatric symptoms such as grandiosity and delusional thinking or magic ritualistic behaviors. For example, a person who demands never to be left alone at home is likely to become progressively fearful and cowardly, truly unable to be home alone even if it is necessary, and there is a danger that the exaggerated babyish dependency and demands on others will develop into a symbiotic exploitation of some other person or even a family group as a whole.

If one must forever achieve some absolute, life can turn into a living hell. Especially noteworthy are the fears that build in people of the rage that mounts in them at whatever seems to be standing in the way of their reaching their absolute quest. The person then resorts all the more to psychiatric symptoms in order to maintain control over threatened eruptions of their aggression, as in cases of obsessional thinking that are unconscious symptomatic maneuvers to protect one from murderous rage at someone else.

On an interpersonal level, a quest and demand for overcertainty often triggers demands on other human beings to act, be, serve, and fulfill the needs and standards imposed on them, which by definition creates a situation that breeds a stressful relationship with the other person and a good deal of emotional tension. For example, when a parent demands that a child fulfill their needs for honor in the community, the demand will weaken the child's freedom and sap the child's energy to achieve and win honor for himself or herself. Similarly, an absolute conception that one cannot bear any sexual-emotional disloyalty in one's mate can set up an awkward situation at best, and a perhaps-fatal situation in the face of a spouse's natural sexual impulses and erotic interest in others (which if enjoyed as a pleasureful tension of some natural attraction to others but without actual disloyalty and acting out, might actually add a tonic of pleasure to the couple's erotic life). Even at the simplest level, a certainty that one's intimates must be there for one at all times can lead to an unbearable sense of a betraying and punishing world, because no machinery is provided for processing the natural waning of attention and retreats to personal selfishness that are true of all human beings.

Sociologist Lewis Coser wrote of the inevitability of a "dialectical tension" in human life and experience, "between order and disorder, between the making and the breaking of internal peace and harmony."

Man's best hope is not the eradication of conflicts, for that is impossible, but rather their channeling and regulation, their domestication if you wish, so that their more destructive impact can be successfully minimized. A great poet once put this in two terse sentences when he wrote: *Without contraries is no progression. Attraction and Repulsion, Reason and Energy, Love and Hate, are necessary to human existence* [William Blake, *The marriage of heaven and hell*].[9]

The democratic alternative to an absolute way of organizing experience is based on an acceptance of uncertainty, possibility, and creative tension and anxiety. There is a valuing of the creative potential of being vulnerable and struggling toward one's goals with alternations of courage and anxiety.

Democratic use of mind even includes a valuing of discomfort. Framed against the prevailing culture in the Western world that seeks, endlessly, to achieve anxiety-free comfort and pleasure, this is a remarkable statement. Paradoxically, in my understanding, an acceptance of discomfort is actually the only way to approach the grand mystery of life without undue distress. The acceptance of unease and distress, including yielding honorably to our vulnerability, imperfection, incompleteness, and even actual experiences of anxiety is the best way I know to reduce, contain, and convert the dread experiences of powerlessness and uncertainty about life and reality into a relative sense of competence for life and comfort about living out our unknown and uncertain futures. Acceptance of anxiety stops a whole slew of runaway secondary processes, such as further anxiety that one is going to be anxious. Discarding the belief that one needs to conceal one's anxiety from others overcomes feelings of shame – external or internal – over being anxious. Accepting that life includes a series of problems that are to be confronted and met with dignity, wisdom, and a combination of potency and humility has the possibility of transforming many of the difficult situations that confront us into challenges and adventures.

  A twelve-year-old girl was ensnared in a terrible logjam of extreme obsessional thinking and compulsive behaviors. Agony was written all over her face. At any given moment she was busy counting away number by number until she would reach whatever was her designated goal, then she would throw her head in a predesigned ritualistic twitch toward the right and roll her eyes, then resume the pattern again, and then the whole pattern again and again. This symptom was accompanied by a variety of other rituals including tapping her fingers in preset patterns, shifting her sitting position through a required sequence of postures, and the repetition of given sentences in silent whispers of her lips.

The poor child was in torment, but surprisingly had little to say about herself and her life when invited to do so by the therapist. It appeared that she was somewhat pleased by the interest shown in her and perhaps able to take some small comfort from his presence to relax the iron grip of the atmosphere attending the obsessions and compulsions that dominated her life, but for the most part she remained so deeply sad and violently imprisoned by the regime of obsessions and compulsions that she could not really converse with him.

Could the parents help? Not at all. The girl's mother was in a state of depression and was undergoing psychiatric treatment. Father hated his wife, and would have long since left her were it not for his wife being in such a weakened state that it was impossible to leave her, as well as the fact that his own highly visible position as a leader in the community would have suffered from the shame of divorce especially when his wife was virtually disabled by her depression.

But liberation did come, amazingly if also tragically, and it was in the form of the mother committing suicide. The relief of the child was absolutely palpable. It was clear that so much of her had wished to be free of the tyranny of her mother's oppressive sadness. In truth, the little girl had wished so deeply in her heart to get away from her mother that she wanted her mother dead, but at the same time she also feared lest her wishes could have the magical power to be translated into actual aggressive assaults. This was the reason she had been utilizing the obsessive and compulsive devices. The obsessive-compulsive devices were magical rituals to ward off her evil feelings and wishes of killing her mother. With her mother's death, the daughter was able to release herself from her rituals and explore the *range of her true feelings for her mother, father, and herself. Amazingly, within a couple of months she reorganized herself as an attractive, friendly girl and began enjoying an all-around natural and wholesome lifestyle.*

In sum, the little girl was protecting herself from feeling responsible for causing her mother's death – which she certainly wanted to happen in order to be free of mother's overwhelmingly depressing and unnourishing presence. The daughter quite likely sensed the death was in the making and she desperately needed not to be held responsible.

3. Censorship and Suppression of Information	versus	Openmindedness to Information, Questioning, and Use of Scientific-like Empiricism

Fascist societies by definition control information. The news that is allowed to reach citizens is the news the regime wants them to have – true or not. Whatever the regime believes can contradict the certainties and absolutes of their rule is variously suppressed, censored, and banished. Thus, many churches and states that advance a given church position disallow as "heretical" informations and publications that might spread "heresy" against the church. Nondemocratic governments fail to allow journalists, presses, and publications to publish the facts and truths about their behavior.,For example, the Serbian people were not informed of the brutal "ethnic cleansing" murders masterminded by Slobodan Milosević, and even after Milosević was ousted, a majority of Serbs denied or didn't know what their leaders and people had done; the Palestinian Authority several times threatened the lives of any TV reporters who would broadcast films of Palestinians celebrating the destruction of the World Trade Center in New York (in Norway there was extensive public coverage of the extravagant celebrations of the devastating blows against the United States by the Palestinians as well as by several other Moslem communities).

To Fascism, every single critic is a danger. He jeopardizes not the continuation in office of the government but its logical foundation

– which does not make the danger any less real. To stifle it in its very beginning, the whole mentality of the people and of every single individual must always be kept in line. Every mental and physical activity must be brought under the dominating influence of the state. That is why there can be no freedom of speech, of the press, of peaceful assembly, why science, arts, trades, professions, sports, everything must show the Fascist coloring. That is the reason for the totalitarian state. If the foundation of the Fascist community is to be firm, every thought and every act in every field of human endeavor must be imbued with the same spirit and reflect the same collective will. . . . The Fascist state, in order to effectuate its organic character, has to rule its members from inside out. They must be so conditioned that a mental process divergent from the proclaimed collective thought not only does not occur, but is *psychologically impossible.*[10]

A courageous Chinese professor of journalism recently described "the still all-powerful department of censors and standard-setters" as "spiteful like the Nazis. . . . It thinks itself infallible like the pope. In the 1950s it covered up the starvation of millions of people. Today, he charged, it lies about SARS. Their censorship orders are totally groundless, absolutely arbitrary, at odds with the basic standards of civilization, and as counter to scientific common sense as witches and wizardry."[11]

In contrast, democratic societies hold as a cardinal principle the dissemination of truthful and accurate information to all people, even if the consequences will hurt people high up in the government and society. Thus the U.S. press battled valiantly to expose the full meanings of the Watergate break-in that in time forced Richard Nixon to resign the presidency of the United States.

The classic illustrations of suppression of information in psychiatry had to do with the original psychoanalytic discoveries that there are hidden sexual impulses that many people do not want to bear in themselves. Thus, the girl who wants to kiss her prince charming lover may develop a very bad taste in her mouth as a hysterical psychosomatic outlet for the suppressed desire she is otherwise banishing from her consciousness. The married man who wants to have extramarital sex with a certain woman but feels too guilty or fearful to do so may experience erectile dysfunction on the same basis. The original classic psychoanalytic paradigm was then extended to include one's connection to inner aggressive feelings as well as sexual impulses, and a whole world of crucial, interesting, and powerful phenomena now became understandable using the same framework of identifying suppressed impulses as underlying various symptoms. Thus, many headaches were understood as derived not from infections and clogged sinuses but from a buildup of a pounding rage and wishes to hurt and kill someone important in one's life. Thus too, many moments of blankness and inability to think clearly were understood to derive from rushes of brooding anger and hatred that one did not know how to acknowledge and release toward whomever one was not allowed to harbor such feelings for.

But the psychology and epistemology of censorship and suppression of undesirable information go further to subtle and profound inner thinking and emotions. For example, inside of everyone there are continuous small voices which, even during our waking hours, bring up signals, symbols, pictures, and thoughts of desires, impulses, and issues in our unconscious mind that are really important to us. These inner mind experiences color and influence the ostensible conscious experiences we are having in our everyday lives to a profound extent. Even as we are ostensibly having a grand time such as at a party, no one else knows what's going on inside of us; for instance, when in our inner mind we may be disturbed by jealousy of a sibling who we always felt was more attractive, and the conscious experience may be in the form of a physical upset, such as "Damn, I suddenly have such a stomach ache!" Many times we sense and even "hear" some of these feelings in the "back of our minds," but most of us do not know how to bring these feelings to our consciousness. Mostly we shake these messages off as annoying discomforts. If only we knew better, acknowledging the small voices and acknowledging the presence of thoughts and emotions inside could make a huge difference in our comfort level. Thus, in the midst of a charitable gathering, the selfish voice inside can have us puffed up and prideful about the charitable contribution we are making to the cause for which we are being honored by our community, and our inner voice may even add that we don't give a real damn about the cause to which we are contributing, and if only we let ourselves know these thoughts we would have a better chance at curbing our preening and pretense. Similarly, a religious person may have licentious thoughts at a peak moment of prayer, a committed educator may find himself or herself thrilled by an experience of power over students even as he or she continues delivering the perfectly correct lesson, or a loving parent may find in their heart indifference or even cruelty to a child to whom they are busily delivering messages of love. Our minds are complex beyond words, and certainly include a continuous flow of dialectical experiences of contradictory thoughts and emotions.

Often enough our inner voices also bring us quite real intuitive information, such as about our spouse being sexually or emotionally involved with someone who is present, say at a community event we are all attending. It becomes more than useful to learn how to sort out one's intuitive feelings and examine them for the information they bring us as well as to understand which emotional reactions are working away in our hearts and minds, and often enough creating false ideas rooted in feelings rather than facts.

A fascist-type mindset suppresses information about thoughts and emotions that do not fit the party line. Such thoughts and emotions cannot be, therefore they do not exist. The thoughts and emotions that stand in contradiction of the announced call are driven into an underground of unknowingness. Insofar as "illegal" sides of our unconscious nonetheless register in the brilliant machinery of the inner experiencing that is our mind, punishment may well be meted out for the forbidden thoughts and feelings.

On the level of interpersonal relationships, this way of censoring and suppressing experiencing extends to denial of our authentic feelings to the other person and not only to ourselves. Feelings that contradict or in any way oppose our stated and expected feelings – of love, friendship, kindness, devotion and so on – are pushed away and denied.

A six-and-a-half-year-old girl was failing first grade and was sent by her teacher for a psychological evaluation. The evaluation proved the little girl was a perfectly bright child who should be able to develop normal mastery in reading and related school tasks on the first grade level, but that she was so busy warding off unpleasant feelings of hurt, resentment, and anger at her mother that she couldn't learn well.

Inside, the little girl felt that mother was regularly scolding and rejecting her. Surprisingly, real life observations of mother and daughter showed what seemed to be the very opposite. In fact, what the examining psychologist saw was that the mother was intensely busy in a tiringly insistent way in maintaining forced smiles and transmitting nice statements to her daughter minute after minute. The immediate impression was that mother was working so hard at proving that she loved her daughter there must be a head of steam of aggressive feelings and displeasures toward the little girl that mother did not know what to do with.

The therapist counseled the mother to tell her daughter each day that she had hateful feelings toward her! Needless to say, this aggressive prescription for mother and daughter was accompanied by a wholesome clarification of its rationale. The naturalness of the bad feelings inside of mother were explained to her at some length; the therapist discussed with her in good humor a basic acceptance of this side of her parenting experience. Mother was helped to accept the naturalness of her resentful and angry feelings at her daughter along with her love.

"Instead of working so hard to smile at her, tell her in good humor, 'Mommy doesn't like you,' the therapist advised the mother to say. As you get braver and you see your daughter can take it, tell her 'Mommy is angry with you'; and then later when you're both stronger, you can even say, 'Right now, Mommy hates you.' But remember all the time you speak to concentrate in your heart on how you really do love her very much. And be sure to be light and humorous when you tell her you can't stand her or you hate her. And every few times, do also tell her that you love her and always will love her even when you're angry with her."

Over a period of a few months, mother delightedly joined in the task of reorganizing herself and her daughter by telling her that she was angry with her as well as assuring her that she also loved her. The mother and daughter succeeded in creating a new music that combined expressions of anger and love toward each other. Over this period, the little girl relaxed and improved dramatically in her schoolwork to a point of moving on to perfectly normal reading skills at her grade level.

DEMOCRATIC MIND cultivates a much greater degree of openness to information from within one's mind, including acceptance of contradictions and ambivalence. The quest for truth is honored by the use of scientific-like methods of questioning in one's mind what is really going on, and how different thoughts, ideas, and emotions are variously truthful statements of different sides of what we really believe and want. One result is that negative feelings are recognized for what they are but so too are positive feelings, and there is less problem in accepting the fact that these feelings alternate with each other and also are experienced simultaneously. The goal of mind is to create reasonable maps of reality rather than maps of reality that are imposed by orders of one's mind in advance of what one must feel and think. Upsetting and contradictory information is sought, accepted, and welcomed.

A manager of a company finds himself increasingly upset in his work. Instead of relying on the fact that he is working too hard, he asks himself how he may be creating the stress in his work. He then realizes he has recently become bossy, controlling, and insulting to workers to a point that a strain is growing in their responses to him and in his own inner experience.

Going further in the quest for information, the manager looks at what might be the sources of his need to run the show so much that he is offensive to the people working under him. He has the courage to track how this side of himself expresses a longstanding style of selfish involvement in which he needs to make other people serve him and feel that they are "under" him, just like his father had treated him as a boy. He concludes that the time has come to cultivate more generous and respectful attitudes toward his workers. The wholesome use of information to which he has opened himself saves him from an enormous amount of tension and results in a dramatically improved atmosphere in the work environment.

CHAPTER FOUR

The Fascist Slave

Obedience, Conformity, and Intolerance of Dissent

1. Obedience, Conformity, Intolerance of Dissent	versus	Freedom, Respect for Dissent, and Responsibility to Make Choices

Abandoning or submerging one's identity to another identity, whether to one's family or a group such as a religious order or nation is an important and almost frightening issue that has been sidestepped in much professional psychological writing.

I suggest that we would do well to add the following to our concepts of psychopathology: descriptions of the extent to which a person abandons their individual identity and self to their family, to a group, or to any collective process or ideology. We should define such situations as problematic, disturbed, and psychopathological.

One of the most significant events in the first decades of family therapy was the identification of the myriad of serious disturbances generated by the patterning of family groups in "pseudomutual" or "enmeshed" patterns.[1] The basic disturbance is a state of undifferentiation, blending or fusion that does not permit individual growth. A variety of serious psychiatric symptomatology can result, including psychosis, severe learning disorders, or severe psychosomatic conditions, conditions that in their own right have long been recognized but not necessarily as having derived from conditions of enmeshment and lack of separation. In family relationships, enmeshment also was found to result in some major family breakdowns, such as a sudden flight from a longstanding conflict-free or conflict-avoidant marriage in which one of the ostensibly happy spouses suddenly announces that he or she is leaving! The abandoned spouse is characteristically left crushed in unexpected horror after years of a "good marriage." Similarly, there are cases of children breaking away from their ostensibly good families and taking on an entirely different lifestyle. To date, traditional psychology and psychopathology have no names for these kinds of behaviors and conditions.

Aborting and withdrawing from relationships has long been "'celebrated" in psychiatry, but I propose that we need to expand definitions of abnormality to include also entering into overly enmeshed relationships in which people abandon and lose their individual identities and integrity within a relationship with another or others.

Many emotional and psychiatric problems are based on and derive from overconnection, overdependence, lack of separation, enmeshment, blind obedience, and surrender of autonomy and personal integrity to an outside identity – whether it be one's family, a group, or a larger societal collective or ideology. Although in conservative traditional psychiatry one is disturbed only after one begins to act disturbed, psychotherapists have always defined disturbance on the basis of earlier unhealthy and unwholesome personality processes and patterns of feeling and behavior, even if major psychiatric symptoms have not yet appeared, or in family therapy terms even if the symptoms as such appear in someone else in the family; for example, in a symbiotic mother who is dependently clinging to her child but whose child looks all put together for now but who surely will show symptoms of emotional disturbance at a later time. A truer map that looks at all parties to overconnection, unseparatedness, fusion, and loss of self will identify emotional disturbances in all parties to the excess, in whoever demands the exaggerated closeness, such as the parents, and in whoever is the object of the demands for closeness, such as the children, even before actual symptoms of psychiatric disturbance show in either party.

Family therapy, in particular, has shown that there are many seemingly normal and even ostensibly outstanding superior people headed for breakdowns because they are too emotionally "enmeshed" in their families. Blending into a family, overreliance on a mate, being part of a "pseudomutual" family in which differences are swept under a rug of continuous unanimity and forced joyousness all prove to be powerful harborings of high risks of emotional disturbances, including as noted earlier sudden irreversible flights from relationships, serious psychosomatic diseases, major learning problems in children, and even psychoses.[2] Although traditional psychopathology does not diagnose disturbances in "healthy" members of families until and if actual symptoms are apparent in their functioning, given an overattachment or blending into one's family at the expense of one's personal identity it is logical to diagnose disturbances long before symptoms of inability to function are evident.

The problem begins whenever one assigns too much of one's identity-maintenance and loyalty to anyone outside of oneself. The classic experiment by Solomon Asch, in which a short line is judged longer than a long line under group pressure, showed how so many people acquiesce to clearly wrong facts under group pressure.[3] The brilliant experimental series by Stanley Milgram in which people believed they were giving serious electric shocks to a subject showed that two-thirds will even do potentially dangerous harm to others when ordered to do so by an authority or when they are placed in a normative context in which people appear to behave that way.[4] Blind participation in cults and orgiastic groups leads to tragic consequences of losses of self, murder, and suicide, as was seen in Jonestown where the killing of a U.S. congressman was followed by mass murder-suicide, in Waco where a tough-out with the FBI led to deaths of the cultists, or in the mass murder in a Tokyo subway station by a cult releasing sarin gas.[5] All of the above are, in my opinion, prima facie expressions of serious emotional disturbances, and not simply "interesting findings" from experiments or remarkable case stories from life that are not to be understood and classified psychiatrically, even though none of the perpetrators came to a mental health practitioner or clinic to ask for help! Acting on otherwise unacceptable values to maim or destroy the lives of human beings – oneself or others – because one is told to do so by someone to whom one has assigned the power to know what is right and must be done is, in my opinion, a serious mental illness, even though it is not listed at this time in the DSM (the standard manual of psychiatric disturbances).[6]

Submerging oneself in other people, such as in one's family or in any

group process, at the expense of one's individual autonomy and conforming blindly to any ideology or authority are personality processes that set
off and combine with other psychopathologies and social psychological
disturbances. As noted earlier, the loss of individual identity in one's
family has been implicated in many cases of mental illnesses. Similarly,
common sense tells us that being silent bystanders when neighbors or
colleagues are marched off to unknown fates, and even more, joining
willfully in blind obedience to orders to massacre people in concentration camps or pogroms should also be recognized as manifestations
of disturbance and psychopathology, and certainly as contributing to a
disturbed society. The same is true in the smaller level of the family, say
when siblings see and allow one of the children to be singled out viciously
as a scapegoat of one or both of the parents. I have seen adults feel guilty
all their lives because they failed to speak up for a brother or sister. These
are hardly behaviors we want to call normal in a value sense.

Traditional psychopathology has allowed for many absurd situations
in which giving over all of one's being to a collective process or ideology
has not been diagnosed as disturbed until it is too late, and being part
of the group has turned into the basis for doing terribly crazy things.[7]
Giving up all of one's earthly possessions to a cult such as the Moonies
and finding refuge in a new life identity as a member of the cult has
not commanded a definition of psychiatric disturbance (unless one's
family could afford hiring psychiatrists to prove that the choice to join
the Moonies was a result of "brainwashing"). Because of grave fears
of tampering with religious freedom in Western democracies, making
oneself an unrecognizable nonperson as part of a cult or group ideology
has been treated virtually as a form of democratic freedom rather than
as an act of self-destruction. Thus, belonging to the Charles Manson
group as a blind robotized devotee of the psychopathic leader was not
considered abnormal until the point in which cult members participated
in their infamous killing orgy. Similarly, relocating with one's family to
the cult headquarters in Jonestown, or to the cult compound in Waco, and
pledging allegiance to their respective leaders, Reverend Jones or David
Koresh, was not considered pathological until the days the Jonestown

group murdered a U.S. congressman and went on to enforce the Reverend Jones's command for mass suicide, and the day the Waco group turned itself into a Masada of self-destruction when it refused the entry of federal officials.

A young man who devotes his self entirely to a passionately anti-Semitic group that distributes the classic anti-Semitic pamphlet "The Protocols of the Elders of Zion" is considered exercising a personal ideological or political choice until, rarely, his anti-Semitic statements are so blatantly irrational that he is perceived as crazy rather than a political person. If this young man succeeds in seizing political power and becomes the designated leader of a whole nation that is to eventually murder millions of Jews as well as millions of Slavs and others, was the mass murdering he espoused and commanded "simply" his chosen political philosophy, or was it also unrecognized madness?

I strongly prefer to think of the above young man as mad from as early a point in time as possible. I hate the idea of simply accepting, what are indeed the facts, that ordinary and normal people are easily genociders. I prefer that we redesign our sciences of psychology and psychiatry to lay down public health rules that whenever a person turns to the rottenness of abusing and killing others, from that point on he or she is not normal but is insanely not human. It seems to me that our attempts at a more civilized society would be strengthened if we had sciences of psychology and psychiatry that were assigned the tasks of defining people who commit themselves to killing masses of other people as disturbed.[8] (Let me add immediately that this does not at all mean that mass killers have to be given any of the protection of those laws that offer more merciful legal punishments to people who are "out of their minds" and unable to restrain themselves from a burst of mad killing.)

Of course, as in many processes, there is a matter of degree. I propose that identification of oneself with a collective group at some real expense to one's personal identity and development be defined as a first or mild level of disturbance. I suggest that going further to greater degrees of giving up one's ability to think for oneself and one's judgment and values in the face of group pressures should be defined as more severe degrees of disturbance. Going along with the instructions of authorities to believe in things that normally are unacceptable to the individual's values, and especially when one loses the ability to discern that one is doing actual physical harm to people, should be viewed as more extreme disturbances of loss of self. And taking the helm to command others to submit to exploitation, and especially to command people to become perpetrators of destruction of the lives of others, should be classified as increasingly severe disturbances.

I suggest that phenomena of loss of self or a readiness to destroy others can be viewed in a schema of parallel and alternating Disorders of Conformity and Obedience, and Disorders of Coercion and Subordination of Others as seen in the table that follows. In one sense, we thus provide for a separation between followers and leaders in processes that involve giving up one's independent identity and judgment. On the face of it, this seems important when it comes to full-blown exploitation, violence, and persecution. For example, there are also legal implications to the degree of responsibility of the leaders versus the somewhat lesser responsibility of followers. But there are also enough situations where individuals who were in one period of time the followers who then are given or seize the opportunity to turn themselves into the cult-masters, brutal commanding officers, and führers of the persecution. In addition, by setting up disorders of conformity and coercion in parallel, we are emphasizing that a common underlying psychodynamic principle is at work – basic violations of the boundary of the self.

Needless to say, the content of the ideology to which one surrenders one's self and one's values has to make a big and even definitive difference. It is still an escape from self to abandon the preciousness of one's identity to, say, a sport-exercise group or a musical group in which one is so immersed that there is no time otherwise to be a "person," but these behaviors are not as serious as joining and being part of a group of goose-stepping murderers. I believe the central question should always be the extent to which human lives are likely to be damaged – beginning with one's own life and continuing with the lives of others.

Table 2. Disorders of Conformity and Obedience, and Disorders of Coercion and Subordination of Others

DISORDERS OF CONFORMITY	DISORDERS OF COERCION
Lack of differentiated self-identity, conformity, enmeshment, and obedience	Narcissistic inability to identify with a common humanity, subordination of others
Renunciation of own ideas and values	Imposition of one's ideas and values on others, coercion and subordination of others
Fusion of self with other, surrender of mind	Charismatic or dictatorial power to command obedience and "mindlessness"
Participation in persecution and destruction of human life	Leadership role in persecution and destruction of human life

A young adult woman gives up her independence to stay forever devoted to her parents, thereby "killing" her potential for love, marriage, childbearing and a satisfying sense of her own dignity as an independent coping person.

Early on, as a young adult, the above woman may very well be a pleasant and attractive "old maid" who seemingly hasn't had the luck to find a mate. In polite society no one would dare identify her as suffering the psychiatric disturbance of hanging on to her parents and nuclear family, but that is the truth being sidestepped by the "nice people" in everyday society who avoid calling a spade what it is, and professional mental health classifications have followed suit in not having a diagnosis for such abandonment of oneself. If the same young woman at some point goes on to attempt to take her life because her existence has turned hollow and empty beyond her ability to bear it, the mental health professions are then obviously ready to define her as seriously disturbed. If she gives herself over to a cult or group whose members threaten to destroy their own lives (for example, a suicide cult), her disturbance will also be recognized as blatant and serious. (Regrettably, if they "only" threaten others, they may be seen as a political group and not as crazies.) The truth is that we should be able to identify this young woman's problems earlier, when it is becoming clear that she is not separating properly from her family. And such commonsense truth might also provide a basis for triggering corrective treatment at an earlier point in her life.

Surrendering oneself "mindlessly" to orgiastic group behaviors, especially with little regard for the safety and welfare of people, is a more advanced stage of loss of self than remaining an immature child to one's family. The cult process existed at Jonestown long before the culminating events of murder and mass suicide. We need to know how to label such processes without fearing that we are violating peoples' political rights and freedom to choose what their lives will be. We should not be afraid to say what common sense tells us: people in blindly dependent relationships to a group are not exactly paragons of mental health.

As suggested earlier, the highest levels of disturbance should be defined in respect of acquiescing to and participating in group programs to do actual harm to other peoples' lives. There are endless examples, including those mentioned of Jonestown, Waco, the cult in Tokyo that used poison gas in the subway, and the Manson-killer group. There are so many others, such as the destruction of lives in the "killing fields" in Cambodia; Idi Amin's murdering in Uganda some years ago; Tutsi orgies of murdering Hutu in Burundi years back, and now more recently in 1994 in Rwanda Hutu orgies of murders of Tutsi; massacres of ethnic Chinese in Indonesia, Malaysia, and other South Pacific countries; anti-Semitic pogroms through the centuries; the incredibly well-organized Auschwitz death factories in the Holocaust; and in the future still newer terrible forms of mass killing that await us, in what has been called man's potential for "ecocide and omnicide – the new faces of genocide."[9]

To sum up, the argument against the prevailing psychiatric establishment in neglect of the subjects of obedience and conformity (no doubt some pundits will correctly observe how much the psychiatric establishment itself is hierarchical, authoritarian, and demands conformity) is that people are disturbed from the time they stop being genuinely autonomous, and not after they show obvious symptoms of emotional distress. The compliant subjects in the Milgram experiments should be defined as disturbed by mental health experts. The fact that fully two-thirds of the subjects showed disturbance in the Milgram paradigm should not be allowed to dissuade us from the truth. If everyone dies in the Black Plague, they were nonetheless all sick. One does not turn plagues into being called normal just because a majority are affected.

Social psychologist Philip Zimbardo notes a high degree of susceptibility to cults and to immoral, ridiculous, aggressive, and self-hurting actions:

The majority of "normal, average, intelligent" individuals can be led to engage in immoral, illegal, irrational, aggressive and self-destructive actions that are contrary to their values or personality – when manipulated situational conditions exert their power over individual dispositions.[10]

There also has been too little attention paid to people's obedience to an inner controlling voice, in other words when people have constructed a prevailing plan or ideology that they must obey: when a youngster does not want to be obese to the extent of becoming anorectic and murdering her or his body; when a person becomes hypnotized by their own construction of an image of suicide as salvation and freedom and feels he or she must complete the suicidal plan; when a married person cannot feel secure without imposing repeated serious humiliation rituals on his or her partner; when a person at work has to step on colleagues and deny them career success in order to ensure their own "success" (in one major Israeli hospital, a distinguished surgeon hid a liver in order to prevent a colleague from having the honor of doing the first liver transplant surgery!). These are situations in which a person is enslaved to his or her inner dictator. The extent of such bondage often does grave damage to the person's health or to others.

To conclude: I propose, as a basic guideline for judging whether obedience and conformity to an inner mindset is to be considered pathological or not, the relatively simple tests of whether or not through such conformity the person is likely to do significant injury to his or her body or emotional health, and whether or not a person is likely to do significant injury to the physical or emotional lives of others.

The Locking of Man's Mind by Obedience and Conformity

It is shocking to take stock of the extent to which people lose their minds by virtue of obedience and conformity. Insofar as the human species is proud of the evolution of mind and so delighted with the brilliance of science and computers advancing and extending man's capacity to think to undreamed of heights, it is shocking to realize how much people become unable to think at the simplest levels of rationality, objectivity, and even self-preservation when they succumb to obedience and conformity. Submitting oneself to the dictates of charismatic or megalomaniacal leaders or the ideas and ideologies of movements and groups often means an end to the possibility of independent reasoning, judgment, and moral values.[11]

How important it is for us to know that even seemingly strong characters, and even people with good leadership skills, can succumb to this terrible phenomenon. Most of us have had experiences in groups in which decisions are made in the rush of a group process that sweeps people into voting with a majority – I have seen this process too many times both in mental health clinical settings and in academia, always the more so in departments where people are overinvolved in the politics of their hierarchies. Irving Janis's studies of *groupthink* have shown that even at the highest levels of government bureaucracies, leaders can be drawn into participating in the power of the consensual political force at work in a group meeting until they are unable to ask themselves, as they otherwise might, what are the true implications and consequences of policies.[12] The implications and outcomes in real-life history are serious, and many lives are lost because of cowardly decisions by governing authorities when some of those present knew better but didn't have the courage (a) to retain their true minds, and (b) to speak up.

We now know that even in democratic societies, for long periods of time a majority of human beings will fail to see the evil of vested leaders who govern corruptly: in the United States the paranoid-persecution era of Senator Joseph McCarthy that left so many lives shattered and the fabric of American society torn to bits; totalitarian leaders of totalitarian regimes such as the Hitlers, Stalins, and Pol Pots. And most difficult are the situations in which a decent leader and governing council are drawn by the passions of their so-serious roles to make wrong decisions such as taking unnecessary or overly harsh military actions, and some of the ministers or senior officials present really know better but lose and give up their individuality and ability to think critically.

One of the recognized fathers of family therapy, psychiatrist Nathan Ackerman, took special note of the readiness of conformists to seek to destroy the person who resists conformity (and saw in this dynamic an important contribution to anti-Semitism, the subject Ackerman was studying at the time).

> Every evidence of individuality in another person becomes a painful reminder of the sacrifice the prejudiced person has made in disowning parts of his self. The fear of the different is, hence, not in proportion to the extent of the objective, measurable differences; rather it grows in proportion to the implied ego threat. Thus, the difference comes to symbolize the fruitless suppression of self in the anti-Semite, the futile effort to achieve acceptance and security through compulsory obedience. It is understandable, therefore, that the prejudiced person should want to destroy the nonconformist. "If only the Jews behaved like everybody else" – this frequently heard remark, with its emphasis on conformity rather than on merits or demerits of behavior, clearly illuminates the resentment that is directed against the person who symbolizes difference.[13]

An intrinsic relationship exists between the surrendering of one's mind to others like a führer or a cult and a readiness to be violent if so ordered. The relinquishing of autonomy means a giving up of one's own judgment and standards. It also means an inability to rely on moral courage to assert one's intuitive knowledge of right and wrong. "Conformity groups" indeed hate the people who defy them, and may well turn violently against them. Thus, the Tokyo Aum cult was reported to have murdered parents who sought to bring legal action against the cult as well as those who showed signs of leaving the cult.

> Like other deceptively easy-to-join cults, however, Aum had an unpleasant fate in store for those who tried to leave: they were told that

they would burn in a Buddhist Hell. Rescuing backsliders, some cult members have confessed, turned into kidnapping them, and, as that went unpunished by the law, kidnapping turned into murder.[14]

Sociologist Meta Spencer has focused on those who exercise obedience to orders to commit aggression as a major contributing threat to the possibility of future nuclear destruction. She writes, "Those at the controls of vastly destructive weapons will only be trying to do a good job when they follow instructions to launch those weapons."[15] Father Thomas Merton, a Trappist monk, wrote vividly of the danger that faces us when some day normal people following instructions, doing what they are expected to do, agree to press the buttons of nuclear destruction.

> It is the sane ones, the well-adapted ones, who can without qualms and without nausea aim the missiles and press the buttons that will initiate the great festival of destruction that they, the same ones, have prepared. What makes us so sure, after all, that the danger comes from a psychotic getting into a position to fire the first shot in a nuclear war? Psychotics will be suspect. No one suspects the sane, and the sane ones will have perfectly good reason, logical, well-adjusted reasons for firing the shot. They will be obeying sane orders that have come sanely down the chain of command. And because of their sanity they will have no qualms at all. When the missile takes off, then it will be no mistake.[16]

Healthy versus Pathological Conformity

Nonetheless, the subject of obedience and conformity is not a simple issue. Some degree of conformity is first and foremost a necessary process for survival of the collective. As Stanley Milgram also pointed out, humans are not solitary animals. We tend to function in hierarchical groups because the individual has the greatest chance of survival when functioning as a member of the group. Obedience and acceptance of one's role in a hierarchy are also positive life-sustaining values. At the same time, Milgram learned and taught that there is something incredibly dangerous in conformity, so much so that Milgram was concerned that in the long run humans as a species may lose their very existence because of the imminent dangers of conformity to policies of destruction of human life. He wrote with severity and concern thus:

> Something far more dangerous is revealed: the capacity for man to abandon his humanity, indeed the inevitability that he does so, as he meshes his unique personality into a larger institutional structure. This is a fatal flaw nature has designed into us, and which in the long run gives our species only a modest chance of survival.[17]

Milgram analyzed the behavior of his compliant subjects who willingly gave what they believed to be severe and dangerous electric shocks; he saw them as having shifted from experiencing life through their own selves or identities into a state of being delegates of a higher power. Milgram called this an "agentic shift" into an "agentic state," which enables people to relinquish responsibility and to follow orders without regard to their morality. "A man [then] feels responsible to the authority directing him but feels no responsibility for the content of the action that the authority prescribes."[18]

The abandonment of self can reach stages of mass psychosis. The psychiatric textbooks contain exotic descriptions of groups of human beings who became transformed into mass hysterical or even psychotic followers, such as legendary tales of groups of nuns who decided they were cats and went outside to dance orgiastically for hours on end, in at least one celebrated case causing the collapse of a bridge in a tragedy that cost many lives. There are more ominous versions of dances around a golden calf of mass experiences, when the very goal of the group is to celebrate the destruction of masses of others' lives. This is what Erich Fromm was writing about in his legendary work. Fromm knew that unless man overcame the capacity to comply, the potential for democratic organization of society is at grave risk. In a radio talk given toward the end of his life, he called for early identification of dangerous credos and leaders, and the courage to stand up against them when there was still a semblance of normality and propriety at work:

> If you begin your resistance to a Hitler only after he has won his victory,

then you've lost before you've even begun. For to offer resistance, you have to have an inner core, a conviction. You have to have faith in yourself, to be able to think critically, to be an independent human being, a human being and not a sheep. . . . Anyone who takes this path will learn to resist not only the great tyrannies, like Hitler's, but also the "small tyrannies," the creeping tyrannies of bureaucratization and alienation in everyday life.[19]

Nowhere are the dilemmas of compliance more dramatic than in religious experience. The religious institutional process by definition calls for devoted blind acceptance of rules, regulations, and inviolate ritualization, in each case according to the dogma of the designated church. It is religious orders that have given humans their sanest and most noble conceptualization of the illegality of killing human life. The spiritual emphasis on good deeds and decency of motivations that religious orders encourage have helped advanced mankind to a high degree. And yet, embedded within the overwhelming obedience and compliance that religion cultivates and demands is also a propensity to command a hypnotic march toward killing other human beings in the name of one's religious gods, when this is what the church and ostensibly one's god tell people what to do. Mature religious philosophies are needed to discern when religious leaders and orders are to be defined as profane and satanic because they are prescribing the destruction of life. Such philosophies of religion for the most part have not yet been developed.[20] In our time at the beginning of the 21st century, the political implications of this understanding again are becoming crucial as the Western world has been brought into a major confrontation with those elements in Islam that call for, legitimate, and actively pursue the deaths of the infidel-Americans and the American way of life, as in the terrorist attacks on New York and Washington on September 11, 2001.

I believe that all religious teaching or teaching in the name of religion that espouses killing the nonbelievers should be declared unlawful in legal and political terms, and entirely outside of the province of the free speech and freedom of religion that democracies practice. In other words, all the institutions of our civilization should be united in defining killing and the espousing of killing as outside of whatever the boundaries of the legitimacy over which that institution presides.

If we return to our focus on psychology and psychiatry, up until now a mature guide to individuality and health has not been worked out in the area of mental health, certainly not in the official diagnostic classifications. We need to encourage and honor normal degrees of obedience and compliance by decent human beings who identify with their families and with the collective needs of the groups to which they belong, but we need to be able to differentiate these from pathological degrees of obedience and conformity that lead people to be slavish robots available to do the worst things against themselves and others. It is important to arrive at an understanding of healthy noncompliance versus pathological noncompliance.

Healthy nonconformists neither obey nor disobey blindly. They are respectful of authority and convention and do participate in the prevailing identificatory rituals and historical continuities of the groups to which they belong, but they do not obey thoughtlessly and mindlessly. They say no to physicians who instruct them to undertake treatments that are patently, on the surface of it, destructive, such as prescriptions of electric shock or lobotomies or mind-destroying drugs.[21] They do not comply with teachers who forbid them to think about alternatives or to research dissenting points of view – be they orthopedists who forbid thinking about chiropractic manipulation or Alexander or Feldenkreis methods of training the body, or psychologists who inculcate authoritatively that all autism is a neurological disease and never has anything to do with parental relationships to children, or economists who command loyalty to a one-and-only model of an instructor or a famous university department. In family life, as parents, if they see their partner rejecting a child, they do not stand by and allow the destructive rejection to continue without making powerful efforts to improve the situation, and they certainly do not stand by and allow abuse of the children. They hold respect for life and potential as a transcending value above all else.[22] They stand up to bosses who push people around insultingly and are interested in showing off their power at the expense of the dignity of their workers more than they are interested in the actual success of the work to which the organization is committed. They say a firm, courageous *no* to Milgram experimenters, and even to police and army officers who command them to do harm to innocent, unarmed human beings.

One professional writer summarized the Milgram study thus: "If Hitler asked you to electrocute a stranger, would you? Probably."[23]

Psychological health calls for people to be nonconformist to the extent they would not electrocute their children, spouses, neighbors, or any other people, no matter who tells them to do so, whether their minds have formulated the crazy rotten idea, or they have been told to destroy other human beings by reputable and impressive authorities outside of their minds, even ostensibly their gods.

The idea of killing unarmed defenseless people is too vicious and disturbed to be honored from whatever source.

Albert Camus wrote thus after the end of World War II:

The years . . . have killed something in us. And that something is simply the old confidence man had in himself, which led him to believe that he could always elicit human reactions from another man if he spoke to him in the language of a common humanity. We have seen men lie, degrade, kill, deport, torture – and each time it was not possible to persuade them not to do these things because they were sure of themselves. . . .

And naturally a man with whom one cannot reason is a man to be feared. The result is that – besides those who have not spoken out because they thought it useless – a vast conspiracy of silence has spread all about us, a conspiracy accepted by those who are frightened and who rationalize their fears in order to hide from themselves. . . .

Before anything can be done, two questions must be put: "Do you or do you not, directly or indirectly, want to kill or assault?" . . . People like myself want not a world in which murder no longer exists (we are not so crazy as that!) but rather one in which murder is not legitimate. . . .

For my part, I am fairly sure that I have made the choice. And, having chosen, I think that I must speak out, that I must state that I will never again be one of those, whoever they be, who compromise with murder [italic emphasis mine].[24]

CHAPTER FIVE

The Fascist Fist

Superiority, Excessive Power, and Violence against Self and Others

1. Superiority, Excessive Power Seeking, and Prejudice	versus	Basic Equality and Respect, Sharing Power with Checks and Balances against Excessive Power

FASCIST MIND "knows" it is superior to everyone else. It is intolerant of alternative ideas and intolerant of the possibilities of leadership and power being vested in anyone other than adherents to its certain and perfect conception of truth and reality. Unfortunately, the belief in one's superiority, and the generally heroic pageantry and choreography of power and superiority make people feel good for quite a while before the destructiveness inherent in totalitarianism catches up with them.

DEMOCRATIC MIND is committed from the outset to sharing power and leadership. With respect to leaders, there is a need for a chain of command, and a democratic organization of power that vests in designated people the right to make major and even world-shaking decisions, but even so control over the leaders is never entirely surrendered. The leader is on notice that he or she is called on to consult and share power with a series of other leaders, cannot impose their decisions one-sidedly on their societies as dictators do, and are subject to critical retrospective review and accountability for their decisions.

Any illusions there once were that totalitarianism is the unique province only of certain cultures, ethnicities, or religions has yielded to the truth that at any given point, all societies are in danger of succumbing to vesting their power in a strong man or junta. At the same time, it is true that some collective groups are more protected and therefore less likely to allow a strong man to gain control, and correspondingly that some societies are more prone to the emergence of a strong-man dictator, and that the study of these characteristics is important. Some religious cultures, for example, speak of a common god for all human beings even as they promote their own chosen godhead or ideology as the true god; other religions call for the destruction of all infidels and heretics who deny the one true god defined by their doctrine. In most religions there is a dialectical tension between both positions. One side of the dialectic strains toward recognition of the universality of a god that is the true god of all human life and is in a sense far greater than any feeble representation of a god that any one religion creates in its efforts to configure and imagine what god might be like. The other antagonistic side of the dialectic involves religions that seek to gain a superior position over other religious groups, banishment of the other religionists and nonbelievers, and perhaps even their destruction and extinction, so that there will be no competition to one's ostensibly true god. It is the balance between these two positions in any given religious culture that defines whether that religious group is likely to adopt crusading-destruction policies toward other religious groups.[1]

Political scientist R. J. Rummel of the University of Hawai'i has done outstanding work in demonstrating that in terms of political organization, democracies are less likely to commit genocide than are totalitarian societies. In other words, given a democratic political organization with checks and balances against excessive power, there is far less likelihood of a dictator overthrowing the democratic regime, and in turn far less likelihood of said society engaging in genocide.[2]

How many fascist dictators has human history seen? Among the numerous names that come to mind are Ghengis Khan, Tamerlane, Hitler, Stalin, Pol Pot, the ruling triumvirate of Ottoman Turkey who created the Armenian Genocide – Jemal, Enver, and Talaat – various rulers of China, certainly Mao Tse-tung, and so many rulers in the Balkans like Milosević. It is an endless parade in which the visible greats are accompanied by an endless parade of many thousands more lesser known heads of state, generals, marshals, commanders, prophets, and holy men, down to the lower levels of field commanders, junior officers, colonizers and settlers, and who-not who did who-knows-what-not to the people under their control. Sadly, democracies also have created their shares of megalomaniac leaders who destroy masses of human beings (for example, the American destruction of indigenous peoples),[3] but democracies characteristically also protect their institutions of free speech, due judicial process, and citizens' rights for criticism, opposition, protest, and censure in order to overcome destructive leaders and restore democracy when it falters.

The Quest for Power in the Human Mind

The human condition with regard to power is not an especially attractive one. In his study of compliant behavior, Max Rosenbaum reported the work of Maurice Walsh, a psychiatrist at the Mayo Clinic who examined 25 leaders in politics, industry, the military, medicine, labor, and religion, all of whom were designated "psychiatrically extremely healthy." Rosenbaum reported that he found "patterns of marked callousness for human life and human rights, a marked tendency to distort the truth to further self-interest, and that the 'pathologically charismatically leader demonstrates . . . an intense narcissism of self-centeredness,' so that . . . 'mass atrocities and murders' are carried out without any guilt!"[4]

What is no less disturbing are the observations that the more people exercise power over others, the more they experience a loss of concern for moral issues. They become more involved in their proficiency and performance, and increasingly devalue the victims of their power. Stanley Milgram noted the tendency of the subjects who gave shocks to the hapless learners to devalue the learners as a consequence of the progression of their shocks. It was not that these people began with a bias or antagonism toward the learner, but rather that they seemed to develop this attitude as a result of their doing harm to the learners.[5] Carl Jung, himself no paragon of virtue in the test of Nazi times when he was known to have cooperated with the Nazis in several ways, noted that Hitler was the symbolic representation of the inferior part of everyone's personality that seeks to compensate for its deficiencies through power over others.[6]

Clearly, power is a basic human need for feeling competent. It is the authority and energy for self-assertion, a capacity and drive for overcoming weakness and obstacles, and a natural means of competition and survival. Yet the capacity of many people to regulate power is distorted. They "electrify" their power system too intensely. Power becomes an end in its own right. It is an aphrodisiac-experience of being liberated from weakness and the threats of limitation and inferiority. Power is a narcotic to quell fears and awareness of mortality. It ends up not as a means for overcoming limitation but as an end in its own right. This is what George Orwell observed when he wrote with a sharp burst of penetrating understanding:

> Power is not a means; it is an end. One does not establish a dictatorship in order to safeguard a revolution; one makes the revolution in order to establish the dictatorship. . . . The object of power is power.[7]

One of the worst aspects of the dynamics of power in human affairs lies in the phenomenon of the destructive leader. So many people are ravenous for dictatorial power, and so many others who rise to leadership for reasons of their competence and decent intentions become tyrannical and dictatorial by virtue of the narcotic of power. The "outstanding" dictatorial leaders become megalomaniacal and psychopathic without conscience. Unfortunately, the masses of people readily "fall" for their leaders. The people generally are hungry for a protector and chief, so that even bad leaders win the support and admiration of their people for a long time, as long as the leader successfully produces with assurance and pomp the narcotic trappings of certainty and leadership. Such leaders often move rapidly to violent control of dissent. The leader becomes the central institution of society, supplanting cooperation and people's identification with a common cause with hero-worship and obedience, which fulfill primitive needs for a parental figure. With or without explicit religious trappings, the leader may also become a kind of deity toward whom people direct their pent-up needs for a godhead to whom they can give their allegiance and devotion, to follow and obey their führers, even with their lives.

An 85-year-old woman was asked how she understood what a dictator is. She replied: "A dictator is a person who must have his way. If he doesn't have his way he himself gets sick because he can't stand people not doing what he wants. And he makes the people around him sick, especially the weak ones who can't fight him."[8]

The power needs of the power seekers and exercisers of power expand and grow on themselves. An intoxicating and addictive process sets in as power corrupts more and more. Making war becomes highly probable.

The growth of a Fascist nation knows no saturation point. Its every expansion, whether justified or not, serves to increase its strength – and every increase in its strength, in turn, calls for new fields to conquer.

No doubt, the Fascists' belief in the inevitability of war is well-founded. The only question is how long prospective victims will oblige them by postponing the necessity for it until the Fascists have really become invincible – either because of a mere distaste for war, or because they fail to realize that the more a Fascist country gets the more *it is bound* to desire.[9]

Perhaps worst of all in the long litany of problems attendant on human use of power may be the fact that once people have exercised destructive power over others, the more damage people have done to the others, the less likely is it that they will be able to experience guilt.

Scholars who have studied warfare agree that when human beings engage in systematic campaigns in which they must kill, something significant happens: a detachment, a numbness to emotion. The enemy becomes less than human. In cases of genocide, the distinction is exaggerated. Enemies are viewed as animals, insects, vermin to be eradicated. This permits ordinary people to embrace a degree of savagery that would otherwise seem unthinkable.[10]

The blood on the hands of the killers corrodes their souls and limits their spiritual experience of the universal value of all human life. Michael Selzer reports a fascinating study of the Nazi leader Albert Speer. Speer was perhaps unusual among the major Nazis in that in the postwar period he seemed to express some contrition and guilt, yet Selzer observes, "He did not *feel* guilt, but only spoke of it."[11]

> Speer was able to express his regrets about the past only in brief, limp, and self-referential remarks. His regrets did not acknowledge the sufferings undergone by millions of people at the hands of the Third Reich, and seemed to imply little more than upset over the price he, Speer, had to pay for his role as a leading Nazi.
>
> "I don't understand myself nowadays, my reactions to Hitler when he humiliated me, for instance, by summoning me back all the way from the South of France when there was no reason to do so. He would play around with me as though I were nothing, and I don't understand why I did not react to that and step down."[12]

The Holocaust has become an ultimate end product of the horror to which man's blind, ugly expression of power can lead. Taking note of the anniversary of the liberation of the camps 50 years after the Holocaust, the popular-culture newspaper, *U.S.A. Today* noted, "When the camps were liberated in 1945 . . . what the Allies found stunned the world. From then on, Auschwitz symbolized the dangers of unfettered power and unbounded hate."[13] Auschwitz also symbolized mankind's inability then, and in a terrible sense still today as well as into in the foreseeable future, not to see the full truth about themselves even when they are ostensibly looking at such atrocities as Auschwitz. Says *U.S.A. Today*, "As a symbol of denial and guilt, Auschwitz has no equal."

If we look at the simple or basic systems of power everywhere in daily life, in families, workplaces, and community life, we see alarming patterns of seeking of excessive power and superiority over others as compared to goals of having respect for others, striving for basic equality, and sharing power in a system of checks and balances. Everyone knows the difference between the chairman of a professional group, however distinguished and capable a professional she or he may be, who is the petty dictator who dominates, insults, and makes the lives of the professionals working in the department utterly miserable. Everyone knows the kind of relief, joy, and wholesomeness that are enjoyed when a leader of a workgroup shows respect for the staff over whom she or he has authority and shares power with them without reneging on his or her responsibilities for being the leader.

In family life, the controlling father is an archetypal figure easily recognized through the ages, and in recent decades in Western society we are challenged to identify a no-less-superior posturing and aggrandizement of power that is increasingly vested in women. As noted earlier, there has been an astronomic increase in mother-led family groups in which there is no father, but the shift in power to women also includes a major shift toward the centering of power in the hands of mothers and wives in intact families. Many men have become increasingly "busy," as well as increasingly passive and dependent, to a point where in emotional terms they are second-class figures relative to the women. Families in which men and women work at sharing power with mutual respect (not a lip-service respect of forced agreement with one another when there really are tense disagreements) are a welcome relief, but are relatively rare.

&⋅ *He was a capable physician, quite well known for caring for patients, who had ambitiously succeeded in rising to the head of a medical service unit. He enjoyed his authority and visibility along with his pleasure at being a healer. But in his beautiful home he was clearly pushed by his wife into a second-class position. He couldn't help it. Her style was one of such a strong flow of energy, volubility, and colorfulness that any space she was in was immediately dominated by her personality. She commented knowingly on all aspects of life and the arts, proposed interesting activities for the two, and was the livewire in organizing and carrying off social events. She told her husband with firm certainty what was right and what was wrong in the way he dressed or talked or in the ideas he proposed. Her style did not manifest malice. It was simply that she had developed a way of being in this world that insisted on centralizing most emotional and social power in her own life space.*

One day it all blew up, and neither of them knew why. The immediate trigger was an absolutely trivial disagreement about a minor purchase, but suddenly they found themselves totally estranged, with the husband absolutely refusing to say a word to his wife day after day, then week after week, and finally into the months. All sexual contact ceased completely, and all mutual social behavior was suspended. He took to "his" part of the house where he sat and listened to his beloved music and read for hours.

In the husband's description: "I married a charming woman who is totally dominating. I liked it though, and had no complaints. Well, that's not quite true. When she overspends insanely, I really get mad at what she is taking from me, but I have never found a way to stop her. Well, that is not quite true either. I go along with a nice smile – incidentally, I also suffer from periodic stuttering – but inside I have a secret coldness and anger toward her. One day, when we were on a vacation in another country, she complained about my spending some money on myself, and I really gave it to her. After that, I didn't sleep with her for over a year. I barely spoke to her, and I made it very clear that I might not stay with her forever. What fun! The truth is I'm not leaving, but what great revenge. To top it all off, I live a comfortable secret life where I really can bear being alone with my vain self. Inside I feel very superior to others in my private world."

What should now be the "happy end" of the story turns out very, very sad nonetheless. After a period of apparently successful marital therapy in which contact between the husband and wife was renewed and a much better accommodation was worked out between them, the husband took suddenly and tragically ill and died of a heart attack. The therapy had brought about demonstrably welcome changes; the husband had become more forthright, active, and genial in his everyday speaking and presence, and the wife had agreed to defer graciously to her husband and to limit her nagging or domineering. At the time of the husband's unexpected death, the couple was enjoying a renewed period of happiness. Yet no one can or will ever know whether the changes the couple made were ultimately bad for the husband. Did the husband have an explosive inner rage for which he now had no outlet because he and his wife were "getting along" so well? Obviously, the reasons for the husband's illness could very well have been physiological. But it also may be that the husband's continuing inner rage exploded in him and caused or contributed to his illness. It is also possible that the accumulated resentment of so many years of the wife having been annoyingly superior to her husband had left too much of a residue of resentment in his cardiovascular system, and he was too worn down to recover. Indeed, one can never know.

On the level of society, DEMOCRATIC MIND shares power with others. On the level of interpersonal relationships, one senses quickly when people want to be with others in mutual equality, and when they genuinely respect others for their fine qualities.

The themes of power over others versus striving for equality with others register in our minds day after day in our relationships. For many people, there is a need to feel superior to members of their family, to colleagues, neighbors, and friends. When they fail to achieve this position of dominance, they suffer from feelings of weakness, shame, self-recrimination, or self-punishment, and from symptoms such as tension, depression, resentfulness, and so on.

If one succeeds in gaining undue power over others, a sense of triumph and even splendor can follow, but the result over time, at least in intimate relationships, may also be a growing sense of meaninglessness and emptiness in the relationship. A heavy price is paid for having transformed the relationship into one of domination of one personality by the other.[14] Some people also feel badly when they sense they have taken the route of power over others in work or other relationships.

But the truth must also be told that, unfortunately for this world, there are many people who just love power and are increasingly intoxicated and addicted to their successes in taking power (fascism has its benefits and successes too), and that is where they remain until and if the people they are dominating rise against them. Some spouses do, many do not; many children do, and many do not. Many professional or work colleagues do, some do not. An intriguing further complication is that many of the people who suffer the domination as ostensibly happy people progressively become weaker and less capable. There may come a time when they become so dependent on their overpowering star-leader that the strong one in effect is left without a meaningful counterpart. Wives or husbands may fade into being virtually nonpersons, children may fail to function independently, and colleagues may quit the race for self-respect they have lost and no longer do the job they were once capable of doing (for example, I've seen some such giving-up adults turn to alcohol or other substance abuse and have also observed adults who chose suicide in protest of being "outsized").

In the workings of the inner mind, a person's ego (meaning overall personal administrator of the self) coordinates and thereby shares its powers with a variety of parts and components of the mind. The healthier a person is, the more he or she remains in touch with and orchestrates the different parts of his or her self, including, for example, contradictory emotions of love and hate, or the contradiction of being able to take a decision confidently while retaining a humble openness to the possibility of being wrong. In the healthier mind, there is less need for "splitting off" or "compartmentalizing" and "dissociating" unacceptable parts of one's feelings and thoughts (psychological processes that enable people to do things with less conscious awareness, which in the experiences many people today are having with computers might be compared to isolating texts from one another in entirely separate files). Thus, in the better integrated person the "good" and "bad," or the caring and rejecting parts of one's feelings toward others, or the generous and selfish parts of oneself, can be recognized and accepted for what they are – all as natural and true.The necessary choices of one's predominant and operational direction and behaviors can be made more fluidly because one is not fighting to conceal shameful and unacceptable parts that do exist in us.

It wasn't that he was actually a dominating person in his professional relationships, although he sought frequently to be the leader or a conspicuous person in an organization. The problem was more subtle; periodically he found himself having nasty thoughts toward others, belittling them, and having thoughts about being Mr. Special and On Top. Slowly but surely he realized that not only were these kinds of thoughts corrupting his own inner experience, but that invariably they appeared at times when he felt especially weak, vulnerable, and unable to succeed in his ambition to be a leader. Slowly but surely he worked out methods for inner mind control in which, with the appearance of superior and power-seeking thoughts, he would consciously acknowledge that he was trying to bolster himself against feelings of inadequacy, and then would give instructions to his mind to stop these superiority-seeking thoughts. To his amazement, most of the time when he did this his mind responded to his direction. The disturbing superior thoughts lessened markedly, and he became more respectful, appreciative, and enjoying of others. What he also learned was that the resulting positive attitude toward others made him feel more relaxed and in touch with his own talents, which he could now express more freely and effectively.

❧ *She was so embarrassed in therapy to admit this, but she absolutely detested her husband's penis. Notwithstanding their three children, the thought of his penis violently disgusted her; touching his penis, which she avoided scrupulously, upset her palpably. Oh, they had intercourse regularly and were to all intents and appearances a successfully functioning couple. Nobody really knew what was going on inside of her mind, ostensibly not even her husband. The fact that each of them suffered from undue levels of anxiety and discomfort in their everyday experiences at work did trouble them. Intuitively, they knew these discomforts might well be linked to other feelings, such as her profound distaste for him and his penis and his implicit or unconscious awareness that she didn't really respect him and love him, which of course hurt him and added to the burden of the inadequate feelings from which he suffered. But they carefully avoided discussing these aspects of their relationship.*

Psychotherapy in this case involved a combination of individual therapy for the two spouses and couple therapy. In the wife's individual therapy, her "dehumanization" of her husband's penis was largely resolved by her being able to discover that the distaste she felt for her husband's sexual organ was also a striking continuation of an even deeper revulsion pent-up inside of her against her mother's breasts.[15] Ugh, the very thought of her mother's nipple standing up from her breast made her shudder in fearful disgust. Behind this representation in the unconscious mind lay a tapestry of feelings of hatred for the mother that had never been accepted. In daily life this woman lived out a slavish kind of overconnection to her mother through an endless series of calls and visits, as if they were caring gestures; she did this with no pleasure but rather from a compulsion to appear dutiful.

The wife was able to separate from much of her compulsive overconnection to her mother and to own the deep anger at her mother that had surfaced in the unconscious disgust at her mother's body, which in turn had then augmented her angry feelings at her husband's "use of her." The husband was able to become more confident about himself, especially as he learned to use his hatred of his father to release anger and to augment his own self-assertiveness. The two spouses moved to better personal mind positions and were able to reencounter each other in a new and happier way. The day came when the two laughingly celebrated a couple session in which the husband's penis was lovingly accorded full political recognition by his wife, to their mutual pleasure and the merriment of all present.

6. Violence against Self and/or against Others, Cruelty, Sacrifice, and Destruction of Life	versus	Nonviolence, Conflict Resolution, Aggression for Self-Defense and Seeking Peace, Kindness, Belief in Humanity, and Goodness of Life

The stories of violence by fascist societies on a societal level are so widely known they hardly require another repetition here. Although this book is not really devoted to totalitarian societies, in my attempt to create a linkage and bridge between concepts of mind and society I am also referring to many examples of destruction by fascist societies, and I confess that each time I do so it is with a renewed burst of rage and protest from deep in my heart at this aspect of humanity.

Violence is an imperative of fascist societies. The drive toward power over others is developed through violent destruction and conquest. The demand for obedience and conformity is backed by threats of violence. The prejudices projected against outcasts are the basis for legitimating policies of massacre and genocide. Susan Sontag has wisely described an aesthetic triumph, as it were, in fascist violence:

> The ss was the ideal incarnation of fascism's overt assertion of the righteousness of violence, the right to have total power over others and to treat them as absolutely inferior. It was in the ss that this assertion seemed most complete, because they acted it out in a singularly brutal and efficient manner; and because they dramatized it by linking themselves to certain aesthetic standards. The ss was designed as an elite military community that would be not only supremely violent but also supremely beautiful.[16]

The violence of fascism begins with total control of the minds of people, beginning with the fascist society itself.

Since the dogma demands that the Fascist consciousness shall prevail exclusively, every other type of group mentality, and especially the hazy kind of social and "class" instinct, is an obstruction which it is imperative to remove. For the making of a Fascist nation, as distinguished from the setting up of a Fascist form of government, it is not enough to issue decrees and create organizations that will fit its ideological frame – it is necessary first to destroy the structure of society that will not fit it. The tearing-down process must precede the Fascist Party's permanent constructive tasks: it must uproot in the people not only individualist trends but also any state-disregarding social consciousness before it can replace it with the uniform collective mentality based on and enclosed in the Fascist.

To Fascism, every single critic is a danger. He jeopardizes not the continuation in office of the government but its logical foundation – which does not make the danger any less real. To stifle it in its very beginning, the whole mentality of the people and of every single individual must always be kept in line. Every mental and physical activity must be brought under the dominating influence of the state. That is why there can be no freedom of speech, of the press, of peaceful assembly, why science, arts, trades, professions, sports, everything must show the Fascist coloring. That is the reason for the totalitarian state. If the foundation of the Fascist community is to be firm, every thought and every act in every field of human endeavor must be imbued with the same spirit and reflect the same collective will.

The Fascist state, in order to effectuate its organic character, has to rule its members from inside out. They must be so conditioned that a mental process divergent from the proclaimed collective thought not only does not occur, but is *psychologically impossible.*[17]

Christopher Bollas brilliantly traces how the very elimination of any opposition also creates a void – and now a new victim must be found for fascist destructiveness.

The moral void created by the destruction of opposition begins to make its presence felt. At this point the subject must find a victim to counter that void, and now a state of mind becomes an act of violence. On the verge of its own moral vacuum the mind splits off this dead core self and projects it into a victim henceforth identified with the moral void. To accomplish this transfer, the Fascist mind transforms a human other into a disposable nonentity.[18]

As noted, one special goal of this book is to see how a kind of fascist punishment system is also at work inside our mind toward ourselves. A closely related goal is to see how this kind of fascist punishment is also applied in our intimate relationships. Seeing the process on this plane of interpersonal activity will be much easier because it is after all a punishment meted out to others, albeit on a much smaller scale than in society but still more comparable to punishments being done to others on the level of society. The more difficult exercise is to see how the processes that correspond to punishment in a fascist society are surprisingly at work also inside our individual minds toward ourselves. For me this is the explanation of a great many of the emotional and mental disorders in which people do serious harm to themselves and to their ability to function in the world.

This conception of many emotional and mental illnesses is very different from a disease model where biological processes are somehow inferred as causing the symptoms. The conception that human beings are often punishing themselves opens the door to interpersonal and spiritual therapies and seeks to reinvest human beings with the rights to protect and love themselves. Similarly in the relational disorders, the implication for treatment is that a major task of psychotherapy is to help people discover and learn the rightness not only of protecting themselves but also of protecting others from harm as an extension of the sacred principle of taking care of one's own life.

The tendency to punish often derives directly from postulating absolute goals. If one sets goals to achieve at all costs, it makes sense that one also has prepared meanings and policies for responding to possible failures to achieve those goals, and quite naturally punishment is going to figure prominently in the repertoire of responses to failures. If one must be or must achieve something or other as FASCIST MIND stipulates, then failure to achieve the absolute definition invites punishment for the error or failure, the more so from a mind that thinks and operates with the militancy of absolutes. Cultural rules enter into the formulation of these paradigms, but every person's mind also is richly capable of creating an infinite number of punishment scenarios without the assistance of cultural templates. Both individual peoples' minds and societies have strong inclinations to punish those who fail to produce what is deemed required and essential.

Students from a culture that requires excellence not only in its own right but in obligation to generations of ancestors are at very high risk for breakdowns, including taking their own lives if they do poorly in their studies. Such a cultural injunction, including approval of suicide as an honorable self-punishment for failure, will be found in any number of Asian cultures, but the same solution also can be played out in other cultures, even where the premium on respecting human life is very high, because the mind of the young person can create the same paradigm from within a repertoire of archetypal meanings that are available to everyone. For example, no few instances of suicide in the vaunted Israeli army are suicides by outstanding young men whose preservice records were excellent. They begin their army careers with high expectations for continuing their excellence, but some failure or problem prevents them from being outstanding – sometimes it is no more than an orthopedic injury that prevents the youth from being able to complete his basic soldiering – and they are then so unable to bear their failure that there seems no way out other than to take their lives.

Any injunction or rule set with conviction as a total truth and necessity sets the stage for punishment of whoever is responsible for failing to follow the holy rule. Any of the paradigmatic rules we have been referring to as requirements will do: requirements of achievement, power, and status; rules against failing; requirements of being loved; not being abandoned or left alone; rules about eating; rules about not having erotic impulses or rules about absolutely needing yes to have such and such erotic experiences; injunctions forbidding aggressive thoughts or emotions; obsessive thoughts of vengeance against an enemy in retaliation for deep injury to one's pride; requirements of reaching a defined level of holiness; rules against being embarrassed; requirements of being devoted and dutiful to whoever in one's family or to whatever cause; insistence on invincible strength or on being the femme fatale of one's era – whatever it is the mind says one must be.

> *An elderly psychiatrist and psychoanalyst nearing the end of his outstanding career as a fine therapist as well as university teacher recalled how in the days of his training there was a colleague resident in psychiatry who made a specialty out of virtually commanding the devotion and attention of females in the department. He described the colleague, who later also rose to some professional fame as a hypnotist, as almost enslaving the women whom he organized to admire him, wait on him, and serve him. But if and when one of the women would step back and away from adoring and serving her master, the young psychiatrist would break out in a flood of sweat and become terribly nervous and unpleasant.*

Punishing Oneself for Failure versus "Failing Successfully"

Obviously the desired alternative is for people to learn how to "fail successfully." We all fail in any number of tasks and challenges. But many people do not know how to ride out their failures. Now they are faced with a situation not only of not having achieved what they wanted, which they may have believed was absolutely necessary but also of having to attribute responsibility to someone or other and exact retribution from whoever caused the failure. In many cases, the natural first candidate is one's own self: "If only I had been more attractive, she wouldn't have left me." "If only I didn't mess up, my buddies in our army platoon would still be alive." Then comes the punishment for failing. The presiding justice is oneself, representing all the accumulated images of authority that a person has retained and built up in his or her mind. The judge pronounces the verdict and sentence. The punishments are as infinite as human suffering. For example, "You shall not love again," is clearly an injunction prescribed by many a person who has failed in love and now will never take a chance again. "You will become sick," is another favorite of the judge in so many human minds. There is, after all, a long list of illnesses that we know can be induced psychosomatically, up to and including the will to induce one's death, which has been described in many folklores as well as in responsible medicine. Many illnesses are made more probable when there is a breakdown in a person's immune system. The variations are endless:

• Not creating again – I won't write, I won't paint, I won't sing, I won't act, I won't do scientific research, I won't play ball.

• Not enjoying life even when all is going well – feeling a brooding heaviness or pulls of despair even when successful.

• Assignment of oneself to mediocrity and banality – staying at a job that means nothing or even is oppressive, or staying in a gray and stultifying relationship: "He doesn't really excite me, but I'll stay even though we don't have much to share and it feels heavy and empty."

I believe that until the ability to "fail well" is learned, everyone undergoes profound experiences of falling from grace into a sense of devastating crushing loss when they fail. Failure is experienced as if life itself is being taken away. But life is such for all of us that from early on we are periodically called upon to stand up to catastrophic emotional experiences of failing at something. In each case we need to work out a process of defining for ourselves that we need not die because we failed, and that as long as we are really alive there is hope and opportunity to try again. This is the meaning of a student or athlete bouncing back from failure to good achievement, or of recovering from the deep hurt of the loss of a relationship. Many people do learn how to successfully translate their hurts and losses into a constructive process of standing up to failure, loss, and pain with renewed commitment to their lives.

For years, I delighted in teaching my graduate students how I had failed my first board examination in clinical psychology, how painful that failure was, and how I decided to overcome the failure by standing for the examination a second time a year later, including how I prepared myself to function differently on that examination in order to overcome the causes of my failure the first time. I hardly ever detected a student who was indifferent or did not pay close attention when I told this story.

A courageous form of accepting "failure" and preparing to survive hellish stress is for parents to prepare for what is possibly the worst conceivable tragedy in their lives, namely, the possible agony of a horrifying loss of a child, or children – tragedies that unfortunately are not rare.

As a social worker, she had attended an intensive workshop on management of crisis interventions in the course of which the lecturer led the group in a powerful and demanding emotional exercise in which each participant was to imagine the tragedy of the possible death of one of their own children under whatever circumstances. The goal of the exercise was to strengthen the participant's emotional resilience in the face of possible catastrophe by doing in advance some of the kind of emotional work that many people succeed in doing after the fact when they have to stand up to terrible agony.

Ten years later, the same social worker was on a wilderness group vacation in the Arctic Circle when her sled became separated from the rest of the group during a severe snow storm. She was appropriately terrified facing her possible death, and then she recalled the experience she had undergone in the above exercise years earlier. To her relief, she felt a surge of acceptance of the inevitability of whatever would be her fate, and she was able to gain a sense of calm during the coming hours as the dogs continued to carry her over the frozen terrain until – luckily and happily – she was again safely in contact with her group.

Unfortunately, at every level of human experience, there is also a close relationship between self-punishment and punishment of others. For example, in the classic syndrome of "murder-suicide," a person combines the murder of one or more other human beings with a clear-cut setup for his or her own suicide. Obviously, the self-punishment we do is regrettable and sad in its own right, but there is an added dimension of immorality and tragedy when we are also inclined to take out our failures and frustrations on others. Sometimes the persecution of others is random. At other times the sacrifice of others is directed at the people closest to us, such as when parents reject or abuse children. Many times the sacrificing of others is done on larger scales of prejudicial discrimination of targeted people (Jews, Blacks, Asiatics, Indians, whoever), active persecution or, worst of all, genocidal murder of the other people.

The ideological use of suicide as the instrument of murder has been perfected and deified in several cultures in the world. Americans learned this to their horror when facing Japanese kamikaze pilots in World War II; in recent years when a seemingly endless number of suicide-bombers appeared in many countries – in Israel in buses and train terminals, a disco, a pizzeria; in earlier years in hundreds of suicide bombings by Tamil in Sri Lanka (one-third of them by women!); on September 11, 2001, in the amazing four groups of Islamic suicide-killers who hijacked civilian aircraft to overwhelm New York and Washington in murderous attacks; and in a long list of additional locations circling the globe, including Russia, Iraq, Indonesia, Turkey, Saudi Arabia, and more, and more.

Smaller-scale events that combine murder and suicide generally follow a reverse sequence, first of murdering whoever and then committing suicide, such as murdering people randomly in a public space and then either killing oneself or clearly awaiting one's execution by the police who arrive on the scene.

If we tear ourselves away from the haunting large dramas of murder-suicide, we can see the pattern of combining hurting others and oneself in a wide variety of lesser forms. For example people have raging and spiteful tantrums directed toward a spouse, leaving both parties shattered, or since the profoundest way to hurt others and oneself is to abandon the other and sentence oneself to loneliness, they break off love relationships that shouldn't be ended (which I have been convinced is the case in a surprising number of divorces that might well have been avoided).

In her childhood she was unhappy and neglected. Her parents were so busy with their own financial and status goals they were unable to recognize emotional needs of their little girl. She grew up into a femme fatale – a highly desirable all-around woman, gorgeous and powerful, and also capable in her work. Soon she landed a husband for a first marriage, and before long they had a first child. But she could not feel the beauty and specialness of their child, much the same as her parents could not toward her. Before long she fell in love with another man who conveyed a stronger heartfelt parental love for her child than she was able to provide. She terminated the first marriage and went to live with her second mate; she married him too, and they had a little girl. A few seemingly harmonious and joyful years passed, and then it happened all over again. By now she was needing to provide emotionally for two children, but she was unable to feel very much for either of them. Although her second husband provided a genuine love connection to both of the children, she was unable to learn from him and unblock the development of her own potential ability to bond, care for, and love themt. One day she met another man who was so beautiful, handsome, and winning . . .

She was impressively honest and self-aware when she met with the therapist to whom her second husband now turned in desperation. She described herself as feeling "a chunk of ice inside of me" toward the children and in general; it was only when she felt the excitement of a new romance that she melted and didn't feel cold inside.

Did she care about the children? Yes, she did, but she couldn't feel actively involved with either of them. She had chosen a life policy in which she said, "I am going on to where I get the love I must have for myself or die."

She was unable to enter a sustained psychotherapy.

In the example just given, it is hard to say who was being hurt the most – the first of the children who had already lost his natural father and who now was on the verge of losing the father replacement who bonded with him so meaningfully, the second child of the second marriage whose life would be shattered as are the lives of most children of divorce, the second husband who was shattered by the dissolution of his happy home and marriage to which he was deeply committed, or the woman herself in her narcotic addiction to serial replacement love experiences, none of which would ever work out.

> ❧ *Something was wrong in their marriage – his second, her first. They were both nice people who liked and respected each other, but he in particular was unsatisfied and wanted his freedom. His style was to be the supervisor who received and graded everyone in the family – his children and especially her. Little was he aware that he loved the opportunities to*

express dissatisfaction and bark disapproval. She in turn tried very hard to please, but was chronically late and incomplete in doing things, continuing a lifelong resignation to the pull of feelings of inadequacy. She was basically a woman of integrity, but she was unduly passive and dependent and fell into his trap of being "deserving" of criticism. Before long, a horrible dance was spoiling their otherwise quite decent relationship, with scenes of repeated "official censure" by the husband, and the wife cowering but also resenting and hating the insults being meted out to her.

In individual therapy sessions, the husband acknowledged that his wife was really a lovely person. He was puzzled by the fact that he felt so uninterested in her and was seriously considering divorce. Could it be that he himself was contributing to this negative atmosphere in the marriage? Of course not, it was mainly because his wife was incompetent.

How had he grown up in respect of domination and equality in family relationships? Well, his father was a shadow figure who barely survived the horrors of the Holocaust in which he lost his first family and then never came into his own again. His mother ruled the family with her vibrant personality and even more with her "generous" criticisms of everyone. She was an emotionally outpouring and active woman who had a word for everyone and about everything. Even when she was well-meaning, the mother happily mandated what was right and wrong for everyone in the family and made it very clear that she would not allow anyone to step out of line. His brother was damaged seriously by mother's dominating ways and to this day was a weak and marginal adult. He resented this sad outcome for his brother, including the fact that as a result he had lost the opportunity of a meaningful relationship with this brother.

What about himself? As a child, he had thought that he was happy. Still, in his teenage years he somehow became aware that he hated the atmosphere of control and humiliation his mother engendered in the house. He worked very hard at leaving home as early as he could to strike out in life away from her domination.

Was it possible that he was now replaying his mother's role in the way he treated his wife? . . .

Aggression for Self-Defense

The most common trap that good people fall into is believing that if they only speak and respond decently to others, they will be reciprocated. But, unfortunately, there are many people on the warpath who don't. They include:

• Ideological killers
• Terrorists
• Professional hit-men
• Lousy, hostile, rejecting parents dead set on hurting a child
• Ugly, demeaning, enslaving spouses with a clear-cut conception of their right to abuse their wife or husband
• Nasty kids who insult or control and exploit one or two parents, or even an entire family group

I prefer to live; and I also prefer to feel a degree of self-reliance in taking care of myself. Unless one is seeking to get hurt or to enjoy a martyrdom or holiness of not having stooped to resorting to "dirty" acts of aggression, one has to fight back in self-defense against known predators and abusers before being clobbered. The challenge in our individual affairs is very much like in our collective lives – to make every possible effort to bring about a nonviolent peace and as wholesome and mutual a resolution of conflicts as possible. The challenge is also to know when the enemy is in no way open to peace and will even exploit the "Munich-agreements" to kill you, à la British Prime Minister Chamberlain's futile efforts to negotiate peace with Hitler at the expense of surrendering Czechoslovakia; and Stalin's infamous alliance with Hitler, who then went on to invade the USSR and was knocked out in what was probably the turning point of World War II by the unconquerable spirit of the Russians' self-defense.

However, even if one accepts the principle of self-defense in theory, one needs to realize that it is a major task, both for individuals and for collectives, to test the belief that one must fight back in self-defense for likely errors of judgment as well as concealed projections of our own nastiness. In marital battles, for example, virtually every husband or wife is convinced they are fighting in self-defense, and in untold cases that experience, however sincere, is not true.[19]

I believe that achieving an integrated balance between peace-seeking and a readiness to protect oneself in self-defense is one of the key challenges to all individuals and to all groups. A philosopher, Frederick Struckmeyer, emphasized the critical distinction between our natural right to defend ourselves, which we must continue even in limited wars, and the fight to impose our ideology on others or to correct their "sinful" ideology:

> It is not our place as men to punish the sins of "mistaken" ideologies of other men. We have a general right, even if not a duty, to defend ourselves as a nation. But we manifestly do not have the right to wage unlimited war, and to seek the destruction of the enemy *because* we think him deserving of death. To fight in self-defense and to fight for this latter reason are two vastly different things. . . . It still seems possible to wage some purely defensive wars, wars which are limited in scope and which do not have the effect of destroying what they originally intended to save."[20]

As I wrote in an earlier essay on "the tragic illusion of self-defense,"

Optimal self-defense is an effort to help all parties triumph over terror. We seek for all of us to feel better, stronger, more equal, more competent, and more open to real aliveness for whatever time we have on this earth.

The effort at such optimal self-defense requires that at least one of the principals seeks to do everything possible to contain the immediate conflict process and to try to develop a momentum toward long-range, no-lose solutions that will strengthen the self-interest of all parties to the conflict. Such a concept of self-defense is patently far more attractive and life saving than are the empty triumphs of murder and subjugation of other peoples, claiming large land areas, or imposing one's religion or ideology on others. Such cooperation can also often lead to agreements to join forces in a common battle against the mutual enemies of disease, pollution, and want. It should also be acknowledged that nothing in these remarks is intended to speak against shooting in self-defense when a blazing gun is firing at you. However, it is far better if one can manage to say before the guns blaze away, "Don't shoot, we're also earthlings!"[21]

Caring for Life

DEMOCRATIC MIND recognizes that what life is all about, first of all, is the sanctity of human life. DEMOCRATIC MIND takes an overriding position of caring for life and the opportunity for life as the definitive prime principle, first of all for oneself and then similarly for others. The sacredness of life is an overriding categorical imperative.

On the level of society, the respected social psychologist researcher of aggression, Albert Bandura, concludes:

> Given the existence of so many psychological devices for disengagement of moral control . . . civilized conduct requires, in addition to humane personal codes, social systems that uphold compassionate behavior and renounce cruelty. . . . If societies are to function more humanely, they must establish effective social safeguards against the misuse of institutional justificatory power for exploitive and destructive purposes. [22]

Slowly but surely, a genuine commitment to care for life can reduce and remove as much as possible all unnecessary forms of doing harm to life, beginning with oneself and then extending to others. One honors one's body and takes care of it utilizing the best wisdoms of contemporary health information and a basic common sense about living healthfully. As one inevitably discovers different ways in which one is nonetheless doing harm to oneself, one strives to reduce these hurts and correct them through the combination of using one's own wisdom and seeking the help of one's doctors, advisors, counselors, teachers, therapists, and other practitioners. The health and welfare of other people is valued similarly. Attention is given to the health and welfare needs of others in the family, and then also to other people in the community and the larger world.

DEMOCRATIC MIND is naturally inclined to be more fair, understanding, and kind – to oneself and to one's fellow human beings. Jean Jaques Rousseau wrote: "What wisdom can you find that is greater than kindness?"

There is sensitivity, kindness, and sympathy for the universal existential spectrum of emotional pain, longing, sadness, loss and grief, regret, shame and guilt, and despair, emotions that variously attend the individual and collective lives of all of us. In contrast, it has been pointed out that fascist thinking denies the various soft emotions. As we read earlier, Alexander and Margarete Mitscherlich, themselves Germans, have attributed to the philosophy of Nazism a denial of regret and mourning and have suggested that the inability to experience these emotions was central to the cruelty of Nazism.[23] Another German scholar wrote (a good many years ago, but already 30 years after the Holocaust):

> Seldom have I heard a word of sympathy for the Jews. . . . So many peoples' capacity for compassion is crippled. The capacity for compassion seems to be stunted in its development not only by instances of cruel early suffering, but also by derision and disregard of helpless pain. Suffering so often is justified, glossed over, ridiculed, or bluntly denied. A great many people . . . distance themselves from the tender voice of mercy. Mutilated self-respect stunts the capacity for empathy; it leave little space or energy for active concern for other people. There is instead much hidden rage. Hurt, self-esteem and corresponding vengefulness of course play leading roles in the power of the Nazi persuasion. Nazism allows its henchmen to feel untouched by human frailty.[24]

Nonetheless, DEMOCRATIC MIND is entirely aware that it too suffers badness and imperfection, and quite distinct inclinations to evil against oneself and others. It accepts the naturalness of all impulses, and even draws on many of them for qualities of playfulness and fun in the course of the human endurance trek through life. Obviously, dissent, differences, criticism, anger or worse of hatred, cruelty, and rage all spring up within DEMOCRATIC MIND too. In the orchestration of DEMOCRATIC MIND, there is first of all an acceptance of the variety of basic impulses that arise, for we are all human and are subject to every one of the human emotions and experiences. In fact, we need them, and we are less than human when any of the major emotions are not present to some extent.

The next step is for DEMOCRATIC MIND to introduce a machinery for weighing, evaluating, and deciding which emotions are to be valued and which are to be reduced through proper management of one's mind. For example, it is one thing to wish to kill someone in anger after having been humiliated or cheated, and it is quite another to actually do so. It is also undesirable to enter into obsessive brooding wishes to kill the other to a point where one's whole life is colored by the presence of such rage. The proper management of mind calls for personal leadership of oneself to feel natural anger and even enjoy it as a source of strength, not to act it out violently, and not to become obsessed with rage and revenge. DEMOCRATIC MIND makes distinctions between feelings and action but then also weighs which feelings should be entertained, augmented, and welcomed and which should be processed out and even stopped by instructions to one's mind to quit engaging in a given thought.

On an interpersonal level, DEMOCRATIC MIND selects those wishes that need, deserve, and can profit from communication and clarification. Not all issues of anger can be handled by talking about them with others. In fact, it is my judgment that a majority of our angers cannot be processed authentically with other people, and that one must work primarily with one's own mind to vent and release much of the anger and at the same time to contain one's anger so that it does not spill over to contaminate a larger range of one's life experience. But obviously, and happily, there are also hurts and angers that definitely can and should be processed with others in real interpersonal interactions, and for these there is a wisdom as to how best to express our anger to others. Not "everything goes." One does not spill the proverbial everything, and one does not tell one's anger in the full vivid language of one's inner mind – at least not if the purpose of telling one's anger is to bring about changes that will improve the relationship with the other. DEMOCRATIC MIND takes care to tap the potential of communication and clarification of angry feelings with others while avoiding doing irreversible harm to the health and survival of oneself and others.

His wife was leaving him because he had concealed from her the financial measures he had taken to manage the economic pressures that had developed in his business. The straw that broke the camel's back was when he got her unknowingly to sign a remortgage of their home. She was inconsolable when she discovered what she had signed. Her sense was that her last security had been taken away from her.

In fact, their married and family lives had been better than average.

They both were positive people who had brought up their several children joyfully in good humor and respectfully, so that the children were emotionally well nourished and capable in their functioning. Although as husband and wife they did not know how to express and savor a poetic kind of intimacy, they nonetheless were decent and friendly. They also frolicked sexually and playfully, to their mutual satisfaction. But this fault of his not telling her what he was doing in financial matters even to the point of deceiving her was absolutely unbearable for her.

For him these acts of economic manipulation were acted out virtually dissociatively. He had grown up in a home so steeped in the selfishness of his parents caring for themselves that he had run away in early adolescence. The way of life he had adopted was one of being a doer and being superbly capable in business, thus to ensure his being admired and loved by himself and his wife and other people because of his virtuosity (deep in his heart, he had no idea that he deserved to be loved for his own self without it being connected to achievement). When business conditions took an unexpected turn for the worse and he became strapped for cash, all he could think of was how to protect himself and his family by taking the kind of strategic moves that would keep money flowing and the business protected. The mortgaging of the house was probably even financially sound. He hadn't meant to trick her. He meant only to protect himself and all of them, and he had no idea that what he did was to her a devastating manipulation.

All through the years he had never spoken to his parents about their emotional coldness, which now continued its characteristic form even in the fact that they paid very limited attention to his children – their grandchildren. Now at a crucial point just before his wife moved to step up divorce proceedings against him, he decided to go see his parents and speak to them for the first time of his anger. He made his final preparation in one of his therapy sessions, and then went off to his meeting with them. The result of telling his parents how he felt was dramatic: they were genuinely alarmed at the decline in their son's life and promptly offered what was for them a remarkable degree of financial assistance. As well, they committed themselves to renewing contact with the grandchildren. The surge in his power to be able to speak honestly to his parents also triggered a wave of new respect from his wife, and she now agreed to put the divorce on hold so they could rebuild their lives together.

Conflict is not bemoaned by DEMOCRATIC MIND, nor is it bullied out of existence. It is welcomed as an expression of the truths of the complexity of life and an opportunity to use oneself to process and resolve conflicts as constructively as possible on behalf of a greater enjoyment of life. Paradoxically, learning to manage the process of conflict becomes so enjoyable that it adds to life, and one is even grateful for one's hard times – damn them.

The largest frame through which to view life is an awareness of ourselves and our life opportunities as wondrous creatures in an incredible universe! Robert Jay Lifton and Eric Markusen urge the cultivation of our "species awareness" and "global consciousness," and that we perceive our relationships to other human beings as "riders on the earth together." These are also our best protections against the possible expansion of our also obviously potential "genocidal mentality."

> Species mentality . . . is full consciousness of ourselves as members of the human species, a species now under threat of extinction. Species consciousness contributes to a sense of self that identifies with the entire human species . . . [in] work, play, religion, ethnic group, and nation. . . . As in many things, only by holding to the particular can one have access to the universal . . . whatever the capacity of an individual self for concern, caring, loyalty, and even love can now be extended in some degree to the human species as a whole – though one need in no way cease being concerned about caring for, loyal to, or loving any smaller unit of human beings or any single human being.[25]

Being a real part of the human race is a way of life that brings much relief from existential anxiety, a sense of much meaning and depth about one's life, and warmth and joy. It is a highly recommended democratic way that competes heartily with the initial glory-offers of fascism.

CHAPTER SIX

The Fascist Denier

"I Never Did Any Harm" – Denials of Doing Harm to Oneself or to Others

7. Denials of Doing Harm to Self and Others	versus	Acceptance of Responsibility for Doing Harm to Self and Others

FASCIST MIND is inherently a liar.

It has to be a liar, beginning with the fact that it sets totalistic goals so adamantly and extremely that it has to fool itself into believing it is as good and completely successful as it insists it must be from the outset. But the issue goes deeper. FASCIST MIND believes it has the right to impose its seemingly true map of reality on reality itself, that whatever it believes to be true is true simply because FASCIST MIND so deemed it, or that it will soon be made to become true by virtue of the force that FASCIST MIND will impose on reality to make it fit the map designed as the truth to begin with. For FASCIST MIND, lying is a matter of honor, avoiding shame, and not losing face. It is also about taking control over any and all aspects of life. Real truth and accuracy are minor obstacles standing before the intention to be powerful and rule over life.

On the level of society, it is hard to think of any government leaders who have not denied the terrible actions governments have done. Sadly, this includes democracies. The United States, for example, denied for many years using U.S. Army troops as guinea pigs exposed to the blasts and radiation of nuclear devices; and concomitant with this denial of historical facts, for many years the soldiers and the families of the soldiers who died of radiation-induced illnesses were denied proper medical care and compensation. Perhaps because the area of nuclear and megaweapons inherently bespeaks archetypal drives toward power, even a democracy that is preparing these weapons for self-defense is seduced into big-time lying about its activities. The deceptions of the United States extended to denials of nuclear accidents and contamination of broad swaths of residential areas in the United States, and there have even been reports of government security agents murdering employees of nuclear facilities or residents of contaminated areas who were threatening to bring out the truth. The U.S. government has also lied about many cooperative ventures with dictator-killers around the world. For example, the CIA is reported to have collaborated openly with Pinochet in Chile in his campaign of "disappearances" in which several thousand people were taken away, tortured, and executed. Another example of U.S. complicity in mass murders is that the United States was a supplier of arms to and a supporter of the Sukarno regime's calculated campaign of "spontaneous killings" of communists and their families in the early 1960s in Indonesia.[1] There are, unfortunately, many more examples of United States deception and lying about its roles in violence.

Nonetheless, the truth largely does prevail in democracies. Built into the fabric of democracy is a trend toward protecting the truth, and a process of bringing about disclosure of policies of cover-ups and denials of destructiveness. The institutions of freedom of speech and especially the freedom of journalistic institutions and the traditions of investigative journalism in a democracy are outstanding guardians of truth. In democratic governments, even the erring government participates in letting the "cat out of the bag" more often than it intends. Thus, in July 2001, the U.S. Government Printing Office inadvertently distributed a declassified report of how the United States had provided the Indonesians with lists of leaders of the Communist Party, people who should be executed. The United States also provided funds. After the report was released alarmed officials sought vainly to recall it (it was already on the Internet), prompting one official to remark, "They're trying to put the toothpaste back in the tube."[2]

In fascist countries free journalism does not exist, and violations of the rule that all the news must fit the dictates of the rulers are met variously with imprisonment, torture, and murder of the offending journalists and closing down of the offending presses and broadcast facilities. Fascist countries do not report the news of reality; they decide what reality is and report their views of the world as if they are reality. It is hardly in the nature of totalitarian thinking to allow for acknowledgment of doing harm. Thus, the Nazi regime in Germany, the Stalinist regime in the USSR, and the communist regime in China never acknowledged killing millions of their own people.[3] And they did not acknowledge the privation, suffering, and desperation of millions more of their citizens under their regimes. Intriguingly, for long periods of time they also did not report straightforwardly the destruction of the other people designated as enemies of the state who were exterminated in massive genocidal campaigns. One would think that having defined the others as vile subhumans and true enemies of all the people and of the state, that the fascist regime might have been proud to announce its glorious campaigns of getting rid of these enemies, but in many cases the murderous regimes did everything to conceal what they were doing.

In the individual mind, denial of doing harm to others is evident even in known torturers and killers. In respect of the Holocaust, for example, there are very few instances of acknowledgment, regret, and contrition by perpetrators.[4] Similar observations have been made of the torturers and killers in other cultures. My own impressions are that beyond a certain point of spilling blood, there is a consolidation of gratification in the power experienced over others along with a reluctance and even inability to acknowledge one has been so evil (in addition to realistic caution about not admitting to one's crimes lest it bring down on one's head retaliation by the victims or legal consequences).

Criminologist Alex Alvarez cites five specific language-logic techniques of "neutralization," or denial of responsibility for doing harm to others, that Gresham Sykes and David Matza identified in their studies of delinquent youths, but which are widely applicable to the denials of many perpetrators of harms to other human beings. These are ways in which the mind of the perpetrator explains to itself, as well as justifies to others, his or her damaging behaviors: internally to avoid suffering an onerous burden of guilt, and externally to minimize the responsibility that will be laid, say by the legal system.

Denial of Responsibility. The delinquent argues the behavior was not his or her fault, that it was caused by accident or by forces beyond his or her control.

Denial of Injury. The offender defines the act as a prank or as mischief, which is socially and individually much more acceptable than something defined as criminal or deviant.

Denial of Victim. The argument here is that the victim caused his or her own victimization or somehow deserved it. This definitional about-face changes he perpetrator's role from that of criminal or delinquent to that of justified avenger. Correspondingly, the victim is transformed . . . into someone who is responsible for his or her own victimization.

Condemning the Condemners. This technique asserts that everyone is corrupt or unfair, so what right do others have to judge the offender?

Appeal to Higher Loyalties. This is the assertion that the offender's actions are not motivated by personal or selfish reasons like greed, but are undertaken on behalf of the group to which he or she owes primary loyalty.[5]

To the above mechanisms Alvarez adds the telltale mechanism of dehumanization:

Dehumanization [or] the denial of humanity [is] a new and separate technique by which internal prohibitions against killing are neutralized. . . . To acknowledge a person's humanity is to recognize that he or she is subject to feelings, emotions, aspirations, dreams, and fears. To destroy another human being is to destroy someone like yourself. In contrast, it is far easier to destroy that which shares no commonality with you, that which is beneath you.[6]

Moving to commonplace everyday life, we all have any number of occasions when we have harmed other human beings, but put off recognition and acknowledgment of having done so. One would like to assume and expect that there are bedrock concepts of decency and humanity available to all human beings, and that these would lead to a perception of what doing harm to others means. The thoughts of causing pain, torturing, maiming, and killing should lead all human beings to feelings of revulsion at the thought of doing serious harm to other human beings, but that

144

is not the case. To this day I do not really understand what it is that prevents an archetypal sensitivity to human suffering and destruction, while allowing another archetype of joy in doing harm to others, to take over, but it is clear to me that I have to face the facts of the cruelty in our species.[7]

Many cases are reported in every society of long-term brutality and physical cruelty imposed on a member of a family. For example, a wife whose husband regularly beats her, or a child who is physically abused by one or even both of the parents. Rarely do spouses or parents acknowledge the manifest physical harm they have done, not to speak of the fact that relatively few husbands and wives and few parents acknowledge their serious, chronic emotional abusiveness. Denials of doing harm extend far beyond the ultimate harm of physical destruction. Millions of parents have brutalized their children with severe rejection but have not taken responsibility for doing so. Millions more have been emotionally abusive and insulting. And beyond them too there is a whole world of different kinds of emotional destructiveness – ways of being with family members that are destructive of their capacity to function and their spirit for life. One especially common pattern involves an ostensible overflowing of love and devotion to a child, but whose concealed intention is to maintain that child as an emotional chattel serving the needs of the parent; for all that this pattern is common, it is rare to find parents who are capable of acknowledging their concealed exploitations of the child.

&. *Both were very attractive people, successful professionals, to all appearances a man and a woman at the heads of their community. But the story at home was different. He was tough as steel and put her in her place regularly with a barrage of strongly rendered commands, observations, and judgments. She paled under the onslaught, but somehow took it. It seemed as if she knew this was what she deserved and what life intended for her, so best to bear it. As is often the case in marriages that have overlays of bitterness, in addition to her own successful career she poured herself into bringing up their beautiful children and told herself that life was satisfying. He also cared about their children, at least in the sense that they should thrive to become attractive showpieces and capable people like* he and his wife were, and he welcomed her devotion to the children (he also welcomed her being busy with the children and therefore making less demands on his time). Ostensibly they were a happy couple organized around social appearances and a mutual pride in their children, and the issues of domination and insults could be accommodated and ignored.

However, the husband didn't limit himself to verbal abuse, and every few months there was an eruption in which he also struck out at her in vicious physical blows. These were the straws that broke her back. She could tolerate the emotional duress, but being physically beaten violated her sensibilities in a way that she was not able to live with. On the issue of his physical violence she put her foot down, and at her insistence the couple came to therapy.

In the individual sessions that accompanied the couple sessions, it became even clearer how the husband had chosen to define his life totally as a fiefdom in which he was the Absolute Ruler. Every space in which he lived was cast to serve him. As an independent professional, he ran his office with an absolute power. He also maintained a mistress in an expensive apartment near his office and led a double life with her that was concealed from his wife. In regard to his wife, it was his conviction that she belonged to him, and that she was to do his bidding. He wanted his pleasures on his terms.

Intriguingly, the clear-cut clash between this man's life script and the therapist's values built up progressively until there came a dramatic day when the husband threatened also to attack the therapist physically. A marvelous showdown took place in the office; the therapist succeeded in standing up to the threats of violence and made it clear that he would stay firmly in charge, beginning with the fact that he would call the police if the man made even one physical move against him. This confrontation was then turned into a basis for empowering the wife in couple sessions, enabling her to take the same stand successfully.

Nonetheless, this couple was not able to go on to a fuller acknowledgment of the harm they were doing. The wife was not able to face how self-damaging she was in allowing herself to be insulted and abused regularly (and she certainly didn't want to know about her husband's mistress), while maintaining an illusion of a successful family life with her good career and dear children, and he was not ever able (willing) to see the *extent of his nastiness on so many levels of his domination of her. But at least the violence was stopped.*

DEMOCRATIC MIND seeks to accept responsibility for any harm done to oneself or to others, harm done intentionally and harm rendered inadvertently and mistakenly.

In recent years, democratic societies have been pioneering new forms of collective responsibility for harms that were done in earlier historical periods.[8] Thus, the American government apologized and paid reparations to Japanese American families who were interred in camps during World War II. German governments have carved a major trail in world history by accepting responsibility for the genocide of the Jewish people in the Holocaust and for many years have paid reparations to survivors. Even so, well over 50 years after the Holocaust it became clear that there were many cases of forced labor that had never been recognized. It also became clear that there were millions of dollars tied up in banks in countries all around the world, Switzerland as the outstanding case, but also even Israel in banks continuing from the period of the Palestinian Mandate, where funds of Holocaust survivors who had perished had never been released to their heirs. There were also millions of dollars in insurance policies that had never been paid because of lack of "proof" of the death of the insured, and only as the 21st century has begun are agreements being reached that deal with many of these issues.[9] Similarly, in recent years American Armenians have also begun to process claims against banks and insurance companies for assets of loved ones who perished in the Armenian Genocide at the hands of the Turks in 1915 and on.

There are also apologies by governments that are not accompanied by reparations. For example, U.S. President Clinton apologized to the Rwandan people for failing to recognize at an early enough time that genocide was taking place in Rwanda, and that this failure had led to a delay of possible international intervention that could have saved hundreds of thousands of lives. Clearly a new mode of international interrelationship is emerging that involves some nations overcoming denials of having done harm to another people, and acceptance of various degrees of responsibility for the harm that was done. In April 2004, the

Secretary-General of the United Nations, Kofi Annan, took responsibility and expressed regret for his role in the United Nation's failure to intervene in Rwanda.

In family life, words of apology can make a huge difference even in the face of emotional damages whose effects still linger. "I am sorry" can be words that release painful feelings and memories in interpersonal relationships. The first test of the authenticity of an apology is in the accompanying demonstration of readiness to stop doing harm if it is still continuing. The "I am sorry" that is a dutiful and ritualistic phrase alongside of which one continues to heap hurt on the other will be violently rejected.

> *"You say you are sorry, but I don't see any improvement whatsoever in the way in which you stamp around and just yell out your hurt and anger and scare the children and me," says a husband to his wife, both of them distinguished professionals, after the wife has screamed at him in a shrill voice. Earlier she grudgingly acknowledged, "All right, I will try to control my anger," but when it came to the test of stopping herself in action she was again out of control.*

The dramatic stories of denials of doing overt harm to oneself or to others are matched by endlessly dramatic stories of these processes on an inner symbolic level inside of us. For the damages we do to ourselves manifest not only in physical and visible ways but also in the ways in which we manage our minds. "Am I allowed to experience the joys of life?" is a basic question for each person. There are many people who cannot allow themselves to experience the pleasures of well-being, and there are many more who can allow good feelings only in limited doses, or which must soon be followed by absolutions in which they "pay" for the good feelings by having absolutely rotten feelings.

> *He was looking better. His face had filled out and relaxed over the year of treatment following the debacle of his previous marriage and in the year or so of his new marriage. The scars of the past were healing, and clearly a degree of loveliness was forming in the present relationship. They had moved to a beautiful new home and were busy furnishing*

and decorating it. Sexual relations were deeply pleasing. They worked together nicely in relating in a mutually caring way with the children from both their previous marriages, and life was good. In many ways, he was behaving more the gentleman and as a nice person in his new marriage. The transition happened after he painfully confronted the fact that he had contributed a good deal to the breakdown of his previous marriage by being a know-it-all, more-confident-than-other, superior-to inferior in that marriage.

Yet a disturbing dark look crossed his face as he reported in one therapy session, "There I was, everything was going good, but I knew that it was all a sham and that I shouldn't be there." A bitter remonstrating look enveloped his face. It turned out that behind his original symptom pattern of being a pompous Mr. Expert, there always had lurked a deep belief that real joy, and especially a mutual respectful love, would never be within his reach. Love and respect had not been present in his parents' lives, and his mother's mandate to everyone in the family was that a genuine caring love between equals simply did not exist, and she virtually forbade her children from seeking to create such a love for themselves in their lives.

Clearly the ways in which people harm themselves and deny that they are doing harm to themselves is unlimited. Abuses to one's health – often at the loss of years of a life span – probably should be placed at the top of the list. The inventory list of how human beings damage their health is long:

People smoke, drink too much alcohol or take other dangerous drugs, overeat to a condition of being overweight or even obese, eat foods that are known to bring on diseases, fail to exercise, fail to rest as much as their bodies tell them to, overwork, work in crazy tension, fail to get medical help, fail to follow sound medical advice, drive too fast, drive recklessly, drive unsafe vehicles . . . the list goes on and on . . .

In most of American society, social conventions forbid or at least mitigate against a person inquiring into another's health practices. It is considered bad taste to advise another person to stop an injurious habit such as smoking or to counsel an obese person to lose weight. As a result, the denials people practice on themselves also are not challenged helpfully by their friends and are even enhanced by the prevailing social conventions.

You have friends who are obviously heading toward joining the growing ranks of the American obese that increasingly concern medical and epidemiological authorities. Do you tell them caringly? Or do you go on with the social sham of proper greetings such as: "You look wonderful"?

We human beings also do harm to ourselves in other nonphysical ways. We may fail to choose a field of work or career that really expresses our genuine interests and talents – and it shows in our sadness or boredom. In our work settings, we try to impose idealistic work ethics on locked-in systems of political hierarchies only to be broken and defeated by the tried-and-true power brokers. We marry the wrong person notwithstanding very insistent inner knowledge that we are heading into big trouble – let alone ignoring good advice from family and close friends who clearly see the disaster that lies ahead. We run our lives without achieving a proper balance between our connections to loved ones and friends versus our work responsibilities (either can be too much or too little). We do not balance out lightheartedness – humor, joy, and playfulness – versus our seriousness, devotion, and persistence.

❧ He is a multimillionaire, have-it-all, happy, handsome blue blood. He is so sure he has it all that he doesn't keep his heart in tune with his wife's emotional experiences. One day he finds her in their bed with the architect they engaged to add a wing to their sumptuous home.

The skill needed for reducing and preventing the worst damages to ourselves and others is maintaining a continuous monitoring and awareness of our methods of spoiling life – our own life and the lives of others. On the surface it is not so hard to do. Inner gauges of vitality, pleasure, and safety are constantly registering what is happening, and these gauges also signal us when our spirits are wounded and when we are frightened, threatened, or perceive dangers to our safety. If only we teach ourselves to receive these notices, process them, and act on them, we would be able to reduce a great deal of the harm we do to our lives. We also are capable of seeing the pain, upset, hurt, injury, and worse happening to others, if only we register the information they convey to people around them.

Generating Courage to Be Responsible for the Harm We Have Done to Integrity and Decency

DEMOCRATIC MIND accepts that it is impossible to be alive without doing harm to oneself and to other people, even unintentionally. DEMOCRATIC MIND accepts that our selfishness and nastiness will be expressed in all manner of unethical and damaging acts to ourselves and other people. The mind is used to monitor when and how we are hurting life. Every one of us will become aware of injurious health habits, for example, after which the challenge is to frame a corrective policy and implement it. Insofar as the leitmotif or driving power for such improvement is rooted in a real caring for life, there is likely to be sufficient strength for overcoming even addictive habits (I think this is the only real basis for successful correction of pathological eating habits, for example). Note how real caring for life was also the strongest basis for the altruism of "Righteous Gentiles" who saved Jews during the Holocaust at great risk to themselves, sometimes even when they personally didn't like Jews! Caring for life gives meaning to life. It is the basis for wholesome value choices and is a source of courage.

As for harm that has been done and cannot be taken back, it turns out that acknowledgment and apology carry considerable power. These seem to work on the level of release from feelings of guilt and shame over what one has done, and also on the level of enabling a healing and resumption of relationship to an aggrieved other party insofar as there still is an opportunity to apologize.

One of the great wonders of family therapy for me has been the immediacy and ease with which many children forgive their parents for emotional damages if and when their parents express genuine awareness of and regret for what they have done. Of course, children intrinsically know the true nature of the relationships in their families – what degree of love if any really is felt, and whether it is linked to efforts to exploit the other, or whether it is true energy intended to bless and empower life and a love of life in the other. The children similarly know whether their parents really understand and regret the errors they have made. When the parents are genuine, the children are amazingly big-hearted in their forgiveness. The hearts of the children seem to open and relax when their parents tell the previously denied truth. I tell families that it is rare that genuine acknowledgment of the truth to their children will bring further damage.

    🙢 *In two cases of autistic children, one of the major goals of treatment was for the mother to acknowledge to the child she had been deeply hurtful.*

    It took many hours of treatment to prepare for the day when the acknowledgment was delivered to each of the two autistic children. To the naked eye the scenes of these acknowledgments were unbelievable, in that in each case the child, who was still symptomatically autistic at the time, continued for the most part in his particular ritualistic pattern – spinning parts of his body, looking vacuously and disjointedly away – even as the mother spoke; as the expression goes, it was as if the mother were speaking to the wall. And yet, it was clear to the child's major therapist and the mother's major therapist, who were both present and working together in the session, that the children showed flickers of eye connection that expressed their realization of the important statement being delivered to them. In both cases there were immediate bursts of aggression in the child's play following the mother's acknowledgment, which the therapists could interpret to the child as his anger over having been cheated by the mother. Both mothers also had been trained to acknowledge to their child that they understood he was very angry with them, and they responded to their child's anger respectfully and with understanding. There is no doubt that both mothers had chosen courageously to acknowledge a terrible destructiveness toward their child. In both cases, these sessions proved to be turning points for major changes that transpired over the ensuing months, in both cases eventually leading toward what could be described as dramatic bona fide recoveries from autism and the development of a degree of ability to function adequately in the world. (It could not yet be reported in the original paper, which described the successful treatments

152

five years after their termination, that both of these children went on to become college graduates). [10]

Silvano Arieti was a famed psychiatrist who edited the *American handbook of psychiatry* of an earlier era. Arieti, who was also deeply concerned with the Holocaust, made the leap to looking at the omnipresence of evil not only as an issue in the kinds of disturbed relationships that come to the psychotherapist's attention but also as a ubiquitous phenomenon in all human life. [11]

Evil has a much larger role in human life than is generally realized. . . . We label as "evil" only the most terrible crimes, like those perpetrated by the Nazis. Actually human existence is pervaded by evil to a staggering degree . . . in the misunderstandings and resulting hostility between parents and children, in the disturbed relations between husband and wife, in the vindictive jealousy between brothers and sisters, business partners, or professional associates, in the heartless behavior between competitors, in academic intrigues . . . , etc. [12]

Arieti did not give up. As a psychiatrist and humanist, he called for corrective emotional-ethical processes in all of us.

The essential activity of man is the good deed. . . . Only when the individual is in full possession of his will and is fully conscious of it can his self flourish and grow. . . . What defines man is not only his nature but also his ability to transcend his nature . . . not only his origin, but also his aims. The most important of them are the striving toward autonomy, the assertion of individuality, and the practice of the common good. [13]

Overcoming and Growing
beyond the Seductions of Fascism
in Mind and Society

CHAPTER SEVEN

Democratic Mind as the Healthy Alternative to Fascist Mind

The Joy of Life Process and Opportunity

In political terms, the alternative to fascism (totalitarianism) is democracy, and I propose that the same alternative awaits us in the management of our minds.

DEMOCRATIC MIND is characterized by acceptance of complexity, diversity, process, contradiction, and paradox. DEMOCRATIC MIND is open to reevaluation and change based on information from reality; it is based on empiricism, and in that sense is like a continuous process of scientific experimentation checking out what does and what does not contribute to healthy living, and uses the information to modify habits and choices. DEMOCRATIC MIND is based on freedom to think, feel, and be as one really wants, but always with responsibility for protecting human life. The founder of the Alexander Technique for postural uprightness and flexibility had a concept about the freedom and responsibility each of us has in our options to make choices.[1] Just as students of the Alexander Technique learn to move their backs and overall bodies flexibly instead of locking them into the rigid positions that cause back pain and other skeletal problems, so DEMOCRATIC MIND stretches toward increasing flexibility in its thinking and openness to new ideas rather than dogma.

DEMOCRATIC MIND stands for feelings of equality with other people in contrast to the superiority position taken by FASCIST MIND. But when DEMOCRATIC MIND experiences feelings of superiority worming their way up inside, it uses checks and balances to say, "Stop! – don't be such a schmuck. You don't have the right to take a superior position. Be humble. You have so much to be humble about in yourself, and so much to

157

appreciate in the leadership and skillfulness of others from whom you gain so much."

In contrast to power strivings, DEMOCRATIC MIND is committed to equality with other human beings. This does not mean *not* being a leader, a mother or father who is a positive authority to one's children, a chairperson of a department or an organization, or any of the other leadership roles that are needed in our family and community lives. Nor does it mean not enjoying being in these leadership roles. It does mean that while being a leader we simultaneously need to hold ourselves in check against excesses of power and remember that we are intrinsically equal to the other human beings we are leading.

DEMOCRATIC MIND is nonviolent and operates according to an injunction of caring for human life, one's own and others, and not doing harm to human life. In fact, human life is sacred. And when inevitably one discovers that one is nonetheless doing some degree of harm to life – one's own or others – DEMOCRATIC MIND is able to accept responsibility for its errors, stop the harm, and follow up with appropriate corrections and regrets, apologies, and perhaps compensation.

DEMOCRATIC MIND is not afraid to feel tense and anxious. Contrary to popular opinion, anxiety is not perceived as an enemy, and one does not rush to take medication to stop anxiety. Insofar as possible, one accepts anxiety as welcome stirrings within us signaling that something potentially valuable is trying to come up in our "aliveness." Of course, beyond a certain degree of upset and distress we all have the right to reduce the pain to a workable level. But when we are psychologically healthy, we are not anxiety-free; in fact, we are free to enjoy being somewhat anxious. I believe that if I am not anxious for a significant period of time, it is time to be afraid, because it means I am getting overcertain and smug and not stretching myself toward my potential. Not having a healthy level of anxiety can mean, variously for each of us, that I am not writing as I want to, or not painting, or not expanding my business creatively. Anxiety in bearable doses is a signal of welcome mystery and complexity. There is a Talmudic saying, "He who goes without a dream six days is considered evil."[2] I treasure this statement so much that I commissioned an artist to create a painting representing it.

DEMOCRATIC MIND lives through uncertainty. "With all that I understand of life, I know that I know nothing; along with the something that I do know, there is so much that I don't know about life."

DEMOCRATIC MIND embraces diversity and complexity. It also allows contradictory feelings to play inside without getting "flipped out." "I can be loving of you (my dearest, my child, my spouse, my friend), and at the same time I am allowed not to like you; I can be angry with you – even strongly, at times even hate you, without feeling rattled, shaken, or guilty because I am being unfair or betraying you." DEMOCRATIC MIND is not afraid of the play of antagonistic processes jarring one another, meeting up with one another, and ultimately complementing one another.

DEMOCRATIC MIND is not afraid of some badness or so-called sinfulness even as it takes a stand against evil. Democracy does not allow violence; democracy does not allow doing harm to life, but democracy does allow the play of some badness as a healthy and ethical kind of pornography, so to speak, inside our minds. DEMOCRATIC MIND enjoys playfulness, libidinousness, and fun. Even serious work has fun aspects. Even in moments of suffering there can be a sense of privilege and sometimes even elements of gratitude in being alive. DEMOCRATIC MIND is fundamentally different from FASCIST MIND in that it includes process. It includes conflict. It includes change. It is not frozen or stuck in an inhibiting way that stops process; on the contrary, it opens and reopens processes to change, new experiences, and new wisdom.

Here is an everyday example:

> A teenager starts getting mad and is talking back in a nasty arrogant way, not because he's that kind of person all the time, but say at this particular time this child of fourteen, fifteen, or sixteen is reaching for his or her developing autonomy in a new kind of way and is testing out a degree of power toward me, his mother, or father (or it might be a school principal or a teacher).
>
> A wise response is, "Oh, this youngster is trying to become more grown up, to separate and individuate – how wonderful." And then we play two roles. On the outside, we play the parent or adult who orders the youngster to stop the excess. We thus represent the rules of our home or society: "No,

you are not going to have the car without having a license. It's dangerous even though you may think that you are a terrific driver, and in fact may be a terrific driver, but I forbid you to drive without a license."

At the same time, we celebrate the emergence of spirit and the struggle of the youngster to be more adult, and more than likely the youngster will sense our inner approval and encouragement even as the battle wages about the excessive privilege she or he has sought. Our authority is firm and unhesitating; at the same time our connection to the teenager is respectful and understanding of his or her inner experience. The result is likely to be an effective disciplining and emotional closeness rather than the estranged separating that often follows parental anger and preaching of morality.

When conflict, process, and change are valued as vehicles through which complexity and antagonistic actions allow our humanness to flow and enable us to be healthier, friendlier, and more loving, we are less afraid and upset when problems arise in our lives. This is a very different point of view from groaning and bemoaning, "My life is ruined by such and such problems." In fact, we learn that instead of our lives being ruined, our lives are often enriched in the course of and as a result of conflicts. Naturally we react with pain and worry as the problem challenges us, but we trust that if we go about solving it well, we may come out all the richer and stronger than we were before. It is like many of us have learned about backaches and sciatica. The symptoms are certainly not comfortable and can threaten to knock us out of commission, yet many of us learn as a result that our bodies are signaling the need for a new kind of learning. If we do that learning, say with the help of an osteopath, Feldenkrais teacher, Alexander teacher, or chiropractor, we have chances not only of getting over the pain but also of finding ourselves dancing, playing tennis, walking, and even breathing better than we did before, and being generally healthier than we were before because we went with the process and were not afraid of it. A human potential for errors and weaknesses is built into all of us, and we need to learn how to overcome our respective faults and potential areas of weakness by doing our best to correct them.

Thus in regard to marriages, even good marriages have regularly difficult and bad times. Are these bad times really "bad," or are they opportunities for growth? The upsetting times provide opportunities for getting feedback about and criticism of unattractive qualities, and give time for a couple to revise ways of living better together. The couple can then make up and enjoy the deliciousness of being friends again.

In psychotherapy the goal should not be to turn out people who have no problems, no anxiety, or no worries. The goal is to turn out people who even enjoy having problems, worries, and anxieties in their lives, alongside of loving, caring, doing, and achieving. Through the combination, one enjoys the miracle of being alive, not as perfect psychiatric specimens – a fascist totality – but as humans.

In the following sections, I enlarge our discussion of the characteristics of DEMOCRATIC MIND in greater detail. I include clinical illustrations of treatment of psychiatric and relational disturbances as efforts at correction and redirection toward these democratic characteristics of mind.

Processing and Containing Complexity, Diversity, Uncertainty, Possibility, and Creative Tension

DEMOCRATIC MIND learns to expect that many different kinds of experiences, emotions, and thoughts will flow through it, many of them contradictory of one another. One loves and one does not love. One wants to succeed and one wants to rest and not exert oneself. One is happy yet at the same time sad. Complex problems bring up thoughts of many different kinds of solutions and attempts at solutions. Humanities professor Vivian Rosenberg explains how she teaches college students to entertain confusion:

> In most of my classes, regardless of the subject, I advise students to "give yourself permission to experience confusion"; I point out that if you're never confused, you probably aren't learning anything new. One student responded to such advice by sending me this note: "Your comment about confusion," she wrote, "was the most comforting advice a teacher ever gave me."
> ... My own conclusion ultimately follows John Stuart Mill's model:

that is, I believe that we will be better off distrusting grand utopian schemes. Those of us who are committed to both humanitarian and humanistic values, to the general welfare and individual freedom, must recognize that the tension between these ideals can never be fully resolved.

It seems to me that an excessive thirst for certainty and control can only lead to fanaticism – or despair. However, while we live with uncertainty and while we recognize that in an open society conflicting values and perspectives are inevitable, utopian dreams can remind us of our better selves. If we cannot have a perfect world, we can still work to cultivate the capacity for empathy, ameliorate human suffering, to refine our negotiation skills, and learn to accept the need for compromise.

In what has been called "The Age of Interpretation," we have to agree to disagree, all the while continuing to search for creative ways to find "common ground" with those whose interpretations and values differ from our own. Utopian thought tells us a lot about human dreams, but it also shows us how dreams can turn into nightmares. Thus the study of utopias raises important questions and fosters thoughtful and even profound insights into the human condition; how to live in our complex world with no answers that compel universal agreement is something we have yet to discover.[3]

Moreover, there are times when we realize there is no solution other than to live with a situation. The realization that there is no solution becomes a kind of solution that brings on possibilities that would not have been present had one continued to try too hard to solve a problem that cannot be solved. For example, many people drop most or all social or sexual activity because they cannot bear the pain of being hurt in the course of intimate relationships, while more fortunate people go on with their social and sexual lives after accepting the fact that personal and intimate relationships can never be entirely smooth and without hurt and pain.

The process within mind is comparable to an orchestra in which each instrument contributes to a harmonious symphony, yet at any given moment there is also a possible cacophony and discord, and the musical voyage moves through alternations and weavings of lyricism and despair, softness and tumultuousness. DEMOCRATIC MIND treats the mystery and marvel of thoughts and fantasies as welcome materials of life even when they make us uncomfortable, and chooses and organizes the paths of thoughts, feelings, behaviors, and experiences we adopt in our efforts to cope with life.

Our minds are like many other variable and changing aspects of nature, and we must bear sequences, tied to the chronology of our personal narratives as well as to the complexities of the historical eras in the societies in which we live, of success and failure, luck and luckless, healthy and ill, prosperous and not thriving. They are all parts of us. For DEMOCRATIC MIND, one does not have to succeed all the time. One does not have to be well all the time. One does not have to be quiet all the time. One does not have to have the answers all the time. One is a process of many processes. One's ability to experience life through thick and thin is valued as the ultimate joy. Sad thoughts, murderous thoughts, ecstatic thoughts, sexual desires, ridiculous ambitions, competitive excesses, ridiculous needs for exhibitionism, and every known impulse and idea and desire are treated as human, accepted with good humor and with a knowledge that they are invariably desirable in moderation, and paradoxically still somewhat welcome even when excessive, precisely because they then become opportunities for correction and integration into a more wholesome way of being in the world.

I am not afraid to be depressed at times. Now that I understand what it is like, I am all the more sympathetic to those who are overwhelmed by chronic depression. Out of my pain, I develop a sense of how I can break out and rebound from depression when it strikes me. I am glad to have had the opportunity to feel depressed a bit, and I know it will happen to me occasionally in the future as well. So be it as a part of my human experience.

I am not afraid to find my mind racing at times in turmoil and with mad ideas. Am I uncomfortable? Very much so. In fact, I feel crazy, and I know that in a sense I actually am crazy now to an extent. It's no longer hard for me to understand how many people can go really crazy, and in my own discomfort I understand and sympathize more with these fellow human beings. But I also learn how with a certain effort I can pull myself back to regain control of my mind and renew my sanity. It feels good. I feel safer about the future, because now I'm less vulnerable to getting crazy; if and when I do lose my bearings, I trust myself more to be able to get over it.

DEMOCRATIC MIND appreciates opportunities to be upset and disturbed similar to appreciating the opportunities to be happy and joyous. In both cases, the joy of being is greater than any specific state of joy or achievement, welcome as they are.

❧ *A minister comes for family therapy with his wife and son "because" of the poor school performance of their son, but before long it becomes clear that the minister is asking for help for himself as well. Sundays at church have become an increasing fright for him, not only in the seriousness of his goal to be a capable and impressive spiritual leader who delivers a meaningful sermon and succeeds in creating an atmosphere of religious reverence, but because his mind has been betraying him into being focused on the cleavages of any number of the attractive women sitting below him seeking his spiritual guidance and communion with their Lord! How could he possibly be so bad that he is all agog with their breasts?*

How fares his ministry in general? Year after year, the archbishop comes to review the work of all the local leaders of the cloth in his denomination, and this minister finds himself spoken to patronizingly and dismissed summarily with hardly any recognition of his efforts, and now for some years with no increase in his salary as well. In short, he is a man afraid of his mind and his being, across a wide range of experience, from the sexual to the assertive.

What does psychotherapy do for this minister? He is invited to learn, and in this case does succeed, to enjoy the range of his mind, beginning with the cleavages of the ladies, and indeed his wife's cleavage, and the fuller play of his sensuality, which has been pent up and is longing to burst forth. He is invited to encounter and re-own the creative impulses in him – to write his interesting ideas about religious themes and have them published. He is encouraged to present himself assertively like an actor when the archbishop arrives. The following year he gets a big raise along with the recognition he yearns for so much.

Ah, yes, I will add that in this case part of the therapy was assisted by having the minister see a very beautiful female psychotherapist. She was asked, in the presence of her patient, to please generate a process with her patient of seduction and pleasure in same, not God forbid in a manifestly sexual way, but in a "sinful" playfulness of libido and attractiveness that even a psychotherapist and patient can share in responsible use of their respective minds and feelings and awareness of each other's body too. In the end, they had a fun time in their constructive professional work with each other.

Welcoming Tension and Even Anxiety

A big problem with DEMOCRATIC MIND is that because it has no defined patterns and answers, it opens human experience to high doses of uncertainty, tension, and anxiety. Not knowing exactly what to do (there are few if any total and perfect truths), and not being sure how to measure success, which is defined more as staying with a process than achieving a final solution, means living with the tension of maintaining boundaries between hopes and always-incomplete achievements, and between inner feelings and choices of actions. DEMOCRATIC MIND leads human beings toward greater qualities of unrest, inner dissension, conflict, and anxiety. Tension and anxiety are respected as progenitors of invention and creativity; controversy and differences are respected as promoting innovation, creativity, and a courage to set out on new paths. By learning to process and contain tension and anxiety as a fuel for growth and innovation, DEMOCRATIC MIND sponsors unfolding and becoming, self-actualization and fulfillment of potential. DEMOCRATIC MIND does not want to feel free from anxiety. In fact, as noted earlier, it becomes anxious over the absence of anxiety. If one has it "all made," and all is under control, secure and assured, then the laws of life are: the unexpected will hit with that much more fury. For who dares have it all together?

• *Jogging, eating healthy foods, keeping calm, and taking the latest cocktail of vitamins prescribed by* Consumers Health Reports *do not mean that one will never develop cancer.*
• *Being a loving, devoted parent, and trying to do one's best for a child*

do not mean that a dear child never gets into the most confusing and distressing kinds of problems.

• Loyal devotion to one's church in its lofty ideals and pageantry does not mean that one will never wake to find that the minister is carrying on with the wife of the minister of another church, or that one of them absconded with the church monies.

• Being a loyal citizen of a democracy does not mean never being pulled into an era in which one's beloved country goes to war cruelly and stupidly out of pretensions of imperialistic grandiosity rather than in genuine good faith to defend human lives that have come under attack.

Life is inherently full of instability, complexity. and surprises. Each individual journey includes successes in becoming more of what we hope to be and can be. At the same time, no matter what we do, the journey also includes weakening and not reaching our potential as we also unravel toward inevitable incompleteness and the end of life. No one is the perfect maestro who can process all of life without being awed and frightened by anxiety about the unknown and signals of major blockages and upsets inside. Rollo May taught many years ago that anxiety, in its essence, is the fear of not becoming what one can become and hopes to be.[4] Harkening to this call is a privilege. Turning off the power of this system is turning oneself off.

DEMOCRATIC MIND welcomes anxiety as an invitation to grow, which makes anxiety less anxious and transforms it into opportunity. Psychiatric treatments that seek to remove anxiety abort this process. They offer a return to certainty through overcontrol of the anxiety process, such as by medications, rather than effectively teaching the patient to respect and even enjoy the anxiety and thus bring it under control and minimize it.

❧ The patient is a 50-year-old psychologist who stumbles in asking for help with major depression. He has already been to several psychiatrists, and the latest one has put him on a regimen of several kinds of medications at fairly high doses, which are justified by the chronicity and severity of his depression and pessimism. Why does he keep changing psychiatrists? Well, he didn't feel so good on the first combination of medications so he switched to a second, and there too it didn't seem to help so he tried a third

person who came highly recommended. Why come to a psychotherapist now? He doesn't know but he senses something is fundamentally wrong.

The therapist recommends that he taper off the medications as much as he can, even to the point of giving them up, and sketches for the patient a picture of how he appears to be devoted to a lifelong way of presenting himself – to himself, let alone to others – as a worried, suffering, martyrlike, joyless person. Does he like being this way? Might he consider raising his head, looking people in the eye, wearing a smile on his face, and speaking up forcefully about all the little things one talks about with other people?

The man does give up all medication and embarks on a – though an incomplete – program of changing his manner of being a depressed loser, and lo and behold over a period of just a few months reports that his depression lifts completely but in fact is then replaced with disturbing bouts of anxiety. At this point the therapist congratulates the patient on his progress, not only because the immobilizing and saddening depression has lifted, but also because a much more vital person is emerging. The therapist explains that the anxieties signal that there is so much more that is useful and vital inside of him that is now begging to come out and make him a more fun person. Will he have the courage and stamina to stay with a period of anxiety until he learns to enjoy being more of a jovial and engaged person?

Openmindedness to Information, Questioning, and Use of Scientific-Like Empiricism

DEMOCRATIC MIND revels in new information, including information that is contradictory to what one has believed. Knowledge is celebrated. The scientific method is one of the finest friends of mind. It asks questions honestly, checks out different conditions rigorously, reports back developing information without fear, faces gaps that remain in the information, and slowly but surely moves to new conclusions.

A physician well known for his scientific excellence, who is approaching the age of 50 and should know better, says he is totally uninterested in stopping smoking, and refuses to have the periodic examinations that are prescribed for all adults as part of a normal health regimen. "I'd rather not know if anything is wrong with me. If I take those tests, they will only find something wrong and then start treating me. I'm going to let whatever happens happen."

The same physician is embroiled in a chronic marital problem because he insists on his right to have other women and haughtily dismisses his wife's angry and pained protests. In all personal matters he is the absolute ruler who dismisses information or feedback from anyone else, including, as we saw, formal health information, professional advice, or the emotional responses of other people. He is the sole Boss even of information.

Because it is open to information, DEMOCRATIC MIND can discover that a person who appeared not to love is in fact, inside of himself or herself, really hurt and afraid to express the love that he or she wants to give. How many couples move into the corner of a staid routine of not experiencing feelings toward each other in order not to be hurt by their conviction that the other does not love them? No efforts are made to love and be loved, but the truth is that both really wanted to love but were afraid to be hurt. Their untapped beauty never emerges, and the marriage becomes progressively gray, grim, and stale.[5]

But DEMOCRATIC MIND can also discover, however painfully, that a person one thought was genuinely loving really has not been feeling for the other person – spouse or child – and has been more involved with their own needs, sometimes including a need to believe and pretend to themselves that they were loving!

❧ He was crazy about her – for the beautiful woman she was. However, he was forced to divorce her after learning she had cheated on him repeatedly. A friend told him it was obvious that the promiscuity in her intrigued him. "I don't understand," said the betrayed husband. "I thought I really loved her, but I guess my friend realized I really was showing her off. She was so beautiful I didn't let myself know how cold she was. If I had known, I wouldn't have talked myself into believing I loved her."

In the give-and-take of relationships, DEMOCRATIC MIND listens sensitively and respectfully to the feelings and reactions of others. One understands that each person participating in a relationship has his or her understanding of what is taking place, and that there are often gross contradictions and disharmonies in the perceptions of people ostensibly sharing the same experience. DEMOCRATIC MIND is respectful of one's own and of the other's experiences, but at the same time presses toward ironing out and correcting gross distortions of reality. The other's point of view is sought and welcomed. It is not shouted down, ruled out of existence, or punished. It is reacted to with a disciplined combination of respect for the other's right to say his or her truth along with respect for one's own right to agree and disagree. There is a sensitivity to the other's different way of experiencing life and a readiness to experience tension and conflict over differing interpretations, but there is also a steady movement toward defining factual and evidential realities accurately. Together, the several modes of respect for oneself, the other, and objective reality lay the groundwork for a combination of personal integrity, decency toward the other, and living according to facts and the truth rather than myths and distortions of reality. In wholesome relationships, such as good marriages, one sees dramas of information processing that slowly but surely bring home to each participant a greater knowledge of each one's tendencies to err and distort, and how to be helpful to oneself and the other to correct each person's distortions.

They are a couple who have been in psychotherapy in the past and know how to work with each other. She says to him: "Have you ever noticed how regularly you complain in the mornings of something being missing, lost, and that you even suspect that someone took your possession? I think you're crying over your mother's death, and don't realize it."

He says to her: "Do you know that no matter if you are aggressive you convince yourself that you're the victim and even the martyr? Isn't this the way you felt as a child?"

With honest feedback like this, one can save a lot in ongoing fees to psychoanalysts and psychotherapists.

DEMOCRATIC MIND asks itself questions about how the person can feel better and more fulfilled. Am I working too hard? Should I be vacationing more? Should I take a new job? Do I want to write the music I have dreamed of through the years? The mind explores, tests, experiments, and slowly but surely derives conclusions from experience.

I was scared when I first started writing music, but I knew that the scared feeling was a good sign for me, and I stayed with it; and slowly but surely I learned that I have no greater joy than to fulfill this dream to compose, which is what I am now doing to my great pleasure.

Over time one learns various ways to treat oneself well to achieve health and personal fulfillment, which should be continued and amplified. One also learns of a hundred and more ways to mistreat oneself, which need to be corrected and changed. The information comes from experience, but only when one is open to the information. Some people become so set in their ways and closed to new information that they cannot make changes in their lifestyles, neither for achieving their better potentials for good living nor for correcting their worst errors. DEMOCRATIC MIND is open and actively seeks corrective information from its observations and investigations of reality: from professionals whom one consults to learn how to better conduct one's affairs – doctors of the body, therapists of the mind, accountants in regard to management of funds and taxes, attorneys for guidance in matters of rights and protection against duress, and so on; and also from one's intimates – spouse, children, work colleagues, friends, in fact anyone with whom one is in contact, since all human contact provides feedback on how we are behaving and what we are communicating.

   ❧ *A lovely young woman who has come to therapy in order to love a man more fully speaks of her inability to be frank with her mother. "A minute after you tell her something, she acts like nothing happened. She will not be able to bear my telling her my criticism. She pushes it off immediately. It is as if I didn't say anything."*

   Mother and her late husband had lived in an armed antagonism. It was a family where straight talk was not allowed.

   ❧ *He hated to face the facts, but he forced himself to remember that his first wife had betrayed him sexually, and he had divorced her for infidelity. His current wife, although sexually faithful, also was furious at him. What was it in him that drew such fury and a need to hurt and insult him?*

   He dares to learn that alongside his nice-guy manner he exudes a denial of the other, talking past the other, and not seeing or hearing what the other person feels.

Was this familiar? From as far back as he could remember, his mother had been a kind of unofficial psychiatric recluse who flitted impotently about their house. His kind father did everything mother should have been doing. Father nurtured the children, fed them, cleaned the house, and took care of his dependent wife, all uncomplainingly. He was wonderful, but somehow he was in a role of the Perfect One, a virtual Angel, and he too didn't really speak to any of the children in a meaningfully connected way about the complexities of their lives.

In therapy, he realized that he needed to be less a ghost figure like his mother or an automaton of angelic goodness like his father. Slowly but surely he trained himself to look at his wife, experience her, speak to her directly, and take in her reactions and opinions.

Freedom, Respect for Dissent, and Responsibility to Make Choices

DEMOCRATIC MIND has "a mind of its own." People with minds of their own eat, sleep, love, study, work, fight for their country's safety, go to church, and more, because they really want to.

Contrast any one of the above functions with the minions of people who do whatever they do because they have to, out of obligation.

• He studies against his will because he has to fulfill his parents' demands.

• She makes love because she has to fulfill her husband's sexual needs.

• He prays devoutly in a routine of blind conformity to the ritual he has been taught.

As we have seen, it is not that obedience and conformity are without gratification. On the contrary. They narcotize, afford a quieting sense of belonging, remove the stresses of choice, and much more. On the surface, obedience and conformity are probably the much better deal for peace of mind and even for getting along effectively in most contexts of human society.

The exercise of freedom is a more complex process involving alternative ideas and emotions, weighing the advantages and disadvantages of alternatives, choosing a course of action, and standing responsibly behind one's choices. There are great pleasures in the exercise of freedom: an opportunity to be true to one's self, a sense of inspiration and wonderment at the opportunities available, satisfaction in working toward and fulfilling goals, and also a stature and dignity earned as the author of one's own destiny. But freedom also brings with it scary levels of anxiety, tension, and impending danger. The biblical awareness that any number of slaves will not want to be set free even when their masters propose to give them their freedom is seen over and over again in everyday life. Making choices is not easy. It is heady and disorienting to choose whom to marry, what work to do, where to place loyalties, how to react to nastiness in work settings or by neighbors, whether to accept a physician's or surgeon's treatment decisions, and more. The easiest way is to take the course of least resistance.

§⅃ *She fell head over heels in love with one man after another. They were all handsome, bright, ever-cheerful, and in truth weakly dependent on her. Because they looked so good, she apparently had nothing to apologize for in any of her choices. She could have taken any one of them to the altar to the acclaim of all (which was very important to her) that she was marrying handsomely, and then gone home laughing all the way that she was the one true boss of the relationship and had a dutiful, adoring slave man to serve her forever.*

Some inner voice nonetheless saved her, and she went for therapy. Unlike many people asking for treatment, she knew from the outset that it would take a lot of time and a high frequency of treatment sessions.

By now she had a serious boyfriend who was not one of her adoring slaves. She respected him and was excited by him, but also felt repeatedly uncomfortable and tense with him. She understood that when he expressed his personality – his wisdom, power for choosing a direction in life, and his strong will power – she felt resentful, overshadowed, and second class. She hated these feelings. Her dream had always been to emulate her w-o-n-d-e-r-f-u-l mother who always was on top, getting people to do what she wanted, always the charmer, and never wrong. Nonetheless, troubling internal voices reminded her that her father had fared poorly with her mother, that he had taken to drink, and had died at an early age, and that a brother also had lost his life in a sports accident because of his bravado and recklessness – which had been the hateful hallmarks of his personality through the years. Who exactly had he been trying to show up and conquer, she wondered. She realized she needed to teach herself to make room for a man who would be free to be himself, truthful, independent, and willful; and that it was she who needed to learn to enjoy a relationship with a man who would be her equal in a concerto of two free people, neither one of them enslaving or enslaved.

Inherently, freedom includes the right and the need for respecting dissent – internally and interpersonally. One needs and wants to hear the dissenting internal voices constantly questioning, challenging, and proposing possible alternative emotions, ideas, and courses of action. And one needs and wants to hear the dissenting voices of one's intimates, beginning with a spouse but also all the other people with whom one lives and works.

It has been observed that the most effective managers tolerate their inner ambivalences and processing of alternatives, and that they are open and even eager to hear the critical voices of their employees and assistants.

🍃 *Some years into conducting my own clinical practice, I decided that any time I felt upset, unsure, even anxious and undecided about how best to treat an individual patient, couple, or family, that I would first of all be pleased that I was uncomfortable! I took my discomfort as a sign that I cared and was potentially trying to do the best, and as a hopeful signal that my best and creative thinking might yet emerge to lead me to wise planning of the therapy.*

An intriguing extension of this way of shaping my personal experience was that I decided not to fear situations in which patients would ask for my opinion or understanding when I really didn't know what I thought. I vowed that I would reply honestly to the question: "I really don't know yet what I think, and I'm not even sure how soon I will have an opinion to share with you, but that is what I am working on as we meet."

When I directed a group psychological practice, we colleagues required of ourselves as a staff a style of sharing differences of opinion with one another without any efforts to convince one another of the rightness of our ideas or the wrongness of one another's thinking. In this group practice our staff shared many cases, combining roles as individual child or adult therapists, couple therapists in parent counseling or marriage counseling, family therapists, or group therapists, so that there were many cases in which we needed and wanted to put together our different views of the people and their cases.

"I really get the creeps with this mother," one psychotherapist might say of the mother of the child he or she was seeing in individual therapy. "She makes me feel bad – like all gray inside and without any appetite for life's pleasures."

"To me she is a nice person, and I find myself feeling sympathetic toward her," another therapist might say. "I sense there is a softness and loving she really would like to bring up from deep inside that she has never succeeded in doing," continued the second therapist who was treating the mother and father in parent counseling as well as the parents and child together in family therapy.

Our working rule was to welcome such differences of opinion as a sign that, hopefully, we were putting our true selves into the case. The working assumption was that there could well be some side of the truth in each therapist's perception and experience. The further rule was that when therapists had different ideas, and especially if they felt a tension between them, they must meet to speak regularly about their opinions, even several times a week, until they reached a point where a clarity – often a synthesis of the differences – emerged for all parties.

This practice was carefully organized not to include formal regularly scheduled staff meetings – which I had come to hate and mistrust as shams of display of hierarchical status and conformity in my earlier work in several psychiatric clinics and hospitals – but to include the expectation of frequent personal collaborative meetings between the therapists sharing cases. For myself, my role in all such meetings was the same as my colleagues' roles, and in no case was I to be deferred to as the director and owner of the practice, nor was I to allow myself to seek to be deferred to.

(I had seen head honchos expecting to be deferred to at staff meetings in clinics and hospitals, and facing them too many sycophantic staff, notwithstanding their MD, PhD, and MSW degrees, currying favor rather *than trying to help their patients. That was how so many electric shock treatments and lobotomies got through in the "Cuckoo's Nest" hospitals of the time.*[6])

Making Choices

The point was made earlier that we do poorly when we function out of coercion rather than choice. If one gets up regularly to work without a sense of choice because one has to go to a job one does not like, work becomes a heavy burden indeed. If one eats food because one is obligated to eat the food that has been served by whomever, eating becomes a choking matter. If one makes love because that is what one is supposed to do with one's mate, or even in order to appear psychologically healthy to oneself, sex becomes sexless and tasteless.

Choice is one of DEMOCRATIC MIND's most powerful means for enriching life with new spirit and vitality. By definition, every act of choice means giving up some alternative that had advantages and an attraction of its own, hence the very act of choice means knowing how to give up the illusion of having everything. Choice therefore also means knowing how to "mourn" what one is giving up, and even to appreciate the privilege of relinquishing whatever it is one has lost in the choice. At the same time, choice is a celebration of the path one has affirmed and the excitement and joy of pursuing it in fulfillment of an energy process one sets in motion with choice.[7]

He cannot choose otherwise. He has been taken over by a role he plays to the hilt. He simply must be top dog. He must be seen. He must be in charge all the time in the business world and come out on top. His family too must go along with him and accept whatever rhythm he introduces into their lives, because his work has to be at the center of his and their universe, and they must always follow his lead. Slowly but surely, his wife becomes hysterically upset, goes off into capricious sexual escapades with a variety of men, and becomes suicidal, not only because she feels alone without her husband's caring for her, but also because she cannot stand the kind of person she has become. Each of the children takes off into extremes of lack of success and emotional irritabilities and crises. Why can't they simply do what they are supposed to do? They cause him so much trouble. There is no end to the problems his family members are making that constantly demand more and more of him and constantly take him out of the office.

Therapy presents this man with a variety of choices he has previously neglected, beginning with the question of whether and how much he is willing to devote to helping each of the members of his family work their way out of the big-time troubles they are in. It will cost him time and effort, and especially that he will have to take time away from the business in which he has anchored himself without knowing he really is in bondage to an addiction. It was an agonizing uphill battle to allow himself to translate the caring that was nonetheless waiting in his heart to pitch in to help each of his family members.

Basic Equality and Respect, Sharing Power with Checks and Balances against Power

DEMOCRATIC MIND regards other people as equals and strives to convey respect for other people. The spaces of life are shared in mutual self-interest rather than in attempts to overpower and overcome others and subordinate them. Differences in status, position, and role are not denied by DEMOCRATIC MIND, but they are not seized on as a basis for humiliating or subjugating others. The cleaning lady is not treated or referred to as a slave or as a member of a derogated minority group. Employees are not treated as servants; junior colleagues and subordinates in professional and business organizations are not ordered about and commanded, and are not subjected to innuendoes of their being in an inferior status. Nor are people patronized and treated equally in a disingenuous fashion.

DEMOCRATIC MIND enjoys competition for success. The drive for a higher status is taken seriously as a proper path to advance to whatever higher levels one wants to attain. But DEMOCRATIC MIND knows that success carries new risks of being corrupted by a sense of importance and power that are dangerous for one's integrity and long-range creativity. In a situation in which there isn't a sufficient play of political forces to constructively check and balance the overuse of power (for example, a university department or a business organization that vests relatively unchecked power in the leader), and when one is not fortunate enough to enjoy structural constraints such as in organizations that maintain a rule of rotating people through leadership positions back into the ranks (for example, the Baha'i faith limits the terms of office of its directors to a specified number of years), DEMOCRATIC MIND itself is careful to provide a person with inner controls against excessive self-importance and abusive power over others.

᪣ *He was one of the most famous psychiatrists in the United States, and many expected that he would be a candidate for President of the American Psychiatric Association. But the truth was that in his home bailiwick as director of a major psychiatric center, he had become progressively removed from his staff. When he met colleagues in the halls of the hospital or in the elevator or cafeteria, he stared icily past them and barely returned their greetings with a curt nod or a choked-off hello if at all. In meetings with his senior staff he sat silently, much of the time combing and recombing his hair in long strokes of self-involvement and peering at a spot somewhere beyond his desk, and he even continued these postures when he deigned to take his turn to speak and act as director of the meeting. Intriguingly, until the very end of his career the content of his professional contributions remained of a very high quality, in fact admirably on the level of the excellence for which he was deservedly known, but the person behind all this excellence was increasingly a brooding paranoid egotist.*

The end of this too-great man came in a brief and intense bout of illness, which had been predicted by one of his senior staff long before there were any signs of the illness. The staff member who amazingly saw the end in advance was a psychiatrist who had enjoyed the formative years of his training under the direction of this senior psychiatrist, had been especially close to him, and in fact loved him. With great pain he watched as his mentor's grandiosity and insulting ways expanded. One day he was asked by a younger staff member, a therapist who had recently joined the staff, to intervene and help bring the chief to his senses. He replied that it was unfortunately too late, and that in his judgment the famous psychiatrist would be so unable to bear himself for the person he had become that he probably would take seriously ill before long, and his illness would prove incurable.

Power, conquest, striving for importance, and all the familiar traits of domination over others are not completely censored out by DEMO-CRATIC MIND. But they are tempered, kept in balance, and subordinated to and teamed with a commitment to respect of fellow human beings. For example, for males fantasies of sexual conquest and power over females are treated in the mind as natural and enjoyable "tribal" themes that empower a certain level of sexual prowess. The fantasies of sexual conquest are not exorcised as inadmissible, as might be demanded by strident feminist therapists (and also well-intentioned women and men who make the mistake of believing that the "rapist" and even plain conqueror in every male must be banished entirely), but neither are those fantasy themes allowed to predominate and take over larger experiences of affection and sharing with one's female friend and partner.

So too men and women as parents are not averse to experiencing some of the pleasures of being "caliphs in their courts," surrounded by children who serve them to some extent in whatever chores or services; but these elements of being feudal masters and family chieftains are softened, made secondary to, and integrated into larger experiences of being caring parents whose purpose is to bring up beloved children with healthy minds and spirits. DEMOCRATIC MIND eschews dominating parenting, whether old-fashioned father bossism or more modern versions of mothers who take on roles as super-leaders of their children, where parents transform their positions into excuses for becoming invasively all-powerful in their children's activities and experiences.

DEMOCRATIC MIND also will not go to the other extreme of being parents who undertake to be democratic to such a fault that they do not exercise any power over their children. They do not remove from themselves traditional symbolisms of being leaders for their children and of their families, for example, agreeing to be called by first name rather than some version of father and mother, and taking pride in being a "friend" to the child rather than a parent. As suggested in an earlier case illustration, in time many of these parents will be faced with one or more out-of-control kids who mock their parent's escape from the responsibility of their roles to be leaders. DEMOCRATIC MIND places parents and children as equals in spirit, but not equals at the expense of parents renouncing their leadership.

In all relationships, DEMOCRATIC MIND joys in reciprocal egalitarian and mutual relationships rather than being more important than others and pushing other people around.

Nonviolence, Conflict Resolution, and Seeking Peace

Welcoming Differences, Conflict, and the Need for Problem Solving

DEMOCRATIC MIND celebrates the rich expressiveness and assertiveness of other people, and appreciates the creative flow of differences of ideas and perspectives in processing ideas with others, including the necessity of differences and conflicts at many points in all relationships.

For DEMOCRATIC MIND, conflicts are treated as welcome opportunities for examination of different ideas, correction of one's errors, and enrichment of one's own contributions by the thinking and wisdom of others. Problem solving and conflict resolution are opportunities for learning more about oneself, they help draw on new inner resources to solve dilemmas, and help develop skills for planning new initiatives. Conflicts are occasions for achieving cooperation and partnership with others, and also for improving one's ability to influence others and provide leadership. Conflicts often lead to the development of novel solutions in the interplay with others that leave a shared sense of well-being and good feelings of having worked together rather than a triumph of one party over another.

DEMOCRATIC MIND is not appeasing, subservient, slavish, or passive. It is alive in its individuality. It represents the pride of authorship of each person's personality and of each person's rights to self-assertion and participation in the various issues of one's life. Numerous studies have shown that at every level of human experience, exercising the right to direct one's own life is good for people's minds and spirits; in studies of old age homes it was shown that when residents have a say in determining policies, such as the hours of meals, the game room, and so on, they live longer than do residents of other facilities in which the decisions are made by staff. Children who are also allowed to make decisions in regard to their lives grow up to be emotionally stronger and also to show more leadership than those who are only demanded to do as they are told or, as the adage had it, were to be seen but not heard.

DEMOCRATIC MIND is open to the sounds of differences, variations, controversies, and contradictions within oneself. DEMOCRATIC MIND is not monolithic. It does not mandate single-dimensional solutions. It does not require obedience and conformity. Mind is an agent of democratic selection and election – it makes choices of policy and action from a range of alternatives, and insofar as possible, subjects emerging choices to further reevaluation and changes based on thoughtful evaluation of realities and possibilities.

DEMOCRATIC MIND is a tool for experiencing, exploration, playfulness, marvel, and joy in one's inner spaces. Disturbing "sounds" – fantasies, ideas, and images – are welcomed, even when disturbing, perhaps even because they are disturbing, for they are understood to illuminate different sides of one's true inner self. "Bad" feelings are accepted as parts of oneself that are not to be denied or suppressed.

As a model of a democratic society, DEMOCRATIC MIND submits for critical review the interplay of its own "legislative," "judicial," and "administrative" departments. Thus, both feeling and thinking are utilized to crosscheck each idea and feeling we have. Thinking is used to review feelings analytically and logically. Feeling is used to review emotionally how an idea sits inside. The audits also include reviewing the ethical implications of thoughts and feelings, and finally a careful analysis of what in the final analysis we want to choose to do.

• Does it feel right?
• What emotions are set off by going further with this direction of thought?
• Does the feeling or thought make sense?
• Logically, what will this lead to?
• What are the cost-benefit implications of taking this direction?
• Even if this is what I feel like doing, is it the fair and decent way to handle this situation?
• In the final analysis, shall I act on this direction or put it aside?

Neither feeling nor thinking are given supremacy over the other, nor is personal gain allowed to override considerations of justice. The full interplay of crosschecking thoughts and feelings intertwined with an ethical analysis concludes one's choice and creates a critical review of our behavior, which, generally, provides protection against being carried away to do heinous acts that do harm either to oneself or to others.

• Maybe it feels right to kill the bastard who slept with my wife, but I know (thinking) it's wrong to do, and I won't do it.

• Maybe rational cost-benefit analysis tells me I'll gain a lot by my becoming a drug trafficker, but my heart (feelings linked to ethical judgments) tells me I can't be party to killing the children who will get hooked, and I won't do it.

DEMOCRATIC MIND seeks and celebrates impulse, passion, and libido. It does not fear joy, which is justly deserved in one's life; it does not flee measures of lust, revelry, and orgy because, like everything else, impulses and fun-seeking are also subject to the checks and balances of considered evaluation and good judgment; and it does not flee aggression or thoughts, knowing they are not the same as actual violence. In fact, they are a wholesome basis for a solid commitment to nonviolence.

The overall responsibility of DEMOCRATIC MIND is to provide for the health, safety, and welfare of oneself and of other human beings, beginning quite naturally, even if apparently selfishly, with concern for oneself and one's closest loved ones, but continuing on to genuine caring for all humanity. Judgments of actions are anchored first and foremost in a commitment to protect life and to improve the quality of life experience. Actions that can cause harm to the physical safety, health, and well-being of human beings – oneself or others – are ruled out by the institutions of DEMOCRATIC MIND. Because inner feelings and ideas are not necessarily the basis for action and are understood not to be equivalents of the actions they describe, a wider range of "bad" feelings and ideas is accepted; but these too are subject to tests, whether the critical mass of concentration in time and energy on such "bad" feelings and ideas will begin to override or dominate the personality and moral meanings of the person entertaining them.

DEMOCRATIC MIND welcomes measures of aggression and anger as a fountain of life, an elixir of experiencing, a statement of involvement, caring, and application of oneself. However, almost all of one's anger is treated first as feelings that are to be welcomed but rarely to be acted upon overtly. Anger is a way of reminding oneself that one is not helpless, one has power, and one could choose to beat the other person's brains in, but also one always has a responsibility to choose what to do in actuality. Healthy minds do harbor fantasies of revenge against enemies, but in most cases do not act on these, certainly not in actual physical violence, and remain open to rediscovery of a forgivable, perhaps poignant or even lovable, humanness in some of those who were hated antagonists and enemies, or at the least to a modus vivendi of nonviolent accommodation to one another.[8]

Needless to say, the suicide-bombers of our times unhappily have a very different philosophy. If there is to be a war between the West and Islam, in many ways it will be over this difference in philosophies.

Acceptance of Responsibility for Doing Harm to Self and Others

DEMOCRATIC MIND is aware that we all do hurt ourselves and other human beings throughout our lives, whether by intention, error in being carried away by ourselves, or even by inadvertence when we are not really aware of the consequences of what we are doing.

We do physical harm to our bodies by overworking, working for the wrong reasons, failing to punctuate our work with rest, using our bodies incorrectly, eating incorrectly, smoking, driving dangerously, not exercising, failing to get proper medical care, and in dozens of other ways. We do major emotional harm to ourselves by being cruel to ourselves, encouraging guilt feelings, or conversely failing to accept guilt feelings that are important for our integrity, striving for a golden calf of power, fame, and fortune at the expense of being at peace with ourselves and others, being overly concerned with the way people perceive us as opposed to centering ourselves in our own niceness as decent and attractive people, and again in an endless list of self-defeating ways of being with ourselves.

We hurt other human beings around us no less. We impose emotional messages on our intimates, friends, and associates. We demand achievements by our children for the wrong reasons. We lose interest in a primary relationship and separate from or divorce a spouse with whom we have lived meaningfully because we are not willing to do our share to maintain and develop the relationship. We hurt one another by being disrespectful of the talent of other people and their dreams and aims to better themselves. Many of us also do actual physical harm to other human beings in the course of our lives. We injure and kill people in automobile accidents, some of which are fully our responsibility, others of which we are inadvertent participants in events beyond our control but where nonetheless we have to accept the fact that we were present at the injury or deaths of others. We do harm to others in our professional lives, such as when those of us who are entrusted with healing are poor healers, and worse when we prescribe interventions that actually harm, in some cases when we could have chosen better based on available knowledge, in other cases because we are trapped in a situation in which what will be known in a few years will show that what we are doing today is wrong or insufficient but we had no choice in our time and era. Worst of all, millions of us human beings do physical harm to millions of other human beings, up to and including torture, murder, massacre, terrorism, and genocide, in some cases as active participants, in many cases as collaborating accomplices and as seemingly unknowing bystanders who do not lift a finger or help the victims.

DEMOCRATIC MIND is aware that we must do everything to prevent and reduce the number of instances and the extent to which we do harm to our own lives and to the lives of others; and it is also aware that we must take responsibility for all those events in which we have done harm to others, even if inadvertently. At the least, the act of taking responsibility is an extension of all the efforts we must make to prevent doing harm in the future. It is also an act of penance for the past. When we correct ways of damaging ourselves, the feeling characteristically described is one of relief that we are taking better care of ourselves. When we try to make amends for the damages we have done to others, confirming our acceptance of the moral imperative that it is wrong to hurt other human beings often makes us feel better too. Making amends, such as apologies or compensation, can reward both individuals and collective groups with memorable spiritual satisfaction and also some release from guilt over the harm that one has done others.

As noted, between the nations and peoples of this world, there have come into play in recent years new forms of apology, compensation, and restitution.[9] The examples given included the U.S. restitution to Japanese Americans who had been interned in camps in World War II. The government prison camps were technically concentration camps, although they were not characterized by cruelty, servitude, or destruction of life. In the early 1990s, the United States Congress voted to accept formal responsibility for the harm done to Japanese Americans. The German government pioneered paying survivor compensation to Jewish victims of the Nazis. I mentioned earlier that in recent years there have been scandalous exposés of how funds of Holocaust victims have been held inaccessible in Swiss and other banks including some Palestinian banks, which means Jewish banks in the period preceding the establishment of the State of Israel![10] Descendants of victims of the Armenian Genocide also have begun to win awards from insurance companies that had long since refused to pay off their policies. Another of many examples is how the New Zealand government denied the destruction it did to the indigenous Maori people, whose leaders were killed and whose people were driven off their lands in the colonization of New Zealand in the 19th century. Around 1996, the New Zealand government accepted responsibility for its past actions in the way of multimillion dollar compensation to Maori residents who were the descendants of the victimized people.

Of course, our world civilization is still marked by an endless series of denials of profound cruelty, exploitation, and killing of other peoples.

• For years, the Japanese government has systematically avoided any kind of recognition of its brutal campaign of torture and killing in Manchuria in the 1930s, including the dangerous precedents it laid down of horrifying medical experiments as well as the production of biological and chemical weapons of mass destruction. In the mid-1990s, a few small cracks of acknowledgment began to appear in Japanese life, but the larger picture of Japanese complicity in the above mass murder still has not been dealt with.[11]

• The Turkish government devotes millions of dollars and some of the best energies of its diplomats around the world to denials of the genocide Ottoman Turkey committed against the Armenian people in the years beginning in 1915. When leaders or parliaments of other countries confirm the historical truth of the Armenian Genocide, the Turks are irate and threaten reprisals, such as canceling major economic relationships or even military and security alliances (for example, Turkey has threatened to stop its participation in NATO, or to stop U.S. planes flying from bases in Turkey if the U.S. Congress so much as ratifies a day of remembrance for the Armenians who perished).[12]

In the everyday lives of plain people, the capacity for taking responsibility for one's errors and hurting others often helps resolve serious conflicts. A real, "I am sorry" or "I apologize genuinely" can go a long way between a couple as well as between parents and children (in both directions of the relationship – meaning children and teenagers who can apologize also can contribute to repairing and enriching their relationships with their parents). There are often doubts about the genuineness of an apology and its reliability, but assuming that the person apologizing works seriously at conveying the authenticity of their taking responsibility for having done wrong, even many serious hurts can be lifted sufficiently to allow for a reconciliation process.

 He meant it. "I'm really sorry I betrayed you," he said to her. "It was a lapse where my sexual passion and the convenience of a trip away from home got the better of me. I had no idea I would hurt you so deeply, and I really understand now how you feel. I'm very sorry and ask you to take me back so I can be loyal to you forever." She did.

 She was inconsolable. She had found out about his brief affair and was shattered. He apologized even if reluctantly, and tried to promise to be faithful in the future. But she would have no part of it. Her rage was cutting and resolute. It went on this way for weeks, and nothing budged in the slightest in the conjoint couple therapy sessions – she was out to avenge her hurt with attack after attack on him.

 The therapist invited her to come to an individual session. The goal was to try to understand whether there was a further personal meaning that was so deeply violated for this woman that she was unable to accept her husband's effort to correct what he had done. Surprisingly, what emerged was that this wife had her own several-month affair long before her husband. Apparently she could not tolerate the apology he was offering her because she could not bear the thought that she might have to apologize to him. She had no intention of his ever knowing, and nothing could be further from her strategy than the thought of her also apologizing to him and the two of them renegotiating a policy of mutual faithfulness for the future. No way.

The wife withdrew from therapy shortly after her admission of her affair in the above individual session.

DEMOCRATIC MIND takes pride in experiencing responsibility for making errors. While it is initially painful to acknowledge a mistake, and worse yet to acknowledge doing harm to human life, it is also uplifting to be able to look at reality for what it is and not be caught up in rushing to justify oneself or to blame others for what has happened. Acknowledging the harm we have done is risky and painful, yet also raises the spirit. It is humbling, yet also strengthening. Although many harms are done to our own or other people's lives that can never be repaired, acceptance of responsibility for having done so and the recommitment of oneself to not doing further harm can bring new kinds of strength and optimism.

The conventional understanding of autism in psychiatry is that it is a congenital neurocognitive defect. However, there have been clinicians who believe otherwise, including in the United States Bruno Bettelheim,[13] and in the United Kingdom Frances Tustin.[14] One psychologist complained that establishment journals refused to publish any of his or other clinicians' works that speak of autism as a psychological and not a physiological disorder,[15] and for many years the traditional or establishment literature on autism has frozen mention of the pathbreaking work of Bettelheim, who reported that a remarkable number of his autistic patients did get better and a surprising number went on to get college degrees.

Following several years in which I treated autistic children very unsuccessfully, I adopted Bruno Bettelheim's understanding of autism that in most cases the baby had experienced the terror of mother's serious death wishes to him or her and then had gone into a self-protective siege not to feel the unbearable threat to life.[16]

In two cases I referred to earlier, on which I reported in a professional article five years after the completion of treatment, the ultimate purpose of the part of the therapy that was devoted specifically to the mothers of the two autistic boys was for each mother to acknowledge, first to herself, and then to her son, that she had rejected the child, and worse had intended psychologically as if to murder her infant son. The full stories of these cases include evidences of the two mothers' murderous feelings – and also the collusive participation of their husbands, the fathers also wanting to see the babies eliminated – and are available to any reader who wishes to see the detailed expressions of the parents' murderous feelings.[17]

As I reported earlier, the time came when my colleague therapists and I – especially the very gifted individual child therapist who worked interactively with each child – organized a session in which each mother told her son how sorry she was for having felt so murderous toward him, and how well she understood the child's return rage at her.[18] Again I have to say that there is no way of proving that the children understood what the mothers said consciously and literally, but in each case the two of us therapists present were impressed that the children did understand and did react with a relief of being able to have their rage confirmed. What is certainly factual is that in the weeks following these memorable sessions there was noteworthy growth in both children.

As reported, both children ended up sufficiently cured to go on in large parts of normal life, including graduating from colleges.

No less than thirty years after the conclusion of the above therapies, I had the opportunity to meet one of these boys – now a man in his early 30s – and take him to a heartwarming and very pleasant lunch. He is living a semiautonomous life in a communal village that offers protected independent living for people who don't function entirely on their own, and works at a professional position outside the village. We continue to be in touch, and recently he called me to say he had moved into his girlfriend's apartment in the same village and they were living together.

Conclusion: The Healthy Alternative of Democratic Mind

To conclude, there is a style of democratic mindfulness that unleashes good energies and a vitality and aliveness. Granted fascist mindsets initially also organize people to feel more secure and safe, but they progressively set off a stuckness and bitterness, and often initiate spirals of punishment and destruction of oneself and others. Democratic mindfulness is not at all immune to disappointments and threatening problems, but by its nature draws on problem-solving skills that are responsive to the factual realities one faces rather than predefined rigid belief systems, and by its nature seeks solutions that enhance and love life for all concerned rather than succumb to destructive power tactics and doing harm to life.

So long as one is able to experience the privilege of being alive, to be open to the wonders of existence, and to enjoy seeking and taking in new knowledge and understanding of life; so long as one is in cooperative, respectful relationships with other human beings and does not allow oneself to become hateful and destructive to others, there is a hum of joy and optimism, and less foreboding and depression in one's daily life.

CHAPTER EIGHT

Psychotherapy as Antifascism and Training for Democracy

Part 1. The Wonderful Psychotherapy Room

And When It Is Good, It Is Very, Very Good

I love the psychotherapy room. As a practitioner these many years, and earlier as a long-term patient in psychoanalysis and subsequent psychotherapy, the psychotherapy room is a marvelous space where I am free to be myself, to think everything I want to, and to encounter the unwelcome thoughts that insist on existing in me seemingly against my will. It is the space in which I, as a patient, toiled long and hard to reach a point where I could willfully choose to sing forth in the loudest voice any and every "song" and "poem" of my true being. It is also a space where I learned to control my voice so I could feel like I was singing and shouting as loudly as I wanted without actually doing so and raising the ire of my analyst's neighbors. I have needed to teach my own patients this trick in the more crowded environment of my treatment room in Israel. The psychotherapy room is a place in which I was helped to recover and generate tools for my self-respect and for loving myself, which I then could direct to becoming more of who and what I wanted to be. It is a "dream-world" room inviting each participant (obviously mainly the patient, but in truth also the therapist) to reach for his or her true self and learn to express unique talents for living well and artfully.

The psychotherapy room is different from any place in a fascist society where by definition, people are forced to comply with orders and dictates from above and are beaten into submission if they do not comply. Psychotherapy is clearly not overcertainty, absolutism, or magical thinking. It is antitotality, final solutions, and perfection. The psychotherapeutic transaction is inherently rooted in an epistemology and pedagogy that train in the use of DEMOCRATIC MIND "software." The structure of the treatment session and the construction of the relationship between the patient and the therapist are designed to create a container – a containing process – in which the patient can explore and process the tumultuous, taxing, and upsetting contradictions that arise from within. In classical psychoanalysis and psychoanalytic therapy, there is no rush to a resolution of problems; on the contrary, a long period of uncertainty and process are welcomed in the course of which the patient is invited to confront a wide range of inner experiences and possibilities from which she or he will eventually choose. It is a process similar to many other creative processes, such as the learning sequence in traditional Zen Buddhism, which invites tension and even strong anxiety as signposts of a mind and a soul engaging and searching the parameters and depths of existence and reality in ways that honor the miracle of human life and its sacredness.[1]

Psychotherapy is against the suppression of information. There is no more inviting methodology for the truths of contradiction, diversity, and complexity within the human mind than the classic free-association technique. It is a way of exploring all of one's mind and of being more open to different thoughts, feelings, and moral interpretations than one had previously been. But the exploration of everything that is within one's heart and mind does not take place as an end in itself. It is a gathering of information that is then submitted to questioning, thoughtfulness, evaluation, and a scientific-like empiricism of checking out what really does advance human life and what does not. Psychotherapy teaches that not "everything goes." One must choose a major policy position and modus operandi while pushing off and relegating to the role of subparts other aspects which, while genuine, are evaluated by us to be less worthwhile or even dangerous and destructive to human life – our own and others.

He came to therapy suffering from anxiety attacks. In the process of therapy, he learned the sources of his anxiety were in his lack of knowing how to be an assertive and strong male, in his flooding torrents of rage toward his parents, and in his deep fears of not being able to be all that he wished to be. Entitling himself to be a stronger male and reducing his anger helped alleviate some of his anxiety, but his way of life of reacting with upset, tension, fearfulness, and panic was still deeply ingrained. For all that he suffered from these experiences, they were so familiar they were subtly comforting, not to be relinquished so easily. In addition, inherent in his anxiety was a degree of sensitivity and an intellectual sharpness that was a welcome lens through which to see the world in its complexity. He also did not know how to preserve the gift of this sensitivity without it being accompanied by anxiety attacks.

The next aim of therapy was for him to make a decision. He chose to instruct himself to stop feeling unduly anxious, and to go about life with a quieter conviction in his right to feel more confident, while continuing to explore sensitively the complexity of life. To his amazement, the decision had an almost immediate payoff with a huge drop in symptoms of anxiety. He buttressed this choice with a further decision that if and when he nonetheless would be subject to bouts of the old familiar anxiety he would not worry about the symptoms as he used to – and in effect increase them by the very worry about whether he would suffer the symptoms. Instead he would take note of the distress, restate his decision to try to feel stronger, continue to build confidence in himself, and continue to have courage to strive to achieve what he really wanted to.

Over the years, he aged well, like a good wine.

৯ From the earliest years of her life she had acted immaturely. Her speech was lispy. Toilet training was very late. Her body language was limping, disjointed, and conveyed a message, "Look at me, I'm a mess." She had learned to delight in being a kind of emotional beggar drawing continuous attention to herself, sometimes real sympathy, at other times a patronizing attention, or even an annoyed anger as she irritated people around her with her ineptness.

Her many symptoms followed one another as she moved up her chrono-logical ladder. Among other problems, she was not free to learn, and her troubles in school mounted. Because of her behavior, the other children mocked her and abused and exploited her. Her hygiene became more disagreeable to her peers. As she approached adolescence, she was still not in control of her toilet functions during the daytime. Characteristically she had a slovenly, unkempt, and almost patently nutty look to her.

Needless to say, there was a long problematic family story, including considerable emotional destructiveness as well as exploitation of this little girl, to explain her sad development. Many experts in mental health, family life, and law attempted to bring some semblance of order and opportunity to the little girl's life. After reasonable conditions were arranged for her life situation, and after the girl had been helped considerably in psychotherapy to express the deep hurt and anger at the core of her life experience, the time came for her to face a choice.

"You can continue to act like you're almost crazy to make an impression on all the other children," said the girl's therapist, "or you can plan to correct your behaviors, make yourself more attractive, and begin to make friends like normal children do. What is it that you would rather do?"

There followed an agonizingly long period in which the girl answered in words that sounded as if she wanted to make herself normal, but she continued in her crazy-making sloppiness and antagonism, as she had done for years. Each social failure and rejection by other children, and each time her siblings and parents became angry with her was taken as a basis for the therapy continuing. She could center on her choice to be a misfit or marginal person forever, or she could put a stop to her regressions and become more normal.

Regrettably, at this writing she still has not made a definitive choice to make herself a winning person, and therapy has been redirected toward placing her in a semiprotected residential facility for people whose ability to live independently is limited.

Therapy had succeeded in organizing her to be more constructive, but only with the aid of a semiprotective environment. Why did the therapy not succeed more? There is no known answer beyond the sad recognition that the original damage to her personality, which was fully understandable, could not be undone.

Psychotherapy is also anti-obedience and conformity, and intolerant, if you will, of a lack of tolerance for dissent. Every patient has an inherent right to decide whether to have therapy or not, with which professional person to have the therapy, whether to continue or discontinue therapy, and most of all whether to improve and get well or not. In therapy the freedom of the patient includes the right to voice differences of opinion with their therapist, to criticize the therapist and oppose him or her, indeed to experience and express powerful anger, and to nurture fantasies of assault and murder of the therapist. In fact, in classical modes of psychoanalysis and psychoanalytic therapies, it is understood that an absence of any dissent, protest, and anger at the therapist is a poor portent of treatment. Paradoxically, the conflict is a basis that enables patients later on to feel more free to adopt ideas, recommendations, and plans of action proposed by the therapist, if only because so many psychiatric problems have their origins in the fact that people were originally forced and in effect coerced in totalitarian ways to eat, sleep, learn, or whatever. It is understood that it is desirable for there to be some degree, and even some extended period, of conflict between the patient and therapist.

Psychotherapy is a renewed opportunity for discovering how wonderfully healthy it is to eat, sleep, and learn, and so on for one's own self, on the basis of one's own choice to do and enjoy being alive, and this freedom to be oneself and to live for oneself can benefit from an experience of fighting off and beating off any vestige of the therapist's control or demands that the patient get better for the therapist's sake, so to speak.

Psychotherapy is also antisuperiority and antiexcessive power seeking and prejudice. There is a catch here insofar as at the outset of therapy, the psychotherapy room hardly looks like it is a setting in which equals are meeting. In many situations, the patient first arrives in such a state of emotional turmoil and need that the therapist is the expert in a superior position to the needy and dependent patient, who at this point is considerably vulnerable to emotional and structural exploitations the therapist may choose to impose on them. However, the essence of good psychotherapy includes the fact that, however much the treatment begins with a natural and necessary dependency on the therapist-professional, the real political definition of the relationship between the patient and the therapist is rooted in a genuine equality between the two persons and real respect for each other. Each newly created team of patient and therapist in effect embarks on a project in which they will share power with each other and slowly but surely move toward increasing their equality.

The process is comparable to a relationship between a parent and a

193

child that, at its best, begins with a gap between the parent as an adult and the child as an immature dependent person, but optimally unfolds stage by stage toward increasing respect for the emergent separateness and individuality of the child, until some day that child becomes the peer and equal of their parent (and later perhaps also a loving caretaker). In the process, from an early age children need to exercise degrees of difference from their parents and express degrees of opposition to them; they need to flex their muscles periodically in rebellion in their thinking and their behavior; as teenagers they need to enjoy developing conscious conceptualizations of their criticisms of their parents personalities and lifestyles; as young adults they need to be able to leave home on their terms and at the right time for their development; in the fullness of their emergent adulthood, they need to make their own choices of who their mates will be and the style of their sexual and familial lives, and so on. A successful parent is one who nurtures this sequence of development and enjoys it, including a certain sense of savoring many of the moments of friction and tension that are inherent in the emergence of a child as an independent person. The happiest ending to the story, of course, is a successful unfolding of the sequence into the period of the child's becoming an adult, where parents and children now have opportunities to experience one another as equals with fascination and pleasure in one another during the overlapping periods of their adulthoods, and then when the parents are older that they enjoy being taken care of by their once dependent children in the final days of their lives.

Psychotherapy is against violence and is adamantly opposed to sacrifice and destruction of life. One of the common reasons for therapy involves situations in which people have erupted into violence against others. Despite the fact that the family should be the safest and most protective place there are many cases of violence in family life, including battering a spouse, abuse of children by parents, and even an amazing number of cases where children, especially teenagers, turn violently against their parents. If the option is open to them, many people will turn to psychotherapists in preference to turning to legal authorities to stop violence that has erupted in their families. (One reader asked me what makes the option open or not? I think that one consideration is that people who know in their hearts that the violence is wrong are more likely to turn to therapists to learn how to get the violence under control rather than go directly to the police.)

Psychotherapy is deeply against violence, first because it is a disruptive symptom that people need to bring under control (the practical side of life), and also because violence is a violation of morality (the spiritual side).

Psychotherapy teaches that the wish to be violent is natural and universal, indeed that failure to be in touch with this wish leaves people unduly passive, weak, and inept and sets them up for a variety of psychiatric conditions, and even sets the stage for more violence. But psychotherapy teaches that the proper channeling of angry wishes is, first of all, to separate them from any and all angry actions. There is an exception when it comes to cases of bona fide self-defense in which one must fight to protect one's life and safety, although there is also a problem of defining self-defense. We all need to learn, individually and collectively, how to evaluate objectively when self-defense really needs to be invoked and when not.[2] Psychotherapy also teaches how to channel angry wishes into healthy power and self-assertion strategies instead of violence. It is inherently committed to the peaceful resolution of all conflicts that can be resolved, and to the creation of the least violent solutions and accommodations to the many situations that cannot really be resolved in peace and love, but where at least the life-destroying elements, against oneself or against another, can be brought under as much control as possible.

Psychotherapy is also against denials of doing harm to oneself and to others. The psychotherapy room is a mirror for how one is mishandling and harming the magnificent opportunity for life for oneself and for other people. The encounter with the truth of how one may be ruining one's own or somebody else's life is evoked either from the patient arriving at self-awareness and self-disclosure, or through the feedback of a family member, or through the assistance of the therapist who feeds back an understanding of the information that is coming from the patient's ways of living their life.

Information of how one may be ruining life involves every aspect of life, including everyday small matters such as how one is messing up in job interviews, inviting rejection in sexual relationships, and damaging one's body in any of thousands of ways including trivial problems such as shaving the wrong way, brushing one's teeth incorrectly, straining too intently in moving one's bowels, or straining to prove one's performance prowess in making love more than loving. The psychotherapy room is also a mirror for seeing how one is damaging the lives of others, such as embittering the life of a sibling or a business associate, humiliating a spouse with endless disparaging remarks, taking the superior position of the know-it-all, or rejecting a loved one at a time of need.

&. *Getting his own way was his way of life. He was a teenager whose vocational dream was to pursue an honorable career in medicine and to attain a degree of excellence. He liked the idea of some day helping people as a physician, but the truth was that his greatest joy in life was in gaining ascendancy over everyone. As a child he had made a specialty out of wrestling with his brothers and other children for the sport of it and loved winning by being the stronger and more skillful, but he also developed himself into an expert "surprise artist" who would suddenly deliver smashing side blows to exposed and vulnerable parts of the body in the most unexpected way rather than continue according to the conventional rules. Some of the blows he delivered were intense, devastating karate blows. He always had an excuse for his toughness by claiming the other had done him harm first. As he grew into a an ominous teenager, he demanded his way more and more to a point where he seemed to radiate a kind of terror and threat that if he were ever stymied in his quest for power, he could do anything, even kill himself – and his death would be on the head of whoever had stopped him from getting what he wanted.*

Needless to say, the youth's therapy was tumultuous. For the therapist, it was crucial to learn to measure each sequence of the buildup of the youngster's inner madness in order to engage and limit him in time before he would go too far. In one intensely stormy session, the patient was threatening to kill himself. He built to a frenzy of disgust with the therapist and got up to leave the office before the time of the session was over. The therapist leaped to his feet and blocked the door. An intense physical and emotional struggle ensued, patient and therapist screaming back and forth at each other, where the therapist refused to allow the patient to leave to fulfill his announced goal of killing himself.

After the successful resolution of that dramatic crisis, there were many sessions in which the therapist would remind the patient of the choices he faced when he was angry. "You feel angry as is your right; you can arrange to tell so and so how angry you are and see if it can lead to any progress toward more of what you want; or you can go to your old routine and threaten to do something extreme to him, or threaten to kill yourself, and maybe even do what you threaten. Which do you want? You need to know and admit how much you have been hurting people, including yourself, if you want to stop these crazy crises and wars in your life."

(Again an early reader of this book when in manuscript form asked to know, "What did he decide?" In the two or so years since this description was written, the young man quieted down considerably, completed high school creditably, and is on a much quieter course.)

Part II. Antifascist Concepts in Psychotherapy

The characteristic kinds of thinking and behavior that we have identified as representative of fascist minds are for me the prime subject matter of much of psychotherapy.

As people tell their tales and pour out their woes, I listen for the ways in which they are constructing their lives and the ways and extent to which they are defining totalities and certainties for themselves or others in their lives, demanding of themselves or others obedience and conformity to whatever notion, seeking undue power, threatening or actually being violent to themselves and others or being unduly available to be victimized by others, and denying the ways in which they are hurting their own life or others' lives. In other words, I am looking for possible expressions of FASCIST MIND in their problems.

This does not mean that I propose a radical overthrow of the method and spirit of listening to people sympathetically that has emerged as the hallmark of psychotherapy; it does mean that I propose a series of shifts in the ways even human narratives of pain are heard and reacted to. The question is extended from not only how a person is suffering, to whether and how a person is contributing to their own suffering, and no less whether he or she is contributing to or responsible for the suffering of another person or family, group, or community.

I believe this kind of thinking about how a person is affecting and shaping life can be used in psychotherapy very meaningfully to assist greater healing. It is a constructive way of thinking about human problems because it addresses what and how people can do to change their lives for the better. I also believe it is a way of looking at people's lives that connects with truths of evil and destruction in our human experience that have their representations in everyday life and not just in major historical events of genocide and mass murder.

Identifying Victims, Bystanders, Accomplices, and Perpetrators in the Psychotherapy Room

After completing my training as a psychologist and after practicing seven years, I experienced a call from inside to try to understand the terrible subject of genocide, and I decided to devote half of my working time to that issue. I have continued this way of work and life now for over 35 years, and along with the satisfaction of my commitment to a meaningful moral cause of genocide prevention have had the privilege of many fascinating intellectual experiences. From looking at the horrible behaviors of human beings on the macro levels of huge genocidal destruction of life, I go on to the level of individual human beings to try to understand how one could agree to commit ugly and evil acts toward other people.

How is it that well-educated human beings could play vital roles in programs such as the Holocaust? Consider the Wannsee Conference, which was, in 1942, where the decision was made to implement the "Final Solution" of the Jewish people. It took place in a dignified hall of a beautiful villa at Wannsee, which is outside Berlin. The villa sits alongside a lake. The fifteen people present made the decision. Each had a highly significant role in the Third Reich. I am sure they were very proud to be invited to this definitive conference. It is shocking to know that about twelve of them had doctoral degrees. Clearly a PhD or any other educational degree at this point in our civilization is no guarantee of decent humanness.

I found myself going back further to the everyday aspects of human behavior and was fascinated with the awareness that understanding the terrible behaviors human beings are capable of was opening doors for me to better understand how human beings organize themselves all the time in so-called normal life. I am not referring to politics now, but to everyday life where a fascist use of mind is opposed to a democratic way of organizing our minds. I found that these conceptual organizations gave me a very useful way of thinking about everyday human behavior and about psychotherapy.

When people come to me with their stories about a marriage that is unsatisfying or about a child that is in trouble, I first of all listen and react respectfully on the level of the information that they are talking about, which is the medical tradition of dealing with the symptoms and the problems of a person. But my secret, as it were, is that ever since I found out about the Holocaust and so many other genocides, I actively look for how the roles in the dramas of genocide may be playing out in the life stories of people who come for everyday psychotherapy. When I meet people, I think to myself: "What is your characteristic role in life? Do you generally choose to be a victim to others' abuse? Are you a bystander to someone else's suffering? Do you make yourself an accomplice to those who hurt others? Or are you a person who is a perpetrator or persecutor who inflicts pain and suffering on others in your life? In other words, I apply to my work as a psychotherapist the concepts I have learned from the Holocaust and genocide, and I look at the classic roles in everyday life of victims, bystanders, accomplices, and perpetrators.

There is, of course, first and foremost in psychotherapy, the role of victims in everyday family life. Some victims in family life are so terrorized and intimidated, such as wives who are beaten by brutal husbands, that they have little control over their fates – and even if they run away, say to a professionally organized shelter for battered wives, they may remain at serious risk even to their lives. There are other family members who take a continuous brunt of rejection, dislike, disparagement, ridicule, and such, and others who are, plain and simple, understood in the family to be the inferior ones lacking in "political power" and a fair portion of respect in the marriage or family. A very important concept in family life is codependency, in which, unconsciously, the victims are playing into their victimization in various ways and varying degrees. Thus, a spouse unconsciously allows and even invites his or her mate to be abusive; a child agrees to remain the weaker and less-favored sibling; or a parent surrenders unconsciously to being chronically insulted by one or more children. These styles become a way of life for the victim that gives them meaning and secret gratifications for all of their genuine discomfort. Here the therapist's role is to empower people as much as possible to throw off their availability to be victims. It is hard work in psychotherapy, especially because much of the time the acknowledgment of any codependency is bitterly resisted and resented by the victims. The day a victim comes to an insightful recognition of their unconscious role in seeking or allowing their victimization is memorable.

Some people are classic bystanders. A bystander sees another person getting clobbered, says not a word, and intervenes not. The story of Kitty Genovese became a tragic classic story.[3] She was a young woman who was murdered in Kew Gardens, a neighborhood in Queens, New York, in the yard of an apartment house when there were 38 people who heard her cries for help. Not one of the 38 came to assist, not only directly, which would have entailed some risk, but also not a single one of them picked up a phone to call the police. By their inaction they all made themselves into bystanders. Bystanders are all around us. Look, for example, at a business situation where you see a person getting fired unfairly, and watch how in the majority of situations the majority of coworkers will not say a word because of their self-interest.

Another role in family life is that of the accomplices. As a parent, one needs to support and stand together with one's spouse so that the children know their parents are united. But there are limits to standing together, such as when the other parent is abusive or rejecting. If you see your partner – the other parent – beating on one of your children, physically or emotionally, and you let it happen without intervening, you become a bystander; if you assist the other parent in the persecution, literally or figuratively holding the child for the beating, you are a more active form of accomplice. There are also children who play roles of accomplices to a parent who is persecuting one of their siblings (and I have seen cases where the accomplice remains painfully guilty about the bad fate of their brother or sister for many years or even their entire life, including cases where the guilt over the sibling is then projected damagingly on to one of their own children years later).

The perpetrators do the direct real harm to others. In family life, they are the husbands who abuse their wives physically, or husbands who abuse their wives emotionally, such as in never-ending insults and disparagement, or in chronic disloyalty and betrayals. And they are the wives who dominate, humiliate, minimize, or betray their husbands. They are also the parents who reject a child or convey disgust or disrespect, or who exploit a child for their own personal needs such as for affection, closeness, warmth, or even sexuality.[4]

What I am revealing is that not all psychotherapists *schmaltz* themselves up into accepting all human beings who come to them with unquestioning regard and love; I prefer to look at people and think, "Do you have any connection to creating, playing, or enabling any of these unwelcome antilife roles – victims, bystanders, accomplices, or persecutors?" This is different from extending carte blanche sympathy to people with symptoms. It is a way of combining seeing who is hurt with seeing who is doing the hurting, also with seeing who is allowing the hurt to be done, and also combinations of all of these even in the same people!

It is well known that therapists minimize traditional religious-like preaching to patients because preaching has its limitations in influencing behavior. Instead therapists listen to and understand people's feelings, motivations, and behaviors. But therapists are also educators who need to help their patients inhibit their destructive behaviors. One accepts all that is human in the inner experiences of one's patients, but never the actual destructive roles of doing harm to other people. Nor does a therapist accept a patient's possible overvaluing of victimhood. When people unconsciously seek suffering, invite suffering, or sanctify suffering, the therapist's job is to say, "Stop! There is a better way to live." When people are hurting others, the therapist says "Stop! It is wrong to do harm to others, although I will help you use legitimate outlets for your anger."

Issues of Power in Psychotherapy

As a therapist I also look at the way people use power. From the time we are born, we need to have the power to cry, call, signal, or otherwise make our needs heard. From the time we are about two years old, we need new forms of power in order to move around and investigate, and we also need to do some of the things we are told not to do. Later we need more power to influence and shape our environments. Power is an essential and desirable vehicle of our energy. But it is also clear that power is often misused rather than used correctly. Too many people, including people who did not intend to be overly power seeking, begin dominating other human beings, first in their own minds and then in behaviors.

> *I was talking with a very nice colleague at his home in the United States. By then we had both passed the 50-year mark. I said to him, "Listen, let's think of all the mental health clinics and hospitals and university clinical programs we have worked in over the years, and let's think of the chairpeople of those departments" (at that point, he and I had both been chairpersons of departments for some years). I said, "Let's think of how they run their departments, and let's think of whether they represent good mental health in their styles of leadership." The results of our survey were disastrous. Many of the chairs of mental health programs, in fact the majority that we recalled, were officious, arrogant, unresponsive to feedback, and created a working atmosphere of terror and fear.*

That is the way it is too often when people are given power. The dynamics are potentially in all of us unless we take heed and work on ourselves. When given power, many people are seduced into arrogance and overuse of power. Power is intoxicating and invites more overuse.

Intoxication with power happens to many parents as well. For example, in their vital roles as mothers who are to organize the lives of the little people who are dependent on them, so many women do not know that they are drawn, slowly but surely, into becoming the kinds of women who are constantly telling other people what to do, rather than being mothers who are lovers of human beings, teachers, and counselors. One hardly needs to add how many fathers have played unpleasant, overbearing patriarchal roles. And there are, of course, all sorts of stories of the unfair distribution of power in marriages. Men's abuses of power, especially but not only in days of old, are legion and well known, while women's abuses of power, which are on the rise today, too often are considered a "no-no" for discussion. (Over the years I have declined to speak in any professional context in which there was a focus only on women or only on men. It is not that I am against advancing either gender's legitimate interests, each and both of which are precious, but I am mainly for a healthy and equitable power that is shared by men and women. I therefore choose to speak about power and gender roles only in contexts in which we work explicitly on both men and women enjoying an equal distribution of power in friendship and cooperation between the two sexes.)

In psychotherapy, issues of power arise in many aspects of patients' situations in their families, work, and social relationships, but also inevitably in the relationship that takes place between the patient(s) and the practitioner. Some patients defer to the authority of the therapist, which is representative of their availability to be pushed around in other domains of their lives. Many people do not realize that the other domains sometimes also include illnesses that "run through them" without encountering sufficient resistance, an issue we have scientific reason to correlate with a reduced or weakened immune system, the causes for which can be both physiological and psychological. One can seemingly achieve magnificent cures in psychotherapy by telling people what to do. They say, "Yes, yes. Oh, you are so wise; oh, you are so helpful!" And they run off, and indeed feel better, but if I had done this I would feel sick, because there is no real processing taking place. I am playing into the appeasing, conforming nonbeingness of those people, and not making a contribution to their longer-term health and vitality.[5]

Other patients are bossy and tyrannical to the therapist. As a supervisor of psychotherapists, I have seen cases in which some high and mighty patients, especially if they are rich and a source of considerable income for a therapist, are allowed to get away with their haughty manner, which is obviously a failure on the part of the therapist.

He came in with his disturbed son for a father-son therapy session. After working with them together for some time, the therapist indicated that he would like to go on individually with the child for the rest of the session. The father went to the waiting room from where the therapist somehow heard that the father was using the courtesy extension phone to make a very long business call, which was an abuse of the courtesy line. However, the therapist sensed something more.

At the end of the session, the therapist came out with the boy.

"You made a long call?" he asked.

"Yea, I guess so," said the father.

"May I ask where to?"

"Oh, I guess I should have told you. It was to overseas." (This was in the days when overseas calls were very expensive – between $2 and $3 a minute.) "Sorry about that," added the father with an "I got caught in the cookie jar" look on his face.

The therapist wasn't amused. He made it clear that he was offended and angry, but also how this self-serving abrogation was illustrative of the father's parenting. For example, the father would go on unannounced business trips and leave the boy alone for long periods of time (and did the same to his wife, who had many symptoms of a deserted woman).

For me, psychotherapy is the cultivation of each patient's individuality and the maximum safety and welfare of oneself and of other human beings. When people do not use sufficient power for themselves, or when they use too much at the expense of other people, the psychotherapist's role is to offer the most effective corrections possible.

Dialectical Processes as Antifascist Techniques

Dialectical processing is key for directing therapists to many treatment decisions, on the one hand to guide patients to reduce excesses in their use and expression of a given aspect of their personality, on the other hand to guide patients to augment or expand reduced or restricted aspects of their uses of themselves. Furthermore, not only should the contradictory aspects of oneself on any dimension of personality optimally be given an appropriate degree of expression, they should also be brought into respectful and playful apposition and then too integration with one another.

In psychotherapy, one sees so many tortured, contorted ways of experiencing and of organizing emotions, just as in the medical professions every day one sees tortured, contorted bodies. For example, many people have to "get it all" correct and perfect. There are people who need life organized so precisely, whether for themselves, their families, or their company, that any exposure to the competing or contradictory influences of others becomes unbearable. Thus, the press explained the shocking suicide of a top U.S. Navy admiral during the Clinton administration as being due to his insistence on perfection.

The family of an admired Israeli army hero came to me shattered with grief and dismay at the sudden suicide of the head of the family. He was, to the best of their knowledge and to all known accounts and purposes, thriving in his "perfect life" at home with his beautiful, adoring wife and their successful children, as well as in the successful business he owned. He had delighted in being a success in everything he did. Yes, he had developed a medical problem in recent weeks, but there was nothing to suggest it was a serious problem. I called and spoke with the deceased man's physician – who is a well-known internist (a top doctor for a top man). The doctor told me that his patient had recently developed a medical problem that was aggravating and not automatically treatable, but not at all serious and certainly not life threatening. But he had responded to his illness very badly, the doctor said; it was like the patient felt his whole being, and certainly his vaunted perfection, were unforgivably blemished.

Similarly, many people strive to be nice, friendly, and loving – which also fulfills one of the prevailing models held up in Western civilization. But in order to release the flow of natural energy of real love, one cannot simply be kind, good, loving, and friendly all the time to one's wife, children, or colleagues; one also needs to acknowledge that at any given moment one also cannot stand one's wife, children, or colleagues. Family members trust the love of a person who is in touch with his or her annoyance and anger more than they trust a one-dimensional person who is invariably positive and loving; the always-loving person generates a question of how do you know when they really mean it. So too with other dimensions of goodness and badness. If you want to know you are dealing with a really honest person, check first that they are able to tell some practical lies when necessary, or that they are capable of being somewhat self-serving, while at the same time they are committed to an overall honesty. A well-known international attorney who was a man of great integrity and a leader in the field of peace research told me, "If you want to know whether you can trust a person who declares he seeks peace, see whether he is honest about being angry at times. If he claims never to be angry, don't give him your trust." He was an attorney who spoke like a psychologist, and I appreciated that.

The kaleidoscopes of our dialectical feelings are rich, poetic, and fascinatingly human:

• I love you.
• I am angry with you.
• I am so much more aware how much I love you when I lose you because of my anger.
• I sometimes get angry with you because I love you so much.
• I can't bear the thought of losing you, also of needing you so much, it's enough to make me want to break away.

The traits and behaviors to which the principle of dialectical processing applies are nearly endless.

What is the optimal psychological response of a patient to serious medical illness?

On the one hand, acceptance of the illness is the best basis for the patient undertaking necessary treatment decisions and dealing well with difficult medical procedures. Acceptance of illness also makes possible a physical yielding or "letting go" that can bring relief from terror and fear, and invites the kind of resting that facilitates the body's potential for healing. The alternative to accepting the truth of one's illness through denial of the illness may look like it brings an experience of calm ("What you don't know can't hurt you," they say), but it complicates every aspect of treatment and healing, and there is hard scientific evidence that denial can extend the amount of time required by the body to heal from surgery.

On the other hand, letting go to an illness to the point of surrendering to it and letting it dictate one's future is a prescription for more serious illness and disability, even of death. "He didn't fight back," says the doctor or a family member, "he just let himself get weaker and weaker, as if he wanted to die." There is a will to live and a will to get well and a fighting back against illness that have been shown to make considerable difference for healing faster and getting well, sometimes tilting bad odds over to a much better outcome than expected, and occasionally even miraculously.

So what is the good and wise patient to do?
Accept your illness (really), and fight back against your
illness with all your will (really).
Both!

Dialectical process, or the interplay of contradictions, is a beautiful concept derived from many sources. For example, in the Alexander Technique, the dialectical process has been called a model of "antagonistic action." Dialectical process means accepting and working with many contradictions in ourselves. It means that many of us need to learn to let go of much of our "end gaining" or living in order to achieve certain goals. Our goal needs to be, first of all, to live for the sheer pleasure of being alive. Yet if one yields to living without goals, purpose, or direction, he or she again faces the prospect of warping the personality and being unable to achieve important goals. It is the combination of giving up ambition for the sake of feeling pleasure in being and living for a meaningful purpose that gives the best chance of moving toward relative wholeness.

The failure to respond with dialectical corrections of excesses or deficiencies in a patient's personality is at the heart of many errors and failures in psychotherapy. In my opinion, the therapist's going along with the patient as he or she is overly tilted to one side of a trait or process is often an act of appeasement or codependency with the patient. One should look twice to ascertain why the therapist is not ruffling any feathers. Often the therapist is sidestepping risking the loss of the patient; in private practice this also means a loss of income, but then again money isn't everything, and just plain holding on to the patient is a priority for many therapists' egos. Not upsetting patients is also based on a philosophical conception that if the patient is comfortable and uncomplaining, the situation is

under control and the therapy is correct. But this should hardly be the case when the patient is all right with:
- smoking
- picking their skin, and descabbing wounds
- staying away from social activity
- avoiding work and relying on being supported by family
- taking unnecessary dangerous physical risks
- being a chronic wearisome complainer
- repeatedly insulting one's spouse
- ignoring one's children
- spoiling one's children
- incessantly abandoning and betraying their spouse
- getting obese

One of the most common errors in psychotherapy is the belief that the purpose of therapy is to remove all inhibitions. What nonsense! Psychotherapy needs to help us be more decent people. The goal needs to be to remove wasteful life-and-fun-spoiling inhibitions, but to keep inhibitions against destructive actions. There are so many wrong ways of thinking and experiencing in the human mind that actually need to be inhibited and stopped.

Thus, when a patient comes to me struggling with repetitive thoughts of which they are unable to free themselves, I teach them first of all "thought-stopping." I am very unhappy about rushing them off for medications unless they are in a palpable agony that might be reduced by the medicine and allow them to learn more effectively in psychotherapy. I don't really see that there is a direct connection between medications and inhibiting the incorrect behaviors.

A very nice man came to me with a terrible obsessive thought as his presenting symptom, which obviously reflected a world of problems beyond that. He repeatedly saw a train coming toward him, and saw that he was about to be demolished by the train. What a horrible thought!

But we all have some horrible thoughts, and we all get somewhat stuck with horrible parts of the perceptual and conceptual associative junk that comes up in our minds. I taught and encouraged the man to say STOP *to the frightening image, and then to battle to erase the thought-picture from the screen. Of course, it was difficult for him, but the effort of battling for himself rather than remaining the helpless victim of the oncoming train already was strengthening him.*

After some time he succeeded in banishing the oppressing thought, and then we were ready to identify and do battle with the more real problems on his "train of life" an oppressive business life that had him in a straightjacket, and a depressed and fault-finding wife who took out her contempt for herself on him by not liking him, his body, and his sexuality.

I believe that one of my major contributions as a therapist is to try to find the way to be a good instructor for healthier living, and that an important aspect of instruction is to be able to say, "Stop!" to our incorrect and unwise behaviors.

If appropriate, the therapist should be able also to say things like:
"Do you know how unattractive you are?"
"Do you know how unattractive you are to your spouse?"
"Behaviors that hurt other human beings need to be stopped."
The therapist is likely to be more effective by balancing unwelcome criticisms and challenges with a friendly, attractive, and especially a humane presence.

I like to tell my patients some of my own not so happy truths, especially as they match painful, shameful, and grievous parts of their lives. The technique is called "self-disclosure," and has been taught by some of the great therapists like the late Sidney Jourard, Carl Whitaker, and Irwin Yalom (each of whom has written marvelous books).[6] I think, however, that the majority of therapists, and especially devotees and loyalists of particular "schools of psychotherapy," eschew telling the truth about themselves like a plague. Many of my patients have learned about me such things as that I

• needed to work hard at becoming a more loving person (and how grateful I am to my psychoanalyst for helping me in many ways)

• failed my specialty board examinations in clinical psychology the first time around, because I was showing off my use of the then-very-new techniques of family therapy most of my examiners didn't yet know about (in fact, I was genuinely excited by the new method of treatment, but I was also busy with displaying myself, a lifelong weakness that has required me to work hard to reduce it)

• was divorced from my first wife after a long and disastrous marriage (but have enjoyed a wonderful loving second marriage for many years)

• have lost out to a large extent on having a meaningful relationship with some of the children from that marriage (but do enjoy a fine relationship with one of the children from that marriage as well as with the children of my second wife whom we brought up together)

• was ill and have recovered fully from a dangerous cancer condition (and am happy about the ways I handled my illness, as well as deeply grateful to my skillful doctors)

When is it correct to use self-disclosure, and when is it not?

Like with any technique, therapist self-disclosure can be hurtful and ill advised. It can remove or attenuate the heroic therapist mystique that is needed, and it can be exhibitionistic and invasive of the patient's space. Yet it can be deeply freeing and encouraging to patients, especially some who appreciate the removal of the therapist's "rank" as a seemingly superior person. So, like with any technique, the therapist is called upon to exercise thoughtful and responsible judgment as to whether, when, and how much the technique is likely to help patients.

Right or wrong, it certainly is clear that therapist self-disclosure is not the usual stuff of therapists who want to maintain a dictatorial control of their patients.

One instance in which I told about some of my pain regarding my children was to two lovely middle-aged people who had come to me for help with their marriage at a late stage of their lives only also to discover in the course of a single year that two out of their five children, both young adults, were each in urgent need of intensive psychotherapy. Beyond their worries about the children, these parents had suffered powerful blows to their sense of themselves and their integrity as parents. I thought it only fair to match my heartaches with two of my children to their two. They appreciated my sharing, and we went on to work well together on their therapy.

Identifying Fascist Paradigms in Everyday Psychotherapy

In applying the paradigm of FASCIST MIND versus DEMOCRATIC MIND to the actual practice of psychotherapy, the therapist brings directly to the patient's attention in as skillful a manner as possible their inherently "dumb," stuck, slavish, or overambitious efforts to coerce life to produce what they demand, and their violent and destructive reactions, whether at themselves or others, when they don't get what they want.[7] The "logic" of such interventions is that for many people there will be a repugnance to totalitarian modes of life once they recognize that this is what they are doing, although, sadly, this is not true for everyone. Some people will redouble their efforts to achieve their fascist goals, but our hope is that most patients will be drawn to more democratic or life-enhancing ways of organizing their mind when the therapist offers them this option. I confess that the above is an assumption I would like to be true, but I also know there are people who will not be shocked and upset to learn about their fascist-type mindsets, and therefore interpretations to them of these behaviors will not be therapeutically effective.

Working with the fascist-type mindset is another promising approach to the mystery of psychotherapy of the human mind, but it is not a new all-powerful curative principle for everyone, nor is it the total and perfect solution many practitioners are always hoping to discover.

The following cases in psychotherapy highlight efforts to modify one or more fascist-type ways of organizing the personality. The second and third cases were presented earlier but are brought back here for a deeper look at the treatment use of the understanding of the patient's organization of self. True to life, not all of the cases reported respond successfully to the therapy. Four of the cases cited show major gains; one shows symptomatic improvement at the time but then a premature breaking off from therapy; one is a case where the patient deteriorates into paranoid accusations against the therapist; and one involves a tragedy of suicide. In other words, attention to fascist certainties in psychotherapy opens the door to new treatment techniques that may be helpful in some cases, but it does not give us the promise of a certain cure.

Will there ever be a method of psychotherapy that is always or almost always successful? Too many case reports of successes in the field cultivate that illusion, if not by the author of the case reports then in the minds of the readers reaching out childishly for new certainties.

> When the Masters and Johnson books appeared
> describing their innovative breakthrough techniques of
> sexual behavior tasks in which patients' skills for sexual
> performance were reconstructed and retrained in sex
> therapy, I sensed that a milestone had been reached in
> our field.[8] But I also was upset by the appendixes that
> reported successes in treatment in over 90% of the cases!
> This kind of success simply doesn't make sense in
> human affairs, and indeed later study of ostensibly
> successful treatment with the Masters and Johnson
> technique showed that only a third of the successful
> cases held on to their gains, and a good number of cases
> required more psychodynamic psychotherapy
> to supplement their sexual therapy.[9]

In psychotherapy, the best treatment techniques must still meet up with a host of realities, including the patients' choices both on conscious and unconscious levels of what they decide to look for in their lives, and it is a fact that a significant number of patients do not want to get well, and another significant percentage simply can't. There is even the paradox that more effective treatment techniques can lead a given patient so much closer to possible happiness and success that they cannot grant themselves that they then must flee all the more and perhaps even become seriously destructive of their prospects.[10]

❧ If We Make Love Well, Then All Has to Be Well in Our Marriage

The first of the cases illustrates the dire consequences of a therapy that subscribed blindly to the romantic belief that if people are only helped to function positively and effectively they will be happy. The patients and therapist accepted the illusory overcertainty. The case also illustrates a heavy price of failing to process information about patients from multiple perspectives.

Overcertainty, Suppression of Information

A couple on a kibbutz (collective settlement in Israel) had been living apart for some years. Although the marriage had not been legally dissolved, each had moved in with a new partner. But after the wife's lover decided to break up the relationship, she returned to her husband and proposed that they make a new start. Since one of their dissatisfactions with each other had been a lack of sexual compatibility, the wife proposed that they get help from a sexual therapist, especially considering the fact that each of them reported enjoying a very satisfying sexual life with their alternative partner.

The sex therapist was a winning and talented man who conducted the sessions artfully. He was one of the first therapists in his region to have learned the then new work of Masters and Johnson, and with impressive skillfulness he proceeded to teach the couple the basic "sexual behavior tasks," beginning with the "sensate focus," or learning how to be mutually aroused by touching and caressing.

The therapist was proud of his work and presented it to a senior consultant.

"Your work with the couple is impressive, including your charm and effectiveness in inducing a good mood in their sexual therapy," said the consultant. "But I am concerned that this couple has not first worked on how they feel about each other after having lived so well and enjoying sexually another partner for so long. And I am concerned that there has been no clarification of how they feel about each other as people, and whether there were other reasons that they rejected living with each other years ago. I think that sex therapy should be slowed down and even postponed until much more work is done on the basic relationship between them as people and lovers in the sense of their inner feelings for each other."

The therapist was clearly disappointed at not being commended and honored by the consultant for his up-to-date knowledge and application of the new Masters and Johnson techniques. Yet before he could meet again with the couple, he received word from the kibbutz that the husband had committed suicide![11]

No one can ever "know" the cause of the suicide, but the reconstruction of the case suggests that the premature resurrection of sexual contact by the couple may have been a key aspect.

❧ You Must Have Your One and Only Way, but Both Your Body and Your Employees Hate That

In the following case a turning point is reached in therapy by the good luck of being able to show the patient how he is using fascist concepts of overdemandingness in an area of life, where his success matters to him very much – his business; and he is then also more able to see how he is hurting himself in his anorexic eating disorder – an arena of experience that is notoriously resistant to insight and improvement in psychotherapy.

Totality, Perfection, Overcertainty

He was a young adult man with anorexia. We had reached the point in his therapy where I could propose that we have lunch together. The purpose of such a meeting around food is to give the therapist an opportunity to interact directly with the patient during the experience of eating. As we were having lunch, I suggested to this man who was a serious businessman that as I listened to some of his business problems, I heard that he was also organizing his business life similarly to the way in which he was organizing his body and his eating regimen.

Needless to say, he was very curious. I explained to him that I saw him setting up his business procedures in rigid ways that he insisted to his employees should never be changed even when problems arose that seemed to call for new procedures. Over and over again his style led him to be stuck. He had recently become aware that many of his workers had come to dislike him, and not only was he concerned for the business, he was also personally hurt and puzzled; he certainly didn't want to be a bad employer. I suggested that it was a "führer" inside his mind who had ordered his employees to work industriously at all times so that "there will not be one minute of goofing off on the job," and that the bad atmosphere that had developed in his work environment was similar to how there was always tension in his anorexic body, which was under command to follow very rigid rules. I said to him, "I don't mean to be insulting, but often, when I think of the way you organize your life, I think of you as something like a Nazi."

My Jewish patient paled and said, "What do you mean?"

I said, "Well, you know, you make so many damned rules both for yourself and now for your employees too, like the Nuremberg Rules: "By my orders, thou shalt do and thou shalt not do such and such!" And you are insistent on having those rules followed to a fault. That's what I think the Nazis did. I think they made some rotten rules; then they got all excited by their own rule making and by their power to insist that their rules be followed; and then they said they would punish anybody who didn't follow their rules, and they got more and more violent. That's what I think happens with bosses who lose their direction and start making so many rules that they are not tuned in to the workers' being responsible and reliable in the first place; and that's what I think happens when a person makes rules for himself of 'Don't Eat!' in the way that you as an anorexic person do."

That day and that lunch were the turning points in that therapy.

❧ You Must Obey the Idea in Your Mind at All Costs Even If It Means Your Very Life

While most psychotherapy of suicide understandably asks the reasons and motives for a person going so far as to attempt to destroy their life, the following case illustrates focusing treatment on how the suicide plan itself became a fascist directive and obligation that took over the patient's mind. Breaking the totalitarian grip of the suicide plan opened the door to a successful treatment process.

Overcertainty, Obedience, Violence against Self

In the case of a young, brilliant, and beautiful teenage girl who tried to kill herself, the interpretation of the fascist way of thinking centered on her rigidity and inability to modify her suicide plan once it had been developed in her mind. The pathology was not only in the suicide as ultimate self-destruction, but also in the way she treated all her mind contents as commanding, inexorable, and inviolable.

This girl really did a serious job in her suicide attempt and would have died were it not for one of those happenstances of good luck – she was found in time and saved medically. She and her family then came for therapy. I did all the things that I know how to do, beginning with family therapy. What I do in the first session is I ask everybody in the family to tell the person who almost died how they would have felt had that person actually died, and also how they feel toward her or him for almost taking their life. Before very long, the problems of insufficient love in that family are out in the open, which is a very good starting point for the therapy. In the case of this young girl, the family session exposed painfully the coldness and ineptness for loving in her mother although she was an entirely "correct" person, and a caring but self-serving, overly busy father who expected his family to function well for him.

The therapy continued with both the family and the girl working away in a combination of individual and family sessions at the subject of the lack of a truer love in the family and at the girl's depression. Months of hard work went by, but it was obvious that the girl was not getting any better. One of the things I learned about the girl was how she had conceived the idea of committing suicide about six months before she had made the actual attempt – and once she had the idea . . .

What happens to many young people and in truth to many people at any age when they get an idea – any idea, and suicide is certainly a potent form of an idea – is that it has the potential of becoming an idea "über alles." People fall so much in love with their ideas that the ideas hypnotize them. The idea becomes the "authority figure" whom they command themselves to obey blindly regardless of the circumstances, even if the end result might be fatal. Many people then become members of a "cult of their own idea." Once the idea has taken root, people say in their own minds, "Now that I have had this idea, I've got to honor it. What kind of a person am I that I won't stand behind my commitments? Once I've got a plan, I have to fulfill it. Otherwise, I am not genuine." This kind of obligation to complete an idea is a form of fascist thinking that is latent in the human mind. The

216

girl explained, "I created a suicide idea, I was committed to it, and I had to plan it and execute it."

I took the suicide plan as a way of trying to break through in the therapy. I started by collecting articles about young people who had committed suicide. I asked my patient to sit next to me on the sofa and I said, "Let's read together and see what happened to the idea of suicide in each case. Let's reconstruct how each person got to commit suicide." Slowly but surely, we picked up from these journalistic stories the threads of conformity and idolatry to the idea once it was conceived. One kibbutz newspaper told a story of another lovely teenage girl who had killed herself after signaling her suicidal intentions for months, and how she had been deeply involved with building up the idea to kill herself in her mind and had even telegraphed her obsession to people around her, but no one knew how to intervene to stop the gathering momentum until she completed her suicide plan.

Finally I could say to my patient: "You know, it's not only that you attempted to commit suicide because you felt miserable; you attempted to commit suicide because you were an idiot who treated your own idea as something so complete and pure that you had to follow it. And, you know, I think you are very rigid in many other ways in your life as well." I then described to her various other aspects of her life about which I knew, such as the way she would become disappointed in a girlfriend and then cut her off totally and forever. Now we were treating the rigidity and the fascism and not only the suicide.

The treatment was ultimately successful, including addressing the girl's failure to love herself and her readiness to be violently destructive of her own self.

❧ Mother, You Can't Control Me (Like You Do Control Father), I'm Going to Blow You All Up

In this case, therapy was hard because of the patient's sour, stonewalling silence session after session. The young patient finally yielded to direct, firm confrontation of his overriding preoccupation with violence as a way of life.

Violence against Self and Others

I don't like this world, and I don't like the people in it, and I show it.

I am a surly 13 year-old boy who refuses to do most things that I am asked to do at home. I am sour, and really unresponsive to efforts to make conversation. Unconsciously, I am enraged by my mother's haughty and dominating ways, and I don't get support from my weak father who is a great guy but busy with his work and with appeasing mother. I hate the way she puts him down, and he just takes it, grins, and never gets mad. I sit and brood for hours. I am fascinated by the idea of making bombs, and I often play with matches and combustible materials in my home when my parents are away. Yes, I would love to set a fire and burn the place down – that would teach them a lesson! I have no friends, but I can't admit it. When my parents complain about my behavior, I complain back. I tell them, and also myself, that I am fine, and everything is fine, and I don't know what they want of me, so everyone get off me and leave me alone. Just leave me alone!

In therapy, over many months the therapist's nicest efforts to make friends with the boy proved relatively useless. The boy was unresponsive, answering in monosyllables, if at all, every possible effort to make conversation. There was little alternative but to interpret the boy's explosive rage as a way of life.

"You are sour, angry, and want to blow up a lot of places and people in this world, if you only could. Even your not talking at home with your family, and also here in my office with me, makes you look like a ticking bomb waiting to blow up and get back at everyone."

The reframing of his pattern of behavior seemed meaningful to the boy, and he began coming around. Slowly but surely he turned more pleasant and friendly in the therapy sessions, and after a while he also began a series of positive changes in his life, including volunteering as a medical corpsman in an Emergency Ambulance Service (which also treated victims of terrorist explosions), becoming a better and better student, and finally also a reasonably pleasant person at home. At this writing the young man is proudly in charge of a medical service unit in the army.

❧ You Chose a Way of Life of Floating Above and Away from All Challenges and Now from Life Itself

This case might be titled, "Treating Mona Lisa's Inscrutability as an Escape." The case tells the story of the dearest, sweetest young girl who secretly developed an iron totalitarian grip on life by refusing to press herself to meet challenges. Increasingly incompetent as a result, she was well on the way to giving up the gift of being alive for permanent tranquility.

Final Solutions, Magical Thinking, Suppression of Information, Violence against Self, Denial of Doing Harm to Self

I began to act so strange and disconnected that my parents decided something must be wrong with me and got me to a therapist. But they had no idea just how close I was to committing suicide until the therapist drew the story from me, and even got me to bring in the copious diary I have been maintaining for over a year in which I recorded the buildup of the black, black despair and my readiness to fly to another world where my beloved dead grandmother awaited me.

What was wrong? I haven't let anyone get beyond the soporific, charm-filled fairy smile on my face for years. They all think I am a dream girl. I know that I am pleasing, and that nobody can be angry with me. I don't even know myself if there is anything else in me. I am not quite sure how it started.

My mother is such a wonderful person. She only wanted to please me. My father was charmed by me, but didn't spend that much time trying to figure out anything about me other than that I was his prettiest-of-them-all daughter. What a shock it was for them to find out that they almost lost me! But the truth is they hadn't bothered to look behind my fixed smile for many years. For a long time now, I have been unable to study in school. I always have excuses. I even got them to a point where they made life easy for themselves by deciding that I had one of those mysterious learning disorders so that I couldn't keep up with my studies through no fault of my own. They never paid attention to the fact that I read many books, that I am a good student of literature on my own, though never at school, and if you look at the diary of my almost killing myself, you will see that I even know how to write very expressively and complexly.

What they didn't want to realize is that I had perfected a method of never coping with pain or struggle or tension. If I don't understand something that I am supposed to learn, I go into a fog, redouble my fairy smile and later on shrug my shoulders when I can't produce the assignment or somehow fail the test. Nobody can say that I am in any way a bad girl or bad student. I am just mysteriously handicapped. I never show any visible signs of disappointment or tension, just a sweet-sick Mona Lisa smile.

The therapy of this Mona Lisa was surprisingly easy but only after firm interventions with her and her family to ensure her getting to sessions (left to her own, she would have missed more sessions than she attended, and for the flimsiest and zaniest "reasons").

"You've created a myth of perfect stillness and tranquility to a point where you are a helpless cripple in regard to most life tasks. You pretend to have all of life under control with your magic of floating away from all unpleasantness and challenge. No wonder you almost killed yourself. There's very little left that you are able to succeed in doing in this real world."

Of course, she protested, but more important she didn't like the picture of herself one bit, and she made a decision to reorganize herself as a person who could learn in school after all, and after that to be a competent soldier when she was called up to the army.

❧ I Am the Boss: Do Everything My Way. I May Leave You, But You Can't Leave Me. My God, What Happened?

This is a case of a young beautiful and bright dictator, but in therapy she fails to give up her "bossism." Although therapy had provided a cushion for her pain over the failure of her marriage, it failed to replace her fascist ways of controlling everyone in sight, and the prospects for her succeeding in entering into a loving relationship remained unpromising.

Absolutism, Superiority, Excessive Power Seeking, Denials of Doing Harm to Self and Others

I am beautiful, capable, and powerful. Whatever I decide goes. I battled my way through childhood and told my mother off harshly and even obscenely as often as I wanted, whatever way I wanted. She's never really been a person I respect. She says I am selfish and loudmouthed. But I won, and she also says that we are best friends. I wonder if she is so involved with me because she can't stand my father's criticalness. No, they are very happy. At least I think so. They had some trouble at the beginning, but they are really a great couple. Yes, I am sure of that.

I myself married a few months ago. First I shocked everybody by marrying some man who is totally out of our circle, and even from another country. But he was handsome, brilliant, and made a terrific impression. It was fun getting married. I liked him. We had good fun getting to know each other passionately and sexually. But not long after we were married, it was time to settle down to the business of letting him know that I was the boss. Not that I realized I was doing this. I simply realized that I had to criticize him for all the stupid, thoughtless, and selfish things he was doing. And then when he got angry at me for being insulting, I simply made it clear that I didn't want him to come close anymore. Well, maybe once a month, but then he finally stopped even that and moved out of our bedroom. I confess I was a bit shocked at that, and one night I tried to get him to come back and to my amazement he wouldn't – I always thought that he would never refuse me! He said that for a while he really tried to send me nice notes and bring me flowers and invite me back, but that I told him I had no interest in him and I didn't feel any love toward him anymore. In fact, maybe I never loved him. Whatever I feel goes, so I told him I wasn't interested. I don't think I was even suffering very much during this time. I mean, it was obvious that our marriage was in trouble, but somehow I was living the kind of life I wanted to, fighting with him, not caring, and then moving in and out of sometimes being nicer to him.

Finally, one day I got the biggest shock of my life. I had been talking to him about the possibility that I would break up our marriage and divorce him, that I didn't know and I would need to take time to figure it out – what fun it was to play with him, even though I didn't know I was doing that. But now he actually dared to say that he was going to divorce me! I couldn't believe it! I insisted we immediately get to a therapist, and I told the therapist that it was I who was thinking of divorcing him, but I was willing to take time to understand more before I made any decision. Was I shocked once again when the therapist let me know that my husband was seriously intending to leave me after all. I also found out that my parents had told the therapist they respected my husband, they thought he was in the right, and they too thought I was an impossible person to live with! I am dumbfounded. I am so accustomed to beating up on others with my love-hate games.

In this case, therapy proved somewhat helpful in that it comforted the young woman in the shock she was in at being left by her husband, and also taught her something about being less nasty and about being softer and friendlier instead. However, the therapy never reached a point of helping her to develop a new healthy relationship with another man. For a while there was another man, but following the initial burst of loving excitement, this relationship too turned into a battle and was dissolved. Shortly afterward the therapist was somehow dismissed and his services terminated. She was again the boss, and the one who did the leaving; and while the therapy may have been somewhat helpful, it was not successful.

❧ I Don't Trust Anybody, But It's Not I Who Causes the Trouble in Relationships, No Way

This case fails despite a sincere effort – even by more than one therapist. The woman is a nice person who inspires a desire to help her, but her entrenched insistence on continuing a life of suspiciousness and bitterness leaves her beyond the reach of people in her family and her therapists who try to help her.

Suppression of Information, Intolerance of Dissent, Excessive Power Seeking, Prejudice, Denials of Doing Harm to Self and Others

I am a negative person, and that is my joy. I have been to quite a few therapists, and they are all jerks. My husband, from whom I am getting a divorce, says that whenever a therapist raises any question about my responsibility for being depressed, which I don't think I am, I become so enraged I fire the therapist, but I refuse to admit there is anything wrong with me. I guess they really mean I am bitter and not nice and not soft.

Now this time we simply had to get help, because our children were apparently having such a bad reaction to the fact that we had separated and were heading for a divorce that I had lost all control of them. Our house was like a zoo with all the children cursing at one another and beating on one another. One of our kids got into throwing himself on the street and just talking about wanting to die. Another of our kids was always in trouble hitting out suddenly, blindly, and much too strongly at other children in school, and complaints were pouring in about him. So off we went to another therapist.

What a relief. The children began to quiet down under the direction of the therapist, who was very firm and even aggressive but loving. Although one thing I didn't like is that the therapist insisted on my husband and me being present together in family sessions when I don't want anything to do with him ever again. Oh, I forgot to mention the fact that it is my husband who wants the divorce. I absolutely do not want it. I did manage to get the therapist to try to convince my husband not to divorce me, but my husband refused. And then the therapist began to talk to me about my part of being a sour person and being weak as a leader to the children, because I don't really try enough to organize them and I just tell them that what they are doing is wrong and stay angry with them.

One day the therapist asked one of my sisters to come to a session with me. I couldn't believe what happened. After all I had said about our parents being horrible, complaining, unhappy people, my sister said that she thought they were not monsters and maybe they were even nice, that she appreciated them and in any case wanted to show them respect in their elder years; and then she also said that I had always been a sour person and negative and never let my parents or anybody in the family or any of my siblings get close to me. That was the end. I knew this therapist was poison and I told him that I was firing him. The only trouble was that my children still needed help, and one of them in particular had become attached to the therapist, and it seemed to be doing him good and stopping him from being so aggressive at home and school. No matter, I still yelled at the therapist that he didn't understand anything and that I was firing him. Anyway, at least I succeeded in turning the therapy into a big sour battle, the way I like to have relationships turn out.

In this case, even devoted therapeutic efforts to extend a loving, helping hand proved of no avail. The patient progressively consolidated her paranoid negative accusations of the therapist and joined them to previously longstanding negative accusation of many other people in her life. The therapeutic efforts in this case had been intensive, with repeated efforts to express and demonstrate caring and availability to the mother, and with careful interpretative work on her mistrust and suspiciousness – including tracing these characteristics to her outstanding early childhood memories. There was also an unusual seemingly lovely joint session organized with one of the mother's earlier therapists, whom the patient had also rejected but for whom she retained a respect and appreciation. The previous therapist was a kind and gentle woman who remained committed to the patient's care even when the patient attacked her. Together, the two therapists, past and present, woman and man, gently and firmly explained to the mother the style of her lifelong bitterness and mistrust and how it caused the dissolution of primary relationships. These traits also endangered the possibility of getting help from any psychotherapist notwithstanding their genuine wishes to help. Yet the intervention of this special session also did not help.

In time the mother discontinued her therapy. At the father's insistence the child selected as the most frequent and intense target of her bitterness continued successfully in his therapy.

The identification of FASCIST MIND concepts and patterns in patients' lives is not a panacea or guaranteed method of treatment, but it is a new and additional way of addressing even tough psychiatric symptoms and complicated life situations; the identification of FASCIST MIND can be meaningful and at times decisively helpful in psychotherapy. There are a lot of people who instinctively don't like totalitarian or fascist governments or dictatorial rule of groups or organizational structures, and if they are made aware that they have become agents of fascist control in the ways they run their minds or relationships, they may become motivated to make real changes.

Intellectually, this way of looking at the lifestyles of all of us, which also brings us closer to the issues of fascism versus democracy in our societies, can lead to a good feeling that our lives somehow make more sense. Now our inner and outer worlds are cut from the same cloth, of our choosing: whether to be more democratic, free, and rationally responsive to information about reality, or to be practitioners or victims of totalitarian thinking, control, and retaliation.

Part III. People, Relationships, and Integrity

Returning to a Psychotherapy of Discovery

Once upon a time people went to psychotherapy to understand and to learn, but now they (too often) go to get fixed and tranquilized.

Once upon a time psychotherapists were masters of exploration and discovery – like other olden-day masters, respected and even beloved for their wisdom and expertise – but now they (too many) are more like service center technicians, and too often like employees of insurance companies.

In days of old, the outcome of a psychotherapeutic venture was known to await and depend on the greatness of spirit and the mutual effort of both the patient and therapist; now there is more of a demand and perhaps even an assumption that the patient will be given a successful outcome, and relief of the presenting discomfort and distress, by the therapist's expertise in doing something to the patient.

Let us assume that a new patient arrives with an unfamiliar symptom of ticks – nervous contractions – of the right ankle – a fictitious symptom for purposes of this illustration that indeed I have never seen or heard of to date.

I suggest that the likely treatment of this ridiculously intriguing symptom by physicians, including the psychiatrists of our day and age, would be to do imaging studies, and then assuming there were no positive findings to inject topical tranquilizers into the area of contractions.

The same patient having turned to a common variety psychotherapist of our time, either before the above medical-psychiatric workup and effort at treatment or after the intervention had proved unsuccessful, would likely be offered some of the following techniques:

• *relaxation technique, such as focusing on different parts of the body and contracting and releasing them, and then focusing on the afflicted ankle area with the intention of inducing sufficient relaxation of the ankle to prevent the involuntary contractions;*

• *behavioral reframing of the involuntary contractions by instructing the patient to tell his mind to replace the contractions before they appear with stretching the area, the intention being to distract the patient from repetition of the contractions through shifting attention to an alternative goal of stretching;*

• *inviting the patient to talk about whatever worries there are in his life to see if relief of the patient's tensions will lead to the symptom going away (this technique comes closest to continuing the old-fashioned psychotherapy tradition of looking for upsetting feelings that are behind symptoms, although it is an unfocused look at feelings without an effort to identify specific psychodynamic connections between the symptom and the patient's feelings as will be described shortly).*

In the more classical dynamic psychotherapies of yesteryear, which are still practiced by an unknown smaller percentage of contemporary psychotherapists, the therapist might smile inwardly at the patient's presentation of an unusual symptom, be genuinely curious how it came about, and would get to work in any of the following ways:

• *listening to the patient's descriptions of his symptoms, the therapist would be attuned to information about when the symptom appears, and also would welcome the appearance of the symptom in the therapy sessions, seeking to understand the thought, contents, and emotions in the patient's mind at the time of the symptom (for example, anger at a loved one or whoever, a possible concern with mother's health, fears about money matters, anger at one's business partner, whatever);*

• *the therapist would teach and encourage the patient to engage in progressive free association and would listen in particular for themes and chains of symbolic meanings that might seem connected to the symptom in question (for example, since the ankle is part of the foot, there might be associations to the patient kicking out at someone in anger; or if the patient was otherwise putting an emphasis on being made an invalid by the symptom, attention might be given to associations that refer to not being able to stop feeling sorry for oneself or seeking to gain sympathy from other people);*

• the therapist would invite and explore the patient's dreams with special attention to the emergence of a possible linkage to the presenting symptom (say the patient dreams of being at bat in a Lou Gehrig Stadium, which brings up associations to the fact that the beloved Lou Gehrig died many years ago of a serious neurological disease, and perhaps this means the patient is concerned these days with fears of illness and serious decline).

Slowly but surely, patient and therapist together would see themselves as detectives and explorers of the hidden terrain of the unconscious feelings and intentions seeking to be expressed through the patient's symptom. Hopefully the time would come that a reasonable explanatory construction would emerge that made sense to the patient of how and why he or she was unconsciously instructing the body to create the seemingly involuntary convulsive movements of his ankle (for example, "I'm kicking out impotently and angrily in protest against my daughter's demands to go out with a crowd that I do not approve of"). With the map of such understanding of the symptom in hand, patient and therapist would then shift to trying to create new forms of self-expression and self-assertion to help the patient achieve a greater sense of control over his or her life in regard to the issue that is so upsetting it had to be processed unconsciously into a symptom (for example, the man resolves to spend much more quality time with his daughter including taking her out to dinners where they would be able to enjoy each other as well as get into more intimate conversation, and would try to channel the improvement in the relationship to influence her to give up being with a bad crowd that could lead her into trouble).

The several alternative treatments that were just sketched move from symptom control through medical means, to behavioral transformation of a symptom, to a shotgun kind of clarification of tensions that may be sitting behind the symptom, to a more patient and certainly more demanding psychotherapy that explores and searches for specific meanings in the patient's unconscious experience that underlie the symptom, and then a retranslation of these meanings into new problem-solving behaviors by the patient acting in his or her behalf. However arduous and lengthy the treatment process, the patient ends up acting in his or her behalf rather than being treated and fixed by the therapist removing his symptom like a surgeon.

The above contrived illustration may sound silly because there is hardly much basis for identifying with the suffering of involuntary ankle movements. The case may seem far-fetched and trivial, but the truth is that if and ever such a symptom developed it could feel as physically painful and disturbing to the patient, as do hundreds of other familiar symptoms such as eye ticks, difficulties in breathing, muscular spasms in the back, or what have you. Besides, the point here was to take any symptom and use it as a symbolic statement of other more familiar psychiatric symptoms. When the patients of our day and age arrive in a state of suicidal fearfulness, or bursting with violent rage, or shaking with anxiety, the therapists of our times have choices: moving rapidly to gain control over the symptomatic disturbance and reduce the immediate agitation through medical techniques, behavioral and cognitive reframing and retraining to gain control over the symptom, short-term catharsis of immediate emotional issues, or to engage the patient in a mutual process of search and exploration for what meanings these symptoms have in the patient's mind and heart.

The Courage to Give Up a Golden Calf of Instant Comforts and Solutions

I like an emphasis on a search for the real meaning of symptoms and a reorganization of self in constructive response to that meaning more than I like gaining control over symptoms either by psychological or by medical means.

I appreciate that we can be suffering so intensely that there are many times we need and deserve a more immediate symptom relief than the old masters knew how to give, but I prefer to look for the least degree of control of symptoms needed to keep the patient relatively comfortable and encouraged to undertake the job of finding the real meanings of their symptoms.

Factually, I suffered a great deal during the several years of my own psychoanalysis, and yet looking back after so many years, I continue to

228

have considerable pride at having been engaged in a process of discovery of truth and the development of a widened range of experiencing my ways of being in the world. I have always felt that my therapy "saved my life," and that notwithstanding many emotional hurts and losses (like most people) over my lifetime, I have been enjoying a wonderful life, much of it thanks to the psychoanalytic therapy I received.

Ailing people go to healers of all sorts with their medical and psychological problems in the hope that there will be an absolute and clear-cut cure. This is how the story begins, but what then follows are many variations on the theme. Somehow in the folklore surrounding psychotherapy, it has remained poorly understood that there is a wide range of possible outcomes. People often present in a great deal of emotional pain or are distraught with anxiety or black depression. They may feel despair over the loss of a relationship, or unbearable grief over a loss of a loved one. They may come to therapy following a bitter failure in their work or in fulfilling their dreams. They are asking for relief, which is a legitimate request, but the possible outcomes vary considerably.

Some psychological problems are incurable, including: "burnt-out" cases of psychosis in which the patient will never lead an independent life again; cases of "giving up" after a terrible loss, say the death of one or more children; many severe personality disorders, especially psychopathic personality disorders and borderline personality disorders that have poor prospects of responding even to strong efforts at treatment (although we are getting better at offering some help); and many relationships that cannot be repaired and must be terminated. Leon Saul was a master psychoanalyst in his time. He served as director of a major psychoanalytic institute in Philadelphia and was editor of the journal *Psychoanalytic Quarterly.* Saul believed in the potential effectiveness of psychotherapy as providing the patient with an opportunity to gain a new freedom from excessive hostility and excessive dependence, which in turn "frees the capacities for the greater satisfaction that life affords the adult human being."[12] But he cautioned that "some patients go so far as to wish to remain disturbed and in the grip of their infantile patterns."[13]

There are many other more hopeful situations in which one of the major implications of the presenting distress is that the time has come for a person to make changes in various behaviors or in their styles of experiencing emotions or relationships and organizing their lives. The cooperative patient who works with the therapist to understand the needed changes and put them into practice is likely to achieve far better results than the patient who is available only to undergo procedures done to him or her, such as through medications, or even through prescriptions for behavior changes that are done in obedience to the therapist's instructions rather than as expressions of changing oneself and how one is living.

I am prejudiced toward the belief that the best results, and the most dignifying and joyous results too, come when human beings engage n a search for understanding what is wrong in their lives that deserves to be corrected. This is a moral process no less than a medical one. It links up with the concepts of spiritual self-correction, self-examination, and accountability that appear in most religions and with time-honored values of decency, humility, charity, reverence for life, devotion to family, friendly and helpful relationships with other people, contributions to one's community, and so on. In Judaism, for example, the word *tikun* refers to a spiritual correction of one's way of being in the world that is a much desired and valued process the wise and good person is urged to undertake.

A full psychotherapeutic process encourages patients to explore how they treat themselves and how they treat other human beings. The process teaches the patient to bear facing the truths of unpleasant and nasty antilife behaviors, and to recommit to being of a good person. The process can produce far-reaching changes in the spirit of a human being and in their behavior that, in my opinion, can go far beyond the calming that medication can produce, or even a valuable reorganization of spirit that is an outcome of being the recipient of helpful support from a caring therapist or loving family members or friends. It is a process of learning, redefinition of one's own choices, and recommitment that is then owned by the person's inner dignity.

᠊ᢀ *They are an outstanding, colorful older couple with children and grand-*

children, but he has recently developed a serious illness that is going to require patience and courage to endure in order to survive for as long as possible. He becomes increasingly insulting and emotionally tyrannizing of his wife, blaming her outrageously and intensely for everything that is discomforting and upsetting, and one day he lashes out at her in physical violence. The news of the violent explosion hits the children like a shock wave, and they rally behind mother who has always been a somewhat more sympathetic figure for them than their father.

He has always been exuberantly positive about whatever he does or believes in. Charming, interesting, and highly successful in his profession, he has won the admiration and liking of many people. He has had little need to question whether there is anything dominating, unfair, or insulting in his bombastic yet charming style of being the kingpin. Now as he ages, becomes ill, and suffers other losses such as the deaths of his parents, what is being driven home to him unconsciously is that he does not have the full measure of control over life that he had pretended he had for so long. In his unconscious panic of awareness that he has entered a phase of life that inevitably leads to death, he reverts to the style he had never corrected, of being a bully and a blamer who takes out his upsets on those around him.

The therapist asks this man, who has agreed to come for therapy because he does not want his wife to leave him, "Is there anything about yourself that you acknowledge deserves to be corrected or changed?"

"No, I don't think so," says the man, and proceeds to tell still another story of how he is well known and widely admired, and how one therapist whom he had seen, albeit unsuccessfully, told him that he was such a great man he did not want to charge him for any of the sessions.

"The answer you are looking for is hidden in your very answer," said the therapist, laughing good-naturedly. Since the man was indeed a good conversationalist who enjoyed mind challenges and good humor, he said quite genuinely that he would try to think about the riddle further.

True to his word he called on the phone a couple of hours later. "I've been thinking about what you said. Tell me, is it possible that what's wrong with me is that there is nothing wrong with me, and that I have to put my foot down harder with my wife when she gets upset about everything and gets so critical?"

231

Not at all surprisingly, the man with no faults never showed up for a subsequent session (and never paid for the session for which he had come).

If coming to therapy is to:
• correct a child's misbehavior without learning to be a better parent;
• discipline a spouse and put them in their place without learning how to be more loving, positive, and fair in one's firmness in response to the spouse's insults;
• overcome a psychosomatic condition through which one is pouring out unexpressed pent-up emotions, but without examining the integrity of one's emotions and relationships to other people;
• stop feeling depressed thanks to the gift of the therapist's interest and caring, but without coming to an understanding of an oppressive relationship and the repeated humiliation and exploitation to which one is submitting;
• overcome a learning disorder by virtue of learning more effective organization of study habits and examination-taking behaviors, but without reaching inwardly for renewed inspiration and empowerment of learning, and without releasing a thirst for new knowledge in its own right rather than as a performance objective;
• overcome bizarre eating habits in order to be able to go out socially without panic at being discovered, but with no intention to learn to eat for the pleasure of nourishing oneself and enjoying eating as a major experience in life;

psychotherapy becomes a service-center, parts-replacement process with little spiritual power and with limited learning about oneself as a person.

While some symptom-controlling therapies do work, and while some cases in which symptoms are relieved also lead people to grow more as persons once they are less burdened by suffering, symptomatic therapies – which remove symptoms – can add to a mistaken conception of life that a person should expect to be free of upsets, problems, defeats, or trying challenges. Feel-better therapies, without learning about oneself, leave people ill-prepared for the inevitable future defeats and challenges that will continue to hit them. They leave people with far less knowledge and methods for future independent problem solving.

Clinical experience and the clinical literature also tell us that too many "successful" treatments end up backfiring, sometimes tumultuously and tragically.

≈ *They were a couple with a longstanding sexual problem, including orgasmic dysfunction for her, and a significant though inconsistent degree of premature ejaculation for him.*

They agreed in a friendly fashion to go for sex therapy. The therapist described the sexual behavior tasks that had been innovatively designed by Masters and Johnson and with their agreement proceeded to instruct them in their use. [14]

They enjoyed their sex therapy and were consistently cooperative with the prescriptions of the therapy. Over a few months, they learned how to be aroused by touches and massages of each other, how to linger in sexual foreplay, how not to worry about the "success" of their performance during intercourse, how to take their time and enjoy his quiet "visiting" when he penetrated her, how to extend intercourse by several minutes by his knowing how to stop his rush toward orgasm before reaching the point beyond control. The wife began to enjoy periodic pleasurable orgasms she had never before experienced.

Sounds wonderful? Obviously a successful treatment case.

Yet a year later the couple was storming at each other and quite seriously on the verge of divorce. They didn't like each other. There was something about spending time with her husband up close that made the wife feel he was a self-involved little boy who had no real feelings for her, and who was too weak in dealing with the children. To him, she was a critical bitch who was never satisfied with him and their good lives, and always had a bone to pick with him; he couldn't stand her. They had been better off when they thought their problem was one of "sexual incompatibility." Now their mutual feelings of being "incompatible personalities" was becoming all too painful, and they might have to break up.

≈ *She had an amazing response to the Prozac and felt much better. A tearfulness that had pervaded her before the drug no longer existed. She now woke up without tears in her eyes and heart and went to sleep lightheartedly as well.*

The only thing that was wrong was that although she was calmer on the

Prozac, she also seemed to have less and less patience for emotional stress, and especially if there were any kind of what she perceived as "criticism" of her. Her husband called to her attention that whenever he had any kind of dissatisfaction with her or criticism of something she had done, she was unavailable to receiving critical comment and treated it spitefully and venomously as if his intention was to humiliate and even trap her. The Prozac had delayed the learning she needed in order to understand her enduring hurt and inner depression, and paradoxically had pushed to the forefront her inability to take criticism and her unrecognized capacity for being nasty.

An increasing number of investigative journalists and official medical groups are now stating that the manufacturers of Prozac covered up for years an amazingly high rate of suicides by patients on the drug, as well as a significant increase in violent outbursts and even actual murders committed by Prozac patients![15]

I suggest that Prozac indeed may be helping a lot of people feel better. Yet the medication should be accompanied by sufficient counseling about the psychological and spiritual meanings and causes of depression and how a patient can cope with a reemergence of bad feelings. In other words, Prozac may help some people feel so much better that once relieved of the physiology of their depression, they are strong and spirited enough to revert to the lousy feelings that made them depressed to begin with. Now they really feel terrible, in some cases so bad that with the strength they have gotten back thanks to the medication they have the strength to kill themselves or more rarely someone else. For with all the pills they have gotten, no one helped them with their deep-down sadness and rage (most often about crucial relationships in their lives).

It is amazing to me that this psychological explanation does not appear readily in the emerging literature about the side effects of Prozac (a lot of suicide and a little murder). In what I shall call the "medical-drug culture" in which psychiatric medications are mushrooming, the thinking about most behaviors is that they are all controlled by specific physiological triggers. The physiological point of view has reached such a point of absurdity that if someone taking medicine commits suicide, it is taken to mean that a physiological suicide switch was directly activated by the medicine. The tradition of psychosomatic thinking is all but forgotten. The fact that feeling less depressed on one level can expose a person to a deeper depression-despair is forgotten, as is the time-honored knowledge that some degree of feeling better means the depressed person has more energy available to take action to harm themselves. In short, even as it really helps many people, Prozac as a perfect solution (here we go again) necessarily will bring on a fair share of disasters, like all promises of overcertainty do.

The Lies and Failures of Psychotherapy

It is such a beautiful profession that one is tempted to invest it with a kind of faith and romanticized trust of the most idealistic hopes. Unfortunately, the profession of psychotherapy is served by human beings, and there is no area of human life and function in which our species has ever proven equal to an ideal hope.

By definition psychotherapists have been entrusted with being guardians and caretakers of the truth of what is going on in human affairs. We are mandated to uncover and overcome lies, manipulation, deceit, exploitation, and abuses of human beings by one another. Yet, regrettably, we psychotherapists too include certain numbers who, notwithstanding proper receipt of whatever advanced degrees in social work, psychiatry, psychology, or whichever counseling profession, engage in the very behaviors we are supposed to police and overcome. Of course, this is hardly a surprise. There are criminal cops, rapist priests, killer physicians, and so on in every profession and walk of human life. Each of these violations of decency and professional responsibility are horrible, regrettable, and need to be fought with all the power within the respective profession and by society. They are the acts of immoral, nasty people that in a larger sense should not discredit the respective professions and the overwhelming numbers of good cops, devoted priests, committed physicians, and fine psychotherapists.

The more serious question is: in any given professional structure are there inherently basic lies and devices for manipulation of the public that, by definition, will draw forth harmful acts toward clients, even by practitioners who are not personally corrupt or particularly disturbed but are simply doing their job as they understand it? For example, it is said that President George Washington died not simply or only of the respiratory disease from which he was suffering, but from the progressive weakening caused by his physicians who, seeing him failing, prescribed more and more leeches to drain his blood to a point that weakened whatever resistance he still had left. If the president had any fight left, it was taken away by his healers who were doing the natural and right thing in their profession at the time!

Regrettably, psychotherapists of our day and age have their leeches too. I believe that the biggest leech of all is when any therapist identifies with or adopts any single mode of psychotherapy as the one-and-only kosher and correct treatment for virtually all cases; similarly, when any therapist practicing a given mode of psychotherapy is unable or refuses to see truthfully that the method in its prescribed form is not working well for a given patient (or couple or family), or is eliciting unwelcome and even dangerous side effects and reactions, but the therapist refuses to modify his or her technique.[16]

Beginning with psychoanalysis, which of the many modes of psychotherapy has not spawned an orthodox catechism and a politics of superior entitlement of its loyal practitioners as the designated elite of the mental health world? Within each of the professional groups and societies devoted to the many different modes of psychotherapy, one hears a style of talking down to and of those who would violate the code of the mandated absolutely correct way of doing therapy. Many therapists are officious, pretentious and sanctimonious, and disparage other therapists who differ from them because they dare deviate from the orthodoxy of their prescribed way of doing treatment. In truth, in the course of practicing psychotherapy, it is naturally hard for therapists to avoid becoming preaching, condescending know-it-alls and pompous or overly do-gooder dispensers of help and wisdom to the less fortunate, less capable, or just plain unlucky people whom they are saving. In these respects, psychotherapists are practitioners of some of the very characteristics of the FASCIST MIND rather than practitioners and teachers of antifascism as they should be.

The practical implication of the above distortions of the role of psychotherapists, I fear, is that there are going to be more failures of psychotherapy than there should be or need to be. After all, the most powerful tool of psychotherapy is the sincerity of the therapist, so that any posturing or role-playing by the therapist in respect of whatever self-serving agenda necessarily takes away from the therapist's presence.

In medicine, it is understood that most treatments cannot be successful with everyone. There is almost always a patient who is allergic to the very medicine that does the job extraordinarily well for the majority of other patients. Many times, patients are not well enough to undergo the life-saving treatments possible for those in better shape. Differences are also found in the skillfulness of individual practitioners and teams of health specialists. At any given point, there are new procedures in the hands of some gifted, pioneering healers that produce God-sent miraculous results while the bulk of patients of that era who receive the standard care of the times suffer high failure rates. To the credit of establishment medicine, slowly but surely, scientific knowledge is developed and medical practitioners are made responsible for applying new knowledge. Simultaneously, it is also true that traditional medicine stupidly pushes away any number of new forms of treatment that don't make it through the political processes (you bet there are politics in medicine and science) of the contemporary medical establishment. However, organized medicine, overall, deserves our respect and love insofar as to a large extent it does study and report back relatively honestly the results of the procedures it employs, and does update procedures based on empirical information.[17]

A major problem with the profession of psychotherapy is that often (if not most of the time) psychotherapists do not have empirical information about the effectiveness of many of their procedures. The impressions that therapists develop on their own of the effectiveness and ineffectiveness of the therapies they are practicing need to be regarded critically. Moreover, the human mind is notorious for its distortions and misrepresentations of reality. Therapists can be so beholden and loyal to a given school of therapy, or caught up in their own narcissistic needs to believe they are doing the right thing, that they are capable of dis-regarding and denying empirical information that contradicts their pet theories and beliefs.

Judging the outcomes of psychological help is an extraordinarily dif-ficult area, and there often are profound questions as to what are the objective results.

❧ After seeing that a prospective bride had a need to be dominant, the therapist helps the prospective young husband break off the engagement. The bride is deeply hurt. The bride's mother, an extraordinarily powerful person with high standing in society, is furious at the therapist for encour-aging the groom to reject her daughter, thus causing social embarrassment to her family.
Was this counseling process objectively a success or failure?

❧ A therapist succeeds over several years of treatment in holding together a disturbed marriage that is characterized by repeated periods of fighting and unforgiving. The children are upset and show different symptoms of poor adjustment; they nonetheless benefit from the further period of continuity of their family structure, and during the time the couple stays together they enjoy some kind of regard for each other, which also strengthens them. The therapist considers his work successful. A time finally comes when the therapy is ended because it has become deadlocked, and there is no promise of further improvement. At this point one of the mates breaks off from the marriage.
Was the period of therapy a success or a failure? Do the benefits of holding the marriage together for some years justify the effort, or would it have been more ethical and beneficial to the adults and children involved to help end the marriage earlier?

I am not offended by the objective failure of some therapies, but by the posturing of psychotherapists, as if everything they did was correct, and as if all aspects of the failures of the therapy issued from the pathology and less-than-admirable characteristics of their patients. It seems to me that being a psychotherapist, like any professional whose purpose is to help people improve their lives, means being able to carry and contain a constantly increasing number of memories of lack of success and failures in the practice of one's profession. Therapists need an ability to bear the truths of their failures and an accompanying sense of regret and honest guilt, without being crushed. Such accumulating information also generates valid questions that need to be asked for future cases as one examines every completed treatment to learn from it and improve treatment procedures for the future. True professionalism is science- or evidence-based and not hucksterism and grandstand salesmanship.

There is another form of manipulation and exploitation of psychotherapy of the client population that has to do with holding people in expensive therapies they do not need. There are too many psychotherapies from which people are not gaining sufficiently to justify their continuation.

Sometimes therapy is what one fine psychotherapist a long time ago called a "purchase of friendship" by lonely, abandoned, or rejected people.[18] Is this a legitimate use of the professional service? I see some situations where the answer can be affirmative, and the service rendered is in the good tradition of supportive treatment, which offers comforts to human beings who are otherwise going to be too lonely and sad. But I can also see the many situations in which the illusion of ongoing treatment that is created is essentially manipulative, to serve the financial or egoistic interests of the therapist at the expense of the client. That patient might well be directed to other family or community social processes to create whatever levels of belonging and connection needed to soften their loneliness and rejection.

There are also cases in which therapists can initiate helping processes, such as through a dialogue between a husband and wife,[19] or an interactive process between children and parents.[20] When couples and family units offer one another mutual loving support and positive criticism, a dialogue process can be created that becomes the vehicle for examining lives more effectively than any reliance on a stranger-therapist. Hearing the truth from the people in our lives can lead us to know what needs to be corrected, for example, stinginess, meanness, or lack of attention to others. The "real McCoy" from loved ones is more undeniable and can be ever more influential than coming to therapy for the services of an expensive stranger.

In sum, I have no problem with the fact that, regrettably, a significant percentage of psychotherapies do not successfully alter people's lives for the better. I am very happy though about the many cases in which psychotherapy is of assistance and helps people live emotionally healthy and meaningful lives. But I am saddened and feel ashamed and guilty about the profession and many of the practitioners insofar as some violate democratic ideals of open-mindedness to empirical information, respect for dissent, and taking responsibility for the choices made, and insofar as practitioners create structures of basic inequality with other people and overuse power to buttress an exploitative position in which therapists earn big bucks and big ego thrills from being false and unhelpful professionals.

Therapists Who Don't Have Their Hearts Genuinely in the Process of Psychotherapy

Too many psychotherapists are not really present in the process for the right reasons or in a right way.

It has always been for me a kind of bad joke to see how some students in the helping professions raise themselves up to a pseudolevel of greater importance when they are given the opportunity to play the role of therapist in their classes and seminars in psychology, psychiatry, and social work. It is also obvious that there are any number of immature and unbalanced people in the psychotherapeutic professions who hide their emotional and mental disturbances by playing the roles of healers and counselors to disturbed people. In psychiatric hospitals, patients have long understood that some of their doctors and attendants in truth are far more nuts than they are. In *I never promised you a rose garden*, the patient-heroine, Deborah, describes an attendant who delights, albeit unconsciously, in instigating distress and madness in the psychotic patients, and who if crossed lashes out with uncontrollable violence in desperate response to the loss of his own pseudo-self-control and superiority over the crazies.[21] In their own madness, psychiatric patients sense the deeper truths about their helpers, just as children know in their hearts the sincerity-insincerity of the helpfulness-exploitation of their parents regardless of the words their parents say. (This inner knowledge of a parent works both ways.

Not only do children know when a parent is hateful no matter how they pretend to be good caregivers, but they also can discern genuine love in the heart of some parents who are behaving incorrectly because they are upset.)

Many forms of exploitation of patients satisfy a therapist's needs for one or another kind of gratification, personal safety, or self-aggrandizement. There are therapists who in their hearts are lording it over the dependent, confused, and lesser people who are their patients. There are therapists who use their "friendship" with their patients to fill their own empty lives and to replace their failures in creating satisfactory relationships with their spouse or children or community with a pseudointimacy with their patients. There are, of course, also therapists who engage in manifestly exploitative relationships such as business deals or sexual liaisons with their patients. Some of the therapists who exploit patients are capable of putting on one hell of a good show of being hard-working, capable helpers.[22]

Other therapists go about their business correctly, in fact so correctly that in truth they are automatons and conformists playing their roles as therapists according to the book, so that they are approved, accepted, and beyond reproach. In the final analysis they are out for success within their professional establishment rather than putting their hearts into efforts at being helpers and healers. They play by the book without spontaneity or creativity; they are busy doing their job and not taking risks rather than investing themselves emotionally in trying to help their patients overcome tough problems. In my experience, many such therapists are also quick to refer for medication and quick to hospitalize. They thus end up not having to work as hard and are seemingly less responsible for the outcome.

Truthfully, some therapists really don't like their patients or their work, and are bored, or angry with their patients – and sometimes it seems at the essence of the human spirit.

A veteran therapist said, "I don't like working with couples. They are always getting so excited and blaming each other. So I sit back and let them talk to each other. They usually end up yelling and insulting each other.

"I wish they would just shut up. I wait them out, and then after a while I make a few remarks about the personality of each of them and how they need to grow up, and sometimes it works, but most of the time they just go on in their ways.

"I much prefer doing individual therapy with well-motivated patients, but they have become far fewer over the years, and it's obvious to me that a lot of the money is in seeing couples, so I do that."

There also are therapists whose main preoccupation in the course of therapy is with the outcome of the treatment as it reflects on their own success and prestige. They are really scared of failures of therapy as if they are blemishes on their records. They also celebrate a happy outcome as a boost for their self-evaluation and public record rather than as a triumph of the patients. In volatile and dangerous situations, such as when there is violence in a family or in the treatment of a possible suicide, the judgment of these therapists can be warped by their narcissistic concern with their position, which overrides the needs of the patients.

The 22-year-old woman leered at the therapist; she was confident of her triumph over him.

"So you have gotten upset about how depressed and bitter I am, I can see the wheels moving in your mind. You want to hospitalize me because you are afraid I am suicidal. Well, let me tell you. They did the same thing with my 20-year-old brother. They put him in _____ psychiatric hospital (a well known teaching institution that was among the best in the field at the time), and what he did is he went and hung himself in the hospital! I promise you that if you put me in the hospital, I will do exactly the same!"

The therapist was struck by the power of the young woman's threat and realized that she meant business. He concluded that he needed to continue to work with her in outpatient treatment. If the therapy did succeed in reaching her and she did decide to save her life, wonderful; if therapy did not succeed in touching her and bringing her to a reaffirmation of her right to live, she would die in or out of a hospital.

The therapist also realized that placing the young woman in a hospital would ostensibly relieve him of being "responsible," for her possible suicide, because her death would appear on the hospital's record, which obviously could absorb the blow more easily than he could as a solo practitioner. But it was also obvious to him that putting her in the hospital would lead her to do exactly what she said, and that she would take her life as a kind of triumph over all the enemy professionals.

The therapist resolved to work hard to bring the girl to caring about her life (and the therapy did succeed).

Some therapies need to be terminated by the therapist, notwithstanding the loss of income to the therapist, because the patient's use of therapy is destructive, unless the patient agrees to cease certain harmful behaviors to his or her self or to another person.

❧ A therapist says to a couple who time after time have orgies of unproductive fighting at home as well as in their therapy sessions, "I won't be able to continue seeing you unless you bring down your rage and your yelling at each other to a more solid kind of argument, where you tell each other what you are angry about, but do not demolish each other. And this means that here in your therapy sessions too, you are going to have to let me be in charge. As soon as I tell you to stop yelling, or even if I instruct you to stop talking, you need to agree to listen to me promptly the same as a player in a sporting match is required to obey the referee or umpire."

❧ I once postponed a couple from coming to couple sessions for close to a year because they were vituperative and out of control. This couple came for help on the referral of the family doctor after the wife had attempted suicide. During the year of waiting, I saw each spouse separately, including in preparation for couple sessions if and when they would be ready. The time came when the couple begged to be seen together, and I agreed somewhat reluctantly with the condition that they would not let their anger get out of control at any time or the sessions would be terminated.

This couple did get together and after considerable therapy went on to enjoy a lovely friendship for many years.

Patients make many requests – sometimes quite insistently – that therapists need to refuse to grant, such as requests for medication that isn't needed, requests for personal attention outside of therapy hours in ways inappropriate to a professional relationship, and requests for entering into a coalition with a patient against somebody in their family such as unfairly casting someone else in an incorrigible bad light ("the family idiot," "the crazy one").

> 🍂 *Already in the initial call for marital therapy, she made a point of conveying that her husband was an unethical person on many levels. She referred to his shady practices in handling their monies, questionable conduct in his profession, repetitive violations of various laws, manipulation and extortion of people, and his chronic insulting of her. When the couple came in, she was indisputably the more colorful and more attractive of the two, and seemingly the less disturbed and fairer. True to her description, he was a brooding, pouting, overly angry man who would blow up at her when he was hurt and soon go over the line to a degree of unpardonable insulting.*
>
> *Nonetheless, the longer-term picture of the therapy showed that he really wanted to learn to correct himself and did so. The person he then revealed was a sweet, idealistic, and fair man who wanted to be loved and was available to love at least in a reasonable give-and-take of romance and positive emotions. It was true though that he did not know how to love in a deeper sense, and it was also somewhat true that he walked too close to the line of questionable self-serving and manipulation in his profession. At the same time, surprisingly, it was she who was given to a degree of uncorrectable tantrums, scathing demands, and scheming manipulations when her dominance or will were crossed in any way or her corruption was threatened with exposure in any way. In the end, he decided to leave her for all that he really wanted to continue their marriage, but he had found her unavailable to any process of correction and forever committed to chronic disparagement and slander of him, both between them and in her references to him to other people.*

Moral Integrity and Being Good to Oneself and to Others – An Effective Prescription for Excellent Mental Health

I have rarely seen instances in which psychotherapy did not succeed if and when the purpose of the therapy was for the patients to become good people. Becoming "good people" means being good to oneself, developing good relationships with loved ones and associates, and living with an integrity and fairness that include being open to being corrected when in error. At the core is a commitment to avoid in any possible way doing serious harm to one's own life or to the lives of other human beings.

When people work for these goals, psychotherapy is a joy. It is a dedicated opportunity for self-discovery and self-awareness in the interests of becoming a better person. The corrections that one discovers almost inevitably reduce and remove most emotional and mental symptoms. In most cases, a theme of a central lifestyle problem is waiting in the background of emotional, psychiatric, and relationship symptoms. A psychotherapy designed (by the agreement of the patient and therapist) to discover such patterns and respond to them with the courage of self-correction almost "can't lose." A person who uses therapy sincerely in this way virtually has to become stronger, and the symptoms have to become weaker. For example:

• Blind retaliatory anger feeds numerous symptoms, from migraine headaches, to triggering epileptic convulsions, to setting off cardiovascular disturbances, to driving away children and mates, to getting bosses to fire you, and on and on. Therapeutic correction of chronic vengeful anger cures and prevents countless problems.

• Playing the conformist, nerd, brainless, or spineless accommodator who allows your mate to walk over you, a child to be disrespectful and abusive to you as a parent, or fellow employees or a supervisor to push you around at work will trigger any of countless symptoms, including flagging and flaccid efforts at erection, lack of self-confidence in giving a public talk, inability to provide leadership and discipline to your children, lowered resistance to illnesses, psychosomatic conditions, and many other symptomatic statements of being unable to carry yourself with pride and pleasure in your identity as a unique and deserving person. Therapeutic correction of overconformity and blending into the power of others or into the surroundings cures and prevents innumerable problems.

• Failure to dream "one's dream," to reach out toward expression of latent talents, or to exercise the self-assertiveness needed in various areas of life will mean a weak, unattractive "loser" kind of person who is deeply unhappy with his or her self and is easily led about, rejected, and ridiculed. Therapeutic correction of denials and walking away from true talents and therapeutic encouragement of self-assertiveness will do wonders in curing and preventing many problems.

It is only natural that people initially turn to psychotherapists because they are ailing, and quite understandably they are asking for relief. It then becomes a matter of the therapist's skill and ultimately the patient's inner character whether the therapy is developed as a quest to find a better person.

Becoming the better person does not mean being a prissy stuck-in-the-mud goody-goody, nor a ramrod stalwart of moral values with never a caprice or spontaneous fun-sinfulness or without a good healthy lust and pleasure-seeking as parts of one's life. I have seen many psychiatric patients who are paragons of commitments to the finest values, who won't lie, cheat, steal, or do harm to others, but who do not benefit from their morality; on the contrary, they are sometimes crazy precisely because they can't even consider lying, cheating, stealing, or doing harm. In other words, they can't even conceive of the possibility of doing something "wrong," because they can't imagine themselves entertaining any "bad" impulses with some degree of pleasure, and this rigid funless pattern actually contributes to making them crazy. Being normally "bad" is being human and is the healthier basis for being a good person. Who, for example, is going to be the better lover? A Mr. Straight-lace who lacks any passion because he knows that he is entering into a holy spiritual communion on entering his lover; or a Mr. Swashbuckler who allows himself to dream of whisking a female off to his ship as a captive whom he will overcome swiftly and powerfully? A Mrs. Goodness who does her sexual duty to her man lovingly; or a Mrs. Excited who is breathlessly in search of orgasmic pleasure? Moral health is too often defined as a rigid, straight-laced way of life for patsies and conformists that excludes natural processes of emotion, sexuality, and a creative flow of passion. In fact, moral health has to do with a fun and joy of living for oneself rather than with a grim asceticism, gray conformity, or self-punishment. Good moral health and mental health are both joyous and decent, and in large part there is a single road that leads to both of them.

Admittedly too, since life is complex, the outcome of therapy isn't always a smooth one vis-à-vis the other people in one's life. For example, if one is married to a person who needs to inflict pain on his or her mate, when the latter breaks out of being the perennial victim, the odds are that the marriage will end because the persecuting or sadistic spouse does not have an ability to change and become a better person. Similarly, there are times when one has to leave a place of work because the manager or director is never going to be the kind of person with whom one can experience a sense of worth. But often the correction of the errors in one's style of living not only builds a new ability to cope significantly with the problems issuing from the limitations of others in our lives, but also can help set off new chains of behaviors that will lead to improvement in those who are partners to the relationships.

Psychotherapy is an exercise of a DEMOCRATIC MIND seeking greater truth about oneself. It stands resolutely against FASCIST MIND's suppression of information and truth. Psychotherapy should not be undertaken in order to win out, outsmart, and take over other people, but should be undertaken in order to discover how to be a better person. Many situations in one's life then get sorted out more effectively. The preferred outcome of psychotherapy is equal and loving relationships rather than domination of a relationship or situation by a person who would use any additional strength gained from therapy to make others cower or be more easily manipulated.

Psychotherapy reestablishes a democratic system of dialogue, discussion, and negotiation. It frees a more healthy competition between different parts of our personalities as well as in our relationships with other people. A gracious conduct of the process of life becomes no less a source of pleasure than successes and acquisitions. In a well-functioning democracy of mind, everyone so to speak – meaning the different parts in our personality, as well as we together with the other people – have an opportunity to share in the wise decisions for living from the vantage points of the skillfulness and beauty each part and person have to contribute.[23]

Returning to a Psychotherapy of Mystery and Discovery

One of the most beautiful aspects of psychotherapy is that it provides a method for exploring both touchingly and scientifically the mysteries of human existence. By listening with patients (whether an individual or couple or family group) to the flow of their experiences, and especially to associative materials from the unconscious by way of interview techniques intending to evoke feelings, free associations, guided imagery, and dream interpretation, patients and therapist together can learn which inner meanings, choices, and ethical values are at work.

I often do not know whether a patient's given medical distress, which has not been clearly diagnosed by physicians, is a product or statement of emotional processes. And when there is a responsible medical diagnosis, I often still do not know if the physiological process has or has not been set off or is maintained by problematic emotions. What I do know is that we are holistic creatures given to an enormous complexity of psychosomatic processes, and that emotions are known (on firm scientific grounds) to be capable of playing major roles in many diseases such as heart disease (see heartbreak, loss of pride, crushing of one's ideals, and so forth), or cancer (see losses of a one-and-only love object, emotional fragility, surrender and collapse).

I often do not know whether it is wiser for a person to continue in or to end a deeply unsatisfying marriage, say given the likelihood that one of the adults may never recover and regroup their ability to create a reasonably balanced life after divorce, or say given that one of the children is likely to be permanently traumatized by the divorce.

I also know that helping people get better in respect of a symptom can actually make them worse. One psychiatric journal reported that there was a lady whose thumb hurt terribly. None of the physicians could help her, then a psychiatrist did remove her pain and she went crazy. Similarly, as we have seen, helping a couple get along better, and even to have pleasurable sexual experiences, can bring on a breakup of the couple and divorce. And helping one person in a family can lead to the exposure of the hidden disturbance in another person in the family.

Altogether, I go into many therapy cases with a sense of mystery, awe, and deep humility.

I appreciate the opportunity psychotherapy gives us to sort out our lives and come to the best decisions we can about our lives – for better or for worse. Clearly therapies that are a priori packaged techniques for removing symptoms, traumas, ambiguities, doubts, anxieties, doubt, and ambivalence can restore a premature order and illusions of wellness – once again the thrill and comfort of clear-cut solutions, but what then? Master existential psychotherapist James Bugental, who was the first president of the Association of Humanistic Psychology in the United States, has written:

> The destructive effect of the psychotherapist who does not recognize mystery is that the worldview transmitted implicitly or explicitly to the client is of a world in which all that is important is ultimately knowable and controllable. Thus arise expectations of one's self which are certain to be disappointed, but the client is likely to read those disappointments as due to her/his own failings. This in turn can lead to self-criticism, depression, and alienation from one's genuine talents.[24]

An approach to psychotherapy as mystery and discovery also expresses a worldview of psychology as an unending process of questioning, criticism, and seeking of new knowledge. One of the great theoreticians of psychology, Sigmund Koch, wrote in what is a powerful antifascist essay that although human beings forever seek (he called it a "poignant human need") to freeze all into frames, systems, maps, and a "set of rules that can seem to offer the wisp of hope for resolving uncertainty," in the end the result is self-deception and no less than "our happy domicile to the death – meaning, in the typical instance, *your* death."[25] What is crucial, Koch asserts, is that the democratic flow of inquiry and criticism never be silenced. "The growth of knowledge and understanding in the sciences has always required criticisms from within. . . . The death knell of scientific progress is sounded at just the time when criticisms is silenced."[26]

Koch also practiced what he preached on himself, and was capable of referring in print to some of his earlier writings as "the silliest most superficial documents I have ever written. They fall into a genre . . . [of] falsetto stipulations of self-righteous but ignorant minds."[27] Koch concludes masterfully:

I have been inviting a psychology that might show the imprint of a capacity to accept the inevitable ambiguity and mystery of our situation. The false hubris with which we have contained our existential anguish in a terrifying age has led us to prefer easy yet grandiose pseudoknowledge to the hard and spare fruit that is knowledge.[28]

What are the optimal aims of psychotherapy? Stated otherwise, what is the desirable mental health for which to strive for in psychotherapy?

• Martin Seligman, a former president of the American Psychological Association, who gave us the meaningful concept of *learned helplessness* as a psychological (and not physiological) organization of self in the genesis of many cases of depression, and his colleague Mihaly Csikszentmahalyi, call on psychology to take as its goals making people – including normal people – stronger and more productive and helping them realize more fully their talents and creativity. They propose that, "There are human strengths that act as buffers against mental illness [such as] courage, future mindedness, optimism, interpersonal skill, faith, work ethic, hope, honesty, perseverance, and the capacity for flow and insight."[29]

• Marie Jahoda was a leading psychologist who was frequently cited in the professional literature. She suggested that, "mentally healthy individuals should be oriented toward the future and efficient in problem solving. They should be resistant to stress and perceive reality without distortion. They should possess empathy and be able to love and to play as well as to work. They should remain in touch with their own feelings. In short, they should manifest anticipation, suppression, altruism, humor, and sublimation."[30]

• From Erich Fromm we have a framing that places the well-functioning individual in a context of relationships with other people, and by his use of the concept *democratic* a description that also reminds us of the connection between personal psychological health and a sane society: "The truly democratic . . . character . . . will refuse both to dominate and to be dominated. For the democratic character the equality and dignity of man are deeply felt imperatives, and such a character will be drawn only to what promotes human dignity and equality."[31]

Taken separately and together, these fine thinkers (and many others in psychology, psychiatry, social work, and additional mental health disciplines) give as the major goal of psychotherapy an ability to live a good life for oneself and with other people, competently, creatively, and decently.

I would add a reminder that life is also very difficult. Even at its best, aging is no picnic, and one's inevitable, ultimate death in many ways is crushing. Moreover, and sadly probably more to the point, many people suffer grave difficulties in their normal existential passage through life. My understanding is that a majority of human beings endure at different times in their lives some of the following personal crises:
• economic privation
• social discrimination
• grievous personal losses
• major developmental and health problems
• trust-shattering traumas
• disloyalty and betrayal by loved ones and personal associates
• bureaucratic horrors and sadism
• historical imperatives of the hells of wars and genocides

I therefore suggest that we add to the goals of psychotherapy a relative ability to live with enormous pain, loss, grief, worry, and stress, from around us and from within.

Depth psychotherapy posited a long time ago that there is at the core of every human being an empty center, meaning a nothingness, and that we all fall short of the evident challenges of our lives, and suffer major personal limitations and continuing vulnerability. But it is also the truth of our being that the reality we experience in life is so huge and majestic that none of us can possibly encompass it, neither can we do justice to life's many-faceted invitations and challenges.[32]

I suggest that especially in regard to the inevitable major stresses of life, we are all challenged:

to yield and accept stress;

AND

to cope with stress and work at improving our lot
as well as we can.

I therefore conclude that whenever possible, the goals of psychotherapy also include the following beautiful experiences, including their built-in contradictions:

• to yield to one's inevitable personal empty center, or human short-comings and vulnerability, honorably, both in humility and with courage: for example, to do one's best to overcome and compensate for lacks and faults (which also goes a long way to gain the appreciation of many of the people hurt by our faults);

• to accept one's being as forever flawed, yet at the same time to celebrate one's beauty and remarkable wholeness;

• to accept one's illnesses and health challenges without denial and yield to necessary treatment and needs for rest and recuperation, while at the same time also fighting hard for one's health and life (doctors and science have long since confirmed that fighting for life makes a difference);

• to experience profound gratitude and awe at the miracle of life and its opportunities for pleasure, joy, and peace, and to do our best to cope with distress and pressure at times of adversity;

• to embrace celebrating and living one's life with vitality, and at the same time to be humble in the face of the gift and mystery of life and its enormous problems for all of us.

It should be emphasized that the underlying and key process-meaning in the above is that mentally healthy living includes an ability to encompass or contain dialectical or contradictory psychological processes in oneself virtually all the time.

Finally, notwithstanding the profound awareness and acceptance of dialectical contradictions, I want to be sure that we don't promote a romanticized version of life and end up expressing a saccharine gratitude for cancers and Auchwitzes, and so I add explicitly that our emotional goals include:

the rights to grieve, wail, protest, curse, and fight back
in self-defense against one's enemies, and even against
one's gods who have betrayed us.

The above goals are also for other human beings on whom we impact to achieve. Life becomes a spiritual commitment to our own welfares, and then to the welfares of other human beings.

To conclude, for me psychotherapy is not intended to help us become entirely free of anxiety, depression, and distress; nor should it be a fake instant overcoming of disappointment, loss, or tragedy; nor should it promise or even seek entirely wholesome marriages or family life or sexual vitality; psychology also should not become a medically-authorized medication-trip into always feeling good; or any other sure-fire method of happiness and self-fulfillment. Psychotherapy for me is learning and improving abilities to love life and be decent people to ourselves and other people – to enjoy all that can be enjoyable in life, and to cope as well as possible with all that is problematic and grievous in life.[33]

CHAPTER NINE

Discovering Applications of Democratic Mind in Everyday Life

How much knowledge is there regarding how a person can best use his or her mind in everyday life? Are there implications for everyday life in the methodology of good psychotherapy?

In psychotherapy, patients enjoy an amazing degree of freedom of thought, feeling, and speech in the therapist's presence. But how much can a person also strive for experiencing their thoughts and feelings by himself or herself? What do we know about the most desirable "operating system" for the basic functions of our mind's experiencing, thinking, feeling, and awareness?

I suggest that an application of psychotherapy to the creative use of mind in everyday living lies in an acceptance of the never-ending associative flow of multiple experiences, thoughts, and feelings in our mind as it continuously screens for the meanings, dangers, and creative possibilities in our life.

It is wondrous to recognize that we have a phenomenal "computer system" in our minds. Someone or other has produced a great model of a computer for the human species! Our mind is at work 24 hours a day, when we are awake and when we are asleep, reviewing the information that enters through the senses. It is capable not only of amazing feats of logical assembly and sorting of data, but also is constantly monitoring the relationship between ourselves and our reality in order to protect against dangers and to enhance and enrich life experiences.

Healthy applications of a DEMOCRATIC MIND in everyday life include: being alert to incoming information and stimulation, feeling what is happening rather than existing passively, feeling different emotions in appropriate responses to events in our lives, and an exploration of new and creative possibilities for redefining and recreating ourselves. An active, well-functioning mind is also devoted to critical quality control used for correcting errors and for turning off any aspect of our machinery that gets out of hand. In a democratically oriented mind, all this takes place within a value framework of overriding respect and appreciation for the sacredness of life, beginning with one's own life and continuing on to other people's.

"Free-Associative" Use of One's Mind and Accepting the Anything That Comes Up in Our Minds

Freud's creation of the free-association technique was in effect a tapping into an existing part of human nature; namely, that our minds are continuously and tirelessly at work registering information about us and our environments, monitoring and checking out potential dangers, registering our true desires, ideas, and emotional reactions, and ceaselessly exploring new possibilities and innovations – all in a marvelous mosaic of a brilliant creative process.

Freud instructed his patients to speak aloud and to tell themselves as well as the therapist all that was going on in their mind. Anyone who has undergone psychoanalytic treatment and has successfully learned to use the method of free association (not everyone succeeds) knows that it is a hopeless task; we immediately acknowledge that the richness of mind activity is so overwhelming, at so many levels, that no matter how hard we try, we can only partially report mind experiences. The thoughts, feelings, and pictorial representations are so rich and plentiful and so amazingly fast moving, one frame following the other in great rapidity, that no matter how fast we speak we cannot keep up with the mind-products. In the process, we sort and select the most important or immediately relevant mind products. This is not the same as sacrificing truth and authenticity, nor is it censorship and concealment. The selection process can be used as a cover for concealing what we don't want to tell our therapist or ourselves, and sometimes this is what a patient does. But patients generally also sense prevarication and concealment, and thereby have a further opportunity not only to go back and tell the truth about their inner knowledge but also to confront which subject they were lying about. Free association is an opportunity to confront emotions and to determine whether to conceal something or to be forthright – and to what extent. The best patients – the most successful learners of the technique and the most committed to the opportunity for probing a wide range of self – sense quite quickly that tuning into the rapid flow of inner experience is not easy or automatic. The skill requires practice and development, and is based on a spiritual decision and commitment to meet the truth. In our everyday lives, we become so accustomed to not being in contact with our inner selves that a whole world of learning is needed in order to install a machinery for being able to turn on inner contact.

Enjoying Experiencing the Anything of the Various Parts of Ourselves

There is, moreover, a contradiction at the core of our inner selves. On the one hand, if we cannot bear making contact with our various "unacceptable" parts, we are forced to split them off and not register them, which means we resist and suppress awareness of these parts when they do turn up in the natural flow of experiences. On the other hand, we can be flooded by inner experiences if we allow uncontrolled access to everything in our minds without monitoring and controlling what we will admit into consciousness and what we won't, and choosing what we will place in the working agendas of our minds and what we will put aside. Without sorting and selecting, we are going to be, variously, flooded or poisoned by the intensity, depravity, and madness of the "primary process" (the technical name in psychology for the bedrock of our mind) of thoughts and emotions taking place inside our minds, which includes every possible mad thought and impulse that human beings can imagine.

In the material that follows in this chapter, I will be talking about regulatory devices that prevent being flooded and poisoned. The concept of self-regulation of mind makes us realize that we have to run the mind with a certain kind of managerial skill, or it can produce bad thoughts and feelings that run wild. But what is less clear to people is that regulation is the other side of a coin that includes trying to stay in tune with what is going on inside rather than posting sentries and guards who exclude ideas and feelings from awareness. To achieve relaxation, one must learn to tolerate and embrace any and all of the thoughts, feelings, and impulses – even magical and spiritual-type experiences – that can occur any time of the day or night, at whatever level of conscious or unconscious experience.

> ໃ Some young people who have never had marijuana – which is a mild psychedelic or mood-changing substance when not overused – experience a severe emotional reaction and sometimes a psychotic breakdown even after their first experience with marijuana. Perhaps there is a physiological explanation in some cases; there are people who are severely allergic to any substance. In these cases the mental breakdown would be an expression of a person's physiological intolerance of the substance. But the cases of psychotic breakdowns I have seen led me to another conclusion: these young people were in no way ready for the bumps and grinds of the different kinds of mental experiences the marijuana set off, and in effect the marijuana exposed their preexisting psychological vulnerability to emotional intensity or to certain kinds of ideas and emotions unleashed that they had no idea how to tolerate and contain.

It has been observed that to be human is to be and think and feel the *everything* we know to occur in human experience.[1] In other words, there is at least a little – a taste or touch – of every known human experience inherent or waiting in everyone. There is a loving, searching, bright, ethical, involved, humane person inside everyone. And there is a dumb jerk, freak madman, zealot, uncaring, cruel and sadistic, impulsive rapist, arsonist, criminal, or murderer waiting inside everyone as well. The goals we set determine which directions we will go in our development and behavior.[2] Our choices determine the extent to which we will or won't be responsive to various messages and stimuli from inside that can be calling us to fine, humane behaviors or to ugly and unacceptable behaviors. Some people really never will rape even when the impulse is riding high and the opportunity lends itself, and never will murder another human being even when a desire to do so is high, and never will respond to the orders of military commanders or government bureaucrats who send them on genocidal missions to destroy an unarmed target people.

The control of impulses is determined by the moral choices we make, but is also a function of being able to bear registration of the very impulses we have to control. Scientific evidence has shown that insofar as one is cut off – split off – from a powerful impulse, there is all the more possibility that impulse will break through and override existing moral convictions in a person's mind to erupt in their behavior.

This is the meaning of Somerset Maugham's story about the minister who dissociated from his sexual impulses, which were then manifested one torrid tropical night when he raped a woman he coveted.[3]

This is the meaning also of research that shows there is a significant number of murderers who are unable to tolerate images of aggression and normal "I want to kill you" thoughts in their minds, which makes them more vulnerable to needing to act out their impulses when a time comes that they are flooded by desires to kill someone else.[4]

On more common levels of everyday life, many social embarrassments occur when we are humiliated and ashamed because we end up revealing something inside that we were trying to conceal even from ourselves – such as jealousy, competitiveness, undue submissiveness to someone we admire in a way that bespeaks our lack of confidence in ourselves, hidden sexual desires, or what have you. We get caught with our pants further down in the public or social situation the more we try to hide the emotional state we were in to begin with.

The capacity to experience the *anything* of our various parts is an important skill needed to organize our minds. It is a skill that must be learned. Many shocks and crises arise as we discover how complex our inner world is. Most people accommodate by invoking censorship and prohibitions of various thoughts and emotions, and the system works even at the cost of a loss of spontaneity, naturalness, and fun. Other people do not work out such limitations, and one sees them sliding into excesses, errors, and disasters. Many artists, for example, have trouble regulating themselves. By definition, the artist is open to a wide range of creative ideas, but like everyone else artists must question whether this openness will flood them with excessive emotions, such as uncontrollable erotic impulses or other demands for gratification that can lead to excessive drinking and drugs, unstable relationships, and poor health management.

The desired solution lies in a combination of acceptance of one's impulses and an ability to contain and regulate one's impulses. It is a joy to encounter people who have put together a reasonably solid organization of themselves that combines an acceptance of the different sides of their emotions and a capacity to inhibit excesses and immoral choices. Some people are lucky enough to be guided into this way of life by healthy and wholesome parents. Others luckily find their guides in good teachers, coaches, trainers, clergymen, or therapists. Some people take over creatively and teach themselves how to be responsibly free in their minds.

It is a pleasure to see graduates of psychotherapy who achieve this kind of maturity and are capable of being good self-managers. With the help of a good psychotherapeutic experience, one comes closer to the flows of the erotic, aggressive, ambitious, selfish, and what not inside, and one comes to sound conclusions about how to monitor and pace these emotions within a framework of a decent life program.

Historically, some psychotherapies have erred in either direction. Some therapies split off the wild and raw primary process from sufficient inhibitory control and let too much of a person's impulses be expressed. Other therapies go too far toward inhibiting impulses and the raw energies of primitive desires so that a person ends up too managed and overcontrolled. Thus, there was a long period in the beginning of psychoanalysis in which graduates of the new medium of treatment were described by observers as rude, gauche, overly aggressive, and even nasty, because they were so involved with being in touch with the flow of their primary impulses they were downright insulting, selfish, and nasty to other people. Yet people in therapies that have emphasized control of their impulses and behaviors without also putting them in touch with the naturalness and legitimacy of the inner whispers of the witches and monsters resident in their beings can be stiffly correct and pompously mentally healthy, as it were, because there is no fun in them.

An ironic variation on the theme involves therapists who have learned procedures for bringing people into touch with their unconscious, which is the mission of the therapy they practice, but the therapists themselves conduct the therapeutic engagement of these inner impulses so dryly, mirthlessly, and without real affection for the fountainheads of human experience they are helping the patient encounter that the therapy becomes tedious and ritualistic.

A well-known and much admired psychoanalyst knew how to talk a good game of the intellectual constructs of psychological theory and was in much demand as a speaker, but in truth he was so cut off from his own real inner world of impulses and from his own erotic feelings that his life was a sham. Psychologically terrified by a possessive mother in his childhood, he had grown up to compensate in academic excellence and in the application of his fine intellectual skills to his chosen profession. He ended up twice with insulting, nonsupportive women who knew and exploited his inner identity as a slave to women. His first wife betrayed him repeatedly and then threw him out. After a flurry of the usual loving experiences at the beginning of his second marriage, his second wife informed him she was no longer interested in sexual contact, which she interpreted as debasing and enslaving the woman. He was so terrified of being left again – for all of the meanings this had for him – that he surrendered and became the accommodating and forever appeasing husband.

Since even this system did not remove all unpleasant tensions between the couple, including periodic black despairs of the wife, which she cast accusingly on her hapless enslaved husband ("It's your fault that I am feeling so terrible"), the couple did come for a brief period of marital therapy, but it was unsuccessful. Any efforts of the therapist to evoke the individuality of the psychoanalyst-husband were met with contempt and rage by the wife and with abject fear by the husband. The therapy was terminated and the husband continued to pour himself successfully into his practice.

The Ability to Turn Off the Flow of Our Inner
Mind Associations: Using the "Switch"

It is also important to develop a means by which to turn off any overly intense contact with our inner worlds in order to carry on effectively with the routine tasks of life.

❧ *When I was a patient in psychoanalysis as a young man in my late twenties, I found myself so shook up by contacting parts of my unconscious that it seemed impossible to go on the rest of the day with my work as a psychologist in a children's psychiatric hospital following my therapy session which took place very early in the morning. The emotional shocks of recognizing unbelievably painful and frightening as well as ugly parts of my inner world threatened to keep me a prisoner all day following the session. The work days looming ahead of me at the hospital where I worked were terrifying enough in their own right for me as a young practitioner, and now the further flooding of feelings and thoughts spilling over in my mind from my analytic sessions left me bedazzled and actually terrified at times.*

One day when I was very upset by my therapy session, the concept of a simple electric switch for turning lights on and off came to me as a metaphor for what I might possibly be able to do with the emotional currents racing through me. I decided I would try to instruct my mind to turn off the intensity of my memory of the session, and that I would direct my full attention and self to what lay ahead of me at work. It worked! I found myself getting through my workday more easily. More than that, I was learning an important tool for self-management at all times, namely, that there were amazing possibilities for self-regulation available inside of me. This kind of turning off thoughts and feelings was not censorship, denial, or escape so long as it was the other side of the coin of my also being ready to tune into my inner world, which I was exercising regularly.

Over the years, I have taught my patients this concept of "the switch" to gain control of themselves, whether at the end of a powerful therapy session, or at any time in their lives when they are in the midst of an emotional or spiritual storm that is flooding them, and they need to get on with whatever normal and routine parts of their lives.

❧ *A lovely young woman who suffered intense bouts of anxiety and depression was unable to complete the major project required for graduation in her last year of college. Only after advising the college that she would postpone the project and her graduation for a year was she able to continue with the rest of her classes and requirements. But she also resolved now in therapy that she would learn how to stop such overwhelming tides of distress and bad feelings.*

"I tried to think how I could handle the situation differently," she explained about the way she approached another project a few weeks after she had given up on the graduation project.

"There I was again starting to worry about what to do just like I used to worry about the graduation project and others before that. I knew the routine, and that if I didn't catch it I would become more and more worried until I would be unable to do anything, and obviously the same thing would happen again to this project. I decided that this time I would stop thinking about my worries and simply go and resume doing my project and let myself be carried along by my feelings in the project rather than my worry."

"I really enjoyed myself," she concluded with a heartwarming smile.

A Quiet Mindfulness of Associativeness When Not Focusing Actively on One's Free Associations

There is a way of staying quietly and sensitively in touch with the hum of our inner minds even when we are busy at other tasks, although there is no question that a more concentrated devotion to listening to ourselves more fully as in concentrated free association gives a better opportunity to touch our more complex and fearsome parts. But there is also a considerable value to listening for the sounds of our inner minds even when we are busy with routine activities.

Messages are being sent from inside all the time. Stop and listen, and be amazed at the small voices and thoughts that we can choose to be aware of. These inner experiences are being broadcast and are bouncing toward us even when we are busy. The truly amazing feature of our "mind computers" is that if we consciously choose not to be aware of these experiences, they nonetheless will continue to be fed into and processed by various parts of our minds. Later they will surface in a variety of ways, including possibly triggering behaviors that express these thoughts. We can bring many of these thoughts into our awareness if, at any given point, we stop to take time to pay attention to our inner selves. A free-associative jet stream of facts, ideas, feelings, analyses of information, and pictorial representations of our lives is present at all times and available to whatever degree we choose.[5]

Accepting and Containing the Many Different Parts of Ourselves

It is all there inside. Among the parts of our minds that we will look at now briefly are our fears, anger, hate and murderous feelings, caring and loving, and feelings of contradiction, confusion, and uncertainty, and experiences of tension and anxiety.

As noted earlier, the trick is not to remove any of these aspects of our human experience. The proper goal of mind is not to be completely fearless – as, for example, in the case history that follows that describes a man who chose this path only to have his unconscious fearfulness, which is a part in all of us that can never be excised completely, drive him into a sequence of behaviors that caused him trouble. Nor is the reasonable and healthy goal of our minds to remove all anger, hate, and murderous feelings; people who attempt to do so may end up all the more poisoned when their inner minds become "dirtier" with the unprocessed sewage of their angers and hates. Nor should mind aspire to give up longing for and needing another person. On the surface one gains the security of not being hurt and rejected when not asking for caring and connection with others, but can end up much too alone and vulnerable and even need to be rescued by others. Even unpleasant mental conditions of being confused and uncertain cannot and should not be removed from our minds. An acceptance of not having all the answers and of periodically finding ourselves unable to rise to a challenge brings us all the more to enlist resources waiting inside for creating new ideas and initiatives that we never would have explored and discovered were it not for our painful inability to deal with a situation.

What comes up in the free association of our minds? *Everything.* To restate what I said earlier, all that is human is possible and present in all of us.

All the parts of our humanness are human. To yield to them, and to learn to admire and enjoy the upsetting and dysphoric and disabling parts of ourselves as aspects of human symphony, is a path from which more pleasurable and even more heroic symphonies and greater mastery of difficult challenges seems to be generated. But we need to know that our mind products are experiences to be processed and not concrete representations of an immutable reality. Our thoughts and feelings are important events in our mindfulness, but at any given moment are not necessarily true, complete, or final maps of reality. The ability to treat one's inner products as a process of experiences and not as factual becomes an essential function of a healthy mind.[6]

Accepting and Containing Fears

Even the bravest have deep fears.

An older man, a top executive, had always taken pride in being fearless. This highly developed aspect of his self-image had served him well. He was a capable manager of his personal and business life, a leader in the community, and he had been a brave soldier when fighting for the defense of his country.

Did he know that, while being so fearless, he was in fact terrified by his wife's dominating and insulting him?

No.

It was a bad unstated joke of his life: this big sure-of-himself executive was led around by his nose by his wife's sharp-mouthed comments and criticisms, and he was so busy making himself appear fearless and unruffled that he didn't know he couldn't stand it. Not knowing he was afraid, he also didn't know he was angry. Not knowing both of these things about himself, he could only huff and puff in pretensions of overcoming her bad-

mouthing of him as "a wife's nonsense," and the wife's nasty remarks in turn only increased with the years.

One day this dignified and important man made a very bad move: he succumbed to an open-and-shut sexual ambush by a woman employee. The woman's come-on was so obvious that he never should have touched her, but apparently here too he couldn't see what a woman was doing to him. All hell now broke loose as the woman and her husband who had together planned the ambush pressed him for money to keep quiet; and no less hell broke loose when the important executive's wife now learned of the sordid incident.

Needless to say, he came to therapy very upset. Under the gun of the threats by the scheming other woman to make a public scandal and bring legal charges against him for sexual abuse, he was motivated in therapy to learn how to experience and use the emotions he had denied for so long. In therapy he began to learn how to feel both afraid of and angry with his wife for her insulting remarks in their everyday conversations. Slowly but surely he also learned how to address his wife with measured and firm statements of his displeasure in response to her attacks.

Even so, he first had to go through falling a second time for a second woman, who was actually a cohort of the first, who laid a similar seductive entrapment. In the final analysis, he pulled himself together to counterattack and beat off both of the entrapping women, and went on to complete learning how he, the ostensibly unafraid and not-angry man, could effectively address his wife about how he was hurt, upset, and angry whenever he felt insulted by her. In turn, the change in his manner also was effective in getting his wife to stop her insults.

Characteristically, the greatest fear in our universal human experience is likely to be that of dying. In the universal machinery of mind, even brave men suffer a degree of fearfulness of dying and moving toward the unknown infinity of nonbeing if only in regret at having to end the too-brief marvel of existence. In any case, dying becomes a major subject for the acceptance and containment of fears. Through the centuries, philosophers have taught us that a key, if not the essential goal of wisdom and philosophy, is to accept our fears of dying as our best way of reducing our fears and coping with the inevitable reality of the end of our lives.

Thus, the French philosopher Pascal proposed epigrammatically that "philosophizing means learning how to die,"[7] which means preparing for death not in resignation but in acceptance of its naturalness and inevitability, and thus reducing unnecessary fear.

Accepting and Containing Anger, Hate, and Murderous Feelings

The range of anger in our minds is endless, including periodic wishes to eliminate and destroy any number of our closest and most beloved ones. At any point, there is in our minds a list of relatives, associates, colleagues, and neighbors, including people with whom we enjoy our finest relationships in addition to those who are our real enemies, that we quite naturally want to – kill.

> The beloved psychiatrist, Carl Whitaker, used to say that he carried in his shirt pocket a list of the eight people he most wished to have die.
>
> When Whitaker was about 70 years old, he was giving a workshop in which he commented wryly, "Oh, I've neglected my list. Several of the people on my list are gone. I need to remember to replace their names with others."[8]

Killing is the imagery at the end of a continuum of angers that includes a fascinating range of emotions: criticism, dislike, distaste, disagreement, anger, conflict, rejection, hostility, hatred, venom, revenge, and more. Already in the minds of little children there are flashing images of obliterating, destroying, and killing the objects of one's anger, including one's otherwise beloved parent. "I wish you were dead," a child may say to a parent; another may have a shocking vivid dream expressing the wish and not talk about it but remember it forever.

Understandably, many good people in Western civilization have eschewed the "negative feelings" of anger and hate. They impose on themselves a discipline of suppressing hate, and they teach this philosophy to their own children and to others in religious and educational settings. Our world has seen hundreds of millions of unwarranted deaths of human beings at the hands of other people. The fearsome pain, brutality, and losses of the right to live that abound everywhere on our planet lead many decent people to want to cultivate only the positive and loving emotions. It takes philosophical and psychological sophistication and wisdom to realize that the problem with anger is not solvable by attempting to exorcise it and to destroy its very existence in our natures, for that is impossible. A Jewish legend tells of the rabbis of the Great Assembly who wanted to get rid of the Evil Impulse. They secured God's agreement to imprison the Evil Impulse for a trial period. After three days of this experiment, with all evil having been removed from human affairs, the chastened rabbis discovered that no chicken had laid an egg. The necessary conclusion was that so long as the Evil Impulse was not a natural part of life, there could be no life, and therefore that the Evil Impulse had to be released and allowed to play its natural part in human affairs.[9]

Anger rises whenever we are hurt, insulted, thwarted, or frustrated. Moreover, it is intrinsically right that this is so. People learn to tap the flow of their anger for a variety of constructive actions: self-assertiveness, healthy competition, efforts at solving problems, expression of anger to loved ones in order to resolve problems and create better relationships, use of anger to contain the aggressiveness of enemies, and more.

A mind at peace with itself allows the registration of a full range of angry emotions. For example, dreams of something terrible happening to people whom we care about but at whom we are angry do not need to be terrifying when we learn to contain or accept the naturalness of angry feelings. At the same time, our minds need to assess in each case whether or not our anger is fair or unfair, and whether or not our anger is a worthwhile or ill-advised emotion. Based on our decisions, we take control and manage our subsequent experiences. For example, say a person dreams of a parent dying in which they covet inheriting the wealth and possessions of the parent. On the one hand, acceptance of the naturalness of such covetous desires can better enable us to take responsibility for this part of ourselves, which is an impulse that has characterized humans from time immemorial. On the other hand, we will do best to renounce such desires for the deaths of people who have their own rights to live, and to renounce our crass desires to gain inheritances as impulses that violate our spiritual decency.

If at first management of our hate through its simultaneous acceptance and control is a painful intellectual-emotional exercise, those who master management of these emotions in time find that the process becomes a friendly, welcome, and even joyous experience.

It is fun to be angry to an extent.

It can be releasing of tension to hate one's enemies to an extent, and to enjoy some thoughts and fantasies of murdering one's truly hated enemies.

There is a sense of mastery in simultaneously accepting and containing angry impulses and submitting them to a larger effort to build a constructive and nonviolent lifestyle in which we disarm explosive emotions and replace them with happier, loving, emotions.

It becomes a dance, with the music and rhythms of enjoying impulses and their mastery in a beautiful flow that brings both power and joy to one's heart.

As a basic system for releasing angry feelings I have adopted a mode of purposeful meditation on one's anger toward selected other people. In this meditation one happily imagines (but does not at all plan to do in any actual way in reality) whatever aggressive acts one wishes toward the other; in clear distinction to violent acts against others that are clearly forbidden, the purpose of the fantasy is a healthy release of emotions.

I give the other person a glancing smack on the face. I punch the other person. I shoot them. I knife them. I create ludicrous situations for them to fall over themselves. It is all my game – a mind game.

But I also hold myself to this game's guiding criteria and rules. One rule is that in my fantasies the release of anger needs to be joyous, heartening, and fun rather than morbid, nasty, or vicious. A second guiding rule is that use of this method has to be limited to a measure of "good taste," which means the release of aggression should not be used too often, or too intensely, and certainly not at the expense of other constructive ideas, emotions, and behaviors . In other words, not only is there a distinction between angry feelings and actions, there is also a requirement that the psychology of emotional expression of anger is in the service of decency. The use of the angry fantasies is for release of feelings accepted as parts of oneself and should not to become an overriding psychological preoccupation.

In psychotherapy with my patients, I often teach the above method. It is at first frightening. It also takes time to learn. Most people don't have the slightest notion of how to enjoy using their angry fantasies. A major emotional lesson teaches that to have angry feelings is not at all the same as taking action against someone; a major ethical lesson teaches that the commission of acts as envisioned is invariably wrong (except in true self-defense). The combination of both lessons is vital for the management of angry emotions.

Many therapists prefer to resolve the causes of angers, in other words to remove the frustrations that develop so that there will be no reason to be angry. Many psychological theories hold that anger is a statement of an inability or a failure to achieve a goal, and that when angry one should redouble efforts to arrive at a constructive expression of innate talent and ambition, rather than be angry. These conceptions of anger as admissions of failure to achieve and manage well in life are, in my opinion, denials of anger as an aspect of humanness that should not be denied, but that should be dealt with effectively and enjoyably. Furthermore, these theories are part of a pleasure-seeking psychology that overpromises happiness, freedom from pain, and complexity, and is in denial of the many aspects of "badness" in human nature. It is a Western pap, opiate, and superficiality that brings little credit to psychology as a more serious science of the mind.

The distinguished psychologist Hans Toch has written of the wisdom of Seneca, a Roman philosopher-educator-statesman around 4 BCE–65 CE, who composed a three-volume treatise on ire or rage, *De ira. Ira* is the process sparked by resentment of a perceived injury, hurt, or affront. Seneca was sensitive to the value of anger as differentiated from cruelty or excesses of anger. He gave explicit instructions on how people should work at reducing their excessive anger, including cultivating "insights into our shared capacity to inflict harm," "modeling a calm demeanor," "encourage[ment of] behavior that is constructively competitive," but also "playing along with verbal aggression." In other words, Seneca's 4th century advice is to use one's aggression, but constructively, wisely, and peacefully.[10]

Accepting and Containing Caring and Loving

In many people the positive, caring, and loving emotions also are driven underground. Many people are afraid to love, and are afraid to desire or long to love, for fear that they will end up being rejected. Traumatic experiences of not being wanted and loved, which many have experienced, leave people suspended in a never-never land where they cannot love themselves and firmly believe that they will never again be loved by others. The rejection in the past plus the anticipation of further rejection in the future are so spirit-shattering that an even more powerful unconscious decision is made not to take any risks of loving or showing a longing to love ever again. Succumbing to this pattern of self-defense can devolve into a life-long solitariness. It can also spread to other aspects of life; for example, to a reluctance or inability to accept compliments or caring statements from others. One can also learn to fear being loved after being the object of overpossessive love, depressive love, or any other perversity that precludes feeling safe and joyous when being loved.

> ❧ He is a charming, interesting, and good-natured man in his early 30s who apparently can't make a connection with a woman. He gets properly attracted and aroused, and does perfectly well initiating the dance of inviting the woman to go out with him. But then, inevitably, everything inside becomes convinced the woman is not attracted to him, and he pulls away prematurely. In therapy he reveals that his father was chronically critical of him, and that his beloved mother who loved him very much sighed and bemoaned the ills of life and the moral foibles and peccadilloes of everyone she encountered. In effect, he had been trained that love was a condition in which all his weaknesses would be exposed to a woman's endless probing.

Millions of long-term conflictual couples live out marriages of chronic desperation because, unconsciously, they agree to protect each other from love and kindness. What never ceases to amaze me in the therapy of such couples is that for all the discomfort and suffering they experience and sincerely want to get rid of, they have often a joined in a mutual defense pact against loving and caring feelings, which they fear more than their pain, and believe it or not, they often secretly appreciate each other for cooperating in this pact. The couple's mutual fears of trying to love and then being devastated by rejection outweigh their upset at being in chronic conflict.

They were both academics, advanced in their respective fields, and at their core they were decent people. Yet neither wasted an opportunity to take a punch at the other with sharp-tongued criticism and disapproval of whatever, and also criticism and disapproval of the other's character and existence. Yet there was no question that they did not want to divorce – and if and when a day would come that they would have to break up, even then it still would not mean they really wanted to leave each other.

In marital therapy, they persisted in what seemed an endless process. This was their life. In truth, each one was protected from the scars of their early neglect and rejection by their parents because they had the other to blame and to use as a punching bag.

"Would you say something complimentary or appreciative to your spouse," the therapist asked in one session.

They each smiled – a wan, hurt, ironical look on each of their faces. "I don't like doing that," said the husband, and then shrugged: "Besides, what is there good that I could say about her?"

"You see," said the wife triumphantly, "What point is there to my saying anything nice to a man like this?"

They looked at each other in hate, but to the therapist, it seemed that their eyes were also meeting in mutual understanding and an appreciation that bordered on secret loving.

Accepting and Containing Contradiction, Criticalness, Confusion, and Uncertainty

The mind holds contradiction and confusion. From adolescence on, there are new levels of complexity, including a progressive development of negative feelings and critical thought that are applied to the previously holy cows of our unquestioned childish love for our parents, siblings, community, nation, our religious faith, or whatever once-sacred ideology, belief system ,or identification.

Unfortunately, rarely are teenagers taught that openness to questioning and criticism is a movement toward becoming a more whole adult person. A mature combination of independent thinking and being loving and loyal gives a person an ability to look critically and see what is wrong and undesirable in a loved one or a beloved ideology, and at the same time an ability to continue caring for, loving, identifying with, and being loyal to the same people – or families and communities, or values and institutions. For many people, the challenge of mixing critical and angry feelings with love and identification with a person or movement can constitute mental health and spiritual crises. Clearly, a balanced and mature acceptance of the beauty and wisdom of one's beloveds together with recognition of their limitations is a preferred basis for being able to contribute and grow in a relationship.

"The more you know, the more you realize that you don't know very much," is a statement one hears from the best thinkers, scientists, and practitioners in many fields.

As humans enter the 21st century armed with knowledge and skills that were not even dreamed of a hundred years ago, it is clear that if we proceed with the changes we are setting in motion with science and technology, we will soon have a planet that is unrecognizable on many different levels. Given cloning and genetic engineering, for two examples, we may soon live alongside of or become part of a dramatically reengineered species. Given the development of tools of mass destruction, we may soon have created spaces on this planet that are not inhabitable (and some fear we may actually destroy life entirely on the planet).

It is also clear that we know little and in a sense actually nothing about our place in a universe that has proven to be increasingly limitless and indefinable. We do not know if we will be in the pathway of a falling meteor that may do untold damage to life on earth. We understand very little about the vastness of black holes in space and what they bode for our futures. We know nothing about the relationship of our species and way of life to possible other species with whom we may soon be in contact and how the contact may impact on the existence of our species.

In an ultimate sense, we already do know that our planet and we are not going to be here forever. The cosmic dimensions of contradiction, confusion, and uncertainty are overwhelming. Were we only to accept that each of us is a creature living in the face of these awesome monumental mysteries, we have reason enough to conclude that healthy minds need to have mechanisms for accepting and containing the fact that much in this world is unknown and uncertain.

In "plain" everyday life too, the more you know about life, the more humble you become about how much is not in our control at all. For those who are believers in the "churches" of mental health, one might comment that even if you have graduated from the best program of psychotherapy in the world, you still are not in a position to manage your health, marriage, the development of each of your children, or the fate of your community, society, nation, and more. It is a rough ride for just about everyone.

Nonetheless, each of the challenging and problematic situations that arise require us to take stands and choose a course of action. A combination of an ability to take charge on the one hand, and humility and acceptance of our fate on the other hand is constantly being demanded of us.

Many painfully worrying and disappointing situations arise in which we are called on to take care of and stand by damaged children who need our wisdom, love, and encouragement in order to live out their potential – in too many cases these also include limitations that cannot be overcome but need to be accepted. In the most grievous cases this means accompanying some of our dear children to their premature deaths. In happier cases of problems that can attain successful and even creative resolutions, there can be long periods of not knowing what is the right thing to do, and how well or poorly all will work out.

Under all these circumstances, the capacity to contain within us and live with the unknown is a vital aspect of being able to know. The ability to incorporate contradiction and uncertainty within choices of direction is essential if one does not want to be paralyzed into inaction or passivity. For example, it seems that new methods and strategies cannot be introduced without the risks of trying and failing.

"How can I let him know that I love him if I'm not sure that he really wants me?" she explains to the marriage counselor.

"That's my point," explains the husband. "I just don't get any signals from her whatsoever that she really wants me. She's like going through a routine of behaving correctly with me, but isn't really there for me."

Nothing adds up in the case. According to all existing criteria in the profession, the child is doomed to autism, and the parents need to place him in a hospital or school for autistic children, which is what the child's pediatrician requested in the referral. But the therapist is haunted by a feeling that despite the fact the 4.6-year-old boy is still not speaking – he's also wetting and defecating like a baby all day and shows all the typical signs of repetitive autistic circular movements – amazingly he is putting out nonverbal signals of a good energy, and might be able to grow far more than can be seen in his manifest condition.

Does the therapist have the right to offer a more ambitious treatment?

It will take so long to know what the outcome is likely to be, it will take so much investment of the parents' time and effort and hopes, and it will take financial investment.[11]

On the personal level, each of our primary relationships suffers contradictory emotions and attitudes. For there is no unadulterated pure acceptance and love without any concern, regret, frustration, criticism, dislike, anger, repugnance, rejection, and more. A capacity to love needs to include a capacity to bear and make use of contradictory emotions and to endure the apparent confusion that results. Similarly, continuity of existence requires an acceptance of ourselves as periodically weak, ill, at times seriously ill, and also of our failures to achieve the distinction and excellence we desired, acceptance of our mediocrity in many things, and our vulnerability, incompetence, and unknowing. For most, there is no respite. The many who don't "succeed" have reason to look enviously at those who rose to the top. But many of those who succeed had still bigger dreams and plans they never managed to fulfill. Some of those who rise to the highest conceivable positions of self-expression and success will have their careers ended by public rejection and humiliation, their weaknesses exposed mercilessly, their career-summarizing books panned, and their lives summed up as failures. Some of their children may hate them, and their bodies may betray them with illnesses and ailments. Being human is not for sissies (a take-off from the common observation among older people that being old is not for sissies).

Accepting and Welcoming Concern, Tension, and Anxiety
and Transforming Them into Their Creative Potential

The free-associative flow inevitably brings with it many streams of concern, tension, and anxiety that are waiting inside our minds. As I note throughout this book, and paraphrasing President Franklin D. Roosevelt, the trick is not to fear being afraid but to accept and welcome the anxiety within.

I teach my patients who are suffering anxiety to look for angry feelings and wishes in their minds that may be causing their anxiety, and to understand that whenever one feels blocked in the use of one's real potential there is a natural and also perfectly desirable anger that surfaces. Accepting this anger and linking it to the wishes to be better may help give us a push to go forward toward our authentic selves. [12]

> *"It is true that feeling anxious makes you feel uncomfortable, and there is a natural instinct of wanting to get rid of this discomfort," explained the therapist. "But what I want you to know is that this anxiety is saying to you that there are bigger and finer things in you that are wanting to develop as more pronounced parts of your personality. If you welcome the essence of your anxiety as the call of your unused talent within, you may find yourself moving from some of the discomfort to a kind of inspiration and an energy for taking on new initiatives that in time will make you feel very good."*

Accepting anxiety as a signal that we are trying to become more of what we can and want to be is likely to reduce and correct some of the anxiety. Accepting anxiety is also a movement toward becoming stronger, more capable, and more creative. A way of facilitating and strengthening this movement is to focus on the question, "What is it that I really would like to do, become, or achieve?" Such a question is a centering of oneself,

275

inviting and directing oneself to tune into one's truest desires, dreams, and ambitions. The answers that come may be thoughts of what we want to do in the coming hours, days, or weeks, or they may be larger thoughts of the unfulfilled purposes and goals we want to attain. In my experience, asking this question inherently reduces anxiety; it moves a person along the trail or path for which the anxiety is intended, namely to bring us out of the doldrums into better contact with what we really want to be.

Anxiety is fear of our selves, including our anger and rage, but it has to do with fulfilling the unused potential that waits within.

Sorting, Selecting, and Discarding the Nonsense in Our Minds as a Basic Tool of Mind Management

Were we to open ourselves continuously to the "jet stream" flow of the rich associativeness of our minds, we would be constantly overstimulated and flooded. What we normally do is focus on a given task or plane of experience and tune out or turn off many other "stations" that are "broadcasting" on the wide band of our minds. Nonetheless, at various times some additional messages of experiences, thoughts, or emotions are allowed to come through by the "master controller" that sits somewhere within our minds and decides that these messages should be brought to our attention. When we relax, and certainly when we go to sleep, our mind goes to work further to bring up more material to our attention – in the course of our sleep the majority of this is in the form of dreams.

What happens if we instruct our mind to open up and bring up every-thing that is waiting to be experienced, seen, and heard?

As discussed earlier, this is the guiding instruction in the free-associa-tive process done in psychoanalysis. The further exciting point is that one can learn to give this instruction to the mind without having the benefit of a therapist being present. The better one gets at being able to tune in and bring up the material, and the better one gets at being able to register, take in, and contain the material delivered by our mind, the wider the range of the band of "stations" (using the metaphor of radio or TV) open to us, and the more "windows" of information (using the metaphor of a computer operating system) available.

However, we also have to return to the problem that if we give our mind an order to open the full range of our inner experiences, the flood of material is endless. In the old days I would compare this situation to a Rolodex card file on which there were hundreds of cards that would flash in quick and immediate succession with the turn of the wheel. Now with the new metaphors of the electronic storing of information, thousands of stored units of memory – call them pages or files or folders – are accessible and flash in rapid succession before our inner minds. The immediate problem is not to be overwhelmed and driven crazy by the amount of information and stimulation.

The human brain is capable of and will exercise every possible combination of ideas and feelings including the most ridiculous, illogical, frightening, unproductive, and destructive constructions possible. So we need to have a mind-management system ready to make it possible to trash the overwhelming amounts of junk, nonsense, and indecent and unethical products that come up.

In my experience the key to not being overwhelmed is to understand that our minds contain and can bring up everything that has been impressed into them. This means that we do not have to take everything that comes up in our minds seriously. It is a relief to know that we are accumulating every impression, observation, and bit of information, and also every association and speculation, that our minds conjure up, not only because we are actively responding to experiences, but also because random experimentation with associations is a hallmark of a living mind as it tries out a wide variety of ideas and feelings. Knowing that our minds are working at a miraculous computer-speed to take in every stimulus as well as to experiment with endless combinations and associations between experiences and ideas should remove the feeling that if anything has come up in our mind, it must be listened to as a message from who knows what supreme being, magical knowledge, or if you are a resident of Berkeley, California, from a true inner self.[13] Not so. The proper management of mind also involves being able to get rid of junk, trivialities, and an endless overaccumulation of superfluous information and impressions.

A series of steps is needed to delete information that prevents us from zeroing in on what we decide is important. The combined information-management process involves (1) sorting the information in our brains, (2) selecting from the huge amount of information that flashes before us, and (3) discarding a large amount of material we decide not to look at. The discarding can be done at various levels. In some cases the information can be put aside but still kept within reach in case one decides to go back to it; in other cases one can permanently delete material that will never be used again.

Do we make mistakes in the process and discard information we will need later on? Of course. After all, we make many mistakes and processing information is no exception.

Do we have the ability to delete and throw out the flotsam and jetsam so that it never returns? I don't really know.

What I have learned is that we generally can put aside what is not important, and that we can select and focus on what is important. I also know that we can stop many disturbed or pathological thoughts and feelings, and this is the next subject.

Thought Stopping or Control of Obviously Wrong and Destructive Ideas

The grand plan of life seems to include an array of problems that beset us. Blatantly incorrect ideas come into our heads perhaps because of an inherent malevolence in the mind. Some very bad ideas press at us urgently and seemingly want to overwhelm us. People of integrity know immediately when those thoughts are patently fascist, prejudicial, discriminatory, or headed in the direction of violence. Liberal and democratic people also have prejudicial thoughts and feelings. All of us suffer from bad thoughts and feelings; we may feel smugly superior to another person, or we may feel like dehumanizing or diminishing and insulting others. We also experience bursts of extreme feelings and fantasies of actual destruction of other people.

We know when our thoughts are too disturbed; they could be obsessively driven repetitions of phrases, sentences, or pictures, or horrifying mental pictures of the destruction of somebody, or crazy thoughts of massive destructiveness such as of destroying a community or poisoning a population. Our inner good sense also can tell us when we are going too far, even with justified angry feelings. For example, we could harbor murderous feelings toward a parent or a child; we could be legitimately quite angry, but the intense passion or excessively angry content of our thoughts becomes too intense and far-reaching.

In all of these instances, from the mild to the severe, including those in which it is a person's own good taste that tells him or her that their thoughts and feelings are overdone or wrong and should be made unwelcome, and including those in which the maddening or psychiatrically disturbed quality of the experience is so clear-cut that the person knows they are in mental trouble, the treatment or intervention is the same: To stop the bad thoughts.

In cases of psychiatric disturbance in which a person feels "crazy" and out of control the odds are that professional help is called for and the person should report to a mental health practitioner to ask for help to stop the unbearable intrusions on his mind. Yet even in the hands of professionals, the truth is that the basic treatment technique is the same one: To stop the bad thoughts.

🍂 *"What do you mean that I should stop my thoughts? If I could do that, I wouldn't be here," says a patient to the therapist.*

"Amazingly, we have a powerful capacity to give instructions to our minds to stop thoughts that are disturbing us," replies the therapist. "Do you know the biblical phrase, 'Let the sun on Givon stop, and the moon on Ayalon Valley stop shining'?[14] *The metaphoric meaning of that verse from the book of Joshua is that each of us has a remarkable capacity for what we have come to call in the mental health profession 'thought-stopping.' I admit that I too am always amazed to find how powerful this capacity is. I have seen people who were actually demented by a recurring thought or recurring picture in their minds successfully reestablish control over their minds and put a halt to the invading thoughts that were driving them crazy."*

🍂 *He was a talented practicing therapist. He had fought long and hard for the degree of mental health he had achieved. From his considerable childhood suffering he had developed a very high degree of sensitivity and understanding, especially for cases of real madness. In his childhood he had been essentially a captive in the hands of his physician-mother, who had a relentlessly driving personality, was garrulous and voluble, and was constantly pouring out an intense emotionalism, especially a sexualized emotional demanding of people around her. Her son was no exception. He too was an object of her demands; he was to be the center of the world and was made the focus of emotional attentions and services to her, including demands by her that he attend her as a kind of sexual queen. Even if she did not go "all the way" with her son and there was no full-blown sexual abuse, she nonetheless often arranged to be naked or partially naked in his presence and would have him lie near her or in some way touch up against him.*

As one would expect, the little boy experienced a hyper degree of stimulation that had him jumping with a nervous energy, and worse, with a brooding rage. Now as an adult, he sometimes found himself flooded with obsessive thoughts of wanting to kill his mother. Therapy for him included an acceptance of the rage he felt toward his mother for invading him so deeply and using him so selfishly, but the legitimization and acceptance of his anger did not stop the obsessive quality of his repeated ruminations of wanting to kill his mother. It was only after the therapist taught him the concept of stopping his obsessive thoughts that he was able to gain relief and to go on to accept more quietly the legitimacy of his natural rage.

Also interesting was that after the obsessive thoughts were stopped, a "clean" slate appeared for him on which he found himself confronting profound inner questions that apparently had been waiting for some time: who and what kind of person did he really wanted to be?

Choosing and Doing

In an earlier discussion of DEMOCRATIC MIND, it was noted that there are many philosophers and psychotherapists who feel that act of choice is perhaps the single most important behavior determining people's mental health.[15] Choice is the affirmation of the intelligence, spirit, and capacity for self-direction with which our species has been blessed. Not making choices is to relinquish much of one's human capacity; it is to be a shadow of oneself, a person in hiding, a person who is dependent on others for deriving a sense of self through their energy and power.

I have also referred to the emotional strength required for making choices, and which in turn is reinforced by the very act of making choices, namely, the ability to relinquish, separate from, and mourn the choices that are not selected.

Many of us have a special someone we can designate as "the one I didn't marry!" Intriguingly, many of us men and women remember this other person throughout our lives – even when we are fortunate enough to be happily married and are truly committed to the person with whom we have chosen to make our lives. (I have a hunch that it would make a fun and instructive project to put together a collection of stories of the special people we did not choose as our mates yet who are not forgotten and in a sense are somewhat loved forever.)

The art of choice includes enjoying the choices that life presents us rather than walking away from them to a false safety of nondoing; respecting ourselves for having the strength to put aside the opportunities and options we choose not to act on or accept; enjoying a sense of hope, excitement, and dedication to the choices we choose to select; and standing responsibly for the choices we do make, including those inevitable times when it becomes clear that our choice was wrong and failed, but rather than blame others we stand responsibly for the fact that we made our choice to the best of our ability at the time.

If I soberly recognize and honor the fact that I am the one who has chosen to marry you and build our lives together, I am armed with greater resolution and wholesomeness when, inevitably, we will need to work on disappointments and tensions in our marriage. Without a clear sense of my responsibility for having chosen you, and without a commitment to giving my best to fulfill this choice, I am more likely to be pushed and driven by our tensions toward an escalation of destructive behavior between us, and to do much less to help us find creative solutions for our angers and differences.

Regulating the Sequences and Momentums
of Our Mindfulness

In addition to sorting, selecting, and knowing how to discard the nonsense in our minds, other principles of mind management pertain to tendencies toward extreme forms of thinking and feeling that are built into the original mind structures we first received at the "factory." In other words, hazards and errors are built into our default human experiencing where we would benefit from more instruction. In many ways we human beings are not given sufficient education in how to use our minds correctly in everyday life. Unless we learn effective forms of regulation and correction of our mind processes, we can remain stuck with wrong ways of thinking and feeling throughout our lives.

In this section I will discuss ways in which we tend to go too far out into extremes of daring, passion, risks, and thrills; how we are pulled toward the completion of structures and processes as if we must only do things "fully," and how often this takes us too far into zones of dangerous excess and overintensity; how we respond to inner demands that we strive for consistency and that everything we do and stand for represents a unified direction or idea; and, most unfortunately, how we are eternally fascinated by the potential and capacity we have for blowing up life and destroying it.

Put together, we are talking about the inherent dangers of "going all the way" in slavish devotion to whatever destructive purpose with a resulting harming of life rather than its advancement.

In the United States the extreme of destruction of life to which people go includes random mass killing. This behavior has become part of the American folk culture, as if it were an "approved" way to vent extremism and madness. We have experienced the wrath of thrill-seeking teenagers in a school, humiliated workers in a former place of business from which they were dismissed, and a random mass murder spree in a shopping mall or other public place. In many places in the world the description also refers to mass murderers in military actions who commit crimes against humanity beyond the legitimate needs of a military campaign by destroying defenseless civilians in a village, or executing surrendered prisoners of war en masse. See, among tens of examples, Algeria, Soviet Chechnya, Sri Lanka with its Sinhalese majority against the Tamil, random violence against unarmed citizens including suicide attacks against Israelis by Palestinians as well as some examples of massacres of Palestinians by Israelis, an explosion of endless attacks against U.S. troops as well as against fellow citizens in Iraq following the U.S. ouster of Saddam, Ireland's battles of Catholics versus Protestants, and evil torturers and killers who caused the "disappearances" of thousands of designated fellow countrymen in Argentina, Chile, and Guatemala. The examples are tragically and infuriatingly endless. See also the genociders who murder millions of designated target people in full-blown genocidal campaigns in the examples that include the Armenian Genocide, the Holocaust, genocides by the USSR, genocide in Tibet by communist China, in Cambodia by fellow Cambodians, or in the former Yugoslavia where over the centuries Serbs, Moslems, and Croatians have variously been pitted against one another (with the Serbs being the prime but not exclusive perpetrators in the genocidal ethnic cleansing of recent years).

In today's world, the above description also includes what I call transnational genocidal terrorism and terrorists such as Osama bin Laden and his al-Qaeda movement who at this writing command the terror and concern of much of our civilized world.

Controlling the Momentum of Activity: Restraining "Going All the Way" to the Full Momentum of Energy

There is a kind of narcotic joy in letting the throttle out and "going all the way."

Every one of us has tasted this joy. Many of us have learned to discipline the attraction of going all the way; for example, we know that driving too fast may kill us and may kill other human beings, and we choose not to do so. But there are many who never get over the thrill of attempting the next and then the next speeds toward a joy of "going all the way." In other words, the momentum of the dynamics of a structural situation can lead people to do terrible things "just because" it is the natural thing to do. It seems so simple, yet this tendency to continue in the direction one is going is a critical force in human behavior.

Perhaps staying with the momentum is psycho-physiologically comfortable because the forward thrust or flow of a sequence can be continued and braking mechanisms are not needed. Staying with the momentum is also easier than choosing a new course. Following the momentum also means that acknowledging that one is going in a wrong direction is not necessary.[16]

There is also an analogue to the orgiastic process that brings us such pleasure in our sexual lives. An experience is built, increased, and increased more; excitement pulsates and intensifies along the gradient of the increasing intensity; and we know from experience that going all the way leads to an eruption of energy that is enormously satisfying. Here may be a structural substrate for our inherent tendencies to veer toward totalities, final solutions, perfection, certainty, and absolutism in fascist thinking: it feels good to go all the way.

Experimenting with the unknown. A related process to letting energy out "the whole way" is the seductive invitation to experiment with the unknown: to do something that has never before been done, to pull the trigger and push the button that have never been pulled or pushed before. Possible concerns – and even factual knowledge of dangers – are pushed aside in favor of the intrigue and excitement of the experiment. The fascination of the experiment can also combine with risk taking and thrill seeking.

Risk taking, thrill seeking, and daring. Other related processes for going with an energy flow to its maximum are taking risks and seeking thrills. Such "highs" seem to be a major attraction for some people even if the known risks are great and even if the known consequences are horrendous.

> *It's the ultimate. Life is boring without thrills. For the Russian-roulette high of it, and for the hell of it, I want to taste the biggest thrills before I check out. What the hell, you only live once, and we're all going to die*

anyway. I'd rather die living than live dead and wooden. Going to the same job, and sleeping with the same woman, and wiping the snot off the faces of the same children day after day is not for me. All or nothing, one last spin of the biggest thrill of all, that's my style.

People who are ideologically committed, say to the Japanese emperor and empire in World War II, or to bin Laden's al-Qaeda in 2001, are prepared to fly their planes and lives into smashing oblivion for their cause and to kill the enemy. And there are many others who will fly their ships of life into black holes of hell because it is thrilling.

Controlling the Gestalt-Pull of Structures and Contents As If Seeking Their Wholeness: Not Being Seduced into Testing the Completion of the "Full" Structure or Process

In addition to the momentum of energy asking to be unleashed to its fullest, there also appears to be an inherent call for incomplete patterns, as if they seek to have us bring them to completion. Gestalt psychologists taught us earlier in the last century about the tensions that perceptual structures bring to our experiencing of reality, and how the eye and mind in many cases will "incorrectly" provide the completion to an incomplete structure in order not to leave an unfinished quality to a percept.

The notion of all-or-none behavior, or the need to take a process to its total completion, is also familiar in regard to human behavior. Thus, some people have got to go all the way toward success, and will be frustrated and miserable when they achieve any given intermediate level of success, because they cannot stop keeping their eyes on total success. (Heaven also help some of them when they reach what they have defined as their ultimate success, because now there is no goal-tension to conceal the meaninglessness of their life, for example, some suicides of Hollywood stars who end up with nothing after they have ostensibly suc-ceeded in acquiring everything.) The all-or-none phenomenon applies to many aspects of human behavior, for example, needing to be loved by all, needing always to be healthy and never ill, needing to exhibit prowess in whatever at a level that is always better than the previous achievement, and so on.

If one looks quietly at infants and toddlers, one sees the dynamic of all-or-none responses present in the sense of the child needing and wanting to achieve completion of any act. Even before larger meanings and conceptual goals have developed for the young child, there is an inherent push to complete an energy sequence. The child becomes frustrated and upset and will cry when he or she is unable to go all the way to their sense of completion of an activity that is underway, whether it is taking a tower of blocks they were building to the bathtub, continuing to catch a ball an endless number of times, finishing a story that they are reading, or watching a TV movie to its end.

In everyday life, the mechanism of going all the way to complete the implied and inherent structure of a situation or activity sequence leads to phenomena in which people do things they are not ready for: people who are not ready to get married who go ahead with a marriage that doesn't have a chance because that's the (next) thing to do in the proper developmental sequence; people who are married and not ready to have children who go ahead and have children because that's the (next) thing to do; people who feel like divorcing their spouse, but who could work out the conflict effectively if they devoted themselves to it, who nonetheless go ahead and get divorced because that's the (next) thing to do in life; people who feel like quitting a job who do so before they have prepared for another job because that's the (next) thing to do; and on and on of people going too far or prematurely to the end of whatever it is that registers in their perception as the next logical step in the experience chain.

These dynamics apply even when the goal of the behavior sequence is unspeakable. Once people get away with a certain amount of whatever they are doing, they seem to go on doing more of the same, not only in terms of power seeking and getting away with the power they develop over others, which of course is a powerful motivational force in its own right, but also on a more elementary level of fulfilling an archaic tendency to go all the way that seems to await deep within. So if there are already masses of prisoners behind barbed wire, and one already has set out on the route of beating and killing some of them, the next "logical" step is to go even further toward the whole way of a "Final Solution." It takes great wisdom and courage to stop fast-moving trains to Auschwitz!

Overcoming a Need for Total Consistency

People tend to have terribly strong needs to be consistent (or not to be inconsistent with themselves), so that once a position or a direction is established they feel a need to pursue that same course consistently in all aspects of their lives.

• If you "have to" love a child, woe be unto you if you suffer hateful feelings toward that child.

• If you are required to be dutifully religious, woe be unto you if you have critical judgments of church policies or of the clergy.

• If you decorate your home in a period style, you may spoil it by mixing in a piece of furniture from a different style.

• If you adopt a given "school" of treating mental problems, you are committing what the classicists call (awesomely) "serious technical errors" if you use a technique of treatment that is identified with another cluster of techniques.

Somewhere or other, the mere idea of being inconsistent with oneself comes to be viewed by many of us as a kind of horror, almost as if it is a felony-level violation of logic, perhaps an act against nature; at the least it is an attack against a sense of a just and well-ordered world. You are either for the good goal – however that is defined – or against it; you can't have it both ways; you dare not contradict yourself.

A driving, insistent need for consistency also dovetails with the previous problematic processes of mental machinery for going too far with the momentum of an energy sequence and having to complete the gestalt of a form; it is as if we are being asked from inside to do more and more of whatever it is that we are doing, and to complete structures and tasks to their fullest.

Consistency to the nth degree is a characteristic of fundamentalists of all sorts: political fundamentalists, like the Marxist ideologues of their time who transformed the quest for social justice into bloodbaths of cruel domination and murder; sadly also some ostensible democrats who end up heading out to kill their defined enemies of freedom with a grim determination that mimics the extremism of their enemies of democracy; and extreme religious fundamentalists of every faith who, slowly but surely, pull many religions more and more toward absurdities of extremisms.

> *Having started out honoring their leader as the "King Messiah," they couldn't stop when he succumbed to his human mortality.*
>
> *Who would have believed that the ultra-right-wing Jewish religious group who were devotees of their venerable Rabbi Menachem Mendel Schneerson, the "Lubavitcher Rebbe," could have adopted the Christian idea of a Second Coming after the Rebbe died in July 1994. To this day a sizable group of believers insists that the Rebbe has not died, that he is immortal and that he is the long-awaited Messiah.*
>
> *Intriguingly, a call by an also-orthodox rabbi and professional of Jewish history asking that the ultra-orthodox establishment take a stand against deification of a mortal human being has been met by "deafening silence."* [17]

Learning to accept, honor, and enjoy degrees of inconsistency in many (though not all) areas of life involves learning to honor a wide range of dialectical processes that are built into our machinery for experiencing. On the level of emotions, it means containing experiences such as both loving and hating a person and being both loyal to and critical of one's people and nation or the cause to which we are devoted. On the level of thinking, an honoring of inconsistency means an acceptance of multiple models for understanding different kinds of realities, and accepting that at any given point there may very well be more than one paradigm that is the explanation. For example, in matters of illness and health, meaningful advances in genetic knowledge of the programming of defects and illnesses do not mean no longer understanding the roles of infections and physical stresses; and knowing both of the above does not mean ceasing to understand that emotional stresses also can invite, make possible, and perpetuate physiologically caused illness; nor should it mean neglecting the truth that there are many illnesses entrenched in our physiology that cannot be banished, and yet that there are ways of living in respect of nutrition, exercise, states of mind, and more that can hold these limitations at bay and give us many years of a reasonably comfortable life and even pleasure despite health problems.

Because the need for consistency leads to polarization and extremism, it also sets the stage for a greater likelihood of using projections. Having pushed myself to the extreme of any position that I demand of myself – love, loyalty, integrity, or patriotism, for example – I am drawn to perceiving the imperfections and incompleteness of others in starker terms: they are hateful, disloyal, corrupt, or traitors. My wrathful criticism is not only that they fail to meet the standard I impose on myself, but is also fed by my own guilt and fears: I may fail to reach and fulfill the consistency and perfection I demand. When we position ourselves at an extreme point of view or position because of a fetish about consistency, we are likely to hate others who fall short of our vaunted consistency at its fullest; and when we hate the other, we are drawn to project or attribute to said other every manner of badness, including our own, which we cannot face.

Sociologist James Coleman described how this process operates in community conflict over and over again and leads to making an opponent's ideas appear totally bad, rather than as alternative ideas to be weighed respectfully based on the dignity of favoring one's chosen point of view. The projections are embodied in serious charges of bad faith and bad intentions that are made against the opponent, individual or group, and the dispute is redefined as if independent of the actual disagreement over the issues. The goal becomes to anchor the dispute in profound feelings of distaste, repugnance, and rejection of the opponent, which in human affairs is all too easily achieved.[18]

"They will go to hell for their fornication and sin. Woe be unto the bigamists and harlots," screams a 21st century minister of a Western church, perhaps even to millions of people in a syndicated television mass marketing of religion. Yet some well-known Western TV ministers periodically are found in bed with prostitutes, who may add spicy reports of the holy man's secret quirks and fetishes.

A zealot Taliban follower orders with biblical authority the stoning to death of an errant woman for her sexual crimes. Yet some of the zealots, who on 9/11 sacrificed their lives in suicide-murder missions in the glory of their gods, spent their last nights on earth drinking forbidden alcohol or at peep shows, striptease bars, and with prostitutes.

Beware, indeed, of extremists. William Allen White (1868–1944) wrote, "Consistency is a paste jewel that only cheap men cherish."[19]

Social psychologist Leon Festinger is credited with having created the concept of "cognitive dissonance" to describe how people seek consistency; this need is so great that it leads to subsequent errors in judgment as the mind tries to keep things fit together consistently.[20] Before it is all over, the argument or feud can exist for its own sake regardless of what set it off. In small instances, it all becomes a bad joke; in larger instances, it becomes a historical process that can determine the life and death outcomes of millions of people for many centuries.

Stopping the Primacy of Destructive and Power-Seeking Tendencies

The human mind needs continuously to occupy itself with and discharge negative feelings. There is apparently a precedence to the negative destructive elements that have to be worked through and discharged before the associative, building, and loving elements of the mind can be released. Many years ago, pioneer psychoanalyst Wilhelm Stekel wrote metaphorically that if two trains of positive and negative emotions are approaching a switching point, the train carrying the negative feelings goes first, which means that when a human being who wants to love and be constructive nonetheless experiences anger and hate, the first order of business needs to be to process the negative.

> I have long ago answered the important question which is primary in man, love or hate, in favor of hatred. . . . It creates its greatest strength from the effect of the contrast. Indeed, pain is unconditionally necessary as a contrast effect for the heightening of pleasure. . . . Our need to hate is just as great as our need to love. At the beginning as there is no one

that can live without love, so there is also no being who can live without hate.[21]

In his analysis of community conflict processes, James Coleman goes so far as to support a Gresham's Law of Conflict:

The harmful and dangerous elements drive out those which would keep the conflict within bounds. Reckless, unrestrained leaders head the attack; combat organizations arrive to replace the milder, more constrained pre-existing organizations; derogatory and scurrilous charges replace dispassionate issues; antagonism replaces disagreement, and a drive to ruin the opponent takes the place of the initial will to win. In other words, all forces put into effect by the initiation of conflict act to drive out the conciliatory elements, and replace them with those better equipped for combat.[22]

Psychiatrist Jerome Frank described the inevitability of the drive for power in human beings:

Neither the drive for power nor the potential for violence can be excised from the human psyche, especially since they are the obverse and reverse of a coin. The drive for power keeps humans perpetually dissatisfied by creating a permanent gap between performance and expectations: since their reach always exceeds their grasp, they will eventually feel frustrated no matter how well off they are; and since as likely as not the source of the frustration will be another human being or group of human beings whose drive for self-aggrandizement might have led them into a collision course, no degree of affluence or self-fulfillment will in itself assure that humans will live peacefully together.[23]

When one accepts the inevitability of negative and destructive processes in the mind, the overriding implication is that people and societies need to lay down a value structure or hierarchy that tells them that they must operate in a value framework committed to the protection and enhancement of human life, and that they need to process negative feelings in order to fulfill their goals of protecting and enhancing life. Otherwise, every Tom, Dick, and Henrietta who gets charged up with negative feelings is going to be an agent of destruction. Looking at the

ways in which many human lives are constructed at this time, it seems
that the dire possibilities of destruction prevail in most of human reality.

Thus, at a seemingly trivial level compared to societal events, but obviously of great meaning to millions of human beings, most marriages are
failures, and most families are failures if only on the basis of the failure of
the aforesaid marriages. So too most human beings are emotionally disturbed. On collective levels, most societies are dictatorships or otherwise
totalitarian and deny the most elementary freedoms to their populations.
Many places in the world are characterized by vicious terrorism, war, and
genocide. It hardly seems far-fetched to say that the human animal as a
whole seems to like doing one hell of a lot of destroying and killing of
life.

Isn't the point of education and civilization for humans to advance
from a sorry state to a treasuring of human life?

Interrelating Negative or Angry and Hating Processes with Positive or Loving Processes of Association, Building, and Loving

Blessed are those capable of integrating the so-called positive and negative emotions into a single unity, without being carried away to the
excesses of either side of emotions. Among other things, this means an
ability to be angry and even roaring mad without "blowing one's gasket."
Similarly, this means being able to feel loving without "losing one's mind"
and ending up enslaved by one's love or lover.

The totality of any emotional direction necessarily defeats it, however
warranted the emotion is at the time. The extremism and purity of
whichever emotion bodes a danger of being excessive in the experience
– overly raging and hot with vengeance or going too far with expression
of one's anger; or overly positive, innocently and naively trusting, and
not being prepared for the disappointment and hurt that are evidently
inevitable in the finest relationships.

Committing to any one direction ("I love him with my entire soul, he
would never, never hurt me"; "I will never forgive him in any way") also
precludes changing over time to use the opposite sides of our emotional
repertoires even if circumstances change, and there develops a reason for

being hurt and angry in an otherwise positive or loving connection or if the time comes when it is possible to forge a reconciliation with a former adversary and enemy.

Extremist use of an emotional direction often ends up capturing and taking over the personality. For all that we are charmed and happy for lovers, many people who have fallen into the stage of being carried blindly away in love are known to be at many high risks, including the risks of awful judgment, as are people blinded with feelings of uncontrolled rage or revenge. Interrelating hating and loving processes means to continue being in charge of one's emotions, to continue regulating and directing choices and intensities of feeling. A greater sense of grace and control of oneself is found in people who know they can both love and hate, and that they can continuously mix an apothecary's elixir of both feelings.

Thus, a parent who can be angry with a child without any self-doubts or without confusing a child about their unquestioned love for the child can pull off disciplinary steps that are simply out of the reach of a parent who becomes too enraged and loses contact with the core of their love.

&❧ *A young man in his twenties told his father that he was going to buy a motorcycle.*

The father, who loved his son very much, was adamantly opposed because of the known high risks of serious accidents. The father's relationship with his son was excellent; the son had just recently enjoyed a trip overseas at his father's expense, at the conclusion of which the two had met up overseas in a mutually happy reunion.

"No, you're not," replied the father firmly.

"How can you say that, Dad, I'm old enough to decide by myself," argued the son. "What are you going to do if I simply go and buy a cycle?"

The father answered sharply: "You can be sure that before a day has passed I will come and burn your cycle. What are you going to do? Report me to the police?"

A husband or wife who is not afraid to move back and forth between positive and negative emotions will be less afraid to deal with any subject in their lives and relationship, and will be in a more commanding position to deal with serious challenges and crises as they arise.

❧ She told her husband she wanted an open marriage. She had a boyfriend with whom she enjoyed parts of herself the husband could never satisfy; moreover, they were all modern adults and it was ridiculous to hold on to old-fashioned rules that in the end defeated many marriages. She did not want to leave him and end their marriage; on the contrary, he was dear to her, and she would limit her extraterritorial pleasures to a single day and night a week.

Historically, the distribution of power in their marriage had tilted toward a disguised supremacy for her. He was a nice guy, who loved her, and could be irked and annoyed, but did not challenge her when she took the upper hand. Both of them knew she was now making her dramatic move for independence on the basis of her being the stronger of the two.

At first he was so confused by the welter of his emotions he couldn't see straight. But after he worked on himself, he succeeded in putting together his "army of emotions," and he proceeded to counterattack:

"I will not agree to any arrangement for you with another man, not one day a week or at any time," he said to her with conviction. I am very angry with you right now, but you know that I love you very much, and I will not agree to sharing you with anyone else. If you don't give up this offensive idea, I will leave you." He was clear and firm.

If he had simply said he refused her demand, she probably would not have bent at all. As it was, she didn't immediately believe he could stand up to her, and she persisted for a time in her demand that he agree to her choice of a way of life. The emotional upheaval and tension continued between them for several weeks, but he held unambiguously to his position that he loved her very much and that he would never agree to her demand to have a boyfriend; if she went that route he would divorce her, he told her again in no uncertain terms. When she realized he had grown strong enough to mean it, she relented. She too did not want to lose him or their marriage. (One can wonder whether in a way she had been bringing home to him that she actually needed for him to become stronger and not allow her to be too much the superior one in their relationship.)

Many years later one sees that the couple went on together increasingly lovingly and successfully.

Summing Up the Regulation of Our Mindfulness

In a broad sense, a mind that is healthily at work and is utilizing a relatively full range of its capacity for experience is one that leaves itself open to a wide-ranging flow of ideas and feelings, and welcomes a flow of stimulation, including confusion and contradictions; is one that sorts out the junk as well as the philosophically and spiritually unacceptable ideas that inevitably come up and discards them; is one that welcomes the tension and anxiety that accompany these processes; is one that proceeds to focus on what is of greatest importance and priority; and is one that formulates its choices of the actions it will take in order to fulfill its chosen goals.

In the process, the constructive mind is careful to regulate the sequences of its activity, including taking care not to go too far capriciously in letting out the full possible momentums of its energy processes; it monitors and stops destructive and power-seeking tendencies that threaten to crush human life and potential; and it overcomes a blind need for total consistencies that can lead to absurd extremes and destructive "final solutions." The basic sequence of a healthy mind is a logical work schedule towards fulfilling its key goals for living which are consistent with the sacredness both of one's own life and of others' lives as well.

Three Applications of Free Association in Everyday Life: Some Everyday Tools for Healthy Living Derived from an Acceptance of the Associative Flow of Our Minds

The use of DEMOCRATIC MIND in everyday life is based on staying tuned in to one's mind with an acceptance of its never-ending stream of activity and its multiple kinds of experiences – the anything of our minds.

The art of managing the mind is to tap its potential for contributing to life rather than to be driven to escapes into fascist certainties – including madness, which I have proposed can often be understood as a kind of fascist certainty – that turn off the beauty and vitality of the life process in return for the security of a prescribed and stipulated way of life. In contrast to FASCIST MIND, which routinely seeks closure and seeks to understand and put together a comprehensible picture of reality, DEMO-CRATIC MIND seeks to gather constantly changing information about reality and to test and reevaluate its understanding and conclusions in light of the new information.

Following are three practical illustrations of how the healthy associative flow in mind can be put to use in everyday life. The first pertains to using the free-associative process as the best "sleeping pill" available (thereby also replacing heavy sleep medication) for falling asleep even when upset, and also for using it to learn more about whatever is "on our minds" and upsetting us.

The second topic continues a productive use of our nights in regard to learning how to tune into our dreams – a topic that has fascinated people from ancient times – as an opportunity for an increased sense of self-direction and greater control of our future. Vital information reaches us not only from our minds but also from the world around us and from the people with whom we live and interact.

The third topic concerns the ways in which we can take in more fully and benefit from the enormous amount of feedback available from other people, and use these truths about ourselves, however unpleasant and unflattering, to improve ourselves and make our lives more productive.

Applying the Free-Associative Process to Falling Asleep

This is a derivative application of acceptance of the free-associative process that can help people go to sleep with little to no sedation, even when they are upset.

> ❧ *After my mother's death when I was a teenager, for a period of some years I suffered from very severe insomnia. I then re-experienced a period of similarly severe insomnia in the course of my psychoanalysis as a young adult, and now I was fortunate to learn the use of the following technique that I have since taught many of my patients, with a very high rate of success:*

Even when you are very tense, do the following when you are unable to sleep:

1. Tell yourself that you want your mind free to bring up whatever is inside of you, in whatever thoughts and preferably in the pictures that are "waiting" inside to come into your consciousness.

2. If the thoughts and pictures that come up make you afraid and anxious, tell yourself that you will not be afraid or anxious about being afraid or anxious. It is O.K. It is amazing how much less afraid we are of being afraid when we accept our fears as natural! Tell yourself that however frightening and disagreeable, you will accept your unpleasant experiences as a part of life and also as bearers of important information about yourself.

3. If you find yourself thinking about any specific aspect of life, such as a business deal, rather than opening your mind to the spontaneity and surprises of a free-associative stream of experience, tell yourself to stop the thought and that you don't want to be dealing with any specific issue. Tell your mind once again that you want to see and feel whatever comes from the more spontaneous "jet stream" currents of your unconscious thoughts and images and not to be stuck with any specific subject.

4. Once you find that thoughts and pictures are beginning to jump into your mind one after the other, especially if they are spontaneous, unconnected, and seemingly not in a logical order, you can rest assured that you will be asleep within just a few seconds or at most another minute or so.

Apropos, some of the images that come to us are like dreams, with rich information from our inner minds and hearts, and will tell us more about what is currently uppermost in our inner experience that is distressing us. I hesitate to mention this because the would-be sleeper should not be focusing on any effort at understanding, just letting the mind-movie of associations happen. However, experienced "mind buffs," who have learned to retain memories of their associations and dreams, will also be able to remember some parts of their associations later when they wake up and to learn from them.

The method is tried and tested. Intriguingly, the method works to a significant extent when one is seriously upset, although that does not mean it brings with it a total reduction in anxiety and discomfort. There are, for example, times when using the method will bring a blessed relief of some sleep, which will be followed by reawakening in the middle of the night, and then one has to reapply the method a second and perhaps even a third time in the course of the night. But even under such rough circumstances, one can get some sleep and more of a rest than would be the case in the classic agony of tossing and turning endlessly for hours and hours. Moreover, at times of great upset, I recommend to my patients (and allow myself as well) to take a very mild, almost homeopathic dose of something like 2 milligrams of valium, not as a "sleeping pill," which actually puts you to sleep, but as a slight tranquilizer that cuts the rigidity or tensing up just enough to enable the mind to let go and bring up everything as previously described and to facilitate sleeping and dreaming in greater ease.

Being in Touch with One's Dreams – A Powerful Basis
for Strengthening Our Sense of Direction in Life

Every night our mind computer dreams. This profound activity takes place in the silence of sleep whether or not we ask for it. It is doing a valuable reorganization of our lives even if we do not manage to be aware of the changing "computer screens" in our brains. Like computers that continue cleaning up and reorganizing long after we leave our offices, our minds are at work cleaning up the events and experiences that took place during the day, and also preparing for events to come. The mind computer scans its inner workings for a variety of messages, including notices of impending illness and other possible dangers, and also creative opportunities and possible ideas for solutions to problems. During our nights we practice how to handle possible emergency situations, for instance, driving automobiles in this terror-filled world; we rehearse the moves we will make in key relationships; and we prepare for examinations in our schools and professions. Our dreaming mind reviews alternative possibilities for future actions, comparing them to accumulated experiences, and sets before us schedules and sequences of priorities for consideration. What a marvelous computer program we have!

Through the ages wise people in many different cultures have tapped the wisdom of their dreaming minds. Records dating back to antiquity, such as in the Western world's bestseller Bible, tell of brave and wise people who have made excellent use of their dreams.

I remember hearing one apocryphal story attributed to a rabbi in an Arab country over 100 years ago who was well-known for his understanding of dreams. Once a distraught Jewish lady came to tell the rabbi of a disturbing dream. He listened and then turned irately against her. "You harlot," he screamed. "Get out of here, for you are carrying on with a man other than your husband." The woman paled and sank fainting to the floor. "How could you possibly know?" she groaned in amazement.

Whether or not the story was true, in this century I have had at least one experience of learning from the dream of a husband that he knew unconsciously that his wife was carrying on with another man, and in point of fact, shamefully, it was no less than with her psychotherapist. Consciously the husband didn't know; unconsciously he did know:

A psychotherapist who was combining his treatment of a woman with sleeping with her regularly learned from her that her husband was becoming increasingly agitated and suicidal. This particular therapist only practiced individual therapy and did not treat the spouses of his patients, and so he also had a legitimate reason for referring the woman's husband to a colleague. Apparently there was some decency left in this therapist if he would not see the husband of the woman with whom he was sleeping!

The distressed husband reported promptly to the second therapist in the greatest upset. He not only described to this therapist serious tensions in his marriage but also reported dreams that suggested that his wife was carrying on with someone. The dream material even suggested suspiciously that this someone might very well be his wife's psychotherapist! But consciously the husband did not dare say to himself that he thought his wife was cheating on him, let alone with her therapist.

The husband's therapist now asked the wife to come in for a private session, and in the course of this meeting the woman did acknowledge she was having an affair with her therapist. In fact, the two of them had set up a way of "working" in which they would meet for a "double session," in the first half of which they would conduct a regular psychotherapy session, and in the second half they would repair to another part of the therapist's comfortable office and have intercourse.

The husband's therapist used his new-found knowledge to guide him in counseling his patient, who in time came to the conclusion that he would divorce his wife.

As life would have it, many, many years later the husband and the former therapist met again as colleagues in an academic setting and were able to spend some time socially reviewing the therapy of many years before. Over drinks, the husband told his former therapist how in later years he came to know about his ex-wife's affair with her therapist; now the former therapist described to his once-patient how years earlier he had come upon the facts of the ex-wife's betrayal from the husband's own dreams at a point when he was not yet able to tolerate knowing the truth consciously that which his inner mind registered so accurately. In effect, the man's unconscious had been able to communicate to the therapist to enable him to act on his behalf.[24]

Western culture's appreciation and knowledge of dreams culminated in Sigmund Freud's brilliant development of a comprehensive perspective of the meaning of dreams as well as the stunning methodology he gave us for approaching the study of the subject by actively remembering dreams and sharing them with a trained dream counselor (therapist) – although again note that any number of religious and folk cultures also have taught people to remember, tell, and relate to the meanings of their dreams. In contemporary Western culture, the surest but not the only place to learn to work with dreams is in the course of psychotherapy, where one has the opportunity to practice remembering as well as to cultivate a truthfulness about one's dreams in the context of a supporting relationship with a therapist; and one learns how to free associate to remembered dreams as a way of decoding their meaning and significance.

Millions of people do not pay attention to their dreams, but people who do learn to recall, and to devote quiet meditative attention to understanding their dreams, are often rewarded with profound knowledge of themselves and a much greater sense of direction and control over their lives. Like other skills, it takes time and patience to learn, practice, and maintain the ability to be in touch with dreams. It also takes a further degree of courage to exercise understanding of dreams, especially to hear what they are saying when their contents frighten or challenge us.[25]

A device I recommend to beginners who want to start on their own to remember more of their dreams is to keep a pencil and pad within immediate reach at their bedside, so that they can write down a dream without having to get up or make large movements to reach a pencil and pad at the time they awaken. More than that, I recommend rehearsing saying to oneself before going to sleep that one wants to be able to remember one's dreams. On awakening in the morning, one should direct one's attention immediately to scanning whatever comes to mind – here too using the free-association process or a letting go to whatever will come up in one's mind as opposed to concentrating on "remembering." Experience shows that remembering many of one's dreams is an art form that can be learned and developed to a high level of skill.

Once a dream is recalled, a basic method for understanding what the dream is telling us is to free associate to any and all parts of the dream. This is different from attempting to decode, understand, and interpret the dream's meanings. The free associations yield a stream of associated meanings, connections, and linkages, and the central implication, meaning, or interpretation is likely to come up to our attention from within the flow of the associations. This method uses the data of experiences rather than imposing interpretations or analytic understanding from the logical part of our mind on the dream. (In therapy, I enjoy seeing people develop skill for understanding their dreams, which I know they will then take with them for the rest of their lives long after their formal therapy has been completed.)

A further useful device we have learned in psychotherapy is for a dreamer to ask himself or herself what part of their self is being represented by each of the figures in the dream. The assumption is that we have a relationship to each of the figures, and that many of our wishes, interests, and concerns are represented by the different figures we have dreamed about. It is confusing at first, for at any given point in the symbolism of our dreams we can be both winners and losers, perpetrators and victims, abandoners and abandoned ones. It takes time to learn how to accept these contradictions, and also how to ask with which parts in our dream we are more identified than others. The ultimate purpose of our dreams is to bring us the information that renews the possibilities of choices as to who and what we are going to be and do in everyday life.

Finally, one must also be prepared to yield to some degree of not understanding, which is a miniature representation of the last word of life and the ultimate fate of all of us that in the final analysis, no matter what, including undergoing the best psychotherapy or psychoanalysis, none of us will ever have complete control of our lives.

Feedback That Comes from Other People in Our Lives: Taking in and Working with Vital Information about Ourselves

There is another powerful way of obtaining a flow of information about ourselves that often will supplement and fill in information we do not dare and are not able to receive from within. It is to listen carefully to the messages about ourselves that we get from other people.

In one way or another, we are all spontaneously getting vital feedback readouts from others about our actions, integrity, and character. Certainly this is true of the information we get from our spouses, who in the final analysis know us fully as no one else does – in a way even more objectively and comprehensively than our parents were able to see us as children. For better or worse, one of the great forces at work in the mystery of the marital process is the communication of one spouse to another of what each one really knows and understands about the other.

However, it is not only our spouses who tell in their various ways the truth about us. The information is also being delivered to us from other members of our families – our children, our parents if they are still alive, and our siblings, cousins, uncles, and aunts. Each family member is also very busy with their own personal agendas, which include their individual degrees of unfairness, selfishness, unreasonable projections of parts of themselves into anger with us, and whatever of the many not-nice sides of any of us human beings. But if we listen carefully, even in the course of an attack guided by one or more of such unfair needs, we are likely to hear from our critics and attackers essential and correct observations of our weaknesses and errors. If we listen in order to learn about the honest and correct criticisms of us, even when they are embedded in a burst of nastiness, we can gain a great deal of information for our self-correction and growth.

The feedback comes not only from our relatives. All of life in effect is a network of feedback information – our friends, business colleagues, neighbors, even spontaneous encounters with strangers – that leads to learning about ourselves, our kindness and cruelty, calm and temper, fairness and pushiness, and so on. A healthy use of mind calls for listening to ourselves critically in order to continue the task of growth as a person, optimally to the very end of our lives.

To enjoy doing this learning and growing is a celebration of the democracy in our mind.

CHAPTER TEN

A Unified Theory of Democratic Mind in the Self, Family, and Society

A Vision of More Decent Human Beings Who Do Less Harm to Themselves and Others

Respect for Human Life as a Categorical Imperative

The guiding value of this work is a concept of the sacredness of life, both for oneself and for all other human beings. This is what I mean by a proposal of a "unified theory" that applies to individuals, to the interactions of people in their marriages, to interactions with their children and families at large, and to the big pictures of collective interactions in society between groups, nations, ethnic groups, and so on. This value of the holiness of human life is a central feature of DEMOCRATIC MIND.

It is my opinion that the value of human life is implicit in the philosophy of all science. I believe that the only valid purpose of knowledge is to promote healthier lives for human beings,[1] and not that science and the pursuit of knowledge exist in their own right for their own sake so to speak, nor that science can be allowed to serve antilife purposes.[2] The fact that science, and scientists, often are employed willingly (and lucratively) by the worst demons of destroyers of life does not mean they are doing the right thing, any more than physicians who are in the employ of old-time outlaws or new-time Mafias to take out their bullets and set their bones, or physicians who were in the service of the Nazi ss camps to do selections and drop the Zyklon-B canisters. From the standpoint of ethical values (how sadly weak such ethical values sound in the face of Zyklon-B canisters and people with power who are out to kill others!), the purpose of scientific knowledge gathering has to be to protect and advance human life.

Moreover, the openness to real information, and not to dogmas, that is intrinsic to scientific thinking fits a cluster of democratic values more than a cluster of totalitarian values. By definition, it takes free people to be open to freedom of information more than an oppressed people and society who are under threats of punishment and extermination by their masters. The conduct of the information-developing process in science is in the tradition of objective inquiry, free of prior assumptions or ideological dictates. Scientific processes of gathering and evaluating information are responsible to the highest standards of impartiality and accuracy. Most important, the reason scientific work is being done, the definition of the purposes of the scientific work and the way the investigation is conducted, should be grounded at the outset in a value-ethic of devotion to protecting human life.[3]

I believe a direct line exists from the above statement of respect for life to the quintessential value principle for definitions in psychology of normal and abnormal behavior. The behaviors that should be defined as disorders are those that do serious harm to the ability to live safely and securely – with adequate food, shelter, biological and emotional security, and dignity. Disturbed, dysfunctional, or disordered behaviors are those that do harm to human lives, and these subdivide into the two categories of doing harm to oneself and doing harm to others. Accepting respect for human life as a categorical imperative is the basis for analyzing human choices, conscious and unconscious, whether or not to do harm to one's own life or to others: Psychologically healthy people protect and enhance lives, while psychologically unhealthy people do harm to life.[4] Thus, laying a wreath at Ground Zero of the World Trade Center site flattened on September 11, 2001, the first leader of post-Taliban Afghanistan, Hamid Karzai, said, "The people that committed this crime here in New York . . . were against life itself."[5]

Correlating Individual and Collective Levels of Behaviors

Many attempts to address social ills through the use of psychological concepts pertain to the individual, and many of these have created stirs of intellectual excitement, I think for the combination of reasons that there is a real kernel of truth in these concepts, and that they stir a dim awareness of some profound relationship between the madness in man's mind and the madness in human society. But many of these ideas have proven limited, and worse have tended to draw intellectual ridicule because something can really be off the mark when ideas that apply to a single human mind are applied to the infinitely larger and inherently greater complexities of societal organization. For example, a notion that rigid toilet training practices can produce an "anal expulsive" or destructive society doesn't make for an impressive explanation of a fascist society. There may be some truth in the connection, but moving from toilet seats to understanding a mass pattern of societal cruelty seems far-fetched.

In Western psychology, some of the seminal ideas about the individual that pertain to societal issues include: Wilheim Reich's view of fascist societies as societies that deny freedom of impulse expression and mind to their citizens;[6] Theodor Adorno, Else Frenkel-Brunswik, Daniel Levinson, and Nevitt Sanford's efforts to identify a relatively pure form of an "authoritarian personality" with the hope of explaining various manifestations of totalitarianism and bigotry by the concentrated presence of many such individuals;[7] Erich Fromm's concept of a "necrophiliac personality" and of people with a "marketing orientation" to one another;[8] Robert Jay Lifton's powerful concept of "psychic numbing," both of victims of grave disasters and of perpetrators of horrors of great destruction, which describes the mind denial and dissociation that underlie the failure of people and societies to grasp major truths of the extent and sources of destructiveness of human life;[9] and various writers, from several fields such as political science and philosophy and not only psychology, such as Ronald Aronson, Ronald Santoni, and myself who have defined as "insanity" the actions of people and societies who are destructive of human life.[10] However, there remains a sense that these and other social science concepts are still only fragmentary parts of a larger picture or conceptualization yet to be formulated. I suggest that the larger unified theory for human behavior be a clear-cut respect for, valuing of, and commitment to protection of human life.

Soviet-communist psychology in its time went to the other extreme of creating concepts of the communal good and the responsibility of the individual to fit into the larger group and society. Individual adaptation and mental health were made virtually synonymous with social adaptation and productivity. Slowly but surely it dawned on the Western world that the Soviets nonetheless were tapping some other truth than what Western psychology had realized, for example that the socialization of children within a communal metaphor produces certain qualities of emotional strength and resilience that are less present in an overly self-oriented society,[11] findings that were strongly amplified by studies of children of the kibbutzim, or socialist collectives, in Israel. In this connection, in his study of the kibbutzim, intrepid iconoclastic psychologist Bruno Bettelheim stood out in his ability to observe the combination of strengths and weaknesses fostered by the collective upbringing, so that along with such fine qualities as leadership and readiness to volunteer he also noted a lack of sensitivity and empathy in personal relationships.[12] As usual, Bettelheim made his observations in an uncommonly aggressive style and with little heed for public relations; his correct observations were too bruising of far too many people, and the result was a concentrated booing and panning of his work that obscures the truths and wisdoms he reached.

In the United States in particular, because the emphasis on the collective was after all "communist psychology," the contribution issuing from a hated enemy was intrinsically suspect and unacceptable. Besides, it was obvious to the Western world that the communist society, which was ruthlessly oppressing the individual, had no legitimate psychology of the individual and therefore could not be trusted in its likely propagandistic exaggeration of the importance of the collective. So a split between concepts of individuals and the collective continued, fed by deep rivalries, suspicions, and hostilities as well as by a failure of the spirit in Western psychology; few dared to undertake efforts at integration of the two split-off concepts. The legendary Jewish exhortation by Rabbi Hillel, "If I am not for myself who will be, but if I am only for myself what am I?" went largely unheeded in formal psychological theory for many years.

Nonetheless, the searches for integrations of individual and collective concepts and of psychological and ethical meanings on a larger level were never entirely stifled. Any number of social scientists continued to do serious thinking toward laying the groundwork for seeing how the same concepts can be viewed as operating on the different levels of human organization of the individual, family, and society.[13] There have also been important theoretical and empirical studies of mechanisms of thinking that are crucial in shaping fascist behaviors both at the individual and societal levels, such as Lifton's very important essay on totalism;[14] Milton Rokeach's studies of rigidity;[15] the stunning researches of Stanley Milgram on obedience and, despite Milgram's avoidance of these terms, I would add destructiveness and cruelty;[16] Zimbardo's dramatic work on the propensity to be evil and cruel when given power over others;[17] Greenwald's penetrating theoretical treatment of the mind as fascist that I described at the beginning of this book,[18] and my own studies with Daphna Fromer of the readiness of students in the helping professions to participate as health professionals in evil societal programs.[19]

In addition, there have been some brilliant applications of societal-level concepts to clinical work such as Bruno Bettelheim's concept of the autistic child as experiencing himself the object of Nazi-like destructive persecution;[20] R. D. Laing's application of the freedom of the mentally ill person to reorganize himself to a renewed choice to be sane;[21] and family therapy studies of scapegoating.[22]

Many attempts also have been made to generalize from understanding the goodness of individuals' wholesome intimate relationships to possible contributions to societal thinking: love, training in respectful, egalitarian, and honest marital relationships;[23] forgiveness, applications of concepts of democracy to marriage and family relationships such as in applied programs for parent effectiveness training;[24] altruism;[25] extending oneself to rescue people in grave distress;[26] and ethical integrity in intimate relationships.[27] Most of these efforts nonetheless flounder in the face of the monumental extent of evil in the world, which can hardly be approached even by many individuals' acts of decency.

While retaining an essential comparability and even degrees of an equivalent identity when thought about in respect of the behavior of an individual and when used as descriptions of societal behaviors, the same psychological concepts sometimes become something different as

308

they are played out in the different contexts of individual and societal behaviors.

Thus, the essential quality of persecuting others in order to escape personal vulnerability and anxiety will be found in the mind of a paranoid person, in persecutions of a hapless family member assigned the role of emotional scapegoat in a family, and in mass movements of bigots who project their pent-up self-hatred and denials of their own vulnerability and mortality in horrible degradation on a minority.[28] But the scope, extent, intensity, and import of the application of the same kind of persecutory thinking is different at each level, and therefore creates a new entity at each of the levels at which the mechanism is at work. There are palpable differences between the small-scale tragedy of a paranoid person who destroys his or her ability to function in society; the unfair-to-another-person psychological cruelty and injustice of a person ganging up on a victim-member of the family, who is assigned a role say as the person in the family who will be the mentally ill (crazy) one; and, notwithstanding both the tragedy and the immorality of both earlier examples, the far more enormous destructiveness of group and societal policies in actual genocidal extermination of masses of human beings.

When we take concepts that have been generated in the study of society and return to see them at work in smaller units of the individual mind or in couples and families, we need to question whether the same concepts that were designed to deal with mass phenomena really apply to smaller units of human experience and interaction. When we apply concepts that have been generated by the study of the human mind to macrophenomena that are taking place on the broad level of society, there is good reason to question whether the same concept, or even the essential core of the concept, really fits phenomena that are on a much larger scale. In each case we also need to ask whether the magnification factor, or the expansion of the concept to describe the large phenomena, and the reduction factor, or the reduction of concepts to describe the smaller phenomena, are introducing degrees of distortion. In other words, the concepts being applied to explain behavioral phenomena may be subject to changes in the process of the stretching and focusing ("magnification" and "reduction") to fit the different plane of activity, and the phenomena being studied are likely to be somewhat different when they take place on vastly different scales and in quite different contexts.

In theory, any scientific lawfulness that we discover on one level of human behavior does not have to have its exact counterpart on other levels of human behavior. There can be laws of processes that are entirely idiosyncratic to one or another arena of human behavior. At the same time, there is a longstanding theoretical consensus in the philosophy of science that, more often than not, one should respect corresponding elaborations of the same phenomena at different levels of organization of reality as probably tapping some degree of the apparent and probable unity of all reality. Indeed, this principle has proven to be a fertile basis for many creative discoveries in which one sets out to seek processes corresponding to an already known principle on another level of organization of life and reality. When the correspondences are confirmed, the fact that parallel phenomena are taking place at different levels of reality is taken to add credence to the likely validity or lawfulness of the original observation. Moreover, in matters of human psychology and behavior, insofar as we determine that people are exposed to the same kind of process at more than one level of their experience, we also have a sense of the far greater power of that process at any single level of experience. More than likely there are additional stimuli and reinforcement for that phenomenon echoing from the resonances of the same dynamic at the other levels of experience.

In sum, the discovery of a correspondence of concepts in different spheres is a welcome advance in scientific thinking, first in the direct yield of explication of behaviors on the new level to which the concepts are now applied; in the contribution of the correspondence to a greater elegance and unification of theories of human behavior on more than one level; and also because of the interesting suggestions of additional synergistic phenomena that, at any given level, the same process may be resonated by inputs from other levels.

I am suggesting that use of the concept of a fascist paradigm in thinking about the emotional problems or psychopathologies of people as individuals and then too about people's relational difficulties in their marriages and families generates a new direction for psychotherapy, not only to deal with the symptomatic problem as such, but also to attack and correct the underlying distortion of thinking that insists on a single way of being a person to the exclusion of all other options and sides of humanness.

Insofar as the correspondence between a societal-fascism and mind-fascism proves useful and true, with the implication that fascism represents a model both in the nature of human mind and on the level of collective minds or societies for coping with reality, new vistas for looking at possible interactions between the individual and society open before us. Insofar as we see parallels to known forms of destructive societal patterns of fascism in personal mind behaviors and models of intimate relationships, we have added reason to suspect and work at correcting these totalitarian patterns of individual psychology and family relationships. Insofar as we see in individuals' personal lives that the closing of one's mind to multiple options and stifling one's ability to change and grow in favor of a ruthless pursuit of a single definition of truth and reality leads to a variety of emotional illnesses and family disturbances, our observations lend new credence to other observations that fascist political thinking creates "sick societies," and that absolutist policy and totalitarian suppression of dissent and difference will create societies of "sick people" who do many disturbed things.

Any contribution of major new bridges between concepts of mind, family groups, and society is a welcome development for practitioners and scientists alike, and can be expected to open doors to new techniques for interventions at various levels. Thus, concepts of appreciation of complexity, tolerance for differences, nonpersecution of dissent but definite limitation of violence against life are useful underpinnings for various innovations in individual therapy, family therapy, family life education, as well as in programs for citizenship education at the societal level. Moreover, this point of view of the desirability of DEMOCRATIC MIND contributes the idea that one should intervene preventively in the life of a person who is becoming locked into any mode of insistence that life be lived in a given single way, long before manifest symptoms are seen.

• Thus, one would hope to nip in the bud the psychotic withdrawal of a previously too-tender, over-intellectualizing youth by spotting him as a loner and intervening to help him make social contacts before a manifest mental illness has appeared.

• And we would hope to reach out well in advance to imminently violent children who can be identified as potentially dangerous by parents and educators, let alone by other children who know or sense what it is the children heading for violence are brewing, on the basis of their being overly and morbidly interested in violence long before having executed a deadly massacre in a school, such as in the Columbine massacre.

• Or one would be happy to have family or friends reach out at a relatively early stage of life to correct the bluster and style of emotional domination of a man or a woman overly sure of themselves, always in charge of their interactions with others, even if with great charm or seductiveness, and convinced that they never err; life shows that in time, either the loved ones of such self-assuming "giants" collapse, or they crumble under their pretensions, and it is not a pretty sight.

• Similarly, couples and families might be guided by ministers or family physicians or caring relatives away from overreliance on any single mode of experience at the expense of its correlative (for example, only loving and not also being angry, or being too firmly united with one another and not fostering separateness) long before the couple or their children report difficulties, such as serious psychosomatic illnesses in either the parents or children or severe learning disorders in the children.

The antifascist point of view also supports the conviction that any society needs to maintain multiplicity and diversity, and that signals of totalitarian suppression must be fought at their earliest appearance. Again we can be reminded of Fromm's inspiring remarks: "If you begin your resistance to a Hitler only after he has won his victory, then you've lost before you've even begun."[29] There emerges an impressive and encouraging consistency of principle that a democracy of mind, family, and society based on a built-in balance and symphonic integration of different modes of experience, thought, and contradictory aspects of human experience is a basis for healthier lives at all levels of life.

Toward a Transformative Relationship between Ethical Values
and a Scientific Mental Health/Pathology Framework

The worlds of mental health clinical practice and ethical values have stood apart from each other for too long.

Although over the years more than a few notable voices in the mental health community, such as in the philosophy and organizational activities of the American Orthopsychiatric Association, have taken stands on important social issues speaking from their consciences as mental health professionals who care about people and society, the prevailing theoretical conception in mental health nonetheless has been that the values that underline the development of healthy minds and sane societies are essentially different. Thus, the early psychoanalytic tradition of cultivation of impulse freedom, and then the prevailing rationale of most psychotherapy as teaching and enabling personal self-fulfillment, have created metaphors of self-assertion and even self-justification and self-indulgence that seem considerably different from the metaphors that underlie a philosophy of a healthy society that emphasizes reduction of conflict, cooperation, equitable distribution of resources, restraint in public policy, the greater common good in society, and justice. The way of thinking that has been presented here about psychopathology opens up what is to me a most exciting if also complex and healthily problematic possibility of a new linkage between ethical concepts and psychopathological concepts.

In the history of psychology, a major differentiation was established between ethical and psychological concepts as if they were entirely different planes of experience. In its time, the field of psychology prided itself on being able to find its way out from the uncontrollable philosophical jungle of speculations about good or bad and right or wrong to move toward an orderly science of observations and empirical interpretations of human behavior. At that stage of development of the science of psychology, it seemed important to maintain a clear-cut distinction between the empirical collection of information and philosophical or nonempirical value judgments. But now, many decades later, it seems that there is a need for a meaningful linkage between the two worlds, which on the one hand still will not erase the differentiation between philosophical thought and empirical observations and fact-gathering, but on the other hand will allow for explicit value judgments about which behaviors facilitate, protect, and enrich peoples' lives versus which behaviors do harm to peoples' lives.

One thoughtful middle-aged woman who had long put off a divorce from her husband who had proven to be both asexual (and she suspected was concealing his being a homosexual) and chronically demeaning and disparaging to her finally turned for help to a therapist and succeeded in bringing her husband in for joint sessions. But now she was appalled by the therapist's stubborn evenhandedness, as all issues were handled as bilateral, interactive, and shared without allowance for and recognition of differences in roles and responsibility between the two mates.

"I finally understood the real source of the problem with the therapy," she said. "The therapist not only was well-intentioned and wanted to help us both, but in truth was also committed to separating all ethics and values from the therapy. My insides were at last screaming after too many years of cowering in silence and fear that I had been tricked and manipulated into a loveless and insulting marriage, let alone lied to about my husband's sexuality. I was finally furious, but the therapist wanted to keep everything quiet! I can't stand a therapy that isn't also anchored in ethical truth and reality."

By using the accepted epistemology and methods of science, we can first demonstrate which specific conditions of human experience and behavior bring on dysfunctions or pathologies. We define these conditions and behaviors as unhealthy. There is little that is speculative and philosophical in these steps. The methods of science are used for observing, testing, and confirming empirically under what conditions human life is protected and thrives, and under what conditions human life is insulted, damaged, and threatened.

For example, it is an empirical fact that a parent's suicide increases significantly the probability/danger of a child's subsequent suicide. Although this is not the core issue in treating an adult contemplating suicide, it is nonetheless relevant information for such an adult who is also known to

314

be a caring parent, and of some therapeutic value for contributing to the prevention of his or her suicide.

Having established the empirical information, we then have every reason and justification to argue against unhealthy behaviors that generate dysfunction and disturbance (for example, although a person on the verge of suicide is by definition caught up in a state of overwhelming self-involvement, in some cases it can make a difference to raise the issue of the impact their suicide is likely to have on their children's lives). The one value judgment we have made is that whatever creates dysfunction, disorder, or in traditional health terms disease, is not acceptable, and after we have used scientific methods to determine objectively what these conditions are, we define them as undesirable. Thus, if we can develop a sound core of empirical observations to show that what we are calling fascist thinking leads to psychopathology, we will have every right and responsibility to take a stronger science-based stand against fascist thinking.

Science studies, observes, and documents the facts of life objectively without succumbing to any favored values and political positions. In a well-ordered society, the professions of medicine, psychology, social work, and others that treat illness and disability then apply the scientific knowledge to methods of treatment and to therapeutic educational programs aiming to prevent illness. Finally, legal and associated agencies of community organization apply the knowledge of science to the development of legal and social policies on a societal level to prevent the conditions that foster dysfunctions and to enhance approaches to treatment and correction of dysfunctions as much as possible.

• Science tells us smoking kills people; professional medicine then tells the consumers not to smoke, and influences legislators to pass laws against smoking in public situations, and to increase taxes on cigarettes.

• The science of psychology proves that early, premature, and traumatic losses of attachments – specific loved ones, and also one's community and reference group and familiar physical surroundings – tear people apart inside and reduce their immunity to psychological breakdown and to physical disease. The implications for child rearing, education, social sciences, and other institutions are that we need to do everything possible to reduce losses of attachments, and that when losses do take place, everything that can be done to enable replacement bonding and attachment is crucial to the health of the aggrieved ones. I have witnessed in a dirt-poor area of Armenia (then still a part of the former Soviet Union) rehabilitation of children who had lost their parents in an earthquake based on defining the extended community as a caring replacement for the missing parents. In Israel, financial compensation and outstandingly caring social work services are available for the lifetime of a child who loses a parent in military service or in the course of a terrorist attack.

• Scientific or objective fact-gathering of history, sociology, and political science tells us that hundreds of millions of human beings have died in a large number of events of genocide; the institutions of law and other institutions such as religion and the international political community slowly but surely are promulgating new codes against genocide, including new codes of punishment and new legal tribunals for judging those who commit the crime.[30]

There are also complex philosophical issues. One should ask, for example, whether in all the above cases, the implications of the scientific findings necessarily are to stop the given behavior that shortens life. Surely the logical possibilities go both ways, and there may be times when the choices adopted are not to extend life, for example, a planned approach to reduction of a too-large population. Perhaps instead of stopping smoking, stopping losses of attachment, and stopping genocide, the conclusions to be drawn from the empirical scientific findings might be for more smoking, more disruption of attachments, and more genocide (some of these "more choices" indeed have been taken by various societies over time).

I believe the correct spiritual answer is that in its essence, the truth-seeking integrity of the scientific method links up with a choice of seeking to protect life as much as possible and to be opposed to promoting destruction and death. There is, I believe, a natural connection between fighting to protect the integrity of facts, evidence, empirical truth, and reality that goes with fighting to protect life, survival, health, longevity, and quality of life. I believe that science qua science is for life and against premature death.[31]

My opinion is that in psychological science, scientific definitions of what conditions make for psychological normality, optimal human functioning, and health in general are intrinsically also statements of ethical imperatives. Scientific psychological and ethical concepts are both useful as different ways for looking at essentially the same behaviors. There are overlapping and complementary meanings between the two sets of concepts. If we want to retain a sense of separation between the two conceptual worlds, we can say that it is our scientific psychology that gives us a way of determining what conditions lead to what outcomes; while ethics enables us to define a positive value for life-enhancing and life-protecting conditions, and a negative value for conditions that lead to doing harm to life or destroying life. Our observations of what behaviors lead to what outcomes are anchored in empirical science. Our definitions of mental health need not be thought of as based on belief systems, but on empirical studies of what is and is not facilitating mental health and life and a philosophical choice of supporting life.[32]

The concept of a model of fascism as underlying individual, family, and societal pathology opens the door further toward bringing together the two worlds of science and ethics that many of us really never were happy about keeping rigidly apart. I believe we are able to demonstrate scientifically that personal and collective overcertainties and absolute truths cause damage to the psychological well-being of people, and, therefore, it is scientifically proper to caution people in the style of Surgeon General's warnings as follows:

> Fascist certainties of all sorts may cause damage
> to the human mind, family life, and society.

To conclude, for those concerned about giving up a distinction between science and values, it should be clear that in our framework we have left the factual and evidential cases of all questions subject to pure scientific investigation, and that there should be no interference with the process of free inquiry. We ask science to investigate many questions:

• What are the conditions that cause premature human death?

• What causes agonizing human death?

• What are the conditions that spread horrible diseases?

After we have the facts, each of us and every society has the responsibility to apply the facts to choices of our positions, whether for more protection of human life or for more destruction and suffering.

Like Albert Camus, whom we quoted earlier as vowing neither to be a victim or an executioner, we opt for the promotion of life.[33]

Correcting Fascist-Type Rigidities

If the concept of a fascist paradigm or mindset as playing a major role in the development of many types of psychopathology is valid, it represents not only an interesting new way of thinking about and understanding emotional difficulties on the level of deciphering of the human mind but also opens the door to the possibilities of new techniques of psychotherapy that may prove to have considerable new power.

Two examples were referred to earlier of the application of this concept in treatment, in one case with an adult anorexic male, in another case with a teenage girl who had made a suicide attempt. In both cases, the message to the patient was that he or she had gotten stuck on an idea and was no longer able to examine the validity of that idea, or even to accept information pouring in from the reality of life. This way of being and organizing the self was inimical to his or her commonsense interests and was affecting their health and even survival. In both cases, not only was the symptomatology severe but also the lifestyle of the patient was problematic. In the case of the anorexic, the pattern was chronic and longstanding, with many indications of poor prognosis; in the case of the suicidal young girl, there had been a recovery from the suicide attempt as such, but it was not clear how long it might be before another attempt, given every indication of a continuing pessimism and rigidity. In both instances the focus of treatment was on the way of thinking more than on the specific symptoms. In both cases this focus brought about palpably powerful changes that at this writing have survived the passage of many years.

How the psychotherapeutic focus on the stuck mindset facilitates change is open to considerable thought.

It may be that the therapist's feedback about the rigid ways of being in the world – accurate reporting and mapping of the stuckness back to the patient – enabled the patients to stop the blind repetition of their habitual programs.

Another quixotic possibility is that the focus on the way in which the mind was operating relieved the patient from exploring more distressing and perhaps more important areas of psychodynamic and relationship problems in their own right, for example, being captive to narcissistic emotional demands of the mother and hostile rejection by the father in the case of the anorexic male, and fearing closeness and tenderness in the case of the suicidal girl. No doubt these were very real issues, but there is also reason to believe that the possibilities of fuller working through of these issues – which were also subjects of the therapies – were limited; in both cases there were also indications that it was too late and quite impossible to make any far-reaching changes in the families of origin of both patients. A fuller working through of these issues would have taken many years more of psychotherapy, with a great danger of the symptoms continuing for longer periods of time, thereby also reinforcing their constituting a chronic way of life. The focus on the problem of the mindset broke through to initiate a meaningful pattern of more immediate change.

Another explanation of how work on the stuck mindset may effect a major change with less psychodynamic work at understanding deeper sources of the behavior is available from the technical concept in psychotherapy of reframing, or changing the set and contextual meaning of repeated ongoing behaviors. The power of reframing often seems to lie in its loosening the stuckness of the compulsion to repeat the same behavior over and over again.[34] The patient in effect is told that he or she is not responsible for troubling behavior because of feelings, motives, and unconscious intentions, but rather that he or she is caught in a mode of stuckness. The concept of being stuck or locked in is archetypically familiar to all of us from earlier experiences in our lives. When given an idea on how to release oneself from stuckness and encouragement to take the step to "start all over again," the patient can be freed from being enslaved by a repetitive context of meaning that has become a trap of doing the same thing over and over again.

It can also be added that the above explanations are not necessarily mutually exclusive. They possibly coexist in the same space and time. It is also possible that a treatment focus on the fascist mindset will trigger the first kind of experience of insight and motivation to stop blind repetition of a behavior in some people, and another kind of experience of reframing the behavior and a change in its meaning releases stuckness for other people.

What was noteworthy in both of the specific cases cited was that alongside of or in addition to the manifest clinical symptomatology, the personalities of both people and their life histories showed evidence of rigid, unvarying styles in their lives. The anorexic young man found it hard to learn from experience how to get along with people. For example, he was often given feedback from business associates in which they told him that he was an invasive, punctilious, fussy mother hen, and a pain-in-the-neck version of his mother, demanding that the world operate according to his terms. In the case of the young woman, her family and especially her friends told her repeatedly that she was always outraged and condescendingly rejecting of any efforts to approach her in friendship or even to give her new ideas. This means that the interventions based on discussing with these patients their ways of thinking and organizing strategies for dealing with problems in their lives went far beyond their specific symptoms to look at many other instances that bothered them, about which they had a good deal of information – albeit thus far unusable – from many sources, where they could now see their inflexibility and the bad results of these styles in their lives.

Nonetheless, it also has to be considered that at this time it is obviously not clear when a psychotherapeutic focus on a rigid way of thinking will and will not be helpful in different cases.

Correcting Rigidities in Intimate Relationships

We have been considering the significance of fascist-type thinking in creating disturbances in the individual mind. Now I also want to explore the impact of fascist thinking on the individual when she or he is engaged in intimate relationships with others, such as a spouse or one's children, or the family.

The treatment of couple relationships and family relationships stands between concepts of individual psychology and concepts of man's relationship to and participation in larger groups of community and society. Paradigms of absolute truth and certainty are not lacking in respect to the ways people seek to organize their intimate relationships. "You *Must* Love Me" demands are pandemic in the minds of many spouses or parents, and the consequences of such demands for love are well known. Another source of stuckness is insistence on absolute integrity in a family relationship, such as demands for absolute truth between couples that leaves no room for human failings, discretion, and privacy. (In fact, I am in favor of total disclosure and truthfulness between husband and wife if it is genuinely possible as an outgrowth of choice and the basic excellence of the relationship, but not on the basis of obligation and requirement, and not for those couples in which one or both cannot handle the full truth and it will only hurt them more.) Another source of stuckness is insistence on unerring justice in whatever plane of family relationships. An insistence on fairness and decency can also be trapping, much like openly exploitative, authoritarian relationships harm people, for it is the mechanism of demand and obligation to serve a given standard that causes difficulty no less than the content of the specific value being demanded. While it has always been obvious that authoritarian relationships that command obedience and subservience in intimate relationships create serious disturbance, it has been less clear, and still today is not entirely understood by many therapists who overidentify with the values of goodness, that overcommitment and being captive to the finest values can also generate disturbances.

A family comes for treatment because they are being drained by the temper tantrums of their oldest child, a twelve-year-old boy. In family ther-

apy it becomes clear that each of the parents had adopted a commitment to positive values that is so far-reaching it has become a basis for continuous disappointment and upset at failures to fulfill the vaunted values.

Mother insists on fairness. Whenever unfairness is present anywhere in her life, she becomes so upset she becomes angry, and her anger is so self-righteous that she tends to become abusive. Father is committed to democratic sharing and equality, and what this means in his case is that even when a child misbehaves, or even when his wife pressures him with her abusive self-righteousness, he retains a calm mien, speaks decently, and above all, does so without imposing any power inherent in his roles as father and husband. The result for the others, such as his son, is that there are no clear messages of displeasure, impatience, or anger regarding abusive behaviors, and therefore the boy's abusive behaviors tend to be reinforced and to continue.

Intriguingly, as soon as changes were evident in the presenting patient, who was the oldest child, each of the remaining children in the family picked up the cudgel and proceeded to act out their versions of inconsolable tantrums; the therapy then helped the parents deliver their new styles of being firmer and more organizing of all the children.

Albert Ellis's contributions to our understanding of the demands people impose on relationships based on the insistent expectations they hold in their mind have been outstanding, although even in his writing on marriages his emphasis is more on what happens in the mind of each of the participants rather than on what happens in the relationship – what family therapists understand to be the systemic pattern that characterizes each relationship.[35] Going back to the pioneering interpersonal theorists in psychoanalysis, several great early thinkers such as Karen Horney and Erich Fromm contributed considerably to our understanding of the decisive concepts around which demands could be organized in relationships, such as power,[36] and exploitation.[37] Irascible psychiatrist-poet Ronald Laing exposed the profound corruptions that are often present in family relationships, and how in many families people feel they are being driven crazy, terrorized with anxiety, or feel threatened with being virtually engulfed.[38] Each of these and other theorists of personality have shed important light on the kinds of concepts that can become the runaway ideas characteristic of a tyrannical invasion and hostage-taking of people in intimate relationships.

Basic Equality in Relationships

A core issue in the complexity of the struggle that takes place between people in all intimate relationships is whether or not the relationship will inherently be one of intrinsic equality and facilitation of each other or will be organized around one person being "more equal" than the other, more empowered, more confident, and more in charge than the other – who is then relegated, even if subtly, to be the less adequate, significant, valuable, or deserving.

People don't necessarily have to intend to seek power over one another. There is in our nature an inherent drive toward differentiation of one's own self and attaining one's potential height of competence in different skill areas that can lead to a superiority of one person over another. Also, an evolutionary battle in human beings for survival of the fittest archetypically pits one person against another in any system or network of relationships. The trick is not in suppressing these natural instinctive forces, but rather in having the good taste and genuine caring for the other that cautions one to correct oneself whenever the sum total of a way of being in the world begins to exceed, overshadow, and dominate loved one(s). At the least, there are always qualities of excellence and leadership waiting in other areas of functioning in the other person. Correspondingly, any family member who in effect is being belittled and placed in a secondary status needs to have the inherent good taste to protest and revolt against such an assignment. Such a refusal to be cast in a lesser role need not be based on a claim to equal talent, but should derive from every family member's right to be experienced intrinsically as equally valid and valuable.

When one spouse or member of a family opts for and holds on to the role of better-than-the-other(s), or when one spouse or family member chooses to find security in playing a lesser role idealizing the more competent mate or overrelying on the other for all sorts of services, the relationship between the family members becomes frozen into a form that must be maintained or else the security of all partners to the tradition of inequalities is threatened. The style of one being "more" and the other "less" becomes a rule that one dare not violate in that marriage or family. The collusive or codependent relationship around inequality takes on a dimension of the way things must be – or else. Like most clinicians, I have seen cases where the punishment of a spouse who dares to change the rules and become more equal is met with relentless punishment.

> ✒ *A woman who, despite being a college graduate, stayed home and played mother and obedient wife while her husband gallivanted about in more senses than one finally decided to learn to drive their car. . . . The symbolic message of her daring to become "more" was obvious to both of them. She was promptly rewarded with her husband's announcement that he was leaving her for another woman.*

Couples committed to a genuine equality move in and out of different facets of their relationship, in which he is the "more" and she is "less," and she is the "more" and he the "less" in different areas of their relationship and at different times. There is a natural shifting between poles; both spouses are honored and grateful to embrace each other in their combinations of strengths and weaknesses, and to appreciate each other, each as a uniquely lovely person and each also deserving of kindness and understanding in his or her frailty and weaknesses that make them more attractive, because they are after all human.[39]

Learning to Care Both for Oneself and for Others

Perhaps the single most powerful force in all human behavior is the compelling desire to preserve and save one's most precious possession – life, but in many instances of pathological family disturbances and mental illnesses, people go about trying to protect their precious possession in the wrong ways.

In fascist or absolute thinking, people in effect are insisting that to survive they must abide by a ruthless, single-minded standard rule. By laying their very survival on the line of the requirement that this rule must be upheld at all times, they are then forced to destroy any and all opposition to their avowed absolute principle, whether from inside or from others, and so they end up hurting human lives, whether their own or others, even though what they intended to do was to save their own lives.

Commitment to life, for oneself and for others, is a precious dimension of human experience, and, not surprisingly, is in itself a source of life.

I doubt that there are many mental health clinicians who will dispute the observation that the single most determining factor of whether or not a patient gets well is the desire to become well, in other words, the desire to live and bestow a decent living experience on oneself. I also doubt that there are clinicians who will dispute the fact that people who care genuinely for others' rights to live not only contribute meaning-fully to strengthening others – as professionals, parents, lovers, in effect in any human connection – but also gain a great deal of pleasure and strengthening of their own power in return.

Learning to care about human life is a psychological developmental process.[40] It begins with an infant caring about itself and the unfolding of its natural narcissism of healthy self-ness. Disturbances of this vital foundation are seen in later years either when people undervalue them-selves or when they overcompensate with overvaluation of themselves (pathological narcissism that represents more selfishness than healthy self-ness).

As the child grows in warm self-regard and as a secure human being, the child's caring extends through a natural progression to take in mother, father, and siblings, and then extends to and becomes a loyalty to the entire family.

However, one must note that these natural loyalties also show up at times as obligatory and forced loyalties to one's "kinfolk" when, in fact, the person does not have a healthy foundation of self-love and there is no genuine love of one's family or people. Unfortunately, as in many other aspects of human nature, people can force an approximation of the subsequent stages of development. Many times people even make unconscious efforts to continue growing, or at least to simulate growth and convince themselves that they are O.K., even though, sadly, they are not really developing. For example, many people get married when

325

they really are not ready for a marriage relationship. People can fool themselves and others by seemingly adopting later stages of development that they have not really reached inwardly. Thus, many people can look like or talk about their apparent caring for other people, but not really feel caring.

For fully alive people, the range of belonging and identification continues to expand steadily with the unfolding of their lives and becomes part of an overall love of life. Slowly but surely, the developing personality becomes aware of new connections that go far beyond the concrete personal connections to which one was born, by chance of one's specific family, tribe, or nation, and one becomes aware of many other human beings and their families, tribes, and nations. A sense of kinship with all other people begins to take form, and a notion of a common humanity begins to transcend identifications with any specific sector of that humanity.

It is entirely natural to care most deeply about one's self and one's own people, and to care more intently for some other people with whom one feels a more immediate kinship, but ultimately the challenge of human development, both for the benefit of individual mental health and happiness and for the benefit of humanity, is for more people also to care about others in a real way.

As noted earlier, the commitment to life needs to be formulated carefully with respect to the choices that are made of the means used to preserve life. One cannot protect life by employing means to the goal that are in themselves injurious and destructive. Once committed to self-defense as the end all and be all, one tends to accept one's own security needs as justifying manipulative and ruthless strategies and policies to eliminate any opposition. If one only thinks about maneuvers and strategies to gain power over people or an organizational structure in order to achieve one's own ends, it is not long before one embraces a philosophy that the ends justify all means. One is no longer able to think straight about responsibility in relationships to other people. Life turns into a veritable jungle.

An illustrative application of the importance of commitment both to one's own life and to others will be seen in marital therapy. In the elusive domain of treatment of marriages, we find that those who are genuinely committed to their marriages, for their own sakes as well as out of real caring for their spouses, have the best chance of working out even difficult problems and of arriving at a way of living together that is genuinely nourishing and fun. The ability to commit to marriage wholesomely is a continuation of the ability to value one's own life as well as that of the other person, so that there is a basic decency and integrity in the way one goes about searching out the causes of pain and dissatisfaction and looking for ways to build a mutually cooperative lifestyle.

When a couple is fortunate enough to share this kind of decency, it is virtually inevitable that they will overcome difficulties and have a wonderful time in their marriage over the long run. Spouses' commitments to the marriage are the single most important determining factor in the outcome of the marital process and in treatment of marital problems.

A Funny Challenging Question: Can One also Turn a Commitment to Life into a Fascist Principle?

Is it possible to become so committed to a commitment to life that it too also becomes a basis for a rigid, unyielding principle? The height of the irony would be that the commitment to life can be turned into the basis for persecution of parts of oneself or of other persons who fail to honor and support what is now a deadly "jealous" overcommitment to life.

If one looks at the history of commitments to life and life values, the answer is that people ostensibly devoted to protecting human life, freedom, liberty, and democracy *have* translated their devotional litany into a basis for inquisitorial persecution and massacre of identified heretics. Blind, ritualistic insistence on devotion to life or democracy or good government or a holy god can become the basis for the heinous guillotining that occurred in the French Revolution, the tortures and murdering by many governments such as in Chile or Argentina in more recent years, the inquisitions and murders by religious zealots and movements like the Crusades centuries ago, the Taliban in our times, or paranoid "purifications" of millions of alleged enemies by Hitlerian, Stalinist, or Maoist-type regimes.

The moral of the story is a very serious one, namely that the commitment to life too must at all times be guarded by built-in safeguards against persecutory or retaliatory acts against other people identified as opposing our values.

The comprehensive *Encyclopedia of world problems and human potential* observes wisely that an "archetypal scapegoat or shadow" is present in every one of us.[41] It is that part of a being that feels vulnerable and under attack, and "feels it necessary to vindicate himself or justify his own behaviour." This vulnerable/attacking-the-other part of the personality springs from fearfulness and vulnerability and "is not normally recognized a part of the self and thus the blame or attack is usually received by someone else who has sparked off the disquieting view of the shadow." To acknowledge and control the vulnerable/attacking-the-other personality "takes courage leading first to humility and *humanness* and eventually to new insight and expanded horizons. It is this mechanism which underlies bias, discrimination and conflict."

The entry concludes:

> Acknowledgement of the collective shadow might well prevent nationalistic or racial over-reactions to atrocities and barbarism which effectively are merely responding in kind. By accepting that everyone, as a human being, holds in himself collective responsibility for every development may well be the key to the next stage in human evolution.

Violence in the name of lofty values must be subject to rigorous controls no less than any other justifications of violence. Killing other human beings needs to be made illegal and morally reprehensible in our civilization except under very carefully defined conditions of self-defense. Claims of self-defense, by people or by nations, need to be subjected to firm tests of evidence, since the objective test of a conviction that one must fight in self-defense is often difficult, and we know that human beings become convinced that harm is intended for them and that they must take preemptive first action to overcome their would-be assailant when in truth there is no such danger. Notwithstanding our devotion to life and a commitment to same, we must be wary of any and all exhortations to protect life and fight for it unless these are also accompanied by a commitment to fight the enemies of life with an avoidance of harsh and brutal acts, and wherever possible eschewing killing, even enemies, except as required in self-defense.

On the small and large levels of life, extraordinary care must be taken to protect other people precisely when they arouse our fears and ire, even justifiably: when a parent feels that a child is draining them; when a married person feels his or her spouse is "killing them," such as in a case of infidelity; when a religious group is convinced that the presence of another faith is deeply insulting and threatens their survival; or when a nation is frightened by the rhetoric and intentions of expansion and domination of a neighboring people, even when a people are in fact being attacked by terrorist forces that ultimately need to be brought down.

Prudence, restraint, and creative alternative strategies for seeking peace are called for on all levels of human relations. Admittedly, on all levels of human life there often do need to be battles in self-defense for peace against very real aggressors, but the battle needs to be joined as nonviolently as possible with the least destruction of life possible, or the battle has already been lost.

The central unifying principle of living is to live and let live. Knowing this also helps make more sense out of our lives.

The Care and Maintenance of the Bridge between Mind and Society

I wish that in the fell swoop of a closing chapter I could make an inspired statement about the care and maintenance of our minds that would really bring us closer to a beautiful new peaceful world. This kind of idealistic dreaming makes me happy. In fact, I will try to make a real-life statement about everyday uses of mind, first to be more sane, resilient, and self-contented; second to be more connected to the people in our lives; and third to contribute to a more sane and life-caring society.

I am talking about the achievement of attributes of DEMOCRATIC MIND and the overcoming of FASCIST MIND.

Staying Away from Totalities and Overcertainties

Foremost in care and maintenance of the bridge between mind and society is staying away from totalities and overcertainties, toward ourselves and toward others. It is our right to be strong and firm in our convictions, but whenever the sound of our voice is adamantly unquestioning or hysterically demanding we are quite likely in a zone of fascist demands for compliance to rules, rituals, and extremisms.

Toward ourselves, I am proposing that we correct overcertainties and totalistic responses in our emotions and thinking, such as always needing to be loved, accepted, successful, admired, strong, happy, unafraid, or wise; or the obverses of needing always not to be rejected, excluded, disrespected, shamed, weak, sad, upset, fearful, or dumb, but which DEMO-CRATIC MIND defines also as natural and inevitable events and parts of healthy and successful lives.

A corollary of the above is to examine our most beloved and intense activities for exaggerations of using ourselves too much in these areas, and also to look carefully at what other parts of ourselves and our lives we are likely neglecting in the process. It is all disconcerting and quite impossible, for to be a real artist or performer or to be competent in any endeavor generally calls for devotion to learning and practicing the skill. On the one hand, my advice would seem to do away with too many of our finest surgeons, ballplayers, musicians, cooks, and just about everybody who falls in love with an area of talent and expertise and becomes really good at something. On the other hand, we do know very well that all surgery and no play, meaning too much work and not enough recreation, and too much time away from home at whatever work and not enough time with family, and too much seriousness and not enough frivolousness, and too much bookworming and not enough sexworming, and busy, busy, busy, and not enough loving; and even the reversals of every one of the above so that you have all play, or too much family, or too much frivolousness, or too much sexworming all make for unhealthy, alienated, and unhappy people.

> *For example, there are data on physicians going way back over the years that shows a high level of personal instability, including suicides, drugs, and marital and family disturbances. The extent to which many physicians' lives get messed up seems to correlate externally with insufficient dedication to quality relationships in the family, and internally with excesses of pride, an illusion of triumph over weakness and mortality, and a failure to yield sufficiently to dependent needs.* [1]

Balancing ourselves on a broad spectrum of activities is a major organizing task. No one I know is exempt from allocating themselves to a wide range of functions, including dedication to health, work, and spouse, children, and community. The self-organization required is hard, and no one really knows how to do it exactly right. The happy news is that just making a meaningful effort seems to bring about a decent enough result.

Toward our families or other people with whom we live intimately, we will do well to scan our minds for behavior rules and requirements we may be imposing on them, such as always to respect us, follow our religious beliefs and practices (I don't mean to step on any toes of committed religionists, some of whom by definition cannot possibly tolerate devi-ation from their one faith, yet life tells us they too must prepare say for children to move to another place on the spectrum of religious practices – sometimes it is even to become more orthodox in the faith of their parent!), not disagree on politics, give us their attention when we turn to them, serve us physically in whatever ways, adore us, believe in us, refrain from criticism or correction, never talk about hurt feelings, and not bother us with such and such needs or problems of theirs. Insisting on an unchangeable reality may work for a while in creating an atmosphere of loving and togetherness, or even a cultist atmosphere of adoration or obedience. Inevitably the situation blows up though, because in princi-ple there is no provision for draining off and discharge of contradiction, dissent, and the necessary expression of each person's individuality.

Toward other people in our work lives, neighbors, community, and larger society, we face the same choices: to blindly succumb to the overcertain-ties, edicts, and ideologies laid down by leaders and groups, or to stand up as spokesmen of a more democratic and pluralistic point of view that is aware of the dangers inherent in going too far in any single direction. We also have a responsibility not to become powerful leaders who demand obedience to our certainties and totalities. Again the task is not an easy one. Many marvelous ideas and causes are deserving of total support. For example, some charitable organizations and movements are dedicated to helping fellow human beings; one can honorably devote "all of oneself" to these. Yet there is a difference between making oneself into a blind loyalist and suspending one's judgments about any possible wrongdoing of a beloved cause and its leaders and a mature identification with a just cause.

In all of their honor and devotion to goals of excellence in helping improve the lives of human beings, is there any one of the professions that has not been revealed countless times to be a hotbed of corruption, exploitation, and even destruction of people?

• There are physicians who are torturers and murderers for killing regimes.

• There are corrupt cops and judges in every legal system.

• Our scheming, swindling accountants and business barons walk off with the food, water, energy, and pensions of millions of people.

• There are priests, rabbis, ministers, and heads of churches in every faith who use people as their slaves, including sexually, who steal church monies and lands, and, most blasphemous to any conceivable concept of a loving God, who engage in collective murders in the name of their church or the government system to which it is linked.

In peaceful times, betrayals by leaders of professions and institutions are shocking stories that explode in any given community with tremendous impact. In times of war or other great social upheaval, it often becomes clear that it is not only individual practitioner-leaders but also the institutions of the given profession that have turned against the values of promoting life for which the profession is supposed to stand. See thus the records of organized medicine in the Holocaust and in other cases of genocide such as the gruesome medical experiments and murders of Chinese by the Japanese in Manchuria in the 1930s;[2] the collapse of the legal system in essentially every country that has engaged in massive torture, brutality, and genocide;[3] the corruption of churches and educational systems of these same societies, whether on the conceptual level of providing explicit or tacit support to the persecutory governments, or even in concrete incidents in which a church leader puts a torch to a church in which frightened people have come seeking protection.[4]

DEMOCRATIC MIND does not relinquish responsibility for critically reviewing the actions of the leaders and institutions of its society that it otherwise admires and supports. DEMOCRATIC MIND does not hide behind admirable qualities of loyalty and identification with a cause to allow suppression of information of gross negligence, injury, exploitation, or sadistic harm to human beings.

To my mind, one of the biggest lies in the medical profession, which has also been accepted as a kind of catchword concept by a number of other professional groups, is that "professional ethics" dictate that one should never express a negative opinion about a fellow practitioner or give any information about malpractice by another practitioner. I think this concept and practice are the heights of unethical behavior. There is some truth to the original concept that any professional will do well to be careful not to allow competitive interests and other grudges and angers to feed into maligning or defaming a colleague, but that is very different from telling the truth about harms done to clients. Many people and families who have been injured by professionals and who have sought recognition and compensation from the courts have been frustrated and maddened by the refusal of other practitioners, who knew what happened, to tell the truth.

No belief system, no cause, no profession, no institution, no ideology, no movement, no utopian scheme deserves to have the blind, unquestioning, slavish support of any person or community (however much they may very well deserve respect and basic loyalty and devotion for all the good they do).[5]

Again there is a paradoxical element inherent in such a call for individuality and integrity of judgment. Great institutions and movements in history often have benefited from the blind devotion of people who believed unquestioningly in the rightness of their cause. Devoted administrators have single-handedly brought about the creation or expansion of a major school, hospital, or treatment center, or a significant social justice movement, or important social legislation that helps people in need. New nations and homelands have been built because great leaders and devoted followers gave their all to the cause of their historical imperative.

Nonetheless, even as commitment and devotion to just and great causes is to be applauded, I propose that the cultivation of an observing mind includes not being afraid to take in information that is critical or even opposed to a cause in which one otherwise believes. DEMOCRATIC MIND evaluates information fairly and rationally, and finds the serious faults that are unfortunately also to be found in good causes and in the best of our democratic governments. The International Red Cross, for example, is an outstandingly deserving cause, but for too long a time the Red Cross engaged in blatantly corrupt actions to conceal its appeasement of and collaboration with the murderous Nazis.[6] Our finest democracies too have records of eras of vicious discrimination and persecution of minorities among them for example, against the blacks in the United States, and against Palestinians in the occupied areas of Israel), and worse of events of manifest genocidal massacres (for example, the My Lai's in Vietnam by the United States,[7] and a number of genocidal massacres of Arabs by Israel, such as Kfar Kassem in 1956[8]).

A great Nazi fighter, Simon Wiesenthal, said in his later years:

> *A school class asked me for a piece of advice for their future which I formulated as follows: "Never let a movement, a political party, or another person persuade you to act against your own conscience."*[9]

The Care and Maintenance of Freedom of Information, Criticism, and Dissent: Taking Responsibility for Our Errors

Resistance to demands for censorship and to suppression of unwelcome information is a further aspect of the bridge between mind and society that needs care and maintenance. It takes courage not to submit to demands for censorship of dissenting, contradictory, or perplexing information that threatens a regime or Establishment, whether in our own minds (for example, extreme eating rules), or in regard to the stability of given relationships (for example, in overcontrol of a spouse or one's marriage, or of a family group), or in the exploitative rules of one's communities and societies (for example, acceptance of exploitation of migrant workers) that have been mandated to persist in an unchanging way.

As we have seen, there are many rules that enter into individuals' minds in mistaken efforts to regulate one's life in some single correct way. Whenever we spot such a rule in ourselves or in the making, we should know that the very method of constructing such rules is inherently mistaken, for there is hardly an aspect of life that does not call for a healthy back-and-forth flow between contradictory and dialectical aspects of an experience. As individuals, we need to regulate our eating, but not to the point that we lose the joy of eating in slavish dieting, nor by stuffing ourselves to avoid feeling empty and uncomfortably alone. We need to be wary of any form of connecting with and even caring for and loving others that becomes unduly sticky, possessive, demanding, and vulnerable to catastrophic upset were anything to go wrong in the continuity of the connection. Any gluing or excessive togetherness of people necessarily suppresses the natural and no less necessary aspects of separateness, individuality, and a resilience of being able to carry on without the persons we love the most in this world. As we have seen, other requirements of oneself always to be any given kind of person and not to deviate from any given mode of behavior or experience are at the root of many mental health and relationship disasters, such as madness, suicide, depression, despair, and breakup of relationships.

I find it amazing to see people turn away when information that is contrary to their devoted beliefs, identifications, and opinions reaches them. In daily life, every one has seen people who simply clam up and walk off when the information they cannot bear comes up. Strange as it sounds, I have become convinced that much of this censorship is an unconscious response, and that many people go virtually into a trance in their belief systems and enter a temporary state of inability to take in any dissenting information.

• One year after 9/11, a Gallup poll confirmed that a majority of people in a wide range of Muslim countries were convinced that Osama bin Laden had not led the attacks against the United States on the deadly day.[10]

• Who then did commit 9/11? In many cases, the blame is laid on the Jews/Israelis being responsible for the suicide bombings of the World Trade Center and the Pentagon![11]

• Moreover, since fascist-hate minds have no responsibility to refer to any empirical sources of information, the sky is the limit for the imagination, ravings, and hate rhetoric of bigots and totalitarians who seek to destroy democracy; so that we even see some bizarre hints if not full attributions of 9/11 to the action of the United States itself against itself![12]

• As a medical patient, I have had too many experiences with physicians who could not acknowledge the errors they made in prescribing medication. (Repeatedly, research has found that up to a third of patients in hospitals at any given time have been the victims of incorrect medication). My impression is that many physicians are not defending themselves against malpractice suits or any kind of claim or external shame of their mistakes, but more simply that they cannot bear acknowledging their errors.

• Psychotherapists who deal with a much softer area of knowledge than medicine are notorious for a quickness to rationalize and defend themselves when information of bad results is brought to their attention, and worse when criticisms are rendered of the ways in which they handled the case.

Thus too, so many people in everyday family life go no less than crazy when criticisms are made of them.

> ⏂ *She literally would lift her nose up to a pronounced angle, lift her eyebrows, and raise her voice to a somewhat shrill and stern tone of a parent remonstrating whoever it was who had dared tell her that she had in any way done something unwelcome or unpleasant. The last thing in the world she was ready to do was to engage in any conversation with her loved ones about her contribution to any problem. And yet this same woman was committed quite sincerely to liberal political causes and human rights, and was sincerely opposed to societal prejudice and totalitarianism.*

Through the centuries, societies adopt policies regarding the flows of information that are contrary to their expressed beliefs. When it comes to denials of genocides that have been committed, for example, there are obviously denials that are based on protecting one's government and one's leaders from prosecution, especially as the world grows in its ability to set up legal machinery for bringing genociders to trial.[13] But it is also obvious that any number of governments are not so much concerned with legal charges or demands for reparations, but are expressing a tradition of demands for respect and blind denial of their wrongdoing.

• The Turkish government has been uncompromisingly adamant there was no genocide of the Armenian people in 1915 and on. It devotes talent and resources to demanding that other governments and cultures and intellectual academies rewrite history and tow their line – and if not they threaten what retaliations they can, such as canceling lucrative business contracts or pulling out of joint military exercises even within an established alliance such as NATO.[14]

• The Japanese government has denied for years several aspects of genocidal persecution of others, including the mass rapes and killings of the Chinese in Manchuria, and including vicious "Mengele-type" medical experiments on prisoners and civilians. When a court case was brought by Chinese survivors against the Japanese government, the government continued in its time-honored contention that there is no proof the Imperial Army spread plague over the countryside of China and infected food with cholera, or engaged in vicious medical experiments of prisoners of war and civilian prisoners. In 2002 a Tokyo district court ruled against the government and concluded officially that Japan had indeed conducted germ warfare in World War II. The court bluntly contradicted the continued insistence by the government that there was no proof. Nonetheless, the same court also continued the time-honored Japanese tradition of refusing to pay compensation to the elderly victims who had brought the case.[15]

We all need a corrective machinery to pick up as early as possible lapses, errors, faults, and systems that are beginning to run crazy in our minds and to look for ways to correct them. Among other things, we correct our errors by disciplined thought-stopping of wrong thoughts, rehearsals of the correct behaviors we want to employ, taking a rest, changing our mindsets and going to another activity, focusing on loving and being loved by dear ones, refreshing the wellsprings of the poetry of life in our souls, and renewing our moral resolution to be good people. Each of these corrective functions is a marvelous experience of mind, which, when truth be told, is fun to employ.

FASCIST MINDS correct stuck functions only in order to achieve their prescribed final solutions. Like every other aspect of fascist society, FAS-CIST MIND is geared to producing conformity to the *über alles* dictates of rules that must be followed unquestioningly regardless of their appropriateness, and to achieving set goals no matter the cost.

DEMOCRATIC MIND exercises its rights for expressing opinions, for dissenting with authority or with "the way things are done in our organization or government," and for demands for obedience and conformity. It also takes an active stand in situations in which a misguided politeness, courtesy, and traditions of "avoiding conflict" lead people to stand by and let bad things happen.

Toward ourselves, first of all, this means proactively managing our own mind and not allowing things to get out of hand without correcting and reorganizing ourselves – the opposite of being "stuck in the mud." If you have ever encountered problems with a computer behaving in a way that it shouldn't (ha!), or in this day and age even with a simple home cable television system in which the complicated controls stop working and lock up and jam up the system (ha! again, since I hardly know anyone among my friends who has not had both of these problems), it is clear that technicians have to be called at times and systems have to be rebooted, reorganized, and sometimes reinstalled. Our minds also periodically go off their deep ends. There isn't a single person who does not wake up to find that an ugly or problematic side of the mind has taken over – be it a jealous, overambitious, overperfectionistic, controlling, competitive, angry, vengeful, murderous, weakling, slavish, confused, or muddled and inept side.

Each of the above disturbing aspects of personalities and a variety of many other weak, lurid, or rotten mindsets in their own right are all human, which means the potential for all of these and still other unwelcome behaviors is in all humans. Periodically some of these behaviors get disturbingly out of hand. Every one, from clergymen to psychoanalysts to government leaders to the healthiest folk, are capable of making the serious mistake of allowing bad parts of his or her character to surface.

The bridge between mind and society needs to be maintained to enable a free flow of traffic, which among other things means that feelings, ideas, criticisms, protests, and corrections need to be expressed and respected at every level of human experience. In relationship to our minds, the trick is to be open to checks and balances against imposition of our overcertainties on our own selves and our reluctances to entertain self-criticism. Many are locked into employing defenses against the ostensible shame, defeat, and failure of having been wrong in one's position or behavior. Some do struggle to be able to hear the dissenting sounds and thoughts in our own minds about ourselves and to work with them for self-improvement, but relatively few of us reach a point at which we are genuinely at ease in accepting and actually treasuring this function of self-correction. In a sense, when we go to a psychotherapist for counseling and consultation, we are seeking help to be able to take in the critical views of another person and emotional support for being able to employ that part of our mind in which we can observe ourselves and see where we are in the wrong. It is almost as if we are afraid to lose our own self if we criticize our own self in a meaningful way!

In our intimate relationships, beginning with our families, there simply is no substitute for the ability to receive feedback, including criticism and anger, uncomfortable as the feedback may be.[16] Here is one of the greatnesses of family therapy: it convenes a forum in which, when a method of genuine criticism and feedback is employed, people speak their minds to one another. This includes children telling the truth of their feelings to their parents. Although very often children's feelings are disguised as complaints and demands, the parent who listens as well as takes the therapist's assistance to translate the fuller metameanings of the child's message, will hear the soul of a child telling truths, such as how they feel unloved, isolated, beat up on, rejected, disfavored, ridiculed, ignored, taken for granted, or exploited. What an incredible opportunity on the bridge of life for making a correction that can change the course of a child's life and relationships with that child!

> I have never seen a case in family therapy in which, after parents listened respectfully to the criticisms of their children, there was anything but an increase in the respect and loyalty of the children toward the parents. Even years of considerable hurt seem to melt away in response to the child's or adolescent's appreciation of their parents' openness to criticism and the parents taking responsibility for the past.
>
> I have a similar though less strong impression of what happens between couples in couple therapy. When the acknowledgment by one spouse of having done something really wrong is rendered sincerely, with a communication of wanting to get past the insult and harm that were done to a more decent relationship, there is often appreciation, and the doors can open to a new level of attachment to each other and a rebuilding of closeness.

A fascinating aspect of our ability to take stands with respect to our families and intimates involves standing up to serious problems in our loved ones, which they do not seem capable of correcting on their own. Of course, respect for another human being involves progressively relinquishing degrees of control. For example, as children get older we instruct them in the ways in which they themselves are to participate and then manage the care and treatment of their own injuries and illnesses. But if we see they do not or cannot take care of themselves, is it ever too late for us to help and attempt to intervene out of love and responsibility?

> *"I really wish you wouldn't have so much fat for*
> *breakfast. Are you aware of the relationship between*
> *this kind of diet and heart disease?" You could*
> *end up paying a heavy price later on.*

A similar continuum of responsibility applies to marital relationships. For example, some people need the help of their spouse or another family member to get to a doctor to see about ominous symptoms. I knew several people who are no longer with us because they did not get to their doctors in time. Others need the help of early feedback about an emerging madness or an escape into an addiction in their behavior, for example, severe depression, withdrawal from relationships, increasing nastiness, crazy or psychotic thinking, failure to work, and gambling. Spouses are often the first and certainly the closest by to spot such trends as they are developing. I strongly believe that a spouse's caring is expressed in bringing disturbed behaviors to the other's attention, first in expressing concern in a loving and caring way, but then progressively in becoming dissatisfied, openly angry, and firmly unaccepting of the increasing tyranny of a spouse's disturbed behavior system.

When anger is employed, it should remain rooted in caring and loving rather than in self-centered complaints. In my experience, the loving anger of one's spouse is a healthy antidote that can be used by some people as a stimulus for their own lacking energy and skill for self-correction. The mate's principled anger raises for the other the danger of losing the respect, companionship, love, and loyalty of their partner if they let themselves go to pot. I do not mean by this that one should rush to disown, separate, get divorced, or otherwise punish a spouse brutally. I mean that one should level with one's spouse and say that one cannot accept blindly and stay forever with an increasingly unattractive, deranged, or unethical person.

The current plague of obesity in America is an excellent example of a point in which caring and firm intervention to stop a spouse from becoming obese early enough in the process might make a difference for enough people that it deserves to be tried. The time-honored cry of the obese that they simply want to be loved unconditionally as they are, and that there is nothing that they can do about their condition, which undoubtedly was programmed by some mysterious genetic force, belies the facts that people can control what and how much they eat, and the involvement of one's intimates can make a difference.

Siblings, too, have opportunities to take stands in family life, certainly as adults but also in their younger years.

Your sister has always been singled out negatively by your mother who yells at her and calls her ugly names. Father characteristically stands by and doesn't intervene – his hands are clean after all, and Mother is less likely to get angry with him so long as she uses their daughter as her whipping post. You are now old enough to see the unfairness of the treatment of your sister and how badly she is hurting. Do you speak up for her? Do you tell Mother she is too harsh? Do you tell Father he needs to stop Mother from abusing your sister? Do you make a point of standing by your sister when she is attacked?

In DEMOCRATIC MIND, there is a tension between one's responsibility to take active stands and the desirability of encouraging other people's freedom to act for themselves, and this is another of the dialectical tensions to be processed by attention to each side of the tension rather than by suppressing either aspect of the conundrum. The same tension between respect for the individuality and the freedom of the other and our obligation to take a stand based on our caring runs through the entire cycle of life, and I believe that there are also many more times that friends and even colleagues and associates could make a constructive difference by providing more authentic feedback on issues of health and safety.

Nonconformity

If there were not a complexity and mystery vibrating within us, there would never be new ideas, invention, and innovation. Each of us would be a robotic mind doomed to repeat the same patterns over and over again. The bridge between mind and society is a safer one on which to walk if one can see from the bridge the streams and gorges where the diversity of human life flows unrestrainedly within our minds and in our relationships with one another.

Granted every new direction and inspiration in our minds sets off tensions and requirements of new choices. Similarly, every difference between people in communities and ethnic/religious/political groups sets off a variety of tensions, including legitimate and natural dislikes and antagonisms, and including legitimate concerns about the possible dilution or loss of historic identity.

The capacity to tolerate the tensions of differences, even more to celebrate and enjoy the pluralism of life, has produced great periods of history where varied cultures have flourished alongside one another and have also enriched one another. Yet these great periods repeatedly break down when fascist forces in a society preach for the singular unity, purity, and superiority of their one-and-only (religious/ethnic/political) identity, and create ominous programs of inquisition, ethnic cleansing, forced migration, enslavement, or outright genocide to banish the now feared and despised bearers of difference. An appreciative enjoyment of differences at all levels of existence, including within our individual minds and in our capacities to respect and appreciate others, seems like the best way to maintain safe bridges over the rivers of life.

Attempting to Play the Role of Critic and Change Agent

With respect to errors, unfairness, and evil in the world, some of the potentially great moments in our lives present themselves when we are faced with onerous commands, rules, regulations, and mandatory procedures by work systems, organizations, communities, and governments with which we do not agree. In the final analysis, some of these are trivial or at least not of overriding importance and can be absorbed and let go of because there is no point in "fighting City Hall." But some issues are serious, and some are so serious they are horrendous.

• The company lets a veteran worker go, and you believe the termination of his employment is unfair and abusive.

• You are employed as a school psychologist by a school whose principal is outrageously dictatorial, insulting, and who intrudes inappropriately on your area of work and expertise, such as ordering you which children to treat and which not.

• It is the infamous McCarthy era in the United States, when serious loyalty witch-hunts abound on the land. You are employed as an instructor at a university, and you witness your university's appeasing conformity to government edicts demanding loyalty oaths that you are convinced are repressive and undemocratic.

• It is the McCarthy era and an FBI agent comes to interrogate you about your colleague's reading habits and his opinions about communists. You know of no seditious or terrorist activities by your colleague – which you certainly would report without hesitation – and you are adamantly opposed to the FBI's invasions of privacy about peoples' reading choices, ideas, and opinions.

• You are a teenager whose cronies decide to warn the girls in the neighborhood that henceforth they are forbidden to enter such and such area or they will be subject to punishment. One night, one provocative strong-willed girl makes a point of being captured in the forbidden zone. The gang takes her to an apartment and begins to strip her. You see that the mood is getting ugly and could build to a serious incident of assault.

From where does one draw an inner assurance to oppose an authority or a group? After all, we are trained to respect leaders and to follow orders. We are likely to believe that it is we who are in the wrong if the majority in our group or society follow a given path. Integrity and courage are called for in these situations to rise and take a stand against an Establishment.

FASCIST MIND delights in humiliation, punishment, and persecution of oneself or of others for failing to obey orders.

344

❧ You hate yourself for failing to become the most celebrated and power-ful person in your field. Your mother demanded that you become super-successful, and thus repay her for the suffering she underwent to give birth to you. You are so burdened by failing the obligation to your mother and so full of anger at your burden, that you become physically ill.

DEMOCRATIC MIND does not tolerate the use of power to scapegoat and subjugate oneself or another person. To the best of one's ability, DEMOCRATIC MIND stands up for the dignity, health, and human rights of oneself and others.

The Care and Maintenance of Equality and Respect, or Not Succumbing to Excessive Power and Prejudice

The bridge between mind and society also needs monitoring with regard to bursts of superiority and efforts at gaining excessive power over other people, beginning with the thoughts we entertain in our minds.

Is there a person alive who has not harbored wishes to lord it over some others and dominate them? Is there anyone of us who has not gone too far in feeling superior to another person, and actually pushed someone around? Most of us have developed images of being superior to others in our own minds, up to and including picturing ourselves Chief Priest, Chief Bottle Washer, Slave Owner, Nazi, or Communist Torturer. How many of our minds have escaped entertaining images of humiliating, persecuting, enslaving, torturing, and even killing members of whatever other group?

As pioneer psychoanalyst Alfred Adler taught, we are more inclined to thoughts of superiority precisely when we feel like shmucks, ne'er-do-wells, losers, impotents, rejected, and other forms of failures.[17] The proper care of the bridge between mind and society calls us to monitor and discipline such mind constructions.

I have learned to take note of my fantasies of superiority, and I require myself first to stop them in my mind, and second, I remind myself that if I am suffering feelings of superiority, it must mean I am feeling inadequate and frightened and am using superiority to overcome my fearfulness. I then concentrate on standing firmly on the ground, and anchor myself by breathing deeply and freely. I generally feel better after going through this sequence. The trick is to utilize sensible parts of our minds as checks and balances against silly, ridiculous, amoral, and totalitarian thoughts and fantasies. That is one of the beauties and powers of democracy in the mind.

Even the meek frequently are covert supremacists extracting from others all manner of overobligation: doles, subsidies, excessive privileges, and exemptions from normal responsibilities.

A minority of mental health professionals have noted that there are some – at times one wonders if not more than is generally acknowledged in the prevailing conception of mental illness as being "just" like any other illness – cases of mental illness in which patients use their condition to get their families and societal institutions to be beholden to them and to cater to them. Small wonder. Is there any context in human life in which people draw resources and support from others that does not get used exploitatively by people "on the take"? Capitalists do it by falsifying books for major corporations; small-time bank clerks abscond with depositors' accounts. Why should there not be exploitation in mental illnesses? But the more important understanding is that such exploitation and power are not only the inadvertent or logical sequels of the mental illness but also can be prime movers in the creation of the mental disturbance as well as in its perpetuation.

In relationships with our families and intimates, we will generally get feedback from our own minds and from our intimates when we become too harsh, dictatorial, possessive, overlording, imperious, highhanded, or exploitative. There will be little to no direct feedback insofar as we impose terror and censorship on our family and ourselves, and everyone – including our mind – has become afraid to tell us the truth. A discipline of listening to the truth coming up from inside our minds (thank heaven, it's always there if one listens), and a style of family life in which everyone exercises the privilege of saying what they feel and are listened to respectfully even if in disagreement are the best antidotes to excessive power, the development of madness, or the onset of any form of abuse. The job of

DEMOCRATIC MIND includes being able to monitor and respond early to feedback and complaints about our superiority and power over others.

The proper care and maintenance of our minds requires monitoring ourselves against being uppity, snippety, braggarts, arrogant, manipulative, exploitative, controlling, dictatorial, or persecutorial. The greatest privilege is to be intrinsically equal to others. When our relationship is with people who objectively are more gifted or mature than we are, an intrinsic sense of equality between people makes it more possible to learn from and be inspired by the excellence of the other as well as to enjoy and honor their gifts. When we are in a relationship with people who are dependent on us in some way – such as our children naturally are – or who are less capable than we are in whatever areas of life, an intrinsic sense of equality between people makes it possible to help, teach, guide, and accompany the other without being patronizing or deriving a superior position.

In work settings, the community, and the society in which we live, it is too pat for me to say carte blanche that every person will do well to acknowledge the errors they have made and the harm that they have caused others. The political realities of life are that there are many settings in society that cannot tolerate a person's acknowledgment of responsibility without translating it into a basis for dismissal, retaliation, or punishment. I think a good and mature person does well to evaluate each situation on its own merits, but I advise that if there seems to be a reason for withholding the truth from others, one would be well advised to seek the counsel of respected advisors, such as a friend whose opinion one really respects, a clergyman, an ethicist, or another professional of high integrity, the only caveat being that the person consulted should not be a priori a rubber stamp who will go along with concealing the truth, nor should the person be a letter-of-the-law-person who never varies their advice from the prescribed and expected social cliché.

Standing up against superiority and excessive power of others at work, where one's job and advancement are at stake, and on a societal level, where one's relationship to authorities with their enormous power is involved, challenges any person's courage. One cannot always fight openly for justice. We do not always need to come out fighting against dangerous people and end up hurting ourselves. There are situations in which one has to go underground. Under circumstances in which we are going to be badly hurt if we protest against fascism, there is every reason to be prudent and look for alternative strategies and timely opportunities for protest and opposition. In fighting a totalitarian government, for example, I see little value in protests that will put us into concentration camps, and would much prefer joining an underground movement that takes courageous actions against the occupiers![18] Similarly, in everyday life one should not automatically ruin one's career around every issue of principle.

I once advised a young surgical resident to go along with a false report of surgery that his senior, who was head of the department, had written. The resident had assisted the senior in surgery that morning. He was very upset that, in his opinion, his mentor had been negligent, in fact in his words, "he butchered the patient." An hour after the surgery was over, the professor called in the resident and asked him to co-sign a report in which he lied about the surgery. He warned the younger doctor that he would never be able to complete his residency and would never get a post in any hospital if he refused to sign the report.

As the young resident's therapist, I was deeply pained at the possibility of his having to go along with such evil, but I also realized there was no way he would survive this incident to be able to practice the medical specialty for which he had been training. I asked the young surgeon to take a vow that he would conduct himself as a physician and surgeon in subsequent years with full integrity, and that the lapse into deceit and exploitation of a patient that he would now make would be an exception for the larger good of his career.

I was reminded that during the three years I was a clinical psychologist intern in some of the finest "cuckoo nest" U.S. government psychiatric hospitals of the time, I had seen countless patients assigned to electric shock therapy as well as too many who were sent for lobotomies, and that I had not opened my mouth in protest at the staff meetings! (If I had opened my mouth, I would have been thrown out of the training program.)[19] In my heart I had felt enraged at the senseless, fascist "treatments," and spent many an hour on my psychoanalyst's couch yelling about these in-

justices. But I knew enough to defer my public opposition to later years, after graduation. Ever since, I have opposed with all my professional vigor any such abusive procedures, and unfortunately I have the personal and professional bruises to show for antagonizing previous friends who used those procedures in their psychiatric practices.

In every society, including ostensibly democratic societies, pressures mount in business, the community, and in response to government to go along with horrible attitudes and behaviors toward other people.

You are a computer engineer. Your company is riding a wave of what its chief executive describes as a "renewed popular interest in World War II." Although for many years there was a taboo among game makers in Western countries against using Nazi protagonists, the company sees that there is money to be made by celebrating the roles of Nazis; it produces a series of games that include Nazi weapons such as Lugers, Hitler Youth knives, prototypes of Hitler inspiring the troops, noms de guerre like "Mein Kamf," "Hitler Youth," and "Zyklon B," and one game player is given the name "Anne Frank."

You question your bosses and they say they are only interested in "insuring historical accuracy in the equipment, weapons, and uniforms, not in providing an outlet for neo-Nazi sentiment."[20] An executive of your company tells you knowingly that the market in Germany "is one we believe is significant."

The national director of the Simon Wiesenthal Center's Task Force against Hate says of such games, "It encourages people to express what are rightly considered to be socially unacceptable sentiments – racism and anti-Semitism and hate."[21]

What do you do as a young engineer newly employed by this company? And if you are higher up in the company hierarchy, with a good salary and stock perks, what do you do as an executive of this company? For the added fun of it, I will ask what do you do if you are the child of a Holocaust survivor, or of a Jehovah's Witness who was sent to a Nazi concentration camp? (My answer is the same no matter what your family roots are.) The real question is do you have the guts and integrity to endanger a lucrative job?

Again my view of our species is that prejudice is natural in our minds. There is no shortage of bigoted and prejudiced people everywhere; this tells us that human minds delight in taking this course of least resistance toward becoming superior and hateful to others as solutions to their own problems of managing the existential anxiety, complexity, and the mortality of it all. I can hardly imagine that there is a human being in any country in the world and in any walk of life that does not find in himself or herself a pull toward some level of agreement and complicity with prejudicial movements. I think that prejudicial attitudes toward other ethnic, racial, religious, minority, and gender groups spring easily in the spirits and minds of all of us some of the time. I am particularly fascinated (and outraged) by instances in which liberal people and groups, such as pacifists and believers in nonviolence, become so militant in their legitimate opposition to groups and governments that engage in prejudice, brutalization, and military suppression that they, the protesters in the name of peace, end up supporting the most brutal and even murderous counterterrorism!

• The Irish fight for religious-political independence hardly justified bombs in the London Underground, which took everyday people's lives and left victims with life-threatening injuries.

• Israel may be engaging in colonization of areas that it should never have entered, and in overly repressive curfews and humiliating checkpoints that go beyond legitimate security needs, but that hardly justifies supporting suicide bombers who leave fragmented bodies in a discotheque or at a community dinner in a hotel where families are assembled to celebrate a Passover holiday.

• An amazing phenomenon took place at the United Nations World Conference against Racism in Durban, South Africa, in 2001. The public setting of the conference became a circus for the most virulent anti-Semitism. For example, one day thousands of South African Muslim demonstrators marched bearing banners proclaiming, "Hitler should have finished the job" – a concept so disgustingly inhuman it should be condemned at every level. The deliberations at the conference produced an insulting reinstatement of the infamous resolution of the United Nations in 1975 that equated Zionism with racism. The United States walked out on this conference.[22]

We are better people if we extend fairness, courtesy, and openness to others' identities and styles of living. To be democratic seems to require an a priori spiritual or ethical commitment to suppress and correct the feelings of intolerance and superiority that surface at one point or another, and we certainly need to head off allowing ourselves to engage in actions of discrimination, repression, or violent persecution.

Whether or not each of our personal mind contributions to society will make enough of a difference to stop a dangerous trend toward fascist hatred and persecution of another people in our society, we need first to do what we as individuals can do. Power collectors and supremacists do manage periods of strutting and derive too much pleasure from persecuting others, but they often pay a large price in a diminution of their ability to enjoy tender emotions of connection, caring, and loving, and they do not feel heartfelt joy and love.

The Care and Maintenance of a Nonviolent Bridge between Mind and Society

Violence is against life. At every level of mind and behavior, violence is the ultimate evil. The goal of life needs to be peace of mind, in intimate relationships and in communities and societies. Wherever possible, the prevailing context of our experiences as human beings should include efforts to resolve the inevitable conflicts in our lives, and as much as possible a seeking of peace and an atmosphere of decency and a belief in the goodness of life.

Since, unfortunately, fascists and destroyers abound, we also need to be able to stand up and fight back, using violence only in self-defense against those who would destroy us.

An Israeli columnist has written a penetrating satire on how the world's objections to Israeli self-defense against Palestinian suicide bombers melted in the face of the spread of Muslim suicide bombings to other countries.

At one point in the satire, Great Britain has been attacked in repeated suicide bombings. People are upset and the government takes up arms by sending out fighting forces against indigenous Muslim groups far off in the world that are believed to be linked to the groups that are blowing up Britons everyday.

Across the English Channel, however, the French self-righteously chide the British for what they consider the Britons' over-response. The writer portrays a marvelous scene on British TV where a BBC announcer is interviewing the French ambassador:

> "What are you saying, then? That we have no right to defend ourselves against murderous terrorism?"
> "What you call terrorism," the ambassador corrected him.
> The veins on the balding brow of the interviewer seemed about to burst. "What do you mean – 'what we call terrorism?' What is it if not terrorism? . . .
> "Attacks," the ambassador replied coolly. . . . "Ostensible attacks by supposed militants."
> The BBC correspondent ends up bursting out and lunging at the ambassador as the screen goes dark.

Soon afterwards, the dread suicide bombings reach Paris as well.

A series of explosions and warnings about suicide bombers – Islamic, Senegalese, Timorese, Algerians and just plain anarchists who seem to have entered a murderous trance – turned the streets of the cities into a maelstrom of blasts, horror, security checks, wailing sirens, flickering blue lights and road blocks.

Before long the French military join the British in bombing Muslim groups somewhere in Asia. The irate president and the government of France do not even rule out a possible use of tactical nuclear arms, and now it is an Israeli broadcaster reporting about France who lifts a critical eyebrow to the point where "the French embassy sent an angry protest to Israeli Television for biased and one-sided reporting."[23]

An important task of decent people is to work at improving our ability to discriminate between the fascists who will not respond to overtures of peace and those who may. The Hitlers, Stalins, Pol Pots, and whatever versions of dangerous would-be murderers, including the fascists among our own leaders and people, have to be stopped in their tracks before they kill others.

Society has an enormous role in educating people for the uses of their mind with respect to violence. Many societies call brazenly for collective attacks against other people. Anthropologist Alexander Hinton, who described the culture of the killing in the Cambodian Genocide, quoted one prisoner:

> "We weren't quite people. We were lower forms of life, because we were enemies. Killing us was like swatting flies, a way to get rid of undesirables."
>
> Hinton describes how the Khmer Rouge indoctrinated their people to have no feeling for the "enemy" – in the case of Cambodia these were their fellow countrymen who were earmarked by the Khmer Rouge as enemies because they did not belong to the revolutionary cadre. "We were brainwashed to cut off our heart from the enemy, to be willing to kill those who had betrayed the revolution, even if the person was a parent, sibling, friend, or relative. Everything we did was supposed to be for the party."[24]

The Media's Contributions to Violence in Our World

In this section I want to address the issue of the horrible (though all too-taken-for-granted) role of the mass media in celebrating, disseminating, teaching, and approving violence. Among the contagious forces that have torn away the images and hopes we once had in Western society for progress toward decent nonviolent lives for the majority of people, I believe that our media stand out as prime contributors to more and more violence.

If some day a mythical jury of the future brings American cultural leadership to trial for teaching millions of people the joy of murdering in endless movies and TV dramas, I would vote for a conviction and tough penalties.[25]

As a culture, we missed the opportunity to use the mass media as agents for a greater decency in human affairs!

In all fairness, there is some element of fantasy to American media violence, while there are other cultures that actually send out citizens explicitly to kill as many civilians as they can. Still, we have created media that teach violence and murder and acceptance of them as natural in human society. It didn't have to be that way.

Some day, I fantasize, the anthropologists of other planets who will be looking at whatever is left of our (in so many ways) beautiful Earth-civilization will scratch their heads (if that is the body language of their other planet) incredulously and wonder what in the name of God led Earth people to destroy the gift of their lives? The assumption in my musings is that Earth will have been destroyed, which of course I pray will never come to be; but it is hard to deny the possibility and probability of this happening. Human beings build more weapons of mass destruction every day, and societal controls are insufficient to overcome a predilection to use such weapons.

Another of my assumptions is that the anthropologists of said other planet will somehow have a greater sensitivity to issues of violence and destruction than many on Earth have. I would like to fantasize that they will be anthropologists from a world that successfully practices nonviolence and has developed culturewide ways for teaching the principles of peaceful conflict resolution.

Violent or nonviolent as the anthropologists looking at the relics of our civilization will be, they will have to conclude that we on Earth destroyed ourselves by cultivating a culture of violence: in respect of our failure to control the development of weapons of mass destruction; in outbreaks of wars; and as if these were not enough, in the butchery of genocides. They will also have to conclude that we had no idea about how to control runaway "failed states" or countries and societies taken over by dictatorial and brutal leaderships that were responsible for wars, terrorism, and genocide; or the overavailability of weapons. They could conclude that violence, revenge, revolution, terrorism, and mayhem was spawned by religions, political ideologies, nationalities, and states; and that as the new tools of communication to mass audiences became available in the 20th century, we failed to convey new standards for a better world and instead propagated an obscene idolatry of murder and violence.

In a satire titled, "Want to raise kids from hell? Here's a how-to primer," Donna Britt wrote:

Just for laughs, let's pretend. Say we wanted to create, in a relatively peaceful society, a nation of youthful killers, or at least just millions of aggressive young jerks.

How could we do it? . . .

We could design, say, an electronic box that beamed seductive, violent images into every dwelling. It would provide fistfights, beatings, rapes and murders.

Now a few troublesome kids would realize that such images are fiction. So we would invent "news" shows, highlighting real-life mayhem from local, national and even international sources. . . .

We invent striking, realistic visual computer "games." Children could shoot, impale or beat to death life-like images of people and monsters. Blood could splatter, "victims" could instantly revive to be killed again and again! We could glorify guns, make folks think they cannot live without firearms. Then we would make it relatively easy for anyone, even children, to get them . . . . We could attach violent, materialistic or overtly sexualized images to music. We could even persuade certain music-makers to celebrate guns, greed and irresponsible sex in their songs! . . .

"How could this happen?" we would [then] wail after each brutality.

With straight faces, we could . . . write shocked editorials, swear to "get to the bottom" of the problem.

So. If a society actually did those crazy things, would children – not every child, just way too many of them – behave in frighteningly aggressive ways?

Maybe. But what intelligent culture could be so stupid? Just thinking about the prospect is scary.

Thank God it's just pretend.[26]

New York Times columnist Bob Herbert has written forcefully:

In the popular culture of movies, television and video games, murder is such a staple we seldom give it a second thought. If a bare breast were shown on network television, it would make headlines from coast to coast. But homicides are fed to us as routinely as commercials for cars and beer. Bang! She's dead. We'll return to this delightful carnage after a word from our sponsor.

. . . The death really means nothing. Americans murder one another by the tens of thousands, and there is no sign anywhere that that is about to change.[27]

The culture of violence the mass media have cultivated has lowered the thresholds of resistance and weakened the moral inhibition of killing that most of our religions ostensibly stand for. Of all of the systems promoting and enabling violence, it seems to me that a proper regulation of the mass media might have been one of the simplest to achieve. After all, the media do not involve actual weapons and real bloodshed, the pounding horror of military equipment, or men armed to the teeth and intoxicated with the power of their arms. The media involve a conception of what is proper and desirable thinking, communication, and behavior. We could have concentrated on showing the far more subtle dramas of peoples' lives in a largely nonviolent society. We could have shown violence in human history as problems society is evolving to control and prevent. And we could have set a limit on the amount of domestic and criminal violence we portray.

It is nonsense to say we did not regulate our media because of our love and commitment to freedom of speech – which is without doubt one of the great cornerstones of democracy and in turn one of our strongest tools against violence, but it is not because we were devoted to free speech that our American and Western civilization left the media open to portrayals of violence. Freedom of speech is not an all-or-none absolute. It would have been possible to set and regulate the boundaries for the extent of violence and the ways in which both news and fictional dramas portray violent events in our lives. Obviously, the good old profit motive played a role in the mass media utilizing the appeal of graphic, lurid, and exciting violence.

Even so, I am not convinced that capitalist profit motives are the entirely to blame. Along with looking for big bucks, the undefined basic defect or flaw in our very character as a species leads too many to enjoy

356

being vicious and creating murderous hell, so that it is fair to conclude that our media plain and simple gave in to represent this rotten side of our human nature.

I also think that the failure of our media to set limits on the extent of portrayals of violence is another statement of fascist thinking; it is a form of going all the way and going too far, whether with the purity of the idea of free speech and avoidance of censorship, or a total dedication to an ideology of capitalist profits justifying anything people are willing to pay for, or pandering to final solutions of violence and cruelty without making efforts to hold up other aspects of humanity that strive for defense and maintenance of life.

Failed Proposal for a New Style of Newscasts That Do Not Celebrate Violence

In the early 1970s, I found myself wanting to be one of the social scientists who might contribute to the reduction of violence on a culturewide level in respect of the mass media. At a conference of the American Orthopsychiatric Association, I gave a talk on a "human language for newscasts of violence," and the proposal was published in a professional social science journal and later in a book as well.[28] I suggested that what was happening in American culture was that our newscasters were telling us in their rich broadcast voices news how and when we killed one another, and that their styles were conveying a subliminal message, "Well, folks, it's happened again, it's still happening, it's always going to happen, and there isn't a damn thing we can do about it!" My proposal was that the news broadcasts about violence should be based on a series of stratagems both for editing the content of the news and for regulating the broadcaster's dramatic style as regards tone and affect, and that even the inner mood of the broadcaster could be addressed in order to achieve a more sober and reverent effect. Among the devices for editing contents, I proposed that news of loss of life be separated from items of sports, commercials, civic developments, and so on; that a local story of violence be used to project the human reality of loss as a context that would give meaning to stories of more distant violence as well; in general, wherever possible, that the story of large violence be taken down to its impact on people's everyday lives with the content edited to convey, even subtly, that there is something wrong with violence against life; and that stories that make a point of respecting life should be used as a counterpoint to the news stories of violent events.

I also suggested that, much as we have emphasized in respect of treatment of actual violence in people's lives, the underlying message in news reports should be that overt acts of violent, destructive events are wrong, for all that feelings of anger and protest are frequent and natural at all levels of human relationships. I therefore suggested that the reporting of news of angry feelings and protests by people and groups and communities be done respectfully, even with humor and affection where appropriate, with a constant separation of the gravity and tragedy of actual violent actions from the legitimacy of anger and protest.

Finally, I suggested that self-defense should be honored. One implication for reporting is that one should be careful not to describe the violence of two sides of a conflict, such as terrorists and a larger society that retaliates against the terrorists, as if there were no difference between the two sides. Wherever a genuine intention of self-defense is the guiding rationale for the behavior of one or the other party or both, even if the application of the concept of self-defense has been exaggerated and wrong, an effort should be made to report and describe the attempt at self-defense and to differentiate it from other violent acts that are more willfully murderous.

Most of all, with respect to the tone of broadcasts, I suggested that one should speak of the loss of life with sadness and reverence. I also proposed that the broadcaster as an artist cultivate a tone of muted anger and hope for the future – which is very different from monotonic indifference or uncaring and from sporting event–like excitement over the violence. At the same time, I suggested to the broadcasters and to their commercial bosses of broadcasting that the process need not be a sterile one; the style of broadcasting I proposed could also legitimately reflect people's natural excitement and fascination with violent events and be commercially effective in capturing audience attention:

Do allow excitement to show in reporting various news of life-and-death encounters and violence (as a mirror of the excitement and potential for violence in all humans; also as relief for our own feelings about possibly being hurt sometime); but move from the element of excitement to restraint, sadness, reverence (as a symbolic demonstration of man's capacity to channel his passions into a fighting commitment for life). Speak of the courage to fight in self-defense with respect and excited pleasure, yet introduce a subtly questioning note that conveys the feeling that one must await a later judgment of history as to whether the sincerity of the self-defense was in fact objectively justified.[29]

Over several years the proposal was reviewed with a number of professional newscasters in the hope of getting some kind of process going in the profession of broadcast journalists. Not surprisingly, the newscasters had many answers to protect their Establishment.

• "The nature of the beast makes these recommendations impractical."
• "The newscaster has to move rapidly from one story to the next."
• "Most stories have to be shortened."
• "The good things people do to a large extent don't make news: It is inevitable that violence is featured."[30]

Various broadcasters were interested in my proposal, and some even humored me by inviting me to come and personally broadcast the news on their station. But they were playing with my proposal as another kind of excitement in their world of broadcasting, not because they took it seriously. Culturally, my proposal was virtually un-American.

I do not believe that the situation has changed to this day in most American newscasting.

Another Even More Colossal Failed Proposal to Regulate TV Fictional Violence

I also hoped in those years to contribute meaningfully to a correction of the contagion of violence in our media, and I drew up another proposal for monitoring, limiting, and shaping the messages of violence in fictional television programs.

It is obvious to anyone who turns on a TV set on any average night of broadcasting that an enormous number of bodies are falling dead at the hands of other human beings, and it is also obvious that the ways and means used for bringing about the deaths have only expanded with the years. Our American media are probably the single biggest educational institution in the world for teaching violence. They lower the moral boundary against the time-honored biblical injunction, "Thou Shalt Not Kill," and they teach and inspire people to embrace bigger and worse ideas of how to kill.

Using the same principle that aggressive and violent instincts and wishes are perfectly natural and human, but that violent actions that do harm to other human beings are ethically abhorrent and unacceptable to decent people and society, I created a manual of about 80 pages for shaping the violent contents in fictional programs on television.

The ideas were really quite similar to those sketched earlier for newscasting. I proposed that it was natural to employ the stories of violence as they very much take place in human life, but that it is important to contextualize them in messages of regret and the basic wrongness of violence; that careful attention be paid to avoiding a pageantry or celebration of violence and its thrills; that there be a focus on portraying positively all forces in human life that constrain violence, such as those who bring violent criminals to justice; and that programming be designed to show respect for and inspire the development of new institutions that will foster justice and nonviolence. I also suggested that the concept of healthy self-defense be honored, while simultaneously teaching people to know how to check themselves and not use self-defense as an illusory basis for attacking others.

In those days, two outstanding social psychologists had served as members of no less than a U.S. Presidential Commission on Violence, and each of these men was in a key leadership and management role in each of two major TV networks.

I arranged to see one of these colleagues at NBC. We ended up sitting together for an uninterrupted stretch of some six hours, in the course of which he read with great care the manual I had prepared – which was purposely in outline form so it could be scanned and read easily and quickly. I was pleased that my senior colleague was most complimentary, and more important to me that he was in full agreement with the principles on which I had based the guidelines. He also agreed with me that the guidelines offered a practical basis for creating interesting and exciting programs that addressed and included the realities of violence in human affairs and therefore would be of interest to audiences that understandably wanted to see and experience exciting shows, but at the same time would significantly reduce the contagion of violence in the culture of viewers.

I was excited and hopeful.

My colleague then said to me, "This is probably the best proposal I have ever read for reducing violence on television, and I can't tell you how much I have enjoyed this meeting with you. You can see that by the way in which we have simply spent hours together and I have put aside all my other work. *But there is no way that I could ever bring this proposal to my network. They simply would not consider it.*"

I was stunned, not only with disappointment but also by the injustice and unfairness of it all. If the proposal made such good sense and really could work, why wasn't the network embracing it?

Obviously, I was young and naive. I now repaired to a second of the then major TV networks in the United States at CBS, where there sat the second psychologist in a senior administrative and management role who had also been a member of a President's Commission on Violence. This time the arrangements for the meeting were much harder to secure; there was a good deal of back-and-forth preliminary correspondence exploring the subject matter of the meeting I was requesting, and I also was sent a legal release form in advance of our meeting that would allow the media psychologist-executive to read my guidelines without it representing an infringement on the copyright or an obligation to adopt the guidelines in any way.

We met first for a cognac-luncheon at a fine French restaurant in Manhattan where we small-talked; we then went back to the network offices. There my host requested that I give him the guidelines to read. He devoted the next two hours to studying the guidelines quietly and intently. When he was finished, he said, "I would like to purchase these guidelines from you for the network, and then I want to hire you as a consultant to the CBS network."

Success! Needless to say, I was thrilled. My dream was coming true. My work was being confirmed. I would enjoy working amidst the excitement of a national network, and I would be contributing meaningfully to reducing the pollution of violence in the media. It couldn't be better.

But now I made the mistake of my life. The media executive took out a checkbook and proposed to write me a check on the spot for $2,000 to purchase the guidelines. He explained that this was the limit of the amount he was authorized to write without getting further approval of higher-up executives. I was disappointed. Since the amount was less than the last advance I had received on a book on the much "plainer" subject of marital love and hate,[31] I thought to myself that it was worth my while to wait for a further negotiation in which I would be able to ask for a larger sum of money. My colleague understood my hopes for a larger sum, and quite graciously proceeded to discuss with me other details of my proposed employment as a consultant for the network. We parted in very good spirits.

A day or so later, I received one telephone call from my colleague to ask for some further details that were needed for drafting the proposed contract for my employment as a consultant to CBS, and he also advised me that purchase of the guidelines was being reviewed by senior network executives.

A couple of days later I received my one further and quite final call. I was now told that the higher-up network executives absolutely refused to purchase the guidelines or to engage me. The reason they had given was that if the network purchased the guidelines or took me on as a consultant, it would represent a commitment and obligation to reduce the number of violent incidents in their programming, and this they absolutely were not prepared to do.

The above interesting story is obviously a statement of capitalism serving its holy cow of profit making at the expense of society's real needs. It is also a clear statement of organizational bureaucracy overriding the judgments of professionals whose genuine concern was with the nature of communication in society and the role of the media in making a better world. But I think the story can also be understood on a structural level to represent a fascist paradigm, in this case how the network's final goal is its own popularity and competitive success at all costs even if it is unleashing new waves of violence. The position of the networks is that they will broadcast the most exciting, salacious violent acts that will draw audience attention in order for them to be successful regardless of the social cost. The network's goal is to propagate megaviolence in a world that hardly needs more instruction in how to be violent. The networks brook no opposition. They censor dissenting information. They demand obedience and conformity of any who seek to benefit from being associated with their establishment. And thus it is that the program content of our media contains so many lessons on how to do harm to life, and the media pander and educate for cruelty and destruction of life to hundreds of millions of people everywhere.

In short, the wiser creatures from another planet some day will understand that the communications industry on Earth was a fascist institution that promoted violence. I think we all understand when we hear a person say they don't watch television much that they want to regulate the programs they watch. Some families even choose not to have a television set in their home in an effort to be more decent than they would be if they watched hours of crime, violence, and murder.

I do want to acknowledge that maybe one of the constructive reasons we Earthpeople have never really looked for ways to monitor and control our media's violence is that if society set up regulatory boards for media content, before long some would probably become censorship boards controlled by fundamentalist groups that gain sufficient political power to control the media according to their extremist values, which is the last thing democracies need. The authorities in China and some other countries restrict and censor access to Internet sources that are deemed unacceptable to their regimes. They are quite convinced they are fulfilling my dream of protecting the common good, and they don't take responsibility for the fact they are protecting their totalitarian power. Actually, every authoritarian and totalitarian society has exercised repressive control over much freedom of speech, expression, and thought. Similarly, large numbers of religious groups and sects forbid all manner of reading, viewing, listening, and thinking that deviate from their prescribed modes of experience. Those of us who want to see violence in the media regulated could very well be opening a door to much more far-ranging totalitarian means of control. I have to face the fact that since the most serious human "disease" is that we have not given up totalistic thinking, if we regulate violence in the media we could well be opening up a door to censorship and propaganda.

Nonetheless, I believe that a democratic society could work at building regulatory devices to stop the violence in the media while carefully protecting freedom of speech and thought. By not regulating the dissemination of violence in the media, we are joining forces with the totalitarians in every era who preach, instruct, and mobilize people to commit the violent acts we hate the most, including going to war. I wonder, for example, where the brilliant idea of flying hijacked aircraft into public buildings first came from. I read of the idea in at least one fascinating novel before 9/11. (The Tom Clancy novel told about a hijacked JAL airliner crashing into the U.S. Capitol during an address by the president to a Joint Session of Congress.) No, I am not against written or media dramas and science fiction and their profound lessons about the future. Yet I am against creating terrible futures by allowing totally free reign in the arts and communications to every imaginable idea of destruction and apocalypse, especially when these are broadcast over and over again as everyday programming in one production after another, especially when there is little control over the goriness, and when the plot fails to include a moral message defining violence as wrong and not deserving of celebration. As individuals we have to impose healthy controls on the mind, and we have to impose controls on a communal level as well. The challenge is to do so in a sophisticated and philosophically mature way, where we simultaneously ensure freedom of speech while controlling incitement to violence.

Cultural Celebration of Violence Is Addictive

The ultimate triumph of a fascist government is to have instructed people to be violent and to celebrate their violence. Fascist culture creates historical venues and contexts that explain and justify killing of genocidal proportions. These include killing in the name of religion, for example, the Christian crusades, or Moslem jihad against infidels; and totalitarian political contexts for violence in the name of progress, for example, Mao's "Great Leap Forward" and "Cultural Revolution" in China, and Stalin's starving of Ukrainians in his battle against the kulak economic class; or dictatorial elimination of protesters and dissidents, for example, Syria's Assad wiping out the 20,000 to 30,000 residents of the town of Hama for protesting against his regime, murderous Chinese suppression of Buddhists in Tibet, and government-ordered disappearances of thousands of civilians in Argentina, Chile, and Guatemala.

> An Islamic religious leader, Fazazi, "preached murderous hatred of the United States to Mohamed Atta and others who planned and executed the attacks on September 11" in a mosque in Hamburg, Germany. Fazazi said that "'Christians and Jews should have their throats slit'" (had the German authorities known of the preacher's call to slit the throats of Americans and Jews, he would have been prosecutable under German laws against racial incitement). Fazazi left Germany sometime before the attacks on the United States on September 11.
>
> When German police subsequently raided the mosque and found tapes of the imam's incendiary sermons on sale to the public, they attempted to question local parishioners and residents, but "questions about the former imam were met with blank stares at Al-Kudz mosque and in the cafes and other mosques frequented by Muslim immigrants."[32]

We have compared the fascist mindset in anorexia that locks in a person's capacity to think and choose not to harm themselves – even to the point of bringing about the end of their life – to full-blown tyrannical orders to kill people in a fascist society. Recently a thoughtful Palestinian psychiatrist also has compared the devastating cult of suicide bombers, which achieved a frightening degree of consensual acceptance in the mainstream of Palestinian society's culture, to the breakdown of the mind in eating fads.

> They are creating a new kind of culture [whose] development is com-

parable to a fad for body-building, gathering adherents by presenting
an ideal that is embraced even unconsciously. Once you create such a
culture, you create something automatic.[33]

Celebrations and rehearsals of violence can foster an addictive readiness to be violent. The passion of the preexisting readiness to be violent
mixes with the immediate precipitating context of excitement about an
inflammatory issue, and together with an added mix of excitement about
fusing with fellow believers and groupies in a collective mob or group
activity leads to progressive conformity, intoxication, and orgies of violence.[34]

Working toward a Less Violent Human Life

It is hard to believe that people can withstand the brainwashing of their
leaders and cultures that calls them to violence. Yet it has to be our
hope that a more humane civilization can still emerge some day on
our troubled planet in which the consensus of people will be, plain and
simple, that murder is wrong. This is in many ways the anthem of the
religious and humanistic ideas we have celebrated in what we refer to as
"civilization."

The bridge between mind and society that I am proposing calls on
each of us to make a choice not to participate in violent acts against life
even when they are strongly sanctioned and impelled by powerful forces.

The choice to avoid violence applies on a personal level too. If we love
ourselves and our lives, we prepare for the moments of grim despair
and dissolution into nothingness that ultimately attend us. We all are
pounded by losses of loved ones, as well as by betrayals of our loves
and ideals, persecution, torture, economic distress, and health disasters.
These are difficult moments when parts of us understandably feel like
dying. However, if we have established enough reserves in our inner
"bank accounts" of love and regard for ourselves, and nurtured our inner
respect for and commitment to life, we have a better chance of riding
out these periods, feeling our despair and even defining within ourselves
some measure of the suicidal statements we feel, but not going too far.
Even as we grieve our losses and worry about our problems, inside we

know we are going to work at recovery and reorganization. The more a person is enriched with a philosophy of loving life and has built up a series of explicit choices to respect its sacredness, the more one is prepared to weather crises of despair that might impel us to hurt ourselves.

The same conviction in the dignity of our own life then stands us in good stead not to sacrifice others to violence. Even when our egos are threatened and enraged by insult and hurt, and everything in us screams out to beat our child, spouse, sibling, parent, or whoever, we do not. Family violence is no laughing matter. In any society, the bruised bones and actual dead from acts of family violence mount up to significant numbers. These runaway events take place not only in the lower socioeconomic classes but also at every level of society. The proper care and maintenance of the bridge between our minds and our relationships to other people includes teaching ourselves not to hurt another person in our circle of family and intimates, even when we really want to do so. No matter how much we hate and want to hurt and kill, we will not do so.

Amazingly, human beings also show a capacity to make their way back from histories of collective violence to renewed efforts and commitments to peacefulness between groups. In the last part of the 20th century, in particular, new mechanisms for change and corrections of past violence have begun to emerge and are shaping new institutional structures such as collective apologies, modes of compensation, restitution, truth and reconciliation processes, and more.[35]

In July 2002, the IRA (Irish Republican Army) issued a public apology to relatives of people killed by them in their battle to unite Northern Ireland with the Irish Republic in the course of 30 years of terrorist guerrilla warfare.

"We offer our sincere apologies and condolences," they said to the families of civilians who did not belong to any of the security forces that the IRA was fighting or to other military groups. According to the New York Times, about 650 civilians were killed by the IRA out of a total of 1,800 people who were their victims.

"We acknowledge the grief and pain of their relatives," the apology continued. "The process of conflict resolution requires the equal ac-

367

knowledgement of the grief and loss of others. . . . We are endeavoring to fulfill responsibility to those we have hurt." The IRA said that it was committed to "the acceptance of past mistakes and of the hurt and pain we have caused to others."[36]

These are new beginnings. The overall international record is uneven and spotty. In 1985 the world's preeminent genocide scholar, Leo Kuper, reviewed the record of the United Nations in responding to genocide and wrung his hands in despair at the impotence and moral dishonesty of the international community.[37] Yet only 15 some years later, at the turn of the 21st century, the world saw NATO intervening militarily to prevent a likely genocide in Kosovo, the United Nations creating international tribunals to bring to trial perpetrators of genocide in Rwanda and the former Yugoslavia, and the creation of a new International Criminal Court in The Hague to prosecute perpetrators of genocide and crimes against humanity.[38] On the tenth anniversary of the genocidal carnage in Rwanda, the UN Secretary-General, Kofi Annan, acknowledged the United Nation's failure in preventing the genocide (the United Nation's own general, Roméo Dallaire, who commanded a small UN force, called for reinforcements but was turned down), and called for the creation of a new UN Special Adviser on the Prevention of Genocide who has since been appointed.[39]

William Shawcross, a tireless reporter of violence in the world, has written a sober account of the inconsistencies and unevenness of international peace efforts, including cases in which it is the peacekeepers who, strangely enough, actually perpetuate violence by preventing the combatants from fighting to a conclusion.[40] Shawcross observes that there is no pattern, and that the United Nations has never developed a formula for defining when it will intervene and when not: Cambodia yes, Rwanda no, Bosnia yes, Chechnya no. He concludes bitterly that more often the determinants of war and peace are money and practical politics, not moral outrage.[41]

Many of us believe that our planet will never be peaceful until and if there is an international peace force dedicated to early military intervention in any case of mass killings of civilians. Just as one hopes to call the neighborhood police officer in the event of a threat to an individual's life, the world needs a planetary police force. Such an international police or military force would best be coordinated with medical and humanitarian efforts to bring urgent relief to victims, as well as a trained corps of community and government administrators whose job would be to reorganize a failed society, including to restart all the governmental systems that have broken down and to bring a message to the constituent peoples of the necessity of living together nonviolently.

I have proposed that an International Peace Army might best be organized as three constituent armies:

1. The International Peace Army Military
2. The International Peace Army Medical and Humanitarian Army
3. The International Peace Army for the Rebuilding of Safe and Tolerant Communities

In this framework, the planning and execution of procedures of any constituent army are to be reviewed by all components of the unified framework and implemented by all of them working together. Thus, military procedures would be evaluated from the outset not only strategically but also from the point of view of their medical and humanitarian consequences. Thus too, successful military conquest and pacification of a warring genocidal society would be less likely to lead to a subsequent power vacuum and an absence of elementary mechanisms of government, or to renewals of ethnic and other violence including revenges of past killings.[42]

Altogether, as we look at Earth's civilization today, winds of change toward a more responsible international community are in the air along with a helter skelter suicidal rush of humanity to put into action the most advanced machineries of inhumane destruction of life. It is an amazing wonderful-horrible race of life against death.[43]

I think that one might argue, with philosophical humor but also seriously, that the way human beings constantly think in extreme and fanatic (fascist) ways, even a firm commitment to nonviolence also could develop fad and cult qualities no less than a commitment to violence. What the hell, humans have killed wantonly in the name of every other wonderful

value (God, peace, liberty, equality, democracy, justice, economic fairness), so why not in the name of nonviolence, notwithstanding the total
word contradiction and absurdity? I have to agree that this can be the case
insofar as a choice of nonviolence becomes a ritualized, slavish response
and doctrinaire belief rather than a genuine celebration of the spirit of
life. But I will also admit that I will opt for and yield to accepting slavish
commitments to nonviolence over slavish commitments to violence –
the former at least seem more likely to leave people alive to be able to
work further on releasing them from their addiction to fascist thinking.

I have always loved and been encouraged by Dr. Martin Luther King
Jr.'s heroic spirit and his faith in the evolution of a better humanity. On
the occasion of his receiving the Nobel Peace Prize, this is what he said:

> [I have] an audacious faith in the future of mankind. I refuse to accept
> the idea that the "isness" of man's present nature make him morally
> incapable of reaching up for the eternal "oughtness" that forever con-
> fronts him. . . . I refuse to accept the idea that man is mere flotsam and
> jetsam in the river of life which surrounds him. . . . I refuse to accept
> the cynical notion that nation after nation must spiral down a militarist
> stairway into hell of thermonuclear destruction. . . . I believe that what
> self-centered men have torn down men other-centered can build up.
> I still believe that one day mankind will bow before the altars of God
> and be crowned triumphant over war and bloodshed, and nonviolent
> redemptive good will proclaim the rule of the land. . . . We are living in
> the creative turmoil of a genuine civilization struggling to be born. . . .
> I still believe that we shall overcome.[44]

My Background Both as a Psychotherapist and as a Peace Researcher Studying Genocide

As a practicing psychotherapist for many years, and for almost as many years also a devoted theorist and researcher of destructiveness and the terrifying phenomena of genocide and mass destruction of human life, my lifework and thinking have been marked by continuous interplays of searching to understand human behavior on both the levels of mind and society.[1]

Experience as a Therapist

I have been practicing psychotherapy "all my life," continuing from earning my PhD in clinical psychology at the University of Rochester (1957); as a psychologist in what was then the only center for treatment of psychotic children and their families in the city of Rochester (1956–1958); as chief psychologist at Oakbourne Hospital (1958–1962), which was the residential treatment center affiliated with the Philadelphia Child Guidance Clinic; then as founder and director of what was certainly the first group mental health practice in the Philadelphia area (1962–1973); and following my move to Israel (1973), I have been Associate Professor of Psychology at the School of Social Work of Tel Aviv University, where I founded and directed both the Postgraduate Interdisciplinary Program in Family Therapy and the Graduate Program in Family Therapy; and in later years Professor of Psychology and Family Therapy, and founder and director of the Program for Advanced Studies in Integrative Psychotherapy of the Department of Psychology and Martin Buber Center of the Hebrew University of Jerusalem.

After arriving in Israel from the United States, I was the founding and first president of the Israel Family Therapy Association in the early 1970s, and then president of the International Family Therapy Association in the early 1990s. Through all these years, I have maintained an active clinical practice that I love and experience as a wellspring of meaning and learning.

When asked to describe myself in terms of professional orientation, I normally identify the kind of therapy I practice as "existential-psychoanalytic-family (systemic)" therapy, and if in a conversation I then add that I believe that the hyphens (which are bridges between the schools of thought) are the most important part of the identification. I have published various papers on family therapy and especially marital therapy, and two books on marriage including *Existential/dialectical marital therapy* (Charny, 1992). I also edited the work of my late colleague psychiatrist Shamai Davidson on the clinical phenomenology of Holocaust survivors (Davidson, 1992).

Some years ago, I found myself discovering a new way for having an impact on some otherwise seemingly intractable cases of serious and long-term psychological disturbances, such as adolescent suicide and chronic anorexia/bulimia, by introducing into the treatment a new focus on the follies of the certainty and totality of the guiding idea in these respective symptoms. Thus, in the cases of teenage suicide, I focus on the obsessive commitment of teenage will and planning to the deadly suicide plan. In the cases of eating disorders, I focus on the bizarre repetitions of rituals, for example, forced vomiting, in order to protect an extreme idea of what one must do. In both instances the patient seeks to destroy any and all sources of opposition to the absolute rightness of their guiding idea – notwithstanding that their health is damaged and even their very life may be threatened (along with whatever suffering they are causing people close to them who also suffer as a result of their vengeful assault on life). Many such cases tend to be "stuck" and intractable.

The therapeutic technique I introduced into a number of these tough and "stuck" cases explores not only traditional issues of the patient's hurt and despair but also addresses the repetitive blind insistence on a single idea, and then the unethical or antihuman life consequences of the totalitarian mind regime based on overcertain and total ideas. I have found that such direct treatment not of the pathological impulse or behavior as such but of the intractable fascist absoluteness and proclivity for destruction has helped break through the *idée fixe* of several of these patients and enabled them to change their mindsets dramatically. Needless to say, I am not presenting this technique in this book as anything like a cure-all, even as I note that the technique seems to help significantly in some cases though not very much if at all in other cases (especially cases of anorexia in which my overall rate of treatment success is not impressive).

Experience as a Peace Researcher and Scholar of Genocide

While being a practicing clinical psychologist, I found myself deeply moved by, mournful of, enraged at, and troubled by the Holocaust, and the result was that I also took on the additional professional identity of a peace researcher, in the 1960s, with a lifelong commitment to being a student of the violent genocidal process to all peoples.

Over several years, I created an interdisciplinary study group that met regularly at my offices in suburban Philadelphia to study the nature and dynamics of individual and societal violence. I then was appointed chairman of the American Orthopsychiatric Association Study Group on Mental Health Aspects of Aggression, Violence and War – under which aegis several pathbreaking meetings were created over a period of some years in which scholars of the stature of Elise Boulding, A. Paul Hare, Herbert Kelman, Robert Jay Lifton, and others participated and from which grew a subsequent book, *Strategies against violence* (Charny, 1978). In 1972, I participated in the founding meeting of the Consortium on Peace Research Education and Development (COPRED) at the University of Colorado and served on its first executive committee. Following my move to Israel in 1973, I continued to be associated with the international peace research movement, such as at first through the International Peace Research Association (IPRA) and in recent years through the International Association of Genocide Scholars, of which I was one of the original founders along with Helen Fein, Robert Melson, and Roger Smith (and at this writing I am president of the association). My work on Holocaust and genocide studies moves me deeply intellectually and spiritually and has made me savor and appreciate my own life so much more.

Most of all, I am widely known as executive director of the Institute on the Holocaust and Genocide in Jerusalem, which I created with Shamai Davidson and Elie Wiesel in 1979 and which I direct to this day. We are credited with being a major force in the creation of the field of genocide studies. Our institute may have been the first to use the linkage of "Holocaust and genocide," and we are very pleased and proud to see the growing use of this linkage in the naming of other institutes, university programs, publications, and other professional thinking and activities all around the world. In 1982 we conducted the world-famous First International Conference on the Holocaust and Genocide which, as reported in many stories in the *New York Times*, other world press, and the Israeli press, required us to stand up against both the Turkish government and the Israeli government, both of which attempted to unsuccessfully censor references to the Armenian Genocide in the conference.

Over the years I have published many papers on genocide and the psychology of violence, including a major new proposal to include the doing of harm to other people as a permanent aspect of all psychological and psychiatric diagnosis (1986, 1996), and a proposal for a new diagnosis of a personality disorder of excessive power strivings (1997); including empirical studies (in the tradition of Milgram) of the psychology of readiness to do evil (for example, Charny & Fromer, 1990; and 1990, studies of the readiness of Jewish/Israeli students in the health professions to authorize and execute involuntary mass "euthanasia" of severely handicapped patients, and the readiness to comply with a program of forced migration of Arabs; and Charny & Fromer, 1992, on attitudes of Israeli viewers of a film on the Holocaust about the mass murder of Arab civilians); and including many studies of the denials of Holocaust and genocide (for example, 2003). I have also published a number of volumes on genocide (Charny, 1982 and 1983 with Davidson, and 1984 growing out of the above First International Conference on the Holocaust and Genocide); founded and edited a series of reference books, *Genocide: A critical bibliographic review*, 1988, 1991, 1994, and see the continuation of the series by Krell & Sherman, 1997, and Totten 2005; coedited with Sherman in 1994 the first database of Holocaust and genocide literature (not included in the Bibliography); coedited a widely used textbook of cases of genocide by Totten, Parsons, and Charny in 1997; and the capstone has been having the heartwarming privilege of serving as editor in chief of the first *Encyclopedia of genocide* in 1999 with a team of associate editors, Rouben Paul Adalian, Steven L. Jacobs, Eric Markusen, Marc I. Sherman, and Samuel Totten, and about 100 contributing editors and other contributors. At this writing, the encyclopedia is in its third printing, has been partially published in a French edition, and is available in an electronic edition on the Internet. Altogether, the *Encyclopedia of genocide* is being hailed as new standard in the field for years to come.

The Present Work

If originally I moved to contribute from my training and work as a psychologist to the understanding of how humans, individually and collectively, commit horrible crimes of holocaust and genocide, in the present work I am going back "home" to attempt to contribute to my original discipline new understanding of mind that has grown out of my work as a Holocaust and genocide researcher.

This work is also a continuation of the Jewish ethical tradition of respect for all human life, and of my lifelong conviction and dream that science – in this case the psychological science of mind – has much to contribute to a more ethical way of life for human beings. As opposed to FASCIST MIND, the evolution of DEMOCRATIC MIND creates conditions for joy in the gift of one's existence along with respect for the privileges and rights of fellow human beings.

Ultimately, my work as a therapist and my work as a peace researcher have been part of a single philosophy and way of life.

Through the years, as I sit with hundreds of people who ask me to be their therapist, I never stop wondering and thinking about who among them would have been, variously, perpetrators, accomplices, bystanders, or victims in the Holocaust (which is the case of genocide that I as a Jew think most about, but I really mean in any of the various cases of genocide), and what the truth is about where I, their respected therapist, would have been and how I would have behaved.

From this understanding there came the next step: realizing that in the workings of my mind I nonetheless remained secretly in some part of me a fascist toward myself and toward others. In other words, there are times when in my mind I become overcertain, rigid and conformist, or demanding others to conform to my dictates, power-seeking and demeaning of parts of myself or of others, or violent to myself or others, or further that I deny the harms I am doing either to my own life or to the lives of others. At such times I am obviously a totalitarian, and also in my understanding of psychological health and illness in these same ways, I became a truly disturbed person.

From there it is a short stop to realizing that in the hundreds of roles I and all of us play in our daily lives as parents, teachers, friends, lovers, spouses, professionals, administrators, officials, and everything else that we do, we are constantly choosing, knowingly or unknowingly, our roles vis-à-vis ourselves and other human beings along gradients of the same roles that people play in the critical historical societal situations of holocaust and genocide. Obviously, my prayer is to be, as much as possible, a person who loves and honors my life and others' lives, who rescues myself and rescues others from dangers, and fights back against the oppressors in every possible way. As a therapist, this is what I want to help people to do in their battles for their mental health and in their personal lives.

The book is dedicated to the alternative of a life-loving DEMOCRATIC MIND. The goal is a genuine openness to ideas and complexity, including not denying the truths of instincts in us toward ultimately undesirable and dangerous emotions and behaviors when they are excessive and harm life, such as competitiveness, anger, and violence. We need to accept the dark shadowy parts of ourselves as natural and to find healthy outlets for expressing their power and vitality, but also to limit and overcome their potentially harmful excesses. We need to draw on other happier instincts we have in us as well for wanting to protect life and treasure it, although these "good" instincts too have to be paced and not overdone. We need also to aspire to the honesty and integrity of DEMOCRATIC MIND in evaluating information, to freedom and individuality, decency and responsibility, cultivation of respect for ourselves and other human beings and a basic equality with others, and certainly to nonviolence toward ourselves and others – with the exception of where the preservation of life requires violent measures in genuine self-defense – as well as to take responsibility for the errors we nevertheless will make of doing harm to life, our own or the lives of others.

If Hitler's favored intellectual position and satanic way of life defined many human lives as undeserving of life, I want to be a person deserving of life and to honor all other people as deserving of life. I want to live my life helping a philosophy of DEMOCRATIC MIND AND SOCIETY to triumph over FASCIST MIND AND SOCIETY.

To life!

Notes

The following notes provide authenticating source information and linkages to the bibliography. But, in addition to providing formal sources of information, they are also a medium for introducing intriguing extra bits of background information, additional interpretations, brief vignettes, and "feature stories," and even some delectable gossiplike comments about people and issues that some readers will enjoy as adding an element of intellectual fun to our discussions of mind and society. I realize that these notes essentially will reach only the eyes of those readers who follow the information trails of the little superscript numbers into the endnotes. Personally, I often begin a book by scanning the bibliography and notes first, and then I go back to study them once again in proper sequence as I read the book. I am happy to give those readers who enjoy such information trails what seem to me like extra gifts that I love myself.

Introduction

1. Asch (1955, 1956).

2. May (1977); Bugental (1965); Becker (1973); Yalom (1980).

3. Fromm (1941, 1964); Arendt (1966, 1969); May (1972, 1977).

4. In the 1950s, leftist French intellectual Raymond Aron criticized intellectuals who were forever criticizing the shortcomings and evils of democracies (as they should), but were "ready to tolerate the worst crimes" of ostensible reformers and revolutionaries and underdogs "as long as they are committed in the name of the proper doctrines" (Rothstein 2003). Review of Aron (2002), *New York Times*, reprinted in *International Herald Tribune*, January 16, p. 18.

Christopher Lasch has criticized the endless skepticism and relativism of intellectuals, a blind adulation of choice and a corresponding failure to honor the public institutions of society that are needed to curb excesses of all sorts. See Lasch (1995).

5. Cited in Seldes, G. (compiler) (1985), *The great thoughts*. New York: Ballantine, p. 155.

6. Smith (1994), p. 408. In his remarks, M. Brewster Smith is directly re-

butting a prominent postmodernist in psychology, Kenneth Gergen (Gergen [1991]).

7. Ellis, J. M. (1998), Poisoning the wells of knowledge. *New York Times*, March 28. Reprinted in the *International Herald Tribune* with title: Out of touch, clichéd and pretentious, academia turns off students in droves.

1. The Original "Mind Software"

1. From the point of view of pure intellectual history, some argue that fascism as such during World War II was not anti-Semitic or bloodthirsty toward anyone; it was Nazism, and some other forms of fascism, that went in these directions.

What then was fascism in its pure form? Here is a description by a scholar who argues that fascism should not be equated with Nazism and that its adherents should not be held responsible for the Nazi effort to destroy Western culture.

Fascism was a rebellion against the universal ideals of enlightenment of the French revolution, rationalism, individualism, equality and human rights. Fascism preached heroic values, a life of danger, violence, the cultivation of new elites and the cult of a leader that would be larger than life. (Sternhall, Z. [2003]. Review of Golomb, & Wistrich [Eds.], *Nietzsche, godfather of fascism? Haaretz* [Hebrew], January 10, p. Heh 4) (Note: The newspaper *Haaretz* for many years used an apostrophe in an English rendition of its name as *Ha'aretz*, but in recent years has dropped the apostrophe, and I am adopting the current usage even when reference is being made to an issue that appeared before the style change.)

Need much more be said? The point of view of this book is that the very essential characteristics of fascism embracing "heroic" violence, elitism, and superleaders dooms it to become deeply destructive more often than not.

2. Hitler said, "Either the world will be ruled according to the ideas of our modern democracy, or the world will be dominated according to the natural law of force; in the latter case the people of brute force will be victorious. [Democracy is the] deceitful theory that the Jew would insinuate – namely, that theory that all men are created equal" (*Mein Kampf*, 1925–1926 p. 186). Cited in Seldes, G. (compiler) (1985). *The great thoughts*. New York: Ballantine, p. 186.

3. Historian and genocide scholar Henry Huttenbach, the founding editor of *The Genocide Forum*, has written:

Utopia, literally, means "No Place"; that is, utopia is a figment of the imagination, an unattainable goal because it simply does not exist, except in the mind(s) of its proponent(s). What does this have to do with genocide? Perhaps everything. . . . Utopianism is a pernicious mode of political thinking in absolutes. It seeks to wrench instantly, by force, today into a tomorrow today and not in the day after tomorrow. It is an ultra-radical ideology of dictatorial social engineering. Utopianism in action depends exclusively on violent action, on violent persuasion. Violence permeates the entire utopian political enterprise. It is a dangerous phenomenon. . . . Those who resort to utopian means are inevitably the merciless practitioners. Genocide is never far from utopianism, their common denominator being the mass application of violence. Both are extreme means to an extreme end, the monopolistic application of all political power in the service of an impossible dream. No wonder that utopianism predictably leads to the silence of the cemetery, with bottomless graves filled with human sacrifices to the goddess of instant "progress." (Huttenbach, H. [2000]. Genocide and utopia. *The Genocide Forum*, 8[4], 3–4)

4. Bugental (1965); May (1972); Yalom (1980).
5. Conquest (1970); Legters (1984, 1997, 1999); Mace (1984, 1997, 1999); Rummel (1990) Rummel (1999), Democide.
6. Leiby (1999).
7. Intriguingly, an editorial statement in an ultra-orthodox newspaper in Israel praised the Taliban and even "took credit" for the timing of its actions as part of the master plan of the Messiah (in this case Jewish, of course) that broke up the Communist empire – "the carrier of the flag of atheism – and since then millions of people across the Soviet empire are free to believe in God and his Messiah [as it is said in the Bible] 'And He will remove the idols from the land.'" From the newspaper *Yated Neeman*, March 9, 2001, translated from Hebrew). Indeed, fascist birds of a feather do flock together with the same nonsense and hatred of any cultures that are not true to their belief system.
8. Brooks (1990, February 22), Looking for a good time in Teheran. *Wall Street Journal*, p. A12.
9. Lifton (1961), p. 436.
10. Fromm (1941).

11. Ashton (1937), p. 17.

12. *Encyclopedia of world problems and human potential* (1986). Encyclopedia entry no: VP55136.

13. Bateson, (1974). Draft: Scattered thoughts for a conference on "broken power," *Co-Evolution Quarterly, 4,* 26–27, p. 27. Cited in Dell (1989, quotation on p. 8.

14. Dell (1989), p. 9.

15. Adorno, Frenkel-Brunswik, Levinson, & Sanford (1950).

16. Forbes (1985).

17. Schlesinger, A., Jr. (1989), The opening of the American mind. Lecture given on April 9 at Brown University on the occasion of Vartan Gregorian's inauguration as president. With permission.

18. Chomsky (1968); see also a description of Chomsky's work in a series on "modern masters": Lyons (1970).

19. Greenwald (1980). The powerful conceptualization by Greenwald was also noteworthy for its having been published in the flagship journal of the American Psychological Association, the *American Psychologist.* I am grateful to Professor Greenwald for having reviewed my present text describing his critical concepts.

Greenwald's conceptualization has since been hailed as a "turning point" in a special issue of the *American Psychologist* 20 years later on "happiness, excellence, and optimal human functioning":

> According to Greenwald, the self can be regarded as an organization of knowledge about one's history and identity. This organization is biased by information-control strategies analogous to those used by totalitarian political regimes. Everyone engages in an ongoing process of fabricating and revising his or her own personal history. The story each of us tells about ourselves is necessarily egocentric: Each of us is the central figure in our own narratives. Each of us takes credit for good events and eschews responsibility for bad events. Each of us resists changes in how we think. In sum, the ego maintains itself in the most self-flattering way possible. (Peterson [2000], p. 46)

20. Greenwald (1980), p. 603.

21. Greenwald (1980), p. 603.

22. Kahneman, D. (2003). Psychology of large mistakes and important decisions. Seventh Oscar Van Leer Annual Lecture, Van Leer Institute, Jerusalem, Is-

rael, September 7. The descriptions, including direct quotations, were recorded by me at the lecture. A video recording is available on the Web site of the Van Leer Jerusalem Institute, http://www.vanleer.org.il/conf/0309_oscar/e_Main_0 309_oscar.htm, accessed June 18, 2005.

23. *Encyclopedia of world problems and human potential* (1986). All quotations are from the Introduction, 10 pp. unnumbered.

24. There are many more observations of the weaknesses of the human mind to be found in popular literature. See, for example, an article on the "mind games" we constantly play, which concludes that "the mind's drive to infer causes can fool people into 'remembering' something they never saw," and that bias, suggestibility and misattributions are frequent occurrences in our minds.

Bias: Your brain rewrites the past under the influence of current events . . . for example, a divorcing couple remember only the bad times together, not the good.

Suggestibility: Leading questions/remarks color your memories or even "create" them . . . for example, parent to child: remember we took you to Disneyland and you talked to Mickey Mouse? Remember? And child "remembers."

Misattribution: You misattribute the source of your memory . . . for example, Joe remembers saying something to Sally when in fact he said it to Sue.

Begley, S. (2001, July 16). Memory's mind games: Absent-mindedness is just the start of memory problems. When the brain distorts the past, our view of who we are suffers. *Newsweek*, 60–61.

25. A helpful reference is Vyse (1997).

26. Sontag (1981), p. 99.

27. Cowley, G. (1997, April 21). Viruses of the mind: How odd ideas survive. *Newsweek*, 12B.

28. Cowley, G. (1997, April 21), 12B.

29. Zimbardo, Haney, Banks, & Jaffe (1974), pp. 61–73.

30. Epstein (1994), p. 712.

31. Grotjahn (1960). An excellent example of the certainty with which the new ideas of family therapy were greeted by the establishment of its day will be found in the various reviews of Martin Grotjahn's then-pioneering book on the integration of psychoanalysis with family therapy. Although the author was an accredited senior analyst and trainer, his daring work was uniformly described and castigated as heresy in one psychoanalytic journal after the other of the time.

32. Palazzoli (1978).

33. See, for example, Brenner (1957) and Menninger (1958).

34. Haley (1976).

35. Janov (1970); Kempler (1981).

36. Franks (1984).

37. Lifton (1986).

38. Kren (1987), p. 56.

39. Kren (1987), p. 62.

40. Arendt (1969, 1966), and Charny (1982), *How can we commit the unthinkable?*

41. Lifton (1986). The healing-killing paradox is that healers too often are prepared to kill the very patients or other human beings to whom they are no less obligated by their healing profession to be protectors of. Killing is often done in the name of healing; in genocide, for example, the victims are regarded as a diseased or eugenically damaging people, and they are to be "cut out" to preserve the larger health of society. A still deeper meaning of the paradox is that given the power to intervene at the most basic level of life, healers are drawn toward the duality that waits in all of us of both wishing to protect life and wishing to harm life, and in too many instances healers allow or succumb to the destructive motivation waiting in them.

42. Fromm (1973), p. 9 (italics in original).

43. Askenasy (1978); Browning (1992); Charny (1982), *How can we commit the unthinkable?*; Charny (1986); Christie (1974); and Lanzmann (1985).

44. "Euthanasia" is a semantic reframing of the murders committed. But this is the conceptualization the Nazis used to protect themselves from knowing they were murderers. They told themselves they were relieving the interminable suffering of the biologically inferior as well as improving the human race. Amir (1977), Chorover (1979), Sachs (1985), and Wertham (1966).

An incredible study that is not well known involved students at the University of Hawai'i who were assembled to hear a brief speech by a professor asking for their cooperation in assisting with the application of scientific procedures to kill the mentally and emotionally unfit. In the course of his remarks, the professor explained urbanely, "Euthanasia, which means mercy killing . . . is considered by most experts as not only being beneficial to the unfit, because it puts them out of the misery of their lives, but more importantly it will be a 'final solution' to a grave problem." The professor then added, "What is not clear, however, is which method of killing should be applied, which method is least painful and who should do the killing and/or decide when killing should be resorted to. For these reasons, further research is required and our research project is concerned with this problem." The results of the study were little short of incredible. Out of 570 subjects, 517 accepted the basic premise; all but 33 even indicated what aspect of the job he or she would prefer to take part in. Not one of these college students said he or she would refuse. See Mansson (1972). A description of the study is also found in the following textbook: Ruch, F. L., and Zimbardo, P. G. (Eds.) (1971). *Psychology and life.* Glenview IL: Scott Freeman, pp. 551–554.

45. Wertham (1966).

46. From a circular printed on the letterhead of the Eugenics Committee of the United States of America dated May 12, 1924, which is found in the M. Carey Thomas Personal Papers, Incoming Correspondence, Reel #40 of the Papers of M. Carey Thomas, Bryn Mawr College Archives, Bryn Mawr PA, and which also appears in *Encyclopedia of genocide,* p. 220.

47. Maslow (1979), p. 269.

48. Maslow (1979), p. 833.

49. Maslow (1979), pp. 1230–1231.

50. Maslow (1979), p. 631.

51. Simpson (1980), p. 913.

52. See the study of couples under age 40 who show reduced sexual activity: Charny & Asineli-Tal (2004). The phenomenon of reduced sexual activity is variously reported in the professional literature at a high estimate of one out of three couples to a low estimate of one out of seven couples. See also Gilligan (2002), and Davis (2003).

53. Miller (1981).

54. Assagioli (1965), Frankenstein (1966), and Neumann (1969).

55. Assagioli (1965).

56. Viorst (1986).

57. Yalom (1980).

58. Mitscherlich & Mitscherlich (1975).

59. Ellis (1962); Ellis & Harper, (1961).

60. Fisher, Anderson, & Jones (1981); Weeks & L'Abate (1982); Weeks (1985).

61. Palazzoli (1978).

62. Weeks (1985).

63. Ivan Boszormenyi-Nagy and Geraldine Spark explain the principle of dialectics thus:

The essence of the dialectical approach is a liberation of the mind from absolute concepts which in themselves claim to explain phenomena as though the opposite point of view did not exist. According to dialectical thought, a positive concept is always viewed in contrast with its opposite, in the hope that their joint consideration will yield a resolution through a more thorough and productive understanding. The principles of relativity and indeterminacy in physics and the concept of homeostatic regulations of living things are examples of increasingly dialectical orientations in natural sciences. (Boszormenyi-Nagy. & Spark [1973), p. 18)

64. Lankton & Lankton (1985), p. 135.
65. Bopp (1985), pp. 273, 295.

2. Choice between FASCIST & DEMOCRATIC MIND

1. Nathan (1943), *The psychology of fascism*, p. 83.
2. Nathan (1943), Fascism makes you feel good, pp. 95–96.
3. Šebek (1994), 105. Winnicott's writing on democracy can be seen in Winnicott (1950).
4. Fascism announces its offers of greatness in no uncertain terms. Thus, a message from Hitler was reported painted on the walls of some of the early concentration camps:

There is a road to freedom. Its milestones are Obedience, Endeavor, Honesty, Order, Cleanliness, Sobriety, Truthfulness, Sacrifice, and love of the Fatherland. (Message, signed Hitler, painted on walls of concentration camps, *Life*, August 21, 1939. Cited in Seldes, G. [compiler] [1985]. *The great thoughts*. New York: Ballantine, p. 186)

Modern fascism also can present itself to us without snarls and venom, dressed in the clothing and posturing of legitimate and acceptable members of our society. Two social scientists who have studied modern fascism offer the following observation:

The modern fascist is no longer a closed-minded bigot, but an intellectual, who is perfectly able to express his/her world-views in such a way that they not only sound acceptable, but also attractive to the general public. This might have important consequences. The presence of racist attitudes . . . is likely to exert more influence on both the output of public policy and the opinions of other people than is the case with the old-fashioned prejudice of authoritarians. (Duriez & van Hiel [2002], p. 1210)

5. Wynne et al. (1958).

6. O'Neill & O'Neill (1972), the O'Neill's are in favor of open marriage; Charny (1992), Charny does not favor open marriage.

7. Boehm (1999), p. 298.

8. Rummel (1990); Rummel (1999), Democide.

9. Chang (1992).

10. Rummel (1999), China, Genocide in: *The Chinese Communist Anthill.*

11. Sydney Schanberg won a Pulitzer Prize for his reporting of the evacuation of Phnom Penh, beginning on April 18, 1975, in the *New York Times.* Schanberg's work was also celebrated in the movie *The Killing Fields*, which was to become the most widespread source of information about the Cambodian Genocide for much of the world. See also Rummel (1999), Khmer Rouge and Cambodia.

12. Anthropologist Alexander Laban Hinton describes vividly the dehumanizing labels Cambodians were ordered to use to designate their victims as subhuman and therein warranting their extinction without mercy. Hinton (1999).

Well-known iconoclastic psychiatrist R. D. Laing wrote about the basic process of projection at all levels of human life:

Because we must defend *reality* against the emptiness, deceit and evil, of *unreality*. This is what we are fighting for. To defend the real against the unreal, the true against falsehood, the full life against an empty life, the good against evil. What is, against what is not. . . . *They* are dangerous, because they *are*. So long as they *are*, we are in danger. So we must destroy them. If we must destroy them, they must destroy us to prevent us destroying them, and we must destroy them before they destroy us before we destroy them before they destroy us . . . which is where we are at the moment. . . .

They exist to be destroyed and are destroyed to be reinvented. . . . There are always more where *they* came from. From *inside Us.* (Laing, R. D. [1972]. The politics of the family. In *The politics of the family and other essays*, pp. 94–95)

13. The soundest clinical practice I know of when one has reason to suspect impending suicide is to conduct a penetrating, and if need be a relentless,

inquiry into whether or not there is a plan, or the beginnings of a plan, to commit suicide. Ronald Mintz writes, "All authorities seem in agreement that *a chief error in evaluating suicidal danger lies in not asking the patient about suicidal thoughts and feelings.*" See Mintz (1968), quotation on p. 277.

14. Reich (1945).

15. There are a number of impressive and instructive writings about failures of psychotherapy, such as Kottler & Carlson (2001), but notwithstanding such compilations the predominant mode in most psychotherapy books is to present successes far more than to report responsibly mixtures of successes and failures.

3. The Fascist Believer

1. Well-known psychiatrist Karl Menninger observed, "Instead of committing suicide because of misfortune, some . . . individuals react in this way to sudden good fortune. They cannot endure certain large successes. I have known men and women to become overwhelmed with depression and attempt or commit suicide immediately following a promotion, an increase in income, or a sudden realization of their importance and prestige in their community." (Menninger [1938], p. 41)

2. Unlike the period of social science research led by the researchers of the "F (Fascism) Scale" (see Adorno et al. [1950]), where the intention was to define a fixed entity of a fascist personality type, my focus here is on the types of thinking and organization of experience at any given time rather than on a designated specific person. Along with the fact that there are relatively enduring characteristics in most of us, we have also learned that people do not necessarily remain the same as they were, especially when people arrive at and make meaningful spiritual commitments not to harm life, or, vice versa, when they do allow themselves or decide yes to be committed destroyers! At any given point, given John Does can present as largely nonfascist persons, but under circumstances such as the adoption of a prejudiced and persecutory policy by their church or government, too many John Does will move over to their available potential to utilize fascist thinking.

The same is true on the more prosaic level of everyday life. Thus, over the course of marriage and family life, various people become more, or less, jealous, possessive, demanding, controlling, encouraging – what have you. Throughout life there are major life cycle transitions. Parenthood, for example, brings out the best, or worst, in a man or woman. Some parents become encouraging and facilitating of children growing for themselves into their identities, while others increasingly squeeze a child to be obligated to function for them, the parents.

3. B. Mussolini. Cited by Ashton (1937), p. 35.

4. Bollas, C. (1992), The fascist state of mind. In *Being a character*, pp. 193–217 (quotation on pp. 200–201).

5. The British psychoanalyst Donald Winnicott taught of

the naturalness and inevitability of every child suffering the hate of his mother. On the simplest level, every mother at some point necessarily will find herself tired, depleted, and challenged beyond her resources to cope. It is an entirely natural fact that she, like all human beings, then turns to anger as a protest against being depleted and as a way of stirring her energy machinery to replenish her. How the mother and child then live out their experience of hating, being hated, and hating in return and how they reconnect their experience of hating and being hated to their loving and being loved become great dramas of the development of the human spirit. Winnicott argues forcefully that in many cases of serious emotional disturbances, the person we now see as a patient never enjoyed a constructive experience of being hated, did not learn to link the experience of being hated with being loved, nor did he learn to link his natural hatred with his also natural capacity and wish to love. Winnicott therefore proposes that one of the most important experiences the psychotherapist can give his patient (especially the very sick ones) is the constructive experience of being hated (along with being loved) by the therapist! This way, the patient may learn of his undeveloped capacity to bear hurts and to bear his own hatred, and to link them to his wishes and readiness to love and be loved. (Section quoted is from Charny [1982], *How can we commit the unthinkable?* p. 142. It is based on a simple and brilliant presentation by Winnicott that was originally published as early as 1949! Winnicott [1965])

See also the wise and helpful treatment of dialectical processes by Assagioli (1965, 1973).

6. Peng & Nisbett (1999), p. 751.

7. Langer & Moldoveanu (2000), p. 2.

8. Bollas (1992), p. 200.

9. Coser (1972), p. 3.

10. Ashton (1937), pp. 42, 56.

11. The quotation is from a news report by Kahn, J. (2004, May 4). A professor strikes back at the censors in China. *International Herald Tribune.*

4. The Fascist Slave

1. Wynne et al. (1958).

2. Bowen (1966, 1978), Dicks (1967), Lidz et al. (1960), Minuchin (1974), Minuchin, Rosman, & Baker (1978), Minuchin & Fishman (1981), and Sprenkle & Olson (1978).

3. Asch (1955, 1956).

4. Milgram (1964, 1974). See also a fascinating follow-up on Milgram's work in Blass (2000).

The same book also goes on to look at a second social science experiment of the last century – Zimbardo's simulation of a prison and his demonstration of the widespread potential for tyranny and cruelty in otherwise (previously) perfectly nice and well-adjusted people. In the process, the book also produces a delicious treat for those who respect both these great studies deeply (and for New York aficionados) when Philip Zimbardo reveals that "Stanley and I were high school classmates at James Monroe High School in the Bronx, he being considered the smartest kid and I voted the most popular" (Zimbardo, Maslach, & Haney [2000], p. 195).

5. Regarding Jonestown, see Levi (1982). Regarding the sarin attacks in Tokyo, see Sayle, M. (1996, April 6). Nerve gas and the four noble truths: How did the guru facing trial for murder in the Tokyo nerve gas attack create himself and a following among the young Japanese elite? *The New Yorker*, 72, no. 6, 56–71. A further subheadline over the article reads (p. 56): The trial of a blind Buddhist prophet for the nerve gas attack in the Tokyo subway is testing a fragile democracy and leaving Japan to wonder how he built his movement among the nation's brightest people.

6. Official psychiatric diagnoses are compiled in the DSM. The following are references to the fourth and third editions of this authoritative bible of psychiatric diagnosis:

American Psychiatric Association (2000). *Diagnostic and statistical manual of mental disorders* (4th ed., rev.). Washington DC: Author [referred to more briefly as *DSM-IV-TR*].

American Psychiatric Association (1994). *Diagnostic and statistical manual of mental disorders* (4th ed.). Washington DC: Author [referred to more briefly as *DSM-IV*].

American Psychiatric Association (1987). *Diagnostic and statistical manual of mental disorders* (3rd ed., rev.). Washington DC: Author [referred to more briefly as *DSM-III-R*].

American Psychiatric Association (1980). *Diagnostic and statistical manual of mental disorders* (3rd ed.). Washington DC: Author [referred to more briefly as *DSM-III*].

7. Practitioners in the field of mental health have vacillated on this issue, even as there naturally have been emotional cries of despair and protest at the madness of these mass killing behaviors. Thus, in 1971, I published a paper on "normal man" as committing genocide based on a lecture I gave to the Israel Psychological Association in Jerusalem in 1969 (see Charny [1971]). Among others, I was basing my work on the earlier findings of the psychologist Gustave M. Gilbert (1950), and the psychiatrist Douglas M. Kelley (1947), both of whom had examined the Nazi killers at the Nuremberg trial. Gilbert, for example, said the majority of the Nazi leaders were not mentally ill as such, but that their overwhelming ambition and low ethical standards joined with their strong commitment to ideology.

In 1972, Henry Dicks, a theorist of marital therapy at the Tavistock Clinic in London, who wrote a major work on understanding couples, *Marital tensions*, published the book *Licensed mass murder* in which he reported on visiting convicted and still-imprisoned killers of the Holocaust in various jails in Europe. His findings were that in the accepted terms of our mental health field these men were psychiatrically normal, but that they suffered personality disturbances as weak-egoed, emotionally deprived individuals who harbored secret resentments, covered by conformity and unquestioning obedience.

In 1978 Hans Askenasy called out in powerful words in the book *"Are we all Nazis?"* the same truth that "ordinary people" are capable of genocidal killing and are the predominant perpetrators. This concept has continued to be developed by researchers over the years, such as in the work of Christopher Browning (1992), *Ordinary men*, in which he studied a German police battalion that was assigned the killings of Jews.

The overwhelming consensus has been that the bulk of genocidal killings in our species are the work of the common everyday human of our societies, who is rarely psychiatrically disturbed, as psychiatry has defined mental illness essentially as an inability to function adequately in society.

My own point of view has been that disturbed mental health needs to be defined either as a disturbance or inability to function for oneself in society or as causing harm to other human beings, which disturbs them and makes them unable to function safely and healthily.

Eureka! If this definition were adopted in formal psychiatry, we would have a way of saying that parents who beat their children, spouses who physically abuse their mates (typically men who beat women but not only), and whichever people humiliate, persecute, or attack others are psychiatrically disturbed – which means opposite to the kind of normality we wish to teach in our societies. We also would have a way of saying that both the people who plan and those who agree to fly the airplanes into skyscrapers to kill thousands of noncombatant civilians are mad, just as their actions are also a profound corruption of the meanings of life, religion, politics, and all the accepted tools of society for improving human life.

As I will note repeatedly, my emphasis that this is psychiatric madness does not then give the perpetrators an exemption from criminal and military justice. But if it becomes a consensual definition that harming others is abnormal mental health, it makes criminal terrorism far less attractive for others to emulate, and provides an important basis for discrediting leaders who preach mass violence. It also gives another way of identifying youths and adults who are turning toward chilling cruelty before they go into action, and in any case it returns to psychology and psychiatry some commonsense meaning: we can't call mass killers normal or we will continue to be a crazy society. Note how when bin Laden attacked New York and Washington, he and his followers were spontaneously characterized by many people as "sick" and "insane," as well as "evil," "terrorists," and "killers," for in common-sense everyday parlance, people don't want to think of genocidal terrorist killers as normal, and they are right.

The following published articles have presented my major proposals for an explicit psychiatric diagnosis of those who harm others. Because of the sensitivity of the subject and the fact that the basic concept is not being accepted in current-day conventional psychiatry, it was important to me to take care to publish these proposals in major publications – two of the following four references are in leading psychiatric journals, one is in an important volume on new methods of relational diagnosis proposed to supplement and replace traditional diagnosis of psychiatric conditions, and one is in an encyclopedia edited by me where it was reviewed by five associate editors as well as the publisher's editorial team. Admittedly, at times the review process of these articles was tense. For example, one reviewer of one of the journal articles wrote that he had a feeling that "the author is laughing at us" (the field of psychiatry), but he nonetheless recommended publishing the paper.

Charny (1986), Genocide and mass destruction: Doing harm to others as a missing dimension in psychopathology.

Charny (1996), Evil in human personality: Disorders of doing harm to others in family relationships.

Charny (1997), A personality disorder of excessive power strivings.

Charny (1999), "Ordinary people" as perpetrators of genocide.

8. For many years, in circles devoted to study of the Holocaust, my writing on the subject of the psychology of genocide contributed to some sense that I was not entirely kosher, for after all the only thing that mattered was to establish that the crime against the Jewish people was the greatest crime in history, and there was little point in getting involved with psychological understanding and definition of the crime. Only after many years can one find in a Yad Vashem publication an article such as "How Was It Humanly Possible?" which describes a new educational unit produced by Yad Vashem under the same title. The author, Arieh Saposnik (2001, p. 8), writes:

> The study of the Holocaust, perhaps even more than any other chapter in history, seems to pose the most penetrating and disturbing questions about human nature. . . . If one of the central goals of Holocaust education is to act towards a human society in which such events do not recur, we are compelled to attempt to comprehend how human beings – "ordinary men" as historian/author Christopher Browning has called them – are transformed into mass murderers.

The author concludes as follows:

> The central axis . . . is the question of individual choice. A choice or a series of choices, led the individual. Where were those crucial crossroads?

9. Somerville & Shibata (1982), Ecocide and omnicide, the new faces of genocide. Ecocide refers to the destruction of the environmental support of life. The term *omnicide* was developed to refer to "the extermination of all human life" (see p. 244), but can be used to refer to "lesser" megaevents of massive multiple genocides of many peoples.

10. Zimbardo, P. (1997). What messages are behind today's cults?: Cults are

coming. Are they crazy or bearing initial messages? Cited in *American Psychological Association Monitor*, May, p. 14.

11. Rosenbaum (1983).

12. Janis (1975), and Goldsmith (1990).

13. Ackerman (1982).

14. Sayle, M. (1996), Nerve gas and the four noble truths, 60. Even following the poison-gas attack in the Tokyo subway that killed 12 people and injured more than 5,500 others, and the leader of the cult (Shoko Asahara) responsible for the attack was behind bars awaiting trial, the cult Aum Shinrikyo was successfully rebuilding its membership. "It's really unbelievable for us," a top official of the Public Security Investigations Agency said. See Sullivan, K. (1997, September 30). Aum Shinrikyo rebuilds its following in Japan. *International Herald Tribune* (*Washington Post Service*).

15. Spencer, M. (1984). Cited in *American Psychological Association Monitor*, November.

16. Merton (1967). Father Merton writes further, "We can no longer assume that because a man is "sane" he is therefore in his "right mind." The whole concept of sanity in a society where spiritual values have lost their meaning is itself meaningless. . . . I am beginning to realize that "sanity" is no longer a value or an end in itself. The "sanity" of modern man is about as useful to him as the huge bulk and muscles of the dinosaur. If he were a little less sane, a little more doubtful, a little more aware of his absurdities and contradictions, perhaps there might be a possibility of his survival."

17. Milgram (1974), p. 188.

18. Milgram (1974), pp. 145–146. Thus, in the fascinating book following up Milgram's work referred to earlier, see the discussion of how perhaps 25% of all airplane accidents are due to excessive obedience of the copilot to the captain!: Tarnow, E. (2000). Self-destructive obedience in the airplane cockpit and the concept of obedience optimization. In Blass (2000), pp. 111–123.

19. Fromm (1986), p. 133.

20. Leonard Glick has written of the positive and negative contributions of religion, on the one hand to the prevention of killing and genocide, but on the other hand to the very opposite of initiation and legitimization of genocide. As the editor of the volume in which his chapter was published, I can attest to the fact that we had earlier gone through inviting several Protestant clergymen who were well known scholars of religion, some of whom promised to write

the chapter but never did, before we secured anthropologist Glick's work. My guess was that it was too spiritually difficult for these scholars who themselves were also noted practicing clerical leaders in their churches. It seemed to me that although they genuinely intended to write a true critical essay, they were unable to tell the truth of religion also being a leading sponsor of genocidal mass killing, and quite probably that it was also politically too dangerous for some of them. See Glick (1994). This story of the resistance of scholars to writing the chapter on religion and genocide will be found in my introduction to the above book. See also Kuper (1990).

21. Perhaps the penultimate case of murderous medical research in the United States was the infamous Tuskegee syphilis study. In 1932, the United States Public Health Service set out to study the long-term effects of syphilis. Four hundred poor, rural African American men in Alabama who had been diagnosed as having the disease were chosen as the subjects. The research was to monitor the course of the disease until death without offering any treatment. Even when in the 1940s penicillin was found to be an effective treatment for syphilis, the patients were not given the medicine. The Associated Press exposed the story in 1972. Allan Brandt, of Harvard University, has suggested: "In retrospect the Tuskegee study revealed more about the pathology of racism than it did about the pathology of syphilis." Cited in Shore (2000). The quotation is identified in Shore's review as the opening chapter by Allan Brandt in Reverby (2000), p. 29.

Not that many years ago, I was honored at a reception in the United States following a workshop I had led on psychotherapeutic management of violent individuals, and I was introduced to a stately local physician who I was told was the head of a local peace organization. Somehow I recognized the name and realized who he was – indeed he was the man who had been in charge of the Tuskegee study! I declined to enter into the usual civilities and instead expressed my outrage at the study.

"You shouldn't criticize us," replied the dignified older man heatedly. "We treated those men [the patients] with full dignity. They were cared for very well by Nurse Rivers [the R.N. who also became famous as the person responsible for patient care in the study], and everyone of them was given a fine funeral that was much nicer than they ever would have had."

I walked away from the man in disgust.

22. Charny (1997), Which genocide matters more?

23. Italics added by me in text. See Meyer, P. (1974). If Hitler asked you to electrocute a stranger, would you? Probably. In Miner, R. A. (Ed.), *Annual editions: Readings in psychology*. Guilford CO: Dushkin, p. 273–279.

24. Camus (1980).

5. The Fascist Fist

1. It is important to realize that the dialectic tension between religion as protecting life and religion as engendering death is present and playing out in many religions. Few religious groups are exceptions that succeed in holding only to a conception of a universal god of all human beings and the need to respect and protect all human life. Two such welcome examples are the Unitarians in the United States and the worldwide Baha'i, both of which stand unambiguously for the sacredness of life. Personally, I do not know of a religion that has been associated with a national or geographic identity that has managed not to be drawn into massacring others in their region. Certainly the acknowledged three "great" religions of the Western world, Judaism, Islam, and Christianity, have records of destruction of others (though not at all equally), notwithstanding and alongside of their calls in the name of their gods for peacefulness and protection of life. See the work cited in the previous chapter by the preeminent scholar of genocide, Leo Kuper, who studied what he called the "theological warrants for genocide" in Judaism, Islam, and Christianity, and especially warned against "religious fundamentalisms" that introduce extremisms.

In the survey of the relationship between religion and genocide also cited in the previous chapter by Leonard Glick, we read as follows: "Religious leaders, whether they be shamans, priests, pastors, mullahs or rabbis, appear on the average to demonstrate neither more nor less compassion for aliens than anyone else. If a few men and women of strong religious faith and moral fiber have indeed taken a stand against genocidal oppression, so have an equal number of people with no particular attachment to religious or 'spiritual' concerns. It appears that if we are ever to reach the point where genocidal massacres will have become a thing of the past, it will not be owing to religions: they are part of the problem" (p. 61).

Glick identified the basic pattern of thought in religions that manifests itself in ethnocentrism and massacre of others thus: "*Ritual affirmation of communal unity and ethnocentric sentiments, belief in deities that belong exclusively to the home group, proto-genocidal attacks on neighboring groups identified as alien or 'other,' conviction that one's own deities approve of such attacks and promote their success* – have been intrinsic components of the human condition since the emergence of our species" (p. 46 [italics in original]).

Nonetheless, the other side of the coin of religious thought cannot be forgotten. In the opinions of many thinkers, a more consistent life-respecting message by organized world religions could offer humanity an enduring framework for greater progress toward reducing killing.

In a forthcoming book by me on suicide bombers, I propose an international "Campaign for Life" that has at its center the leaders of many of the world's religions standing together in affirmation of life. See Charny, (unpublished manuscript), *How can the suicide bombers do it? Can we fight back?* Robert Jay Lifton and Eric Markusen note that all major religious traditions have been instrumental in inspiring and guiding some of the great leaders for nonviolence:

> In their humane, nonviolence struggles, Mohandas Gandhi and Martin Luther King, and the movements they inspired, drew heavily upon Christian tradition, and Gandhi upon Hindu and Muslim tradition as well . . . we can also include such modern Jewish figures as Martin Buber and Abraham Joshua Heschel. Indeed, all of the world's great religions contain principles of universalism or species consciousness, however these have been violated by religiously inspired conflicts, wars, and massacres. (Lifton & Markusen [1990], p. 263)

2. Rummel (1999), Democide; Rummel (1997, 1994); Rummel (1999), Power kills, absolute power kills absolutely.

3. For a masterful scholarly and moving summary, see Churchill (1997).

4. Reference is to a paper by Walsh, M. (1980), Symposium on political uses of psychiatry. Presented at American Psychiatric Association, San Francisco CA. Cited by Rosenbaum (1983), p. 17.

5. Milgram (1974).

6. Jung (1970).

7. Orwell (1949), p. 266.

8. A proper academic reader of this manuscript asked that the source of this quote be identified. It was from a very plain and simple woman with no academic or literary identity with whom I had a good conversation.

9. Ashton (1937), p. 209.

10. Leiby (1999).

11. Selzer (1983), p. 224.

12. Selzer (1983), p. 219.

13. Special report, 50 years after the liberation of Auschwitz. *U.S.A. Today,* January 26, 1996, p. 10A.

14. Many writers have addressed the human need for superiority. I have always been instructed and helped by the book by psychoanalyst Karen Horney (1937), whose marvelous title, *The neurotic personality of our time,* makes it ring contemporary forever – certainly its statements about human strivings for power remain entirely current. See also my proposal to identify a personality disorder of excessive power strivings: Charny (1997), A personality disorder of excessive power strivings.

15. Early on in the psychoanalytic literature there were reports of this powerful symbolic connection between reactions to the penis and reactions to a breast. It sounds funny "on paper," that is, in words, but lo and behold it is of such symbolic constructions that our unconscious mind is made. Certainly in this case the classic symbolic paradigm fits. This is the linkage that came up in the patient's associations, which is how one establishes likely knowledge in psychotherapy.

16. Sontag (1981), p. 99.

17. Ashton (1937), pp. 83, 42, 56, respectively.

18. Bollas (1992), p. 203.

19. Charny (1992).

20. Struckmeyer (1971).

21. Charny (1982), The tragic illusion of self-defense, p. 181.

22. Bandura (1990), p. 191.

23. Mitscherlich & Mitscherlich (1975).

24. Hartman (1984), p. 198.

25. Lifton & Markusen (1990), pp. 258–259.

6. The Fascist Denier

1. See for example, Curtis, M. (1996). Democratic genocide. *The Ecologist,* 26(5). Excerpted in *Encyclopedia of genocide* (1999), p. 355. See in the next note how this story was inadvertently let out by the U.S. government in 2001, and then the government vainly tried once again to suppress it.

2. See Lardner, G., Jr. (2001, July 30). U.S. tries to call back account of role in Indonesia killings. *International Herald Tribune.*

3. Rummel (1994); Rummel (1999), *Statistics of democide*; Rummel (1999), Democide.

4. Around 1980 I tried canvassing hundreds of physicians in Europe to inquire about their experiences in treating perpetrators of the Holocaust at points of medical crisis in the perpetrators' later years when they would suffer conditions such as heart attacks or other life-threatening situations. The theory was that such anxious, humbling moments in the lives of the perpetrators might naturally turn into "confessional" experiences. No such luck. Very few physicians reported they had treated known perpetrators; of those who did, almost nobody reported the patients expressing guilt or remorse. Dan Bar-On reported similarly that when he was on repeated field trips in Europe in connection with his pathbreaking study of children of perpetrators of the Holocaust, he was unable to make contact with a significant sample of physicians or clergymen who had direct experiences with the perpetrators of the Holocaust (personal communication). See Bar-On, D. (1989).

5. Text is excerpted from Alvarez (2001), pp. 114–115; it is based on Sykes & Matza (1957).

6. Alvarez (2001), pp. 125–127.

7. There are today many descriptions of the unending cruelty and genocide humans perpetrate, but not too often are there clear-cut descriptions of the joy and rewards so many people do experience in being killers. For an unusually straight-on discussion of the considerable joy many human beings experience in killing others, see Bourke (1999). Also useful are discussions of how human beings who normally would not kill do so under circumstances in which moral norms are destroyed and restraints are lifted. Thus, see Glover (2003). Glover rejects the opinion that human evil is not inherent in human nature but derives from political institutions. He argues that sadism and cruelty occur over and over again throughout history, and therefore we must examine the human soul with no illusions. See also Bartlett (2004). The author, a physician, proposes that evil be regarded as a pathological condition, within a framework of a theory of disease, similar to my proposal to define doing serious harm to others as psychopathology.

8. A comprehensive analysis of emerging new forms of reparations and apologies by governments will be found in Barkan (2000).

9. See the comprehensive work by Bazyler (2003).

10. Charny (1980).

11. Arieti (1972).

12. Arieti (1972), p. 223.

13. Arieti (1972), pp. 228, 242, 252, respectively.

7. DEMOCRATIC MIND as the Healthy Alternative

1. Alexander (1987).

2. "He who goes without a dream six days is considered evil" will be found in *Brachot*, 14:1 (book in Talmud).

3. Rosenberg (2001), p. 9.

4. May (1977).

5. Gordon, with Frondsen (1993).

6. Kesey (1962).

7. Greenwald (1973). There are many fine works on the process of choice. Among classic works, see the existential approach in Bugental (1965), a philosophical-theological analysis in Tillich (1952), and a Jungian approach in Wickes (1963).

8. In a later chapter, practical ways are described for using healthy anger in one's mind first for "good living," and second as the basis of a technique of treatment of some people who become violent because they don't know what else to do with their violent emotions.

9. Barkan (2000).

10. The issue of Palestinian banks such as the Anglo-Palestine Bank, which was the predecessor of the formidable current Bank Leumi in Israel, has surfaced in various press reports. According to Holocaust restitution expert Michael Bazyler, the issue has yet to reach its peak of full exposure. Source: Address by Michael Bazyler, "Suing Hitler's Business Partners: The Battle for Holocaust Restitution in America's Courts," to the Jerusalem Center for Public Affairs, July 19, 2004. See Bazyler. (2003).

11. Japanese Unit 731 – Dread medical experiments that preceded the Nazis. In *Encyclopedia of genocide* (1999), p. 413.

12. Smith, Markusen, & Lifton (1995). This is not only an excellent paper but a very funny one in that its origin was the mistake by a secretary at the Turkish embassy who enclosed with a letter from the Turkish ambassador to Robert Jay Lifton a confidential document showing the research, bigotry, and scholarly malfeasance of a well-known academic, who for many years was in the employ of the Turkish government as a propagandist, which was the basis for the ambassador's critical letter to Lifton.

13. Bettelheim (1967).

14. Tustin (1972, 1988).

15. Well-known psychologist Victor Sanua wrote such a complaint in the

publication of a professional organization: Sanua, V. D. (1986), Letter to the Editor: The organic etiology of infantile autism: A critical review of the literature. In an interesting letter to me, he describes the above as "originally a 40–50 page report which I had submitted to many journals dealing with infantile autism. They all rejected my paper because I had expressed doubts about autism being an organic disease. I finally sent it to the editor of the above journal with the request that he evaluate it on its merits and not on the prevailing philosophy on the subject. Surprisingly, he wrote to me that I was wrong, that it is an organic disorder, but he was angry because I was not given the opportunity to express my opinion on the subject. Therefore, he decided to publish it as a letter to the editor, which would circumvent the need to send it to 'experts' for evaluation subject to getting a lot of critiques from readers. My letter to the editor was thirty pages long! For your information, I got most positive reactions and no critiques. And although letters to the editor in journals are not normally indexed, a specialist of the American Psychological Association made sure that it was indexed [like an article in the professional literature]."

16. Bruno Bettelheim's beleaguered voice stands out as very different from the mental health establishment's claims of an organic etiology to all autism. Bettelheim's central thesis shatters normal conventions: "The precipitating factor in infantile autism is the parent's wish that his child should not exist," Bettelheim dared to say gravely. Bettelheim emphasized that it is not simply parental ambivalence to the autistic child that develops once the child is already autistic and therefore a source of terrible pain to the parent, but "only the extreme of negative feelings in the parents can set the autistic process in motion." The autistic child lives out a "single-minded preoccupation with a specific issue . . . his unremitting fear of destruction." Bettelheim (1967), quotations on pp. 125, 127, 459.

17. Charny (1980).

18. The gifted individual child therapist was Ellen Gillespie, EdM, a special education teacher and psychoeducational therapist.

8. Psychotherapy as Antifascism

1. Zen Buddhism has a well-developed technique for inducing an anxiety of "unknowing" and confusion. For a collection of koans, or the riddles that are the grist of confounding students of Zen, see Hoffman, (1975). There have

been interesting comparisons and connections made between Zen and Western thinking about psychological treatment such as that by Suzuki, Fromm, & De Martino (1960). In the Western world too, psychoanalytic treatment was calculated to induce greater anxiety in the patient so that the patient would be led to deeper aspects of his or her inner self. See for example works on psychoanalysis such as Menninger (1958). In family therapy too, there are times when anxiety is purposely increased; see Minuchin & Fishman (1981), for a discussion of increasing intensity and unbalancing. Regrettably, many therapists today are so beholden to "successful" short-term solutions to problems (per the dictates of managed-care insurance reimbursements on the one hand, and per a culturewide insistence on avoiding stress and pain on the other) that they operate as if therapy is a straight-line logical clarification and clearing up of problems, and refrain from using techniques that might upset and destabilize patients, which, heaven forbid, might lead to their complaining.

2. Charny (1982), The tragic illusion of self-defense; Struckmeyer (1971).

3. The story of Kitty Genovese is vividly told in the reports of 38 witnesses, the neighbors in the building in which she lived, who heard her screams and came to their windows to see what was happening; none came to her assistance nor did any call the police for help. See Rosenthal (1964).

4. My colleague, Pnina Blitz, and I have systematically spelled out many ways in which people do harm to their loved ones in family life in the flow chart "Disorders of Incompetence and Pseudocompetence in Marital, Family and Parental Relationships," which will be found in Charny (1996), chart on pp. 484–487.

5. I remain with an old-fashioned school that believes that while resistance in therapy looks like and can be antagonism and refusal to allow a process of counseling, frequently it is a legitimate and natural resistance to learning and change that presages the effective progress in treatment that is to come. As much of modern psychotherapy has turned toward a kind of "what works" pragmatism and has moved away from the dramas of emotional and spiritual discovery, there has been more of an equation of resistance with patient noncompliance and noncooperation, and more emphasis on the smart tactics therapists should adopt to overcome resistance. Thus, a good "how-to-overcome-resistance-book" by Anderson and Stewart refers to a claim of as-if total victory over all resistance by one of the outstanding master teachers of what-and-how-to-do-to-treat-them-victoriously-in-family therapy, Steve de Shazer, who proclaimed

no less than "the 'death of resistance,'" and that "there are no resistant families only misunderstood families." See Anderson & Stewart (1983), p. 23.

For examples of a more respectful approach to the naturalness, legitimacy, and even usefulness of resistance, see the extensive treatment of resistance in the classic work on individual therapy by Lewis Wolberg (1954), *The technique of psychotherapy.*

It has also been proposed that a strong self with a capacity to resist encroachment by foreign bodies so to speak will express itself in healthier boundaries even on the level of greater psychobiological immunity against illness and disease. There is today a significant literature on "psychoimmunology."

Resistance is also a phenomenon of the personality in one's being relatively protected and safe from emotional invasion, domination, and control by others. Thus, individuals who have their own minds can stand up better against seductive ideologies, cults, or coercion. See, for example, Rosenbaum (1983).

6. Jourard (1964); Whitaker & Keith, (1981); Whitaker & Bumberry (1988); Napier & Whitaker (1978); Yalom (1980).

7. Such analyses of repetitive unproductive styles of emotional functioning may be seen in the continuing tradition of character analysis first pioneered by the brilliant if later eccentric and troubled Wilhelm Reich in his classical work (1945), *Character analysis.* This method of psychotherapy of reflecting truthfully the ways in which a person is conducting their life has been elaborated by many therapists over the years, for example, including the training psychoanalyst, Leon Saul (1956), in *The hostile mind*, where he emphasized helping the patient to be aware most of all of their anger, hostility, and hatred. While treatment is respectful and accepting of the humanity of the patient, it is based on truth and a search for integrity more than it is concerned with accepting all the patient's desires and impulses.

8. Masters & Johnson (1970).

9. Levay & Kagle (1983).

10. This was one of the startling issues Wilhelm Reich (1945), dealt with in his amazing work. The phenomenon of a "negative therapeutic reaction" in patients who have done very well in their psychotherapy and even are nearing successful completion of their therapy is one I have learned to respect and even to fear. I often refer to such cases as living out the biblical legend of Moses who is allowed by God to see the Promised Land but forbidden from entering it. Like Wilhelm Reich reports, I too am not always successful in overcoming these negative therapeutic reactions and leading these patients across the finish

line that had seemed so approachable when they were progressing well in their therapy before the impasse developed. Needless to say, I celebrate heartily with those patients who succeed in overcoming their impasse to achieve a full-blown successful completion of their therapy.

11. Some years after Masters and Johnson introduced their pioneering technique, psychiatrist Helen Kaplan taught adamantly, and I believe correctly, that one should never proceed with sexual behavior tasks so long as there are any indications of basic emotional rejection in the couple's emotional relationship. See Kaplan (1974). Indeed, there have been clinical observations that some couples break up precisely because their successful sex therapy enables them to succeed in resuming pleasurable intercourse, and what then happens is that their experience of renewed closeness brings them in touch with their underlying more basic rejection of each other, lack of compatibility, and lack of basic acceptance of one another.

12. Saul (1972), p. 31.

13. Saul (1972), p. 322.

14. Masters & Johnson (1970).

15. Ah, Prozac. How can one possibly speak critically of a joy-wonder drug that at any given point is bringing real relief to millions of people?

Prozac sounds like a good wine or cognac, which are certainly welcome to this writer. And yet there are other sides to the phenomenology of what one writer called "the Prozac that ate America" (Morford, M. [2003, June 25]. The Prozac that ate America. Are you massively depressed? Sure you are. Survey says so. No really, you are! Stop resisting! The Web site www.SFGate.com of the *San Francisco Chronicle*, June 25). As noted, there have been reports of many patients on Prozac being suicidal and some homicidal. There are also allegations – and plenty of legal suits, and big financial settlements by the drug manufacturers that confirm that they are genuinely vulnerable – that the manufacturer made various efforts to suppress known experimental and clinical data about these lethal side effects.

One investigative journalistic source that perhaps played a significant "Watergate-exposing" role in respect of Prozac was the reputable *Boston Globe* (for example, Garnett, L. R. [2000, May 7]. As drug gets remade, concerns about suicides surface. *Boston Globe*), whose reports of some 50,000 suicides by Prozac users were widely reprinted in other papers around the world (including no less than a front-page story in the distinguished *Haaretz* in Israel).

Estimates and projections of Prozac damages have varied widely but have included alarming numbers. One FDA document projected the probability of "108,900 suicides" and "188,500 suicide attempts" (www.petitiononline.com/lil pro/petition.html, accessed July 8, 2003).

You might argue (as have the drug manufacturer's representatives in a way that has reminded me of the arguments of the super-rich law firms for the tobacco industry not long ago, although this is also an unfair comparison since it is clear to me that Prozac is a very helpful and constructive medication for millions of people), that most people who take Prozac are depressed to begin with, so there are bound to be any number of them who commit suicide.

A fair answer to the argument certainly has to include a policy that users, and prescribing doctors, need to be warned that the medication is no sure-fire preventive of suicide; that in one way (physiological) or another (psychological), the medication may bring the patient closer to a fatal action; and that clinical reports and studies show that "the Prozac class of anti-depressants can make *healthy* men, women and children *with no history of depression* feel suicidal" (italic emphasis mine) (Bosley, S. [2000, May 23]. Happy drug Prozac can bring an impulse to suicide – British study. *London Guardian*).

The Mental Health Foundation of the United Kingdom reported in hearings before Britain's Department of Health on the possible prescription of Prozac to "people under 18," that evidence from nine studies showed "an increased risk of suicidal thoughts and self-harm among those under 18 and that the drug was ineffective in treating depression in this group." The chairman of the regulatory agency who was testifying concluded, "The balance of risk and benefit is unfavourable. The drug should not be used in young people" (www.connects.org.uk, which is the Mental Health and Learning Disabilities portal, accessed July 8, 2003). Prescription of the drug to children under 18 has since been forbidden by law in the United Kingdom, while in some other countries increasing cautions have been issued to physicians.

Personally, I believe on the basis of the available evidence that Prozac – and perhaps other SSRI's, or Selective Serotonin Reuptake Inhibitors, the class of medications to which Prozac belongs – does work, and even dramatically so for many millions, but that there are flaws as well that need to be faced honestly. The writer for the *San Francisco Chronicle* cited earlier writes sarcastically about "doctors who absolutely swear they have no direct affiliation to the multibillion-dollar pharmacological industry ha-ha yeah right have taken *a big survey* and discovered that a shockingly huge number of Americans are apparently just totally bummed about one helluva lot of things" (Morford, M. [2003, June

25], *San Francisco Chronicle*). The basic flaw with Prozac is that, like with any medication including the most wonderfully helpful substances, some people – in this case probably a small percentage that adds up to a lot of people – react badly. In the case of Prozac, known possible side effects include agitation; akathisia, which is a severe form of anxiety and agitation; depression; suicidal thoughts; self-harm; suicide; and aggressive behavior including assault and murder.

I suggest further that these side effects derive from two possible sources. The first can be the physiological influence of the drug; it is often the case that a medication that has the power to act on a crucial physiological mechanism, in this case let us say on the capacity to feel calm and unfrightened, may trigger a contradictory effect in some people.

The second source, which personally interests me even more, is psychological. It involves the mechanism that we have long known is triggered in depressed patients precisely when they feel better. It is a clinical fact that many suicides occur after depressed patients have begun to improve, so much so that the responsible therapy of depressed patients requires a therapist to caution and warn the patient and, I believe, to actively coach the patient how not to despair when they relapse into depressed feelings, how to cope with the return of depressed feelings, and organize oneself in advance to be promptly in touch with the therapist. See the further discussion that follows in the text of how Prozac may be helping some people feel so much better that they can feel bad!

16. Florence Kaslow has called wisely for an integrative approach to knowledge and practice in psychotherapy rather than adherence to set beliefs or schools of thought:

> The problem arises when adherents of a school become totalistic purists – exuding a fanaticism purporting that their way is the only right way. As has happened throughout the history of the psychiatric professions, brilliant, charismatic leaders attract those who have a longing to become worshipful true believers. They carry the gospel with them – unquestioningly – and any deviations from the master's catechism is heresy. (See Kaslow [1981], p. 347)

17. Arthroscopic surgery for the pain and stiffness caused by osteoarthritis is performed on "225,000 middle-age and older Americans each year," said one report. A tall lanky friend of mine who suffered intense knee pains was told that he would need surgery in both knees. He decided to do one knee at a time,

but then to his amazement, and to the consternation of his doctor, following the successful surgery of the first knee his other knee also stopped hurting! Some time later a report in the *New England Journal of Medicine* reported a study from Houston Veterans Affairs Medical Center and Baylor College of Medicine that "while patients often said they felt better after the surgery, their improvement was just wishful thinking." The study was a remarkable one in that half the patients actually were given placebo surgery where surgeons took them through the whole operating room mystique and made cuts in their knees and the patients did not know they did not have the real surgical procedure! (Kolata, G. [2002, July 12]. Surgery found useless for arthritic knees. Study suggests a placebo procedure is as . . . effective as arthroscopy. *International Herald Tribune*, with attribution to the *New York Times*.).

18. Schofield, (1964).

19. See the focus on activating husband-wife healing of each other in the imago therapy created by Harville Hendrix (1988).

20. Boszormenyi-Nagy & Spark (1973), for a basic procedure of having family members tell one another "straight" their good and bad feelings and "settling accounts" with one another.

21. Green (1964). See also a book about Hannah's inspiring therapist "Frieda," who was the famous and beloved Frieda Fromm-Reichmann: Hornstein (2000). See also a fascinating review of the book, by Bloch, (2001).

22. See Tapping (1996) for a review of a satirical novel by Leonard Szymczak about corrupt, inane, and incompetent mental health practitioners. There is a slapstick quality to it all, but it also touches too much on truths known to practitioners in the field and to laymen – patients who dare to let themselves know the truth:

> Set in suburban Sydney, the novel sets out to satirise the therapy profession, while chronicling the journey of its main character (an ingenuous male psychologist) towards maturity and manhood as he struggles with his first counselling job in the department of child and adolescent psychiatry at the Royal Prince Andrew Hospital.
>
> The department is peopled by mental health professionals who are, with the odd exception, awesome in their incompetence, arrogance and bigotry. No profession escapes a mauling. The team leader is an arrogant child psychiatrist separated from his third wife and desperate to make a name for himself, hopping on and off every family therapy fad with

the assistance of the highly paid family therapy consultant who positively oozes charisma. The psychiatric nurse, red haired, loud mouthed, "built like a footballer" and abandoned by her husband twenty years before, specialises in helping women vent their rage against ex-husbands. The child psychologist is a health and fitness freak who lifts weights obsessively and is in thrice-weekly psychoanalysis. She is supervised by a stereotypically sexless, matronly analyst, and they interpret *ad nauseum* the behaviour of a six year old boy in his 122nd unstructured playroom session. The social worker, a fishnet stockinged, glamourous clothes horse, sells her soul for the team leader's sexual attentions.

On the margins of the team is the semi-retired psychiatrist in an advanced state of dementia whose clients have long since ceased turning up but who nevertheless draws a huge hourly salary while she does her knitting. The pastoral care counsellor ineffectually tries to defuse team conflict while dispensing fatuous religious advice. The psychiatric registrar is constantly stoned and preoccupied with finding ways of sexually exploiting female clients while pathologising and discrediting any complaint they make. The head of the psychiatric department, an expert on the Australian experience of suicide, keeps overdosing on his antidepressant medication yet is protected by the hospital administration who fear a scandal should his condition come to light.

All the therapists create havoc in their clients' lives – whether by inept cook-book family therapy interventions or by interminable analysis to the point of stagnation – yet each is able to interpret the resulting butchery as a resounding success. . . .

It would be nice to be able to dismiss this bunch of nasty pasties as over the top and unbelievable. Sadly though, I suspect we've all met people just like them at one time or another, and as an exposé of the abuses in our profession. Mr Szymczak has done us all a service by submitting them to such squirmingly uncomfortable scrutiny. (Carmel Tapping, Private Practice, Adelaide, Australia. See Tapping [1996], p. 240)

23. This point of view of psychotherapy as intended to help people live more constructively both with themselves and as productive members of their communities is also consistent with a worldview of psychological science as a whole having meaning only insofar as it contributes to a betterment of human life. The great psychologist Gordon Allport said in his inaugural speech as first

president of the Division of Personality and Social Psychology of the American Psychological Association:

> The test of our fitness to exist and to prosper will be our ability to contribute substantially in the near future to the diagnosis and treatment of the outstanding malady of our time . . . the fact that man's moral sense is not able to assimilate his technology. (Allport [1947], p. 182. Cited in Kipnis [1994], p. 166)

24. Bugental, J. F. T. (1985, March), Seek a wild god. *Association of Humanistic Psychology Newsletter*, p. 8. See Bugental (1965).

25. Cited by Robinson (2001), p. 421.

26. Cited by Robinson (2001), p. 421.

27. Cited by Robinson (2001), p. 420. Quotation is from Koch (1999), p. 32.

28. Koch (1992), p. 429.

29. Seligman & Csikszentmahalyi (2000), p. 7.

30. Vaillant (2000), p. 98. See Jahoda (1959).

31. Fromm (1986), p. 126.

32. See the writings by many existential philosophers and various spiritual leaders, including in psychology James Bugental, Ernest Becker, Rollo May, and Irving Yalom.

33. An important critique of humanistic psychology as striving too much for highs in therapy and life and unmitigated joy for patients and therapists alike was presented years ago in the newsletter of the Association.

The author recognizes the positive potential of psychological experiences aiming at enhancing personal growth:

> Encouraging development of human potential . . . means questioning all those structures (whether internal or external) which limit and constrain people. The main internal constraints seem to be rigid patterns of behavior which have been set up as answers to the problems of living; however effective these may have been at the time, they have now turned into handcuffs or blinkers which prevent movement or awareness. Through the process of therapy counselling, personal growth and general self-discovery, these patterns are questioned in such a way that they can undergo change.

At the same time, the author, John Rowan, cautions against extremes, especially when one pursues the too much of any good style of experience:

> *Peakism.* In this aberration, people get hold of the bit about peak experiences

and somehow turn it into something to *strive* for. . . . The trouble with it is that it does inevitably lead on to the idea of the superman.

Instrumentalism. This is the one where people use the methods developed within humanistic psychology to oppress other people in new and more effective ways. This can happen in management training, in encounter groups . . . in transpersonal psychology . . . and in many other fields [like] . . . education.

Peace-and-Love-ism. This is the way in which group leaders and others aim at warmth, truth and openness in a way which seems to suggest that if you're not being warm, trusting, open and loving, you're not getting it right. . . . If we aim directly at validation, we run the risk of getting a false sweetness which itself becomes oppressive because it becomes a norm which cannot be challenged. We may then project all our "badness" into the world outside.

Expertism. Here people take their patch and try to become the great expert on it.

Spiritual-ism. This is where one gets *so very* spiritual that one loses touch with the ground altogether. One puts one's trust in a set of higher functions, which rise above mere rationality.

Feelingism. One of the best ways of getting into the subjective realm where therapy is done is by going deeply into feelings. Unfortunately, this can all too easily turn into a worship of passion for its own sake, as if it were an end rather than a means. I have seen people bullied and intimidated because they weren't expressing feelings, or weren't expressing the *right* feelings (usually anger). But worse than that, I have seen people criticized because they weren't expressing feelings *all the time!*

Autonomy-ism. One of the key things about humanistic psychology is the emphasis it places on "taking responsibility for yourself," on "creating my world" and so forth. *As a therapeutic stance*, and taken in a *first-person way*, this can be extremely valuable and indeed necessary. But if it is idealised as a total answer to life, it can turn into a pathological wish to be independent of everyone else in the world. Such a person becomes quite incapable of love because this involves some element of dependency on the other person, whether we like it or not.

Eclectic Mish-Mash-ism. One of the strengths of humanistic psychology is its adventurousness – the way in which it is prepared to try things out and see whether they work or not. But pushed to a one-sided extreme, this becomes a nervous search for novelty and the latest thing. And it also results in a set of practitioners who are using a mutually contradictory set of theories and practices and trying to turn them into a whole – which can only be a false-whole, held together unstably by the idealised wish of the user. (See Rowan (1980), pp. 5–7)

9. Discovering Applications of DEMOCRATIC MIND

1. To be human is to think and feel everything. It has been said that nothing that is human (that which has been experienced by human beings) is foreign to all the rest of us – at some level the spectrum of all potential psychological experiences is present as a possibility in all of us. Thus, William Blake (1757–1827) wrote:

Cruelty has a human heart,
And jealousy a human face;
Terror the human form devise,
And Secrecy the human dress.
—From *Songs of innocence and of experience*

Existential psychologist James Bugental writes of our "valuing the entire range of our emotions from the most unpleasant to the most satisfying." Indeed, much emotional disturbance is brought about by "the attempt to deny or alter certain feelings the person fears to have." Bugental (1965), quotations on pp. 386, 387.

2. "Mankind needs peace more than ever, for our entire planet, threatened by nuclear war, is in danger of total elimination or destruction; an annihilation only man can provoke, only man can prevent. Peace is not God's gift to his creatures. Peace is a very special gift – it is our gift to each other." Wiesel, E. (1986). The Nobel Peace Prize. Nobel Presentation Speech delivered by Egil Aarvik, Chairman of the Norwegian Nobel Committee in Oslo on November 10.

Psychiatrist Viktor Frankl wrote, "There are two races of men in this world, but only these two – the 'race' of the decent man and the 'race' of the indecent man, . . . Psychotherapy and education . . . must . . . focus their attention upon man's lingering and groping for a higher meaning in life" (pp. 86 and 111). See Frankl (1959).

3. W. Somerset Maugham's novel *Rain* is set on a remote Samoan island, and tells how a girl incites first the religious zeal and then the sexual lust of a

reform-minded cleric. The novel was also made into a movie in 1932 starring Joan Crawford and Walter Huston.

4. Psychiatrist August Kinzel studied people who were imprisoned for violent behavior. He found a striking absence of fantasies of violence in them. "They did not seem to dream, daydream, or attach much value to thought. Instead, they seemed to express themselves by body action almost exclusively. It is particularly striking that although they spoke relatively freely about their violent pasts, they almost totally denied their own aggression, so that none actually considered himself a violent individual." Kinzel (1971), p. 161.

The principle of a greater proclivity for aggressive behavior in people who are not connected to – express or own up to – their aggressive feelings is also seen in relation to aggressive behaviors that fall short of the ultimate of killing. Thus it has been reported that twice as many priests who have committed sex-offending violations show "overcontrolled hostility" than nonoffender priests show. The offending priests are characteristically passive, highly controlled, and compliant and obliging toward others – especially people in authority. Study attributed to Thomas Plante, Gerdenio Manuel, and Curtis Bryant who examined 160 Catholic priests, half in treatment for sexual misconduct and the other half for nonsexual psychiatric problems. DeAngelis (1996), p. 51.

5. Bugental (1965), sees much of psychotherapy as teaching the patient to expand their "genuine" and "nonfocal" awareness. "Many patients are quite cut off from genuine awareness of processes within themselves." See chapter 13, Awareness: The basic process of being, pp. 217–234; and chapter 14, Ontologic aids to expanding awareness, pp. 235–244 (quotation on p. 239).

6. Segal, Williams, & Teasdale (2002). The authors teach a "'decentered' relationship to experience in which negative thoughts or feelings can be viewed as events in the mind, rather·than 'self' or as necessarily true" (book jacket).

7. Pascal (in French): "Philosopher c'est apprendre a mourir."

8. Whitaker & Bumberry (1988).

9. The Evil Impulse argued back on his own behalf in the hearing before God: "Said The Evil Impulse: See here if you kill me, the entire world will be destroyed." The legend is from the book *Yoma*.

In a similar rabbinical legend, the hatched egg is expanded to additional life-giving and life-celebrating activities: "Were it not for the existence of The Evil Impulse, men would not build homes, they would not marry women, they would not sire children, and they would not engage in trade." The legend is from the book *Breisheet Raba*.

10. Toch (1983). Toch refers to a classic work on Seneca from the 17th century: L'Estrange, R., *Seneca's morals by way of abstract* (13th ed.). London: Straham, Bettesworth, Tonson, Lintot, Molte & Brown, 1729 (originally published 1623).

11. This is an especially dramatic real case that is referred to a number of times in the book. The child was specifically referred by his pediatrician for the therapist to help gain his parents' cooperation in placing him in an institution after the parents had rejected two earlier efforts by two other psychologists to hospitalize him when he was 2.3 and 3.5 years old. At the time of referral to me at age 4.6, the child – who was urinating and defecating without control, had no speech, and engaged in continuous ritualized movements – presented with totally inappropriate behavior in just about any context (nursery school, play group, neighborhood, even at home), and it seemed quite clear that he had to be taken away to an environment designed for autistic children. Nonetheless, at the end of a therapy session that was intended to convince the family to hospitalize the child, I was amazed and deeply touched by a sense of wordless contact with the child's eyes. I decided to propose treatment, at first in small testing steps and then increasingly in a full-scale program of multimodal treatment, and over a period of some years the child reached many aspects of normal functioning. This is one of the two cases reported fully in my "Recovery of two (largely) autistic children through renunciation of maternal destructiveness in integrated individual and family therapy" (1980). As reported earlier, at the time of the publication of this case report which told of a promising renewal of development in the child, it was too early also to report that the child eventually even went on to graduate successfully from college (as did the second child in this report).

12. See earlier reference to the core notion of anxiety as concern over one's unused potential in Rollo May's (1977) classic *The meaning of anxiety* (originally published in 1950).

13. This is a potshot at the California tradition of taking everything so seriously about being only and totally natural, healthy, and peace loving, which for me is another example of a very good try that is taken to an extreme.

14. From the Bible, Joshua 10:12.

15. See psychotherapeutic writing on choice, including Harold Greenwald's proposal of "direct decision therapy" in Greenwald (1973), Yalom (1980), and Bugental (1965).

16. Aeschylus said, "The high strength of men know no content with limitations." There is a deep primordial pull in our minds toward going to whatever is

the "ultimate" of a structure or experience. See in the psychoanalytic literature: Levy (1962), and Spitz (1964).

17. Dan, Y. (2002, January 4). *Haaretz English Edition*, B8. See Berger (2002).

18. Coleman (1957).

19. *Emporia Gazette*, November 17, 1923, cited in *Bartlett's Familiar Quotations*.

20. Festinger (1957).

21. Stekel (1953), pp. 24, 29.

22. Coleman (1957), p. 14.

23. Frank (1967), p. 288.

24. I was the second therapist who treated the husband in this case. Our reunion took place some 30 years following the therapy, when I had the privilege of speaking at the university where he teaches. In our mutually delightful reunion after all this time, we both reconstructed our memories of his therapy. To add to the drama, his wife's former therapist also teaches at the same university and turned up for one of the lectures I gave; I cold-shouldered him despite his so-happy-to-see-you greeting.

Agh, for those who ask, I did report the erring therapist to our professional society at the time, but in those years there still were no laws or sanctionable rules against sexual exploitation of patients, a situation that happily has changed for the better since then.

25. Among the classic books on dream interpretation, see Freud (1955), Gutheil (1967), Fromm (1951), Hall (1959), and Hall & van de Castle (1966) There continues to be considerable attention paid to the understanding of dreams. An interesting recent work that emphasizes the relevance of dreams to management of our lives is Langs (1999). The author sees many dreams as based on triggering events that are then worked into a narrative, first at a superficial conscious level that still seeks to conceal many truths about us and others, but then also at a deep unconscious level where we move toward telling more of the truths.

10. Unified Theory of DEMOCRATIC MIND

1. See psychiatrist Jules Masserman's statement on the three fundamental needs of all humans – physical vitality and longevity, interpersonal security, and existential faith. Masserman casts a comforting vision of idealistic expectations for the evolution of man to greater wholesomeness: "All mankind as

a single species . . . is slowly evolving towards the status of homo sapiens – man the wise. . . . In essence . . . we are a species reaching towards universal fellowship on a still salvageable planet." To his own profession of psychiatry Masserman adds, "Certainly we in the World Psychiatric Association must remain profoundly dedicated to this objective." Masserman (1990), pp. 155, 160.

2. Do I know what a hornet nest of complexity and controversy I am stirring up? Of course. I especially know that our definitions of "antilife" forces and behaviors will be co-opted and distorted by every one of the endless ideological cults that abound in human society, so that even people who take others' lives will swear they are doing it in order to protect life. Nonetheless, I dare hold to a commonsense definition of opposition to all forms of destruction of the lives of unarmed people. Any means of knowledge and science that are devoted to or facilitate the destruction of the lives of unarmed civilians (I have to exclude cases of clear-cut self-defense, and reluctantly, I am also excluding conditions of organized warfare between official combatant soldiers, although if I really could have my idealistic ways, I'd get rid of wars too!) should be defined by all institutions of knowledge-gathering and science and by all associations of professionals as flagrant violations of the codes of these institutions and professions. For example, in my professional world, I would unhesitatingly defrock any psychologist, psychiatrist, or social worker who assists a police regime in torture or executions. Famed scientist Jonas Salk, who created the polio vaccine, wrote that "new values and new ethics are required . . . lest men in their greedy competition . . . destroy themselves and their planet." See Salk, (1972), p. 101.

3. For a relevant discussion of the goals defining and "governing" narrative in scholarship, see Des Pres (1986).

4. Writing in a special issue of the *Journal of Pastoral Counseling* devoted to the "Psychology of Evil," Edward Shafransky called for recognition and identification of both evil "deeds and, perhaps, persons." See Shafranske, (1990), quotation on p. 1.

5. Hamid Karzai is described as paying "an emotional visit to Ground Zero in New York City" when he made these remarks. See Purdum, T. S. (2002, January 31). On Washington stage an Afghan star: Kabul's chic leader flashes a style that U.S. politicians would envy. *International Herald Tribune*.

6. Reich (1946).

7. Adorno, Frenkel-Brunswik, Levinson, & Sanford (1950).

8. Fromm (1941, 1964, 1973).

9. Lifton (1967).

10. Aronson (1984), Santoni (1984), and Charny (1986).

11. Bronfenbrenner (1970).

12. Bettelheim (1969).

13. Singer (1968).

14. Lifton (1961).

15. Rokeach (1960).

16. Milgram (1974).

17. Zimbardo et al. (1974).

18. Greenwald (1980).

19. See two studies of evil in the health professions in Charny & Fromer (1990) and Charny & Fromer (1990). In both of these studies of Israeli students of medicine, psychology, and social work, we demonstrate a considerable readiness of (a) students in the helping professions who are (b) Jewish-Israeli nationals, well aware of the Holocaust, to imagine themselves as future professionals participating first in a program of mandatory collective euthanasia of severely handicapped patients – the use of the concept of mercy killing here is contrived camouflage, of course – and then in a program of forced expulsion or population transfer of Arabs out of Israel.

In another study of readiness to identify with or exonerate evil, Fromer and I approached the good people queuing at the box office of the Tel Aviv Museum to buy tickets for the monumental 9-hour film on the Holocaust, *Shoah* (Lanzmann (1985)), and in effect investigated how they felt about a genocidal massacre of some 49 unarmed Arab men, women, and children at Kfar Kassem in 1956. See Charny & Fromer (1992).

The results of both studies upset and saddened us (there were many people supporting or approving the taking of other peoples' lives); and simultaneously relieved us (the percentages of people ready to do harm were less than in many other studies, such as Milgram's).

20. Bettelheim (1967). An earlier reference to Bettelheim's work in chapter 7 presented Bettelheim's startling thesis that the parents of autistic children did not want the child to exist! Beyond my modification that I believe Bettelheim's thesis to be true of many though not all cases of autism, the question is can we conceive of any parent who would want their child dead? But then again, can we conceive of many human beings in many cultures and eras murdering their

neighbors and other countrymen, infants and young children, unarmed men and women – with machetes, hammerlike objects, bullets, or then burying them alive or gassing them? I fear that in all cases the answers based on the hard facts are a terrible yes. This is an appallingly true aspect of the human mind that we need to study honestly and resolutely.

21. Laing (1967, 1970, 1972).

22. Vogel & Bell (1968).

23. Gordon, with Frandsen (1993).

24. Gordon (1970).

25. Axelrod (1984).

26. Latané & Darley (1970); Oliner & Oliner (1988); Staub (1996).

27. Boszormenyi-Nagy & Spark (1973).

28. Becker (1973); Charny (1982), *How can we commit the unthinkable?*

29. Fromm (1986), p. 133. A fuller excerpt containing this quotation will be found in chapter 4.

30. In recent years, there are major new developments of legal tribunals for judging those who commit genocide. See Bassiouni, (1999) and Krieger (1999).

31. The *Encyclopedia of world problems and human potential* proposes a definition of humanness as the purpose of all human civilization. "Humanness is generally taken to be that quality which is proper to human beings and which differentiates them from other entities and species. In particular, it describes the moral and ethical attitude including love of one's fellow men and human understanding which, as opposed to use of force and coercion, is thus the aim of civilization and the development of moral and political life." *Encyclopedia of world problems and human potential* (1986), quotation from HH0203.

Nobel Prize–winning scientist Niko Tinbergen wrote about scientific research as a whole as a comforting answer to the dread concern that the human species may be destroying itself:

Those who share the apprehension . . . of mankind destroying his own species . . . might perhaps . . . derive strength from keeping alive the thought that has helped so many of us in the past when faced with the possibility of imminent death. Scientific research is one of the finest occupations of our mind. It is, with art and religion, one of the uniquely human ways of meeting nature, in fact, the most active way. If we are to succumb and even if this were to be ultimately due to our own stupidity, we could still, so-to-speak, redeem our species. We could at least go down with some dignity, by using our brain for one of its supreme tasks, by exploring to the end. (Tinbergen [1969], 48–49)

Tinbergen in effect poses the knowledge-acquiring process against the prospects of global destruction. Certainly the Constitution of the United Nations Educational, Scientific, and Cultural Organization (UNESCO) calls explicitly for the application of psychological science to the prevention of destruction of life when it promulgates its famous statement, "Since wars begin in the minds of men, it is in the minds of men that the defences of peace must be constructed."

32. Existential psychiatrist Viktor Frankl said definitively, "Psychotherapy and education . . . must . . . focus their attention upon man's longing and groping for a higher meaning in life" (Frankl (1959), p. 111). In "A profession of moralists: Of values, science and other therapeutic power plays" (1995), Jay S. Efran and Mitchell A. Greene reviewed several works in psychotherapy and morality, including Cushman (1995), Doherty (1995), Fancher (1995), and Wright (1994). The authors, clinical psychologists, conclude:

Surprisingly, even clinicians . . . who comprehend the folly of pretending that morals can be excluded from the consulting room shy away from "imposing" their value judgments on others. That sort of hands-off position was all well and good a few decades ago, but today's moral crisis demands bolder leadership. . . .

As social scientists, we know that one pathway is not just as good as another, that certain actions and conditions lead to human satisfaction while other choices are inimical to achieving a sense of fulfillment and purpose. Clients need education in these matters. Personally, we have no compunction about defining psychotherapy as a specialized form of moral instruction and, in our own work, were quite willing to question the adequacy of a client's goals or suggest that he or she entertain an alternative worldview. . . . Ultimately, the worth of therapy is contingent on our ability to use that knowledge base to help clients craft workable solutions to their dilemmas, and perhaps enrich the culture at the same time. (quotations on pp. 80, 81)

In *The mystery of goodness and the positive moral consequences of psychotherapy*, Mary W. Nicholas (1994) concluded that psychotherapy is concerned with the enhancement of goodness – and concern about others in altruism, responsibility, justice, egalitarianism, and honesty, and that the typical conduct of psychotherapy on the basis of a moral neutrality may block genuine therapeutic goals.

33. Camus (1946). The fuller excerpt containing this quotation will also be found earlier in chapter 4.

34. Weeks (Ed.) (1985); Weeks & L'Abate (1982).

35. Ellis (1962); Ellis & Harper (1961, 1968).

36. Horney (1937).

37. Fromm (1941, 1964, 1973).

38. Laing (1967, 1970, 1972).

39. Charny (1992).

40. Charny (1997), Which genocide matters more?

41. *Encyclopedia of world problems and human potential* (1986), quotations from HH0204.

Conclusion

1. The subject of the mental health of physicians has long been intriguing. It is clearly important in its own right to the large group of our healers, as well as the fact that the dynamics of physicians are instructive for many other people as well.

Stress-related problems among physicians have been high for many years. Depression and suicide rates are higher than in the general population (source: American Foundation for Suicide Prevention in *Surgicenteronline*, posted June 12, 2003). Amazingly, "over a third of physicians have no regular source of health care, and physicians frequently fail to identify depression and mental health disorders in themselves" (American Foundation for Suicide Prevention in *Surgicenteronline*, attributed to an article in *Journal of American Medical Association*, June 18, 2003).

A study of physicians who graduated from Johns Hopkins Medical School from 1948 to 1964 – a period when divorce was less socially acceptable than has since become the norm – over 30 years showed overall a divorce rate of one out of three, which in its own commonsense terms was high, even though it also was less than the U.S. average. The psychiatrists among the doctors reached a high rate of 51% divorces (source: Physicians' divorce risk may be linked to specialty choice, *Johns Hopkins Medical Institutions*, March 13, 1997). Psychiatrists are also known to be high in suicide risk. But they are not the only troubled physicians. Thus, an ophthalmologist writes with concern that his specialty is at particular risk: "As ophthalmologists, we are more at risk than many of our colleagues" (source: Hagan, J. C. [2003]. When good docs go bad: The impaired physician, March, p. 84, posted on the Web and attributed to an editorial by the author in *Missouri Medicine: Journal of the Missouri State Medical Association*).

Why do physicians exhibit such heavy loads of mental distress?

The last author cites the arduous study and work of the physician, the cultivation of "pathologic and unhealthy extremes [of] compulsiveness, competitiveness, perfectionism, physical and emotional stoicism, delayed gratification and a workaholic lifestyle." But behind the above, which the author calls the physician's "emotional armor plating," there are often also a variety of painful and disturbing emotional problems of "inadequacy, depression, hypochondria, self-doubt, fear of death or failure and inability to self-forgive."

Many observers have also commented on the reluctance of physicians to seek and receive help for themselves. Self-imposed demands for excellence and service create many pressures, but most problematic is that when physicians become pressured by the demands on them, they succumb to "mental models [learned] during their medical training that keep them from reaching for help" (source: Musick, J. L. [1997]. How close are you to burnout? *Family Practice Management*, April, posted on the Web). There are also observations of the "denial and machismo that characterize the medical profession," and a reluctance of physicians "to accept the fact that professional competence allows for compassion," including "towards themselves" (quotations from Hagan (2003). One might say Dr. Hagan is an ophthalmologist who *sees* life with considerable sensitivity).

Finally, it has been suggested that by accepting responsibility for the life and death of patients, physicians expose themselves to death anxiety as well as to characteristic human defenses of denial of death (see Becker [1973]) and compensatory feelings of superiority, arrogance, and harshness that ultimately do harm to many of them as well.

2. See the report on "Japanese Unit 731 – Dread medical experiments that preceded the Nazis" in the *Encyclopedia of genocide* (1999), p. 413; also in the Encyclopedia: Rummel, China, Genocide in: *The Chinese communist anthill*, pp. 149–151; see also Chang (1997).

3. See the section on "Law and the perpetration of genocide" in Balint (1999), pp. 395–397.

4. In the recent genocide in Rwanda in 1994, there were several terrible

incidents of mass killing of Tutsi who had gone to seek refuge in churches, and in some cases priests and nuns were directly implicated. One infamous incident that took place in a church in Nyange, Rwanda, on April 16, 1994, involved a priest who later escaped to Italy and was accepted for a post in a church in Florence. This priest is reported to have ordered the bulldozing of his own church, crushing to death all those who remained alive inside; 2,500 Tutsi had sought refuge in the church. One description of the incident is given by James Smith, M.D., a founding director of the Aegis Trust, a worldwide antigenocide organization based in England:

> The church is in a place called Nyange. In 1994, in April, 2,500 people took shelter in this church. The militia and the gendarmes, they broke through the windows, and they threw in grenades; they tried to set fire to the building with everyone inside, and still there were people alive. And so the priest gave orders to bulldoze the church with his own congregants inside – yes, the priest gave orders to bulldoze the church. . . . Tom Ndahiro, the Human Rights Commissioner in Rwanda calls the place where that church once stood "Rwanda's Ground Zero". Almost the same number of people were killed here as in the World Trade Centre. (Source: Smith, J. [2003]. A day to remember, posted on the Web: www.aegis.tv, July 15)

Other priests were implicated in the killings; they mobilized militias, led hunting-killing parties, or provided other killers with weapons, transport, and encouragement. Still other priests refused to allow refugees to take shelter at their churches and sent them directly to the hands of the Hutu killers, to be massacred.

Here is one report by the director of African Rights, a human rights organization, directed to Pope John Paul II:

> Archbishop Thaddée Ntihinyurwa was Bishop of the diocese of Cyangugu during the genocide. Anxious to safeguard the buildings, the bishop refused to allow Tutsi refugees to hide in the cathedral, with the exception of some clergy, some helpers and a few acquaintances. Accompanied by the notorious préfet of Cyangugu, Emmanuel Bagambiki, and soldiers, he forced them out to be driven to a football stadium. Bagambiki was the man who massacred Tutsis in Bugesera in 1992; on the way to the stadium, the refugees sang funeral songs, knowing the fate that awaited them. He also stated publicly that three copies of the list with their names on it had

been made; one copy for him, one for the préfet and the third for the gendarmerie. Over the next few weeks, the lists were used to abduct Tutsi men and boys from the stadium – particularly the educated and businessmen – who were murdered. Between 15–17 April, several thousand refugees were massacred at the Parish of Nyamasheke in killings sanctioned by Bagambiki. The bishop visited them on the 13th and 14th, with the parish surrounded by well-armed militiamen and villagers. Sensing their death was imminent, the bishop gave them communion and departed, but took no other action, not even an attempt to save the people who remained at the stadium whom he had "entrusted" to Bagambiki. Nor did he visit them again, despite the proximity of Kamarampaka stadium to the bishopric. Throughout April, May and June 1994, Bagambiki organised and participated in massacres of Tutsis sheltering in Catholic parishes that belonged to the bishop's diocese, as well as massacres elsewhere, but the bishop remained silent. (Source: Omaar, R. (1998). An open letter to his holiness, Pope John Paul II, May 13, posted on the Web. The author is identified as the director of African Rights in London: "working for justice – Africa's problems seen from an African perspective")

5. The traditional call to the faithful to have no other gods before their one and only god is a painful challenge to the critical thinking and independent dignity of every human being and group who believe in their need and right to evaluate critically every pronouncement by their leaders – including their religious leaders, officials, teachers, or parents – and to reject calls, orders, instructions, or whatever directives to injure or kill human beings except in clear-cut self-defense.

In many Western armies it has become a matter of law that soldiers are legally responsible not to follow patently illegal orders that constitute crimes against humanity in respect of unnecessary killing of unarmed civilians. In effect, the concept proposed here is that all human beings should be "soldiers for life" and take on responsibility not to obey blindly the orders of any authorities that may command us harming life.

I would add that in no way do I propose anarchy or the adoption of a policy of never following leaders and honoring the various authorities in our lives. ("Pray for the welfare of the government," says Rabbi Chanina in *Sayings of the elders [Pirkei Avot]*, "since but for the fear thereof men would swallow each other alive.") But there is a line to be drawn when any of our governments, state leaders, political heroes, religious leaders, or whoever tell us to go and harm and kill unarmed people in the name of ideology.

6. There are many studies of the relationship of the International Red Cross to the Nazis. See, for example, Dworzecki (1977).

7. There are many writings on the My Lai–type murders in America's questionable war in Vietnam, for example, the chilling account of the actual My Lai massacre by the U.S. officer in charge, including his explanation of his willingness to obey orders. Calley (1972).

8. See the study referred to earlier of the responses of Israelis attending a showing of Claude Lanzmann's monumental 9-hour film on the Holocaust to the Israeli massacre of innocent Arab men, women, and children at Kfar Kassem. Charny & Fromer (1992).

9. Wiesenthal, S. Information Bulletin No. 42, Documentation Center of the Association of Jewish Victims of the Nazi Regime, Vienna, Austria, January 31, 2002, p. 2 (italics in original).

10. Gallup polls were conducted during December 2001 and January 2002 of 9,924 residents in nine Muslim countries: Indonesia, Iran, Jordan, Kuwait, Lebanon, Morocco, Pakistan, Saudi Arabia, and Turkey. Although all 19 of the September 11 hijackers were known to be Arab men, only 18% of those polled in six Islamic countries say they believe Arabs carried out the attacks, 61% say Arabs were not responsible, and 21% say they don't know who did it. The respective percentages of the respondents who stated their belief that Arabs did not carry out 9/11 were as follows: Lebanon: 58%; Turkey: 43%; Kuwait: 89%; Indonesia: 74%; Iran: 59%; Pakistan: 86%. In Jordan, Morocco, and Saudi Arabia, the pollsters were not permitted by the governments to ask who was responsible (source: *USA Today*, February 27, 2002).

11. A cbs story on *Sixty Minutes* reported that

the vast majority of Middle Easterners, including most intellectuals . . . mostly think the Jews did it. . . .

A cbs reporter, George Crile, reported accepting an invitation to a wedding party in a small town in Pakistan. All the town's leading citizens were there. . . . The Jews did it. That's exactly what they are saying: the mayor, the businessman, the journalist, the baby doctor . . . everyone. And, as one of them said, "Osama is totally innocent!" . . . As the Gallup poll later confirmed, that's exactly what most Muslims believe. "I was surprised that very few, even among the elites, believe that bin Laden did it," says Dr. Shibley Telhami, the man whom Gallup commissioned to analyze the findings of its survey. (Source: MMII, CBS Worldwide Inc., cited by Australia/Israel & Jewish Affairs Council, September 12, 2000, posted on the Web)

In the United States, David Duke, shamefully once a member of the state House of Representatives of Louisiana and since then periodically a bona fide if minority candidate for the presidency who is of course a rabid anti-Semite, wrote in his newsletter:

> The Internet had many claims that 4,000 Israelis "did not show up for work," after the September attacks. The problem was that the sources for these claims were all from the Arabic media, and the mainstream press dismissed the concept of early warning for Israelis as ridiculous. On the surface it would seem ridiculous, but when you begin to put the facts together, there seems to be ample reason for suspicion that the Mossad had foreknowledge and warned some Israelis, while they murderously let the attack proceed against America (source: Duke, D. (2003). Price of supporting Israel. Updated January 7, 2003. How Israeli terrorism and American treason caused the Sept attacks. David Duke online: www.davidduke.com, www.davidduke.org, www.davidduke.net)

The full research article in Duke's quite well written hate piece illustrates only too well the step-by-step stretching of innuendo, insinuations, lying, and bigotry:

> Powerful evidence is mounting that Israelis had foreknowledge of the September 11th attack on America. And, if indeed they had foreknowledge of these murderous acts of terrorism – and then had the bold-blooded mentality not to warn the United States, because they saw a horrendous massacre of thousands of Americans as good for Israel – it follows that they would have felt no restraint from actually instigating and covertly aiding this terrorist plan through their own agents provocateurs.

12. If one does an Internet search for "9/11 and CIA knowledge," an enormous amount of garbage is available that suggests – in fact as if "proves" – ominously that America was forewarned by its own intelligence operatives and the Israeli Mossad, but mysteriously ordered intelligence agents not to take action; that the American government knew of the forthcoming 9/11 attacks (in fact, it is

assumed that not-to-fly warnings reached chosen personalities such as Mayor Willie Brown of San Francisco, a group of Pentagon officials, and Salman Rushdie, who canceled flights planned for the infamous day); that after the event America again mysteriously did not pursue investigations of obvious suspects; and more. The implication of many such "reports" is that not only were major incompetence and negligence shown by U.S. agencies, but that something far more ominous was at work by some U.S. government agency. The reports steadily build an atmosphere of mystery and conspiracy to a point where it is clear, in the words of one writer, that not only "incompetence" and "bureaucratic blocking" were involved but that "innocent American civilians paid with their lives in order to fulfill and protect another agenda." The meaning conveyed is that the American "intelligence failure" was not really a failure at all, but a result of a full-blown directive to suppress the available information about the forthcoming attack that America itself somehow sought to have happen. Source: Ahmed, N., who is identified as a "British political analyst and human rights activist" in London. The material, taken from a book by the above author, is presented in an attractive serious-looking Web site and is accompanied by 134 references in a style of as-if legitimate documentation. Posted on the Web May 18, 2002, at www.mediamonitors.net (MMN), which is identified as an organization in California.

13. Balint (1999).

14. Smith, Markusen, & Lifton (1995).

15. Struck, D. (2002, August 28), Tokyo court confirms germ warfare: But judges find that no law allows victims to claim compensation. *International Herald Tribune*, p. 7. Reprinted from the *Washington Post*.

16. A memorable story of personal courage in an intimate relationship is told by the wife of many years of Philip Zimbardo, the social psychologist who was the responsible investigator in the Stanford Prison Experiment and later became a president of the American Psychological Association. Zimbardo's wife was then his fiancée. She had gone to see the study when it was early into its process:

I talked to one of the guards there who was waiting to begin his shift. He was very pleasant, polite and friendly, surely a person anyone would consider a really nice guy.

Later on, one of the research staff mentioned to me that I should take a look at the yard again, because the new late-night guard shift had come on, and this was the notorious "John Wayne" shift. John Wayne was the nickname for the guard who was the meanest and toughest of them all; his reputation had preceded him in various accounts I had heard. Of course, I was eager to see who he was and what he was doing that attracted so much attention. When I looked through the observation point, I was absolutely stunned to see that their John Wayne was the "really nice guy" with whom I had chatted earlier. Only now he was transformed into someone else. He not only moved differently, but he talked differently. . . . He was yelling and cursing at the prisoners as he made them go through "the count," going out of his way to be rude and belligerent. It was an amazing trans-formation from the person I had just spoken to – a transformation that had taken place in minutes just by stepping over the line from the outside world into that prison yard. With his military-style uniform, billy club in hand, and dark, silver-reflecting sunglasses to hide his eyes . . . this guy was an all-business, no nonsense, really mean prison guard.

Deeply shaken, the young lady then met her fiancé later that night and insisted that he had to stop the experiment! She writes that she knew she was putting their engagement at risk, but she had no choice but to speak of her convictions; on his part, for all his enormous investment in his study, Zimbardo agreed to learn from her critique and concluded he would terminate the study. See Maslach (2000), pp. 215–216.

17. Adler (1917), *Study of organ inferiority and its psychical compensation*; Adler (1917), *The neurotic constitution*. See also Ansbacher, H. & Ansbacher, R. (1956), The individual psychology of Alfred Adler.

18. Armin T. Wegner (1886–1978) was a remarkable German journalist who has captured my admiration and love for his principled stands against the Armenian Genocide to which he was an eyewitness. He even photographed several scenes. Wegner was also against Hitler's initial anti-Semitic policies leading to the Holocaust. He is best known for his public letters in respect of each of the above evils, the first to U.S. president Woodrow Wilson in 1919 ("The Armenian Question is a question for Christendom for the whole human race"); and the second to no less than Adolf Hitler in 1933 ("The fate of our Jewish brethren . . . also concerns the destiny of Germany. . . . The shame and misfortune [of the Jewish victims] will not quickly be forgotten, even in the future"). Of course, Hitler and the Nazi regime were not of a kind to which one writes any letters of protest(!); and for the latter Wegner was tortured and

imprisoned by the Gestapo in a series of concentration camps. Some people who knew him well say he never recovered from these experiences, and some say that what especially affected him were the bitter blows to his pride in being a German and the idealism that he attributed to German culture, as well as the physical suffering he endured. See Milton (1999). Wegner's letters are presented in a feature story accompanying Milton's entry on p. 611 of the *Encyclopedia of genocide*.

19. See Kesey (1962).

20. Kaye, J. (2002, January 9). Swastikas invade video combat games: Once taboo themes attract players who express neo-Nazi sentiments. *International Herald Tribune*.

21. Kaye (2002, January 9), p. 7.

22. Cooper, A. (2001, December 16). Anti-Semitism. *Los Angeles Times*, p. M1.

23. Rosenblum, D. (2002, July 1), Who's sorry now? A scenario. *Haaretz English Edition*.

24. Hinton (1999), p. 135.

25. For a recent meaningfully comprehensive review of research on the implications of media-rating systems, see Bushman & Cantor (2003). The authors note in summary with respect to children that "meta-analyses have confirmed that exposure to media violence promotes aggressive behaviors, engenders attitudes more accepting of violence, increases hostility, and results in other antisocial outcomes" (p. 130). Would we allow the continued production of medications that have such scientifically confirmed side effects? Hardly.

26. Britt, D. (1998, April 1), Want to raise kids from hell? Here's a how-to primer. *International Herald Tribune*, Opinion/Letters. p. 9.

27. Herbert, B. (2002, October 30), In a culture of violence, every citizen suffers. *International Herald Tribune*, p. 7, with attribution to original article in the *New York Times*.

28. "We need a human language for reporting the tragedies of current violent events." Presented at the Annual Meeting of the American Orthopsychiatric Association in 1970 in New York, in a Symposium, Psychosocial design for nonviolent change, with a summary published in *American Journal of Orthopsychiatry*, 1971, pp. 41, 219–220. See Charny, 1972, "We need a human language," and 1978 for later publications of this work in full.

29. Charny (Ed.) (1978), p. 205.

30. Charny (Ed.) (1978), p. 209.

31. Charny (1972), *Marital love and hate*.

32. Frantz, D., & Butler, D. (2002, July 17). Hamburg imam preached hatred to September 11 pilots. *New York Times.*

33. Bennet, J. (2002, June 21). A rash of new suicide bombers showing no pattern or ties. *New York Times.* The Palestinian psychiatrist is identified as Dr. Iyad Sarraj.

34. Le Bon (1903).

35. Barkan (2000).

36. Lavery (2002, July 17). IRA apologizes for killing civilians in effort to unite Ireland. *New York Times.*

37. Kuper (1985).

38. On the development of the International Criminal Court, see Krieger (1999); and Bassiouni (1999); and in the *Encyclopedia of genocide*, Establishment of the International Court: Statement by M. Cherif Bassiouni, p. 363.

39. See Dallaire (2003). Kofi Annan's statement was made in a message to the Symposium on the Media and the Rwanda Genocide at Carleton University School of Journalism and Communications in Ottawa, March 13, 2004, and is available at www.un.org/News/Press/docs/2004/sqsm9197.doc.htm, accessed April 10, 2004.

40. The example given is in Angola where neither the government nor the rebels were treated conclusively, and UN efforts at peacekeeping were defeated because the combatants would resume shooting at the first opportunity. See Shawcross (2002).

41. Shawcross (2002).

42. Charny (1999), An International Peace Army.

43. Carl Sagan expressed the truth of our vulnerability as a planetary civilization in a way that gripped the imagination and sensitivity of many readers:

Sixty-five million years ago, the proud possessors of this planet were the dinosaurs. They were everywhere, land, sea, air. If you had dropped down on the Earth then, you would of course have predicted that they and their descendants would continue into the far future. They had already been around for one hundred and twenty million years.

They are all gone. They were snuffed out, all over the planet in what in geological time is an instant. It makes you wonder, if they, so immensely successful for such a long period of time could be destroyed, what about us? Our genus has been around for only a few million years; our species for only a few hundred thousand years – we who have created world-transforming technologies.

The key difference is that the dinosaurs, whatever else you want to say about them, were not responsible for their extinction. If there's an epitaph for us, it very likely will not be, "They bore no responsibility for their own demise." That's not what it would say.

We find a similar lesson in space and in time. Nothing is guaranteed. No organism on Earth has its tenure warranted. (See Sagan (1994), pp. 1–2)

44. Excerpts from text of Dr. King's acceptance speech on the occasion of receiving the Nobel Peace Prize in Oslo, Norway, on December 10, 1964. King (1991).

Epilogue

1. The following are two invited autobiographical chapters about my life and work, the first in a work honoring psychologists who contributed to the development of the field of family therapy and the second a work devoted to the autobiographies of scholars who contributed to the development of the field of genocide studies: Charny (1990); Charny (2002).

Bibliography

Ackerman, N. W. (1982). Anti-Semitic motivation in a psychopathic personality: A case study. In D. Bloch & R. Simon (Eds.), *The strength of family therapy: Selected papers of Nathan W. Ackerman* (pp. 121–130). New York: Brunner/Mazel. (Original work published 1947 in *Psychoanalytic Review*, *34*(1), 76–101)

Adler, A. (1917). *The neurotic constitution: Outlines of a comparative individualistic psychology and psychotherapy* (B. Glueck & J. E. Lind, Trans.). New York: Moffat, Yard. (Original work published 1912)

Adler, A. (1917). *Study of organ inferiority and its psychical compensation: A contribution to clinical medicine.* New York: Nervous and Mental Disease Publishing.

Adler, A. (1924). *The practice and theory of individual psychology.* New York: Harcourt.

Adler, A. (1932). *Individual psychology and its results in the practice and theory of individual psychology.* New York: Harcourt Brace.

Adorno, T. W., Frenkel-Brunswik, E., Levinson, D. J., & Sanford, R. N. (1950). *The authoritarian personality.* New York: Harper.

Alexander, F. M. (1987). *The use of the self: Its conscious direction in relation to diagnosis, functioning, and the control of reaction.* London: Victor Gollancz. (With an introduction by Professor John Dewey; original work published 1932)

Allport, G. (1947). The emphasis on molar problems. *Psychological Reviews, 54,* 182–192.

Alvarez, A. (2001). *Governments, citizens, and genocide: A comparative and interdisciplinary approach.* Bloomington: Indiana University Press.

American Psychiatric Association (1980). *Diagnostic and statistical manual of mental disorders* (3rd ed.). Washington DC: Author.

American Psychiatric Association (1987). *Diagnostic and statistical manual of mental disorders* (3rd ed., rev.). Washington DC: Author.

American Psychiatric Association (1994). *Diagnostic and statistical manual of mental disorders* (4th ed.). Washington DC: Author.

American Psychiatric Association (2000). *Diagnostic and statistical manual of mental disorders* (4th ed., rev.). Washington DC: Author.

Amir, A. (1977). *Euthanasia in Nazi Germany.* Unpublished doctoral dissertation, State University of New York at Albany.

Anderson, C. M., & Stewart, S. (1983). *Mastering resistance: A practical guide to family therapy.* New York: Guilford.

Ansbacher, H., & Ansbacher, R. (1956). *The individual psychology of Alfred Adler.* New York: Basic Books.

Arendt, H. (1966). *The origins of totalitarianism.* New York: Harcourt Brace Jovanovich. (Original work published 1951)

Arendt, H. (1969). *Eichmann in Jerusalem: A report on the banality of evil.* New York: Viking. (Original work published 1963)

Arieti, S. (1972). *The will to be human.* New York: Quadrangle Books.

Aron, R. (2002). *The dawn of universal history: Selected essays from a witness of the twentieth century* (Reiner, Y., Ed.; Bray, B., Trans.). New York: Basic Books.

Aronson, R. (1983). *The dialectic of disaster: A preface to hope.* London: Verso.

Aronson, R. (1984). Societal madness: Impotence, power and genocide. In I. W. Charny (Ed.), *Toward the understanding and prevention of genocide* (pp. 137–146). Boulder CO: Westview Press; London: Bowker Publishing.

Aronson, R. (1987). Social madness. In I. Wallimann & M. N. Dobkowski (Eds.), *Genocide and the modern age: Etiology and case studies of mass death* (pp. 81–96). New York: Greenwood.

Asch, S. E. (1955). Opinions and social pressure. *Scientific American, 193*(5), 31–35.

Asch, S. E. (1956). Studies of independence and conformity: A minority of one against a unanimous majority. *Psychological Monographs, 70*(whole of #416), 3–45.

Ashton, E. B. (pseudonym for Ernst Basch) (1937). *The fascist: His state and his mind.* New York: William Morrow. (Reprinted by AMS Press, New York, 1972)

Askenasy, H. (1978). *Are we all Nazis?* Secaucus NJ: Lyle Stuart.

Assagioli, R. (1965). *Psychosynthesis: A manual of principles and techniques.* London: Turnstone Books.

Assagioli, R. (1973). *The act of will.* Baltimore: Penguin.

Axelrod, R. (1984). *The evolution of cooperation.* New York: Basic Books.

Balint, J. (1999). Law responds to the Holocaust and genocide: Redress and perpetration. In I. W. Charny (Ed.), et al., *Encyclopedia of genocide* (pp. 389–397). Santa Barbara CA: ABC-CLIO Publishers. (Oxford UK, 2000).

Baltes, P. B., & Staudinger, U. M. (2000). Wisdom: A metaheuristic (pragmatic) to orchestrate mind and virtue toward excellence. *American Psychologist, Special Issue on Happiness, Excellence, and Optimal Human Functioning, 55*(1), 122–136.

Bandura, A. (1990). Mechanisms of moral disengagement. In W. Reich (Ed.), *Origins of terrorism: Psychologies, ideologies, theologies, states of mind.* Washington DC: Woodrow Wilson International Center for Scholars and New York: Cambridge University Press.

Barber, J. D. (1995). *The book of democracy.* Englewood Cliffs NJ: Prentice-Hall.

Barbour, I. G. (1990). *Religion in an age of science: The Gifford Lectures, 1989–91.* Vol. 1. New York: Harper Collins.

Bargh, J. A., & Chartrand, T. L. (1999). The unbearable automaticity of being. *American Psychologist, 54*(7), 462–479.

Barkan, E. (2000). *The guilt of nations: Restitution and negotiating historical injustices.* New York: Norton.

Bar-On, D. (1989). *Legacy of silence: Encounters with the children of the Third Reich.* Cambridge MA: Harvard University Press.

Bar-On, D., & Charny, I. W. (1990). The logic of moral argumentation of children of the Nazi era in Germany. *International Journal of Group Tensions, 22*(1), 3–20.

Bartlett, S, J. (2004). *The pathology of man: A study of human evil.* Springfield IL: Charles C. Thomas.

Bassiouni, M. C. (1999). Prosecution and punishment of perpetrators of genocide. In I. W. Charny (Ed.), et al., *Encyclopedia of genocide* (pp. 475–476). Santa Barbara CA: ABC-CLIO Publishers. (Oxford UK, 2000).

Bateson, G. (1972). *Steps to an ecology of mind: Collected essays in anthropology, psychiatry, evolution, and epistemology.* New York: Ballantine.

Baumeister, R. F., & Leary, M. R. (1995). The need to belong: Desire for interpersonal attachments as a fundamental human motivation. *Psychological Bulletin, 117*(3), 497–529.

Baumeister, R. F., Boden, J. M, & Smart, L. (1996). Relation of threatened egotism to violence and aggression: The dark side of high self-esteem. *Psychological Review, 103*, 5–33.

Baumrind, D. (1964). Some thoughts on ethics of research: After reading Milgram's "Behavioral study of obedience." *American Psychologist, 19*, 421–423.

Bazyler, M. J. (2003). *Holocaust justice: The battle for restitution in America's courts*. New York: New York University Press.

Beck, A. T. (1976). *Cognitive therapy and the emotional disorders*. New York: International Universities Press.

Becker, E. (1973). *The denial of death*. New York: Free Press.

Bennett, W. L., Gressett, L. A., & Haltom, W. (1985). Repairing the news; A case study of the news paradigm. *Journal of Communications, 35*(2), 50–68.

Berger, D. (2002). *The Rebbe, the Messiah and the scandal of orthodox indifference*. New York: Littman Library of Jewish Civilization.

Bergin, A. E. (1991). Values and religious issues in psychotherapy and mental health. *American Psychologist, 46,* 394–403.

Bettelheim, B. (1967). *The empty fortress: Infantile autism and the birth of the self.* New York: Free Press.

Bettelheim, B. (1969). *The children of the dream: Communal child-rearing and American education*. Toronto: Collier-Macmillan.

Blass, T. (Ed.) (2000). *Obedience to authority: Current perspectives on the Milgram paradigm*. Mahwah NJ: Lawrence Erlbaum.

Blitz, P. (1993). Parental collusions in destructiveness towards a child as a cause of subsequent psychiatric and emotional disturbance. Unpublished MSW dissertation, Bob Shapell School of Social Work, Tel Aviv University.

Bloch, D. A. (2001). A very special type of fun [Review of the book *To redeem one person is to redeem the world: The life of Frieda Fromm-Reichmann*] *Readings: A Journal of Reviews and Commentary in Mental Health, 16*(1), 6–11.

Boehm, E. H. (1999), The fates of non-Jewish Germans under the Nazis. In I. W. Charny (Ed.), et al., *Encyclopedia of genocide* (p. 298). Santa Barbara CA: ABC-CLIO Publishers. (Oxford UK, 2000).

Bollas, C. (1992). *Being a character: Psychoanalysis and self-experience*. New York: Hill & Wang.

Bopp, M. J. (1985). Contradiction and its resolution among the psychotherapies: Results of a preliminary investigation. In G. R. Weeks (Ed.), *Promoting change through paradoxical therapy* (pp. 271–301). Homewood IL: Dow Jones – Irwin.

Boszormenyi-Nagy, I., & Spark, G. M. (1973). *Invisible loyalties: Reciprocity in intergenerational family therapy*. Hagerstown MD: Harper & Row.

Bourke, J. (1999). *An intimate history of killing: Face-to-face killing in twentieth-century warfare*. New York: Basic Books.

Bowen, M. (1966). The use of family theory in clinical practice. In B. N. Ard

Jr. & C. C. Ard (Eds.), *Handbook of Marriage Counseling* (pp. 139–168). Palo Alto CA: Science and Behavior Books. (Original work published 1966 in *Comprehensive Psychiatry, 7,* 345–374)

Bowen, M. (1978). *Family therapy in clinical practice.* New York: Jason Aronson.

Brenner, C. (1957). *An elementary textbook of psychoanalysis.* New York: International Universities Press.

Bronfenbrenner, U. (1970). *Two worlds of childhood: U.S. and USSR.* New York: Russell Sage Foundation.

Browning, C. R. (1992). *Ordinary men: Reserve Battalion 101 and the Final Solution in Poland.* New York: Harper Collins.

Bruner, J. (1986). *Actual minds, possible worlds.* Cambridge MA: Harvard University Press.

Buber, M. (1953). *Good and evil, two interpretations: I. Right and wrong.* (R. G. Smith, Trans.) *II. Images of Good and Evil* (M. Bullock, Trans.). New York: Charles Scribner's Sons.

Buber, M. (1963). *Pointing the way* (M. Friedman, Ed. & Trans.). New York: Harper.

Bugental, J. F. T. (1965). *The search for authenticity: An existential-analytic approach to psychotherapy.* New York: Holt, Rinehart & Winston.

Bushman, B. J., & Cantor, J. (2003). Media ratings for violence and sex: Implications for policymakers and parents. *American Psychologist, 58*(2), 130–141.

Calley, W. L. (1972). Lieutenant Calley: His own story. In J. W. Baird (Ed.), *From Nuremberg to My Lai* (pp. 213–234). Lexington MA: Heath.

Camus, A. (1980). *Neither victims nor executioners* (D. MacDonald, Trans.). New York: Continuum. (First appeared serially in fall 1946 in issues of *Combat;* republished July–August 1947 in *Politics*)

Chang, I. (1997). *The rape of Nanking: The forgotten Holocaust of World War II.* New York: Basic Books.

Chang, J. (1992). *Wild swans.* New York: Doubleday.

Charny, I. W. (1971). Normal man as genocider: We need a psychology of *normal* man as genocider, accomplice or indifferent bystander to mass killing of man. *Voices: The Art and Science of Psychotherapy, 7*(2), 68–79.

Charny, I. W. (1972). *Marital love and hate.* New York: Macmillan.

Charny, I. W. (1972). We need a human language for reporting the tragedies of current violent events: Towards a model for the content, tone and dramatic mood of the broadcaster reporting the news of human violence. *International Journal of Group Tensions, 2*(3), 52–62. (Reprinted as A human language for newscasts of violence in *Strategies against violence* (pp. 200–211). Boulder CO: Westview Press)

Charny, I. W. (Ed.) (1978). *Strategies against violence: Design for nonviolent change.* Boulder CO: Westview Press.

Charny, I. W. (1980). Recovery of two (largely) autistic children through renunciation of maternal destructiveness in integrated individual and family therapy. In L. R. Wolberg & M. L. Aronson (Eds.), *Group and Family Therapy, 1980* (pp. 250–281). New York: Brunner/Mazel.

Charny, I. W. (1982). *How can we commit the unthinkable? Genocide: The human cancer.* In collaboration with C. Rapaport. Introduction by E. Wiesel. Boulder CO: Westview Press. (Republished as *Genocide, the human cancer: How can we commit the unthinkable?* New York: Hearst Professional Books [William Morrow], 1983. Translation into Portuguese, with new Introduction to this edition by the author and updated Bibliography: *Anatomia do genocídio: Uma psicologia da agressão humana.* Rio de Janeiro: Editora Rosa dos Tempos, 1998. Translated by Ruy Jungmann.)

Charny, I. W. (1982). The tragic illusion of self-defense. In *How can we commit the unthinkable? Genocide: The human cancer* (pp. 167–182). Boulder CO: Westview Press.

Charny, I. W. (Ed.) (1984). *Toward the understanding and prevention of genocide.* Boulder CO: Westview Press; London: Bowker Publishing.

Charny, I. W. (1986). Genocide and mass destruction: Doing harm to others as a missing dimension in psychopathology. *Psychiatry, 49*(2), 144–157. (Reprinted in Friedrichs, D. O. (Ed.) (1998), *State crime. Vol. 1. Defining, delineating and explaining state crime.* In *The international library of criminology, criminal justice and penology* (pp. 461–474). Dartmouth UK: Ashgate Publishing. (Originally presented in 1984 as: Genocide and mass destruction: The missing dimension in psychopathology. In *Toward the understanding and prevention of genocide* (pp. 154–174). Boulder CO: Westview Press; London: Bowker Publishing.)

Charny, I. W. (Ed.) (1988, 1991, 1994). Series: *Genocide: A critical bibliographic review.* London: Mansell and New York: Facts on File, Vol. 1, 1988, Vol. 2, 1991; New Brunswick NJ: Transaction Publishers, Vol. 3, *The widening circle of genocide,* 1994. See Krell, R., and Sherman, M. I., 1997 for Vol. 4 in the series, and Totten, S., 2005 for Vol. 5 in the series.

Charny, I. W. (1990). Marital therapy and genocide: A love of life story. In F. W. Kaslow (Ed.), *Voices in family therapy* [invited autobiographies of psychol-

ogists who contributed to the development of the field of family therapy]
(pp. 69–90). Beverly Hills CA: Sage.

Charny, I. W. (1992). *Existential/dialectical marital therapy: Breaking the secret code of marriage*. New York: Brunner/Mazel.

Charny, I. W. (1996). Evil in human personality: Disorders of doing harm to others in family relationships. In F. W. Kaslow (Ed.), *Handbook of relational diagnosis and dysfunctional family patterns* (pp. 477–495). New York: Wiley.

Charny, I. W. (1997). A personality disorder of excessive power strivings. *Israel Journal of Psychiatry, 34*(1), 3–17.

Charny, I. W. (1997). Which genocide matters more? Learning to care about humanity. In S. Totten, W. S. Parsons, & I. W. Charny (Eds.), *Century of genocide: Eyewitness accounts and critical views* (Foreword, pp. xiii–xix). New York: Garland.

Charny, I. W. (1999). Editor's Introduction: The Dawning of a New Age of Opposition to Genocide. In I. W. Charny (Ed.), et al., *Encyclopedia of genocide* (pp. lxi–lxxiv). Santa Barbara CA: ABC-CLIO Publishers. (Oxford UK, 2000).

Charny, I. W. (1999). An International Peace Army: A proposal for the long-range future. In I. W. Charny (Ed.), et al., *Encyclopedia of genocide* (pp. 649–653). Santa Barbara CA: ABC-CLIO Publishers. (Oxford UK, 2000).

Charny, I. W. (1999). "Ordinary people" as perpetrators of genocide. In I. W. Charny (Ed.), et al., *Encyclopedia of genocide* (pp. 451–454). Santa Barbara CA: ABC-CLIO Publishers. (Oxford UK, 2000).

Charny, I. W. (2002). A passion for life and rage at the wasting of life. In S. Totten & S. L. Jacobs (Eds.), *Pioneers of genocide studies* (pp. 429–478). New Brunswick NJ: Transaction Publishers.

Charny, I. W. (2003). A classification of denials of the Holocaust and other genocides. *Journal of Genocide Research, 5*(11), 11–34.

Charny, I. W. (unpublished manuscript). *How can the suicide bombers do it? Can we fight back?*

Charny, I. W., & Asineli-Tal, S. (2004), Study of "sex-less" (sex avoidant) young couples. *Contemporary Family Therapy, 15*(1–2), 197–217.

Charny, I. W., & Davidson, S. (Eds.) (1983). *The book of the International Conference on the Holocaust and Genocide. Book one. The conference program and crisis*. Tel Aviv: Institute of the International Conference on the Holocaust and Genocide.

Charny, I. W., & Fromer, D. (1990). A study of the readiness of Jewish/Israeli students in the health professions to authorize and execute involuntary mass euthanasia of "severely handicapped" patients. *Holocaust and Genocide Studies, 5*(3), 313–335.

Charny, I. W., & Fromer, D. (1990). The readiness of health profession students to comply with a hypothetical program of "forced migration" of a minority population. *American Journal of Orthopsychiatry, 60*(4), 486–495.

Charny, I. W., & Fromer, D. (1992). A study of attitudes of viewers of the film "Shoah" towards an incident of mass murder by Israeli soldiers (Kfar Kassem, 1956). *Journal of Traumatic Stress, 5*(2), 303–318.

Chomsky, N. (1968). *Language and mind.* New York: Harcourt, Brace & World.

Chorover, S. L. (1979). *From Genesis to genocide: The meaning of human nature and the power of behavior control.* Cambridge MA: MIT Press.

Christie, N. (1974). Definition of violent behaviour. In *International course of criminology: The faces of violence* (Vol. 1) (pp. 25–34). Maracaibo, Venezuela: Universidad del Zulia.

Churchill, W. (1997). *A little matter of genocide: Holocaust and denial in the Americas 1492 to the present.* San Francisco: City Lights Books.

Coleman, J. C. (1957). *Community conflict.* New York: Free Press.

Conquest, R. (1970). *The nation killers.* New York: Macmillan.

Coser, L. A. (Ed.) (1972). *Collective violence and civil conflict. Journal of Social Issues* (whole issue), *28*(1), 3.

Crocker, J. (2002). The costs of seeking self-esteem. *Journal of Social Issues, 58*(3), 597–615.

Cushman, P. (1995). *Constructing the self, constructing America: A cultural history of psychotherapy.* Reading MA: Addison-Wesley.

Dallaire, R. (1993). *Shake hands with the devil: The failure of humanity in Rwanda.* New York: Random House.

Darley, J. M., & Batson, C. D. (1979). "From Jerusalem to Jericho": A study of situational and dispositional variables in helping behavior. In A. Pines & C. Maslach (Eds.), *Experiencing social psychology: Readings and projects* (pp. 149–156). New York: Alfred A. Knopf.

Davidson, S. (1992). *Holding on to humanity – The message of Holocaust survivors: The Shamai Davidson Papers* (I. W. Charny, Ed.). New York: New York University Press.

Davis, M. W. (2003). *The sex-starved marriage: A couple's guide to boosting the marriage libido.* New York: Simon & Schuster.

DeAngelis, T. (1996). Psychologists' data offer profile of abusing clergy: Clergy who engage in sexual misconduct range from sexual predators to those who act in a time of weakness. *American Psychological Association Monitor*, August, 51.

Dell, P. F. (1989). Violence and the systemic view: The problem of power. *Family Process, 28*(1), 1–14.

Denes-Raj, V., & Epstein, S. (1994). Conflict between experiential and rational processing: When people behave against their better judgment. *Journal of Personality and Social Psychology, 66*(6), 819–827.

Des Pres, T. (1986). On governing narratives: The Turkish-Armenian case. *Yale Review, 75*(4), 517–531.

Dicks, H. V. (1967). *Marital tensions: Clinical studies towards a theory of interaction.* New York: Basic Books. (Paperback: London: Routledge & K. Paul, 1983.)

Dicks, H. V. (1972). *Licensed mass murder: A socio-psychological study of some ss killers.* London: Heinemann.

Doherty, W. J. (1995). *Soul searching: Why psychotherapy must promote moral responsibility.* New York: Basic Books.

Duriez, B., & van Hiel, A. (2002). The march of modern fascism: A comparison of social dominance orientation and authoritarianism. *Personality and Individual Differences, 32,* 1199–1213.

Dworzecki, M. (1977). The International Red Cross and its policy vis-à-vis the Jews in the ghettos and concentration camps in Nazi-occupied Europe. In Y. Guttman & E. Zuroff (Eds.), *Rescue attempts during the Holocaust: Proceedings of the Second Yad Vashem International Historical Conference, Jerusalem, April 1974* (pp. 71–110). Jerusalem: Yad Vashem.

Efran, J. S., & Greene, M. A. (1995). A profession of moralists: Of values, science and other therapeutic power plays. *Networker*, November, December, 75–81.

Eidelson, R. J., & Eidelson, J. I. (2003). Dangerous ideas: Five beliefs that propel groups toward conflict. *American Psychologist, 58*(3), 182–192.

Ellis, A. (1962). *Reason and emotion in psychotherapy.* New York: Lyle Stuart.

Ellis, A. (1987). The impossibility of achieving consistently good mental health. *American Psychologist, 42,* 364–375.

Ellis, A., & Harper, R. A. (1961). *A guide to rational living.* Englewood Cliffs NJ: Prentice-Hall.

Ellis, A., & Harper, R. A. (1968). *A guide to successful marriage.* Hollywood CA: Wilshire.

Elshtain, J. B. (1995). *Democracy on trial.* New York: Basic Books.

Encyclopedia of genocide (1999). I. W. Charny, Editor-in-Chief, et al. Santa

Barbara CA: ABC-CLIO Publishers. (Oxford UK, 2000). *In 2003 an e-book or electronic edition of the Encyclopedia was published on the Internet.*

Encyclopedia of world problems and human potential (1986). (2nd ed.). Munich: K. G. Saur. "Orchestrator" (Ed.), A. Judge. Published by the Union of International Associations [40 rue Washington, B-1050 Brussels, Belgium].

Epstein, S. (1994). Integration of the cognitive and the psychodynamic unconscious. *American Psychologist, 49*(8), 709–724.

Fancher, R. T. (1995). *Cultures of healing: Correcting the image of American mental health care.* New York: W. H. Freeman.

Ferguson, C. J. (2000). Free will: An automatic response. *American Psychologist, 55*(7), 462–463.

Festinger, L. (1957). *A theory of cognitive dissonance.* Evanston IL: Row-Peterson.

Fisher, L., Anderson, A., & Jones, J. E. (1981). Types of paradoxical intervention and indications/contra-indications for use in clinical practice. *Family Process, 20*, 25–35.

Forbes, H. D. (1985). *Nationalism, ethnocentrism, and personality: Social science and critical theory.* Chicago: University of Chicago Press.

Frank, J. D. (1967). *Sanity and survival: Psychological aspects of war and peace.* New York: Random House.

Frankenstein, C. (1966). *The roots of the ego: A phenomenology of dynamics and of structure.* Baltimore: William & Wilkins.

Frankl, V. E. (1959). *From death camp to existentialism: A psychiatrist's path to a new therapy.* Boston: Beacon Press.

Frankl, V. E. (1963). *Man's search for meaning: An introduction to logotherapy.* New York: Pocket Books. (Originally published in German in 1947.)

Franks, M. (1984). On conceptual and technical integrity in psychoanalysis and behavior therapy: Two fundamentally incompatible systems. In H. Arkowitz & S. B. Messer (Eds.), *Psychoanalytic therapy and behavior therapy: Is integration possible?* (pp. 223–247). New York: Plenum.

Freud, S. (1952–1974). *The complete psychological works of Sigmund Freud* (24 Vols.). Standard edition. London: Hogarth Press.

Freud, S. (1955). *The interpretation of dreams.* Reprint of Vols. 4 and 5 in *The standard edition of the complete psychological works of Sigmund Freud* (J. Strachey, Trans. and Ed.) London: Hogarth; New York: Basic Books. (Original work published 1900.)

Friedman, M. (1960). *Martin Buber: The life of dialogue.* New York: Harper.

Fromm, E. (1941). *Escape from freedom.* New York: Rinehart.

Fromm, E. (1951). *The forgotten language: An introduction to the understanding of dreams, fairy tales and myths.* New York: Grove.

Fromm, E. (1964). *The heart of man: Its genius for good and evil.* New York: Harper & Row.

Fromm, E. (1973). *The anatomy of human destructiveness.* New York: Holt, Rinehart & Winston.

Fromm, E. (1986). *For the love of life* (H. J. Schultz, Ed.; R. & R. Kimber, Trans.). New York: Free Press. (Originally broadcast in 1974 in a West German radio interview with Hans Jurgen Schultz, titled, "Hitler – wer war er und was heifst Widerstand gegan diesen Menschen?" ["Hitler – Who was he and what constituted resistance against him?"])

Gergen, K. J. (1991). *The saturated self: Dilemmas of identity in contemporary life.* New York: Basic Books.

Gergen, K. J. (1994). Exploring the postmodern: Perils or potentials? *American Psychologist 49*(5), 412–416.

Gilbert, G. M. (1950). *The psychology of dictatorship: Based on an examination of the leaders of Nazi Germany.* New York: Ronald Press. (Reprinted in 1979, Westport CT: Greenwood Press.)

Gilligan, C. C. (2002). *A new map of love: The birth of pleasure.* New York: Knopf.

Gilovich, T. (1991). *How we know what isn't so: The fallibility of human reason in everyday life.* New York: Free Press.

Glick, L. (1994). Religion and genocide. In I. W. Charny (Series Ed.), *The widening circle of genocide. Vol. 3 in the Series: Genocide: A critical bibliographic review* (pp.43–74). New Brunswick NJ: Transaction Publishers.

Glover, J. (2003). *Humanity: A moral history of the twentieth century.* New Haven: Yale University Press.

Goldfried, M. R. (2001). *How therapists change: Personal and professional reflections.* Washington DC: American Psychological Association.

Goldsmith, J. (1990). *McCarthy* (A Play). Milwaukee Repertory Theater, February 17. (Originally produced by Ron Sossi and Lucy Pollack at the Odyssey Theater Ensemble, Los Angeles, July 1988 through February 1989.)

Golomb, J., & Wistrich, R. S. (Eds.) (2002). *Nietzsche, godfather of fascism? On the uses and abuses of a philosophy.* Princeton: Princeton University Press.

Gordon, L. H., with Frondsen, J. (1993). *Passage to intimacy.* New York: Fireside (Simon & Schuster).

Gordon, L. H., with Frondsen, J. (1993). The art of anger; The art of fighting fair. Chapters in *Passage to intimacy* (pp. 111–119, 120–139). New York: Fireside (Simon & Schuster).

Gordon, T. (1970). *Parent effectiveness training: The "no lose" program for raising responsible children.* New York: Wyden.

Green, H. (1964). *I never promised you a rose garden.* New York: Holt, Rinehart & Winston.

Greenwald, A. G. (1980). The totalitarian ego: Fabrication and revision of personal history. *American Psychologist, 35*(7), 603–618.

Greenwald, A. G. (1988). Self-knowledge and self-deception. In J. S. Lockard & D. L. Paulhaus (Eds.), *Self-deception: An adaptive mechanism* (pp. 113–131). Englewood Cliffs NJ: Prentice-Hall.

Greenwald, H. (1973). *Decision therapy.* New York: Wyden.

Grotjahn, M. (1960). *Psychoanalysis and the family neurosis.* New York: Norton.

Grotstein, J. S. (2000). *Who is the dreamer who dreams the dream? A study of psychic presences.* Hillsdale NJ: Analytic Press.

Gutheil, E. A. (1967). *The handbook of dream analysis.* 2nd ed. New York: Washington Square Press.

Haley, J. (1976). *Problem-solving therapy: New strategies in effective family therapy.* New York: Harper.

Hall, C. S. (1959). *The meaning of dreams: Their symbolism and their sexual implications.* New York: Dell. (Originally published in 1953)

Hall, C. S., & van de Castle, R. L. (1966). *The content analysis of dreams.* New York: Appleton-Century-Crofts.

Hardcastle, V. G. (Ed.) (1999). *Where biology meets psychology: Philosophical essays.* Cambridge MA: MIT Press.

Hartman, D. D. (1984). Compliance and oblivion: Impaired compassion in Germany for the victims of the Holocaust. In I. W. Charny (Ed.), *Toward the understanding and prevention of genocide* (pp. 197–201). Boulder CO: Westview Press; London: Bowker Publishing.

Hendrix, H. (1988). *Getting the love you want: A guide for couples.* New York: Harper & Row.

Herman, J. L. (1992). *Trauma and recovery: The aftermath of violence – From domestic abuse to political terror.* New York: Basic Books.

Hinton, A. L. (1999). "Comrade Ox did not object when this family was killed." In I. W. Charny (Ed.), et al., *Encyclopedia of genocide* (p. 135). Santa Barbara CA: ABC-CLIO Publishers. (Oxford UK, 2000).

Hoffman, Y. (1975). *The sound of the one hand: 281 Zen koans with answers*. New York: Basic Books.

Horney, K. (1937). *The neurotic personality of our time*. New York: Norton.

Horney, K. (1942). *Self-analysis*. New York: Norton.

Horney, K. (Ed.) (1946). *Are you considering psychoanalysis?* New York: Norton.

Hornstein, G. A. (2000). *To redeem one person is to redeem the world: The life of Frieda Fromm-Reichmann*. New York: Free Press.

Jahoda, M. (1959). *Current concepts of positive mental health*. New York: Basic Books.

Janis, I. (1975). *Victims of groupthink: A psychological study of foreign-policy decisions and fiascoes*. Boston: Houghton Mifflin.

Janov, A. (1970). *The primal scream; The primal therapy: The cure for neurosis*. New York: Putnam.

Johnson, S. M. (1994). *Character styles*. New York: Norton.

Jones, R. (1979). The third wave. In A. Pines & C. Maslach (Eds.), *Experiencing social psychology: Readings and projects* (pp. 203–211). New York: Alfred A. Knopf.

Jones, S. L. (1994). A constructive relationship for religion with the science and profession of psychology. *American Psychologist 49*(3), 184–199.

Jourard, S. M. (1964). *The transparent self: Self-disclosure and well-being*. Princeton: Van Nostrand.

Jung, C. G. (1970). The fight with the shadow. In *Collected works of C. G. Jung* (2nd ed.) (pp. 218–226), Vol. 10. Princeton: Princeton University Press.

Kahneman, D. (1973). *Attention and effort*. Englewood Cliffs NJ: Prentice-Hall.

Kaplan, H. S. (1974). *The new sex therapy: Active treatment of sexual dysfunctions*. New York: Brunner/Mazel.

Kaslow, F. W. (1981). A diaclectic approach to family therapy and practice: Selectivity and synthesis. *Journal of Marital and Family Therapy, 7*(3), 345–351.

Kaslow, F. W. (Ed.) (1996). *Handbook of relational diagnosis and dysfunctional family patterns*. New York: Wiley.

Kelley, D. M. (1947). *22 cells in Nuremberg: A psychiatrist examines the Nazi criminals*. New York: Greenberg.

Kelly, G. A. (1955). *The psychology of personal constructs* (2 Vols.). New York: Norton.

Kelman, H. (1973). Violence without moral restraint: Reflections on the dehumanization of victims and victimizers. *Journal of Social Issues, 29*(4), 25–62.

Kempler, W. (1981). *Experiential psychotherapy within families.* New York: Brunner/Mazel.

Kesey, K. (1962). *One flew over the cuckoo's nest.* New York: Viking.

King, M. L. (1991). *A testament of hope: The essential writings and speeches of Martin Luther King, Jr.* (J. M. Washington, Ed.). San Francisco: HarperCollins.

Kinzel, A. F. (1971). Violent behavior in prisons. In J. Fawcett (Ed.), *Dynamics of violence* (pp. 157–164). Chicago: American Medical Association.

Kipnis, D. (1994). Accounting for the use of behavior technologies in social psychology. *American Psychologist, 49*(3), 165–172.

Kirsch, I., & Lynn, S. J. (1999). Automaticity in clinical psychology. *American Psychologist, 54*(7), 504–515.

Koch, S. (1992). The nature and limits of psychological knowledge: Lessons of a century qua "science." In S. Koch & D. E. Leary (Eds.), *A century of psychology as science* (pp. 75–97). Washington DC: American Psychological Association. (Original work published 1985, New York: McGraw-Hill)

Koch, S. (1999). Vagrant confessions of an asystematic psychologist: An intellectual autobiography. In S. Koch (Ed.), *Psychology in human context: Essays in dissidence and reconstruction* (pp. 21–48). Chicago: University of Chicago Press.

[Kohlberg, L.] (1996). Focus on Lawrence Kohlberg. Whole issue of *World Psychology, 2,* 3–4.

Kohut, H. (1984). *How does analysis cure?* Chicago: University of Chicago Press.

Kottler, J. A., & Carlson, J. (2001). *Bad therapy: Master therapists share their worst failures.* Philadelphia: Brunner-Routledge.

Krell, R., & Sherman, M. I. (Eds.) (1997). *Medical and psychological effects of concentration camps on Holocaust survivors. Vol. 4 in the Series: Genocide: A critical bibliographic review.* (I. W. Charny, Series Ed.) New Brunswick NJ: Transaction Publishers.

Kren, G. M. (1987). The Holocaust and the foundations of moral judgment. *Journal of Value Inquiry, 21,* 55–64.

Kren, G., & Rappoport, L. (1980). *The Holocaust and the crisis of human behavior.* New York: Holmes & Meier.

Krieger, D. (1999), International criminal court for genocide and major human rights violations. In I. W. Charny (Ed.), et al., *Encyclopedia of genocide* (pp. 362–364). Santa Barbara CA: ABC-CLIO Publishers. (Oxford UK, 2000).

Bibliography

Kuper, L. (1981). *Genocide: Its political use in the twentieth century.* London: Penguin Books; New Haven: Yale University Press, 1982.

Kuper, L. (1985). *The prevention of genocide.* New Haven: Yale University Press.

Kuper, L. (1990). Theological warrants for genocide: Judaism, Islam, and Christianity. *Terrorism and Political Violence. 2*(3), 351–379.

Laing, R. D. (1967). *The politics of experience.* New York: Pantheon Books.

Laing, R. D. (1970). *Knots.* New York: Random House.

Laing, R. D. (1972). *The politics of the family and other essays.* New York: Vintage.

Lakoff, G., & Johnson, M. (1980). *Metaphors we live by.* Chicago: University of Chicago Press.

Langer, E. J., & Moldoveanu, M. (2000). The construct of mindfulness. *Journal of Social Issues, 56*(1), 1–9.

Langs, R. (1999). *Dreams and emotional adaptation: A clinical notebook for psychotherapists.* Phoenix AZ: Zeig, Tucker.

Lankton, S. R., & Lankton, C. H. (1985). Ericksonian styles of paradoxical treatment. In G. R. Weeks (Ed.), *Promoting change through paradoxical therapy* (pp. 134–186). Homewood IL: Dow Jones – Irwin.

Lanzmann, C. (1985). *Shoah: An oral history of the Holocaust.* New York: Pantheon.

Lasch, C. (1995). *The revolt of the elites and the betrayal of democracy.* New York: Norton.

Latané, B., & Darley, J. M. (1970). *The unresponsive bystander: Why doesn't he help?* New York: Appleton-Century-Crofts.

Latané, B., & Darley, J. M. (1974). The unresponsive bystander: Why doesn't he help? In Z. Rubin (Ed.), *Doing unto others: Joining, molding, conforming, helping, loving* (pp. 113–123). Englewood Cliffs NJ: Prentice-Hall.

Le Bon, G. (1903). *The crowd: A study of the popular mind.* London: F. Unwin. (Translated from the French.)

Legters, L. H. (1984). The Soviet gulag: Is it genocide? In I. W. Charny (Ed.), *Toward the understanding and prevention of genocide* (pp. 60–66). Boulder CO: Westview Press; London: Bowker Publishing.

Legters, L. H. (1997). Soviet deportation of whole nations: A genocidal process. In S. Totten, W. S. Parsons, & I. W. Charny (Eds.), *Century of genocide: Eyewitness accounts and critical views* (pp. 113–135). New York: Garland.

Legters, L. H. (1999). Soviet deportation of whole nations. In I. W. Charny (Ed.), et al., *Encyclopedia of genocide* (pp. 521–523). Santa Barbara CA: ABC-CLIO Publishers. (Oxford UK, 2000).

Leiby, R. (1999, December 31). The enemy is us. Why do we hate? For the same reason we love. Because we are human: Born to hate. Born to kill. *Washington Post*, M09.

Lerner, M. J. (1980). *The belief in a just world: A fundamental delusion.* New York: Plenum.

Levay, A. N., & Kagle, A. (1977b). Ego deficiencies in the areas of pleasure, intimacy and cooperation: Guidelines in the diagnosis and treatment of sexual dysfunctions. *Journal of Sex and Marital Therapy, 3,* 10–18.

Levay, A. N., & Kagle, A. (1983). Interminable sex therapy: A report on ten cases of therapeutic gridlock. *Journal of Marital and Family Therapy,* 9(1), 1–9, 15–17.

Levi, K. (1982). *Violence and religious commitment: Implications of Jim Jones's People's Temple movement.* University Park: Pennsylvania State University Press.

Levy, D. M. (1962). The act as a unit. *Psychiatry, 25,* 295–314.

Lewin, K., Lippit, R., & White, R. K. (1939). Patterns of aggressive behavior. *Journal of Social Psychology, 10,* 271–299.

Lidz, T, Comelson, A. R., Fleck, S., & Terry, D. (1960). Schism and skew in the families of schizophrenia. In N. W. Bell & E. F. Vogel (Eds.), *A modern introduction to the family* (pp. 650–662). Glencoe IL: Free Press.

Lifton, R. J. (1961). *Thought reform and the psychology of totalism: A study of "brainwashing" in China.* New York: Norton.

Lifton, R. J. (1967). *Death in life: Survivors of Hiroshima.* New York: Random House.

Lifton, R. J. (1986). *The Nazi doctors: Medical killing and the psychology of genocide.* New York: Basic Books.

Lifton, R. J., & Markusen, E. (1990). *The genocidal mentality: Nazi Holocaust and nuclear threat.* New York: Basic Books.

Lindner, R. M. (1976). *The fifty-minute hour: A collection of true psychoanalytic tales.* New York: Bantam Books. (Original work published 1955)

Lowry, R. J. (1977). *A. H. Maslow: An intellectual portrait.* Monterey CA: Brooks/Cole.

Lynch, A. (1996). *Thought contagion: How belief spreads through society.* New York: Basic Books.

Lyons, J. (1970). *Noam Chomsky.* New York: Viking.

Mace, J. E. (1984). The man-made famine of 1933 in the Soviet Ukraine: What happened and why. In I. W. Charny (Ed.), *Toward the understanding and prevention of genocide* (pp. 67–83). Boulder CO: Westview Press; London: Bowker Publishing.

Mace, J. E. (1997). Soviet man-made famine in Ukraine. In S. Totten, W. S. Parsons & I. W. Charny (Eds.), *Century of genocide: Eyewitness accounts and critical views* (pp. 78–112). New York: Garland.

Mace, J. E. (1999). Ukrainian genocide. In I. W. Charny (Ed.), et al., *Encyclopedia of genocide* (pp. 565–567). Santa Barbara CA: ABC-CLIO Publishers. (Oxford UK, 2000).

Mansson, H. H. (1972). Justifying the final solution. *Omega, 3*(2), 79–87.

Maslach, C. (2000). An outsider's view of the underside of the Stanford Prison Experiment. My role in the Stanford Prison Experiment. Section in Zimbardo, P. G., Maslach, C., & Haney, C. (2000), Reflections on the Stanford Prison Experiment: Genesis, transformations, consequences (pp. 214–220). In T. Blass (Ed.), *Obedience to authority.* Mahwah NJ: Lawrence Erlbaum.

Maslow, A. H. (1943). The authoritarian character structure. *Journal of Social Psychology, 18,* 401–411.

Maslow, A. H. (1979). *The journals of A. H. Maslow* (R. J. Lowry, Ed.). 2 Vols. Monterey CA: Brooks/Cole.

Masserman, J. H. (1990). The dynamics of world concordance. *Journal of Contemporary Psychotherapy, 20*(3), 155–161.

Masters, W. H., & Johnson, V. C. (1970). *Human sexual inadequacy.* Boston: Little Brown.

May, R. (1972). *Power and innocence: A search for the sources of violence.* New York: Norton.

May, R. (1977). *The meaning of anxiety.* New York: Norton (Originally published in 1950 by Ronald Press)

Menninger, K. (1938). *Man against himself.* New York: Harcourt, Brace & World.

Menninger, K. (1942). *Love against hate.* New York: Harcourt, Brace.

Menninger, K. (1958). *Theory of psychoanalytic technique.* New York: Basic Books.

Merton, T. N. (1967). A devout meditation in memory of Adolf Eichmann. Reprinted in *Reflections, 2*(3), 21–23 (Merck, Sharp, & Dohme).

Milgram, S. (1964). Group pressure and action against a person. *Journal of Abnormal and Social Psychology, 69,* 137–143.

Milgram, S. (1965). Some conditions of obedience and disobedience to authority. *Human Relations, 18,* 57–76.

Milgram, S. (1965). Obedience (A Film). University Park: Penn State Audio-Visual Services [distributor].

Milgram, S. (1974). *Obedience to authority: An experimental view.* New York: Harper & Row.

Miller, A. (1981). *Prisoners of childhood: The drama of the gifted child and the search for the true self.* New York: Basic Books.

Miller, A. G. (1986). *The obedience experiment: A case study of controversy in social science.* New York: Praeger.

Milton, S. (1999). Wegner, Armin T. In I. W. Charny (Ed.), et al., *Encyclopedia of genocide* (pp. 610–612). Santa Barbara CA: ABC-CLIO Publishers. (Oxford UK, 2000).

Mintz, R. S. (1968). Psychotherapy of the suicidal patient. In H. L. P. Resnik (Ed.), *Suicidal behavior: Diagnosis and management* (pp. 271–296). Boston: Little, Brown.

Minuchin, S. (1974). *Families and family therapy.* Cambridge MA: Harvard University Press.

Minuchin, S., & Fishman, H. C. (1981). *Family therapy techniques.* Cambridge MA: Harvard University Press.

Minuchin, S., Rosman, B. L., & Baker, L. (1978). *Psychosomatic families: Anorexia nervosa in context.* Cambridge MA: Harvard University Press.

Mitscherlich, A., & Mitscherlich, M. (1975). *The inability to mourn: Principles of collective behavior.* New York: Grove.

Mowrer, O. H. (1961). *The crisis in psychiatry and religion.* New York: Van Nostrand.

Napier, A. Y., with Whitaker, C. A. (1978). *The family crucible.* New York: Harper & Row.

Nathan, P. (1943). Fascism makes you feel good. In *The psychology of fascism* (pp. 95–106). London: Faber & Faber.

Nathan, P. (1943). *The psychology of fascism.* London: Faber & Faber.

Neill, J. R., & Kniskern, D. P. (1982). *From psyche to system: The evolving therapy of Carl Whitaker.* New York: Guilford.

Neumann, E. (1969). *Depth psychology and a new ethic.* New York: G. P. Putnam. (Originally published in German in 1949.)

Nicholas, M. W. (1994). *The mystery of goodness and the positive moral consequences of psychotherapy.* New York: Norton.

Oliner, S. P., & Oliner, P. M. (1988). *The altruistic personality: Rescuers of Jews in Nazi Europe.* New York: Free Press.

O'Neill, N., & O'Neill, G. C. (1972). *Open marriage: A new life style for couples.* New York: Evans.

Orwell, G. (1949). *Nineteen eighty-four: A novel.* New York: Harcourt, Brace.

Palazzoli, M. S. (1978). *Self-starvation: From individual to family therapy with the treatment of anorexia nervosa.* New York: Jason Aronson.

Park, D. C. (1999). Acts of will? *American Psychologist, 54*(7), 461.

Peck, M. S. (1983). *People of the lie: The hope for healing human evil.* New York: Simon & Schuster.

Peng, K., & Nisbett, R. E. (1999). Culture, dialectics, and reasoning about contradiction. *American Psychologist, 54*(9), 741–754.

Peterson, C. (2000). The future of optimism. *American Psychologist, Special Issue on Happiness, Excellence, and Optimal Human Functioning, 55*(1), 44–55.

Phillips, D. P., & Hensley, J. E. (1984). When violence is rewarded or punished: The impact of mass media stories on homicide. *Journal of Communications, 34*(3), 101–116.

Piaget, J. (1973). The affective unconscious and the cognitive unconscious. *Journal of the American Psychoanalytic Association, 21,* 249–261.

Power, M., & Brewin, C. R. (1991). From Freud to cognitive science: A contemporary account of the unconscious. *British Journal of Clinical Psychology, 30*(4), 289–310.

Rapoport, A. (1974). *Conflict in man-made environment.* Baltimore: Penguin, quotation on p. 73.

Reich, W. (1945). *Character analysis.* New York: Orgone Institute Press.

Reich, W. (1946). *The mass psychology of fascism.* New York: Orgone Institute Press. (3rd, rev. and enl. ed. Translated from the German manuscript by Theodore P. Wolfe.)

Reverby, S. M. (Ed.) (2000). *Tuskegee's truths: Rethinking the Tuskegee syphilis study.* Chapel Hill: University of North Carolina Press.

Robinson, D. N. (2001). Sigmund Koch – philosophically speaking. *American Psychologist, 56*(5), 420–424.

Rokeach, M. (1960). *The open and closed mind: Investigations into the nature of belief systems and personality systems.* New York: Basic Books.

Rosenbaum, M. (Ed.) (1983). *Compliant behavior: Beyond obedience to authority.* New York: Human Sciences Press.

Rosenberg, V. M. (2001). Utopian thought: Between dreams and disasters. In A. B. Shostak (Ed.), *Utopian thinking in sociology: Creating the good soci-*

ety (Syllabi and other instructional materials) (pp. 8–12). Washington DC: American Sociological Association.

Rosenthal, A. M. (1964), *Thirty-eight witnesses*. New York: McGraw-Hill.

Rowan, J. (1980). Heresy-hunting in the AHP [Association of Humanistic Psychology]. *Humanistic Psychology Newsletter*, 4–7.

Rowan, J. (1976 and 1978). *Ordinary ecstasy: Humanistic psychology in action.* London: Routledge & Kegan Paul.

Rubin, Z. (Ed.) (1974). *Doing unto others: Joining, molding, conforming, helping, loving.* Englewood Cliffs NJ: Prentice-Hall.

Rubinoff, L. (1978). In nomine diaboli: The voices of evil. In I. W. Charny (Ed.), *Strategies against violence: Design for nonviolent change* (pp. 34–67). Boulder CO: Westview Press.

Rummel, R. J. (1990). *Lethal politics: Soviet genocide and mass murder since 1917.* New Brunswick NJ: Transaction Publishers.

Rummel, R. J. (1992). Power kills, absolute power kills absolutely. *Internet on the Holocaust, Special Issue 38*, 1–10.

Rummel, R. J. (1994). *Death by government: Genocide and mass murder in the twentieth century.* New Brunswick NJ: Transaction Publishers.

Rummel, R. J. (1997). *Power kills: Democracy as a method of nonviolence.* New Brunswick NJ: Transaction Publishers.

Rummel, R. J. (1999). China, Genocide in: *The Chinese communist anthill.* In I. W. Charny, (Ed.), et al., *Encyclopedia of genocide* (pp. 149–151). Santa Barbara CA: ABC-CLIO Publishers. (Oxford UK, 2000).

Rummel, R. J. (1999). Democide: A new inclusive concept proposed. In I. W. Charny (Ed.), et al., *Encyclopedia of genocide* (pp. 15–34). Santa Barbara CA: ABC-CLIO Publishers. (Oxford UK, 2000).

Rummel, R. J. (1999). Khmer Rouge and Cambodia. In I. W. Charny (Ed.), et al., *Encyclopedia of genocide* (pp. 132–136). Santa Barbara CA: ABC-CLIO Publishers. (Oxford UK, 2000).

Rummel, R. J. (1999). Power kills, absolute power kills absolutely. In I. W. Charny (Ed.), et al., *Encyclopedia of genocide* (pp. 23–34). Santa Barbara CA: ABC-CLIO Publishers. (Oxford UK, 2000).

Rummel, R. J. (1999). *Statistics of democide: Genocide and mass murder since 1900.* New Brunswick NJ: Transaction Publishers.

Ryan, R. M., & Deci, E. L. (2000). Self-determination theory and the facilitation of intrinsic motivation, social development, and well-being. *Ameri-*

can Psychologist, Special Issue on Happiness, Excellence, and Optimal Human Functioning, 55(1), 68–78.

Sachs, S. (1985). Action T4: mass murder of handicapped in Nazi Germany. Tel Aviv: Papyrus Publishing House, Tel Aviv University (Hebrew).

Sagan, C. (1994). Nuclear war: The perspective of a planetary astronomer. Santa Barbara CA: Nuclear Age Peace Foundation, Booklet 36 in the Waging peace series.

Salk, J. (1972). Man unfolding. New York: Harper & Row.

Saltzman, A. L. (2000). The role of the obedience experiments in Holocaust studies: The case for renewed visibility. In T. Blass (Ed.), Obedience to authority (pp. 125–143). Mahwah NJ: Lawrence Erlbaum.

Santoni, R. E. (1984). Nuclear insanity and multiple genocide. In I. W. Charny (Ed.), Toward the understanding and prevention of genocide (pp. 147–153). Boulder CO: Westview Press; London: Bowker Publishing.

Sanua, V. D. (1986). Letter to the Editor: The organic etiology of infantile autism: A critical review of the literature. International Journal of Neuroscience: An Interdisciplinary Journal of Brain Behavior Relationships, 30(3), 195–226.

Saposnik, A. (2001). How was it humanly possible? Yad Vashem Quarterly Magazine, 23 (Summer), 6–8.

Saul, L. (1956). The hostile mind. New York: Random House.

Saul, L. (1972). Psychodynamically based psychotherapy. New York: Science House.

Schofield, W. (1964). Psychotherapy: The purchase of friendship. Englewood Cliffs NJ: Prentice-Hall.

Schwartz, B. (2000). Self-determination: The tyranny of freedom. American Psychologist, Special Issue on Happiness, Excellence, and Optimal Human Functioning, 55(1), 79–88.

Šebek, M. (1994). Psychopathology of everyday life in the post-totalitarian society. Mind and Human Interaction, 5(3), 104–109.

Segal, Z. V., Williams, J. M. G., & Teasdale, J. D. (2002). Mindfulness-based cognitive therapy for depression. New York: Guilford Press. With a foreword by Jon Kabat-Zinn.

Seligman, M. E. P., & Csikszentmahalyi, M. (2000). Positive psychology: An introduction. American Psychologist, Special Issue on Happiness, Excellence, and Optimal Human Functioning, 55(1), 5–14.

Selzer, M. I. (1983). Compliance or self-fulfillment? The case of Albert Speer. In

M. Rosenbaum (Ed.), *Compliant behavior* (pp. 213–228). New York: Human Sciences Press.

Shafranske, E. P. (1990). Evil: A discourse on the boundaries of humanity: An introduction. *Journal of Pastoral Counseling 25*(1), 1–7.

Shawcross, W. (2002). *Deliver us from evil: Peacekeepers, war lords and a world of endless conflict.* New York: Simon & Schuster.

Shedler, J., Mayman, M., & Manis, M. (1993). The illusion of mental health. *American Psychologist, 48*(11), 1117–1131.

Sheehy, G. (1976). *Passages: Predictable crises of adult life.* New York: E. P. Dutton.

Sheleff, L. S. (1978). *The bystander: Behavior, law, ethics.* Lexington MA: Lexington Books.

Sherif, M., Harvey, O., White, B., Hood, W., & Sherif, C. W. (1961). *Intergroup conflict and cooperation: The robber's cave experiment.* Norman: University of Oklahoma, Institute of Group Relations.

Shore, M. F. (2000). Swimming in an empty pool: Research ethics in an unethical society. *Readings: A Journal of Reviews and Commentary in Mental Health, 15*(4), 11–15.

Simpson, E. L. (1980). Self-report of a complex simplifier. [Review of the book *The journals of A. H. Maslow*]. *Contemporary Psychology, 25*(11), 913–914.

Singer, J. D. (1968). Man and world politics: The psychocultural interface. *Journal of Social Issues, 24*(3), 127–156.

Smith, M. B. (1994). Selfhood at risk: Postmodern perils and the perils of postmodernism. *American Psychologist, 49*(5), 405–411.

Smith, R. W., Markusen, E., & Lifton, R. J. (1995). Professional ethics and the denial of the Armenian Genocide. *Holocaust and Genocide Studies, 9*(1), 1–22.

Somerville, J., & Shibata, S. (1982). Ecocide and omnicide, the new faces of genocide. Presented at the *International Conference on the Holocaust and Genocide.* See Charny, I. W., & Davidson, S. (Eds.), (1983), *The book of the International Conference on the Holocaust and Genocide* (p. 43, also pp. 27, 46, and 244). Tel Aviv: Institute of the International Conference on the Holocaust and Genocide.

Sontag, S. (1981). *Under the sign of Saturn.* New York: Vintage. (Original work published 1972, Random House)

Sperry, R. W. (1988). Psychology's mentalist paradigm and the religion/science tension. *American Psychologist, 48*(3), 607–613.

Sperry, R. W. (1993). The impact and promise of the cognitive revolution. *American Psychologist, 48,* 878–885.

Spitz, R. D. (1964). The derailment of dialogue: Stimulus overload, action cycles, and the completion gradient. *Journal of the American Psychoanalytic Association, 12,* 752–775.

Sprenkle, D. H., & Olson, D. H. L. (1978). Circumplex model of marital systems: An empirical study of clinic and non-clinic couples. *Journal of Marriage and Family Counseling, 4*(2), 59–74.

Staub, E. (1996). Preventing genocide: Activating bystanders, helping victims and the creation of caring. *Peace and Conflict: Journal of Peace Psychology, 2*(3), 189–201.

Stekel, W. (1953). *Sadism and masochism: The psychology of hatred and cruelty.* New York: Liveright.

Sternberg, R. J. (Ed.) (1990). *Wisdom: Its nature, origins, and development.* New York: Cambridge University Press.

Sternberg, R. J. (1997). *Thinking styles.* New York: Cambridge University Press.

Sternberg, R. J. (2000). Images of mindfulness. *Journal of Social Issues, 56*(1), 11–26.

Struckmeyer, F. R. (1971). The just war and the right of self-defense. *Ethics: An International Journal of Social, Political, and Legal Philosophy, 82*(1), 52–53.

Sutherland, S. (1992). *Irrationality: The enemy within.* London: Penguin.

Suzuki, D. T., Fromm, E., & De Martino, R. (1960). *Zen Buddhism and psychoanalysis.* New York: Grove.

Sykes, G. M., & Matza, D. (1957). Techniques of neutralization: A theory of delinquency. *American Sociological Review. 22,* 664–670.

Tapping, C. (1996). [Review of the book *Cuckoo forevermore.*] *Australia-New Zealand Journal of Family Therapy, 17*(4), 240.

Tauber, E. S., & Green, M. R. (1959). *Prelogical experience: An inquiry into dreams & other creative processes.* New York: Basic Books.

Tillich, P. (1952). *The courage to be.* New Haven: Yale University Press.

Tinbergen N. (1969). On war and peace in animals and man. *Reflections, 4*(1), 48–49.

Toch, H. (1983). The management of hostile aggression: Seneca as applied social psychologist. *American Psychologist, 38,* 1022–1025.

Totten, S., Parsons, W. S., & Charny, I. W. (Eds.) (1997). *Century of genocide: Eyewitness accounts and critical views.* New York: Garland. (Original work published 1995 by Garland as *Genocide in the twentieth century: An anthology of oral histories*)

Totten, S., & Jacobs, S. L. (Eds.) (2002). *Pioneers of genocide studies.* New Brunswick NJ: Transaction Publishers.

Totten, S. (Ed.) (2005). *Genocide at the millennium: Genocide: A critical bibliographic review, volume 5.* New Brunswik NJ: Transaction Publishers.

Tustin, F. (1972). *Autism and childhood psychosis.* New York: Science House.

Tustin, F. (1988). The "black hole" – a significant element in autism. *Free Associations: Psychoanalysis, Group Politics, Culture, 11,* 35–50. [Free Association Books, 26 Freegrove Road, London N79RQ]

Vaillant, G. E. (2000). Adaptive mental mechanisms. *American Psychologist, Special Issue on Happiness, Excellence, and Optimal Human Functioning, 55*(1), 89–98.

Viorst, J. (1986). *Necessary losses: The lives, illusions, dependencies, and impossible expectations that all of us have to give up in order to grow.* New York: Fawcett Gold Medal (Ballantine Books).

Vogel, E. F., & Bell, N. W. (1968). The emotionally disturbed child as the family scapegoat. In N. W. Bell & E. F. Vogel (Eds.), *A modern introduction to the family* (pp. 412–427). Rev. ed. New York: Free Press.

Vyse, S. A. (1997). *Believing in magic: Psychology of superstition.* New York: Oxford University Press.

Wallerstein, J. S., & Blakeslee, S. (1995). *The good marriage: How and why love lasts.* Boston: Houghton Mifflin.

Watchel, P. (1991). From eclecticism to synthesis: Toward a more seamless psychotherapy integration. *Journal of Psychotherapy Integration, 1,* 43–53.

Weeks, G. R. (Ed.) (1985). *Promoting change through paradoxical therapy.* Homewood IL: Dow Jones – Irwin.

Weeks, G. R., & L'Abate, L. (1982). *Paradoxical psychotherapy: Theory and practice with individuals, couples, and families.* New York: Brunner/Mazel.

Wegner, D. M., & Wheatley, T. (1999). Apparent mental causation: Sources of the experience of will. *American Psychologist, 54*(7), 480–492.

Wertham, F. (1966). *A sign for Cain: An exploration of human violence.* New York: Macmillan.

Whitaker, C. A., & Bumberry, W. M. (1988). *Dancing with the family: A symbolic-experiential approach.* New York: Brunner/Mazel.

Whitaker, C. A., & Keith, D. V. (1981). Symbolic-experiential therapy. In A. S. Gurman & D. P. Kniskern (Eds.), *Handbook of family therapy* (pp. 187–225). New York Brunner/Mazel.

Whitehead, A. N. (1911). *An introduction to mathematics.* New York: Holt.

Wickes, F. G. (1963). *The inner world of choice.* New York: Harper & Row.

Winnicott, D. W. (1950). Some thoughts on the meaning of the word democracy. In D. W. Winnicott (1986). *Home is where we start from: Essays by a psychoanalyst* (pp. 239–259). New York: Norton.

Winnicott, D. W. (1965). Hate in the countertransference. *Voices: The Art and Science of Psychotherapy, 1*(2), 102–109. (Originally presented in 1947 and published in *International Journal of Psychoanalysis, 30,* in 1949.)

Wolberg, L. R. (1954). *The technique of psychotherapy.* New York: Grune & Stratton.

Wright, R. (1994). *The moral animal: The new science of evolutionary psychology and everyday life.* New York: Pantheon.

Wynne, L. C., Ryckoff, I. M., Day, J., & Hirsch, S. I. (1958). Pseudomutuality in the family relations of schizophrenics. *Psychiatry, 21,* 205–220. (Reprinted in Bell, N. W., & Vogel, E. V. [Eds.] [1968]. *A modern introduction to the family* [pp. 628–649]. New York: Free Press.)

Yalom, I. D. (1980). *Existential psychotherapy.* New York: Basic Books.

Zimbardo, P. G. (1973). On the ethics of intervention in human psychological research: With special reference to the Stanford Prison Experiment. *Cognition, 2,* 243–256.

Zimbardo, P. G. (1989). *Quiet rage: The Stanford Prison Experiment video.* Stanford CA: Stanford University.

Zimbardo, P. G., & Funt, A. (1992). *Candid camera classics in social psychology: Viewer's guide and instructor's manual.* New York: McGraw-Hill.

Zimbardo, P. G., Haney, C., Banks, W. C., & Jaffe, D. (1974). The psychology of imprisonment: Privation, power, and pathology. In Z. Rubin (Ed.). *Doing unto others* (pp. 61–73). Englewood Cliffs NJ: Prentice-Hall.

Zimbardo, P. G., Haney, C., Banks, W. C., & Jaffe, D. (1973, April 8). The mind is a formidable jailer: A Pirandellian prison. *New York Times Magazine.*

Zimbardo, P. G., Haney, C., Banks, W. C., & Jaffe, D. (1975). The psychology of imprisonment, privation, power, and pathology. In D. Rosenhan & P. London (Eds.), *Theory and research in abnormal psychology* (pp. 270–287). 2nd ed. New York: Holt, Rinehart & Winston.

Zimbardo, P. G., Maslach, C., & Haney, C. (2000). Reflections on the Stanford Prison Experiment: Genesis, transformations, consequences. In T. Blass (Ed.), *Obedience to authority* (pp. 193–237). Mahwah NJ: Lawrence Erlbaum.

Index

Aarvik, Egil, 411n2
abnormality: definition of, 305
absolutism, 86–91
accomplices, 200–201
Ackerman, Nathan, 107
Adalian, Rouben, 375
Adler, Alfred, 341
Adorno, Theodor W., 306, 388n2
Aeschylus, 413–414n15
Afghanistan, 305
"agentic state" (in Milgram experiment), 109
aggression, for self-defense, 134–135. *See also* self-defense
Ahmed, N., 424–425n12
Alexander Technique, 157, 207
all-or-none behavior, 282–295
Allport, Gordon, 408–409n23
al-Qaeda, 283
Alvarez, Alex, 143–144
American Orthopsychiatric Association, 313, 357, 373
Amin, Idi, 101, 104
Anderson, Carol M., 402–403n5
anger, 205–206, 275–276, 292–295; disconnection from, and tendency to violence, 412n4; fantasies of, and how to enjoy using, 268–269; feeling, versus committing actual violence, 7, 266–270; along with hate and murderous feelings, acceptance of, 266–270; healthy, at unfairness of life, 252; as natural, 181–182, 266–270, 341–342, 358, 360, 400n8; proper communication of, to others, 138; proper uses of, 195–197
anger and love, integrating. *See* love and hate, integrating
Annan, Kofi, 148, 368

anorexia: fascist mindset within, 63, 214–215, 318, 365–366, 372–373
antifascist tools and interventions in psychotherapy, 19, 49–52, 189–253, 318–321
anti-Semitism, 101, 107, 349, 350
anxiety, 3, 6, 70, 86–91; acceptance of, and falling asleep, 296–298; accepting and welcoming, 158, 165–167, 173, 275–276; and complexity, uncertainty, and humility, 20–22; disconnection and escape from, 20–22; inducement of, 401–402n1; and tapping unfulfilled potential, 275–276; and Zen Buddhism, 401–402n1
apologies for doing harm, 141–153; in family life, 185; in family therapy, 151–153
Arendt, Hannah, 7
Argentina: disappearances from, 327, 365
Arieti, Silvano, 153
Armenian Genocide, 147, 283, 316, 337, 374, 426–427n18; denial of, by Turkey, 184–185, 337, 400n12. *See* Wegner, Armin T.
Aron, Raymond, 379n4
Aronson, Ronald, 306
Asch, Solomon E.: and Asch experiment, 6, 99
Asineli-Tal, Shlomit, 385n52
Askenasy, Hans, 391–393n7
Assad, Hafez, 365
Atta, Mohamed, 365
Aum cult, 99, 104, 107–108, 390n5, 394n14
Auschwitz: as symbol of denial and guilt, 117
authoritarian personality, 22–24, 388n2
autism, 152–153, 274, 308, 413n11, 416–417n20; understanding, 186–188, 400–401n15, 401n16

church and destructiveness, 333

Clancy, Tom, 364

codependency, 323–324; in family life, 200; in psychotherapy, 203, 207–208

coercion and subordination: disorders of, 102–105

cognitive dissonance, 290–294

Coleman, James C., 289, 291

complexity: and anxiety, uncertainty, and humility, 20–22; disconnection and escape from, 20–22; processing and containing, 81–86, 161–171

conflict: avoidance, 219–220; community, 289–292; Gresham's law of, 291; process as valued, 159, 179–182; resolution and DEMOCRATIC MIND, 179–182

conformity and obedience: and danger of human extinction, 109; and religious experience, 110–111; resistance to, 108–112. See also obedience, to authority and conformity

confusion: accepting and containing, 161–162, 271–275

consistency: overcoming need for total, 287–290. See also cognitive dissonance

Consortium on Peace Research Education and Development (COPRED), 373

contradiction: acceptance of, 81–86, 251–253, 271–276; experiences of, and DEMOCRATIC MIND, 162–163; and healthy minds, 27; inability to bear, 335–343; as symphony of opposing feelings, 84; working with, 204–210

Coser, Lewis A., 89

couples. See marital relations; marital therapy

courage: to be responsible for doing harm, 151–153

Crawford, Joan, 411–412n3

Crile, George, 423–424n11

criticism and critical feelings: acceptance of, in couple therapy, 340; as creative, 69–70; integrating, with caring, 271–275; and loyalty, 288; role of critic and change agent with regard to, 343–345;

teenagers' developing ability for, 271–272. See also freedom of speech and dissent

cruelty, 144–145

Csikszentmahalyi, Mihaly, 250

cults, 99

Cushman, Philip, 418–419n32

Dallaire, Roméo, 368

Davidson, Shamai, 372, 374

Davis, Michelle Weiner, 385n52

DeAngelis, Tori, 412n4

decision to die, 3

definitionalism: example of, 8

dehumanization: and devaluing victims, 115, 117, 143–144, 387n11; and devaluing even relatives, 353

De ira [ire] (fourth-century book on psychology of anger), 269–270

Dell, Paul F., 21–22

demands of children and marital partners, 55–56, 60, 65–66, 88, 97–99, 145, 178

De Martino, Richard, 401–402n1

democracies: and denials of destructiveness, 141–142; and protecting truth, 142

DEMOCRATIC MIND, 2–7, 58, 65–66, 69–71, 84, 86, 96; acceptance of basic impulses as, 137–138; acceptance of contradictory ideas and experiences as, 70, 161–171; accepting anxiety in, 165–171, 173; accepting responsibility for doing harm in, 147–153, 182–188; and anger and aggression, 137–138, 181–182; and appreciating being upset, 164; and conflict resolution, 179–182; and controls against power, 176–179; and criticalness of one's own cause, 334–335; discovering applications of, in everyday life, 254–303; and equality, 176–179; and feedback about superiority, 346–347; fostering awareness of badness and imperfection, 122, 137; and the imperative of caring for life, 136, 140; and joy and libidinality, 181;

DEMOCRATIC MIND (*cont.*)

and learning and growing, 303; and machinery for evaluation of emotions, 138; and management of conflict in life, 140; in marriage and family life, 65–66, 70–71; and nonviolence, 179–182; and objective reality, 168–169; as openmindedness, 91–96, 161–171, 305; and orchestrating different parts of oneself, 122, 137, 254–303, 312; and realizing greater fulfillment of life, 70, 169–170; and recognizing criticism as creative, 69–70; and recognizing distinctions between feelings and actions, 137–138; and sharing power and leadership, 113, 121; in standing up for oneself and for others, 345; summary of, 157–159; and training for democracy and psychotherapy, 189–253; in unified theory of self, family, and society, 304–329

DEMOCRATIC MIND versus FASCIST MIND, 81 (Table 1), 157–188, 330

denial: of doing harm to oneself or to others, 141–153; language-logic techniques of, 143–144; of genocide, 337–338, 374 (*see also* Armenian Genocide)

destructiveness, 292; as insanity, 306; stopping tendency toward, 290–294; as a strategy to protect one's life, 324–325. *See also* ordinary people and destructiveness

dialectical processes, 52, 89, 93–94, 204–209, 251–253, 386–387; as antifascist techniques, 204–209; compared to logical processes, 84–85; used to enhance diminished traits, 204; used to reduce excessive traits, 204

Dicks, Henry V., 391–393n7

dictators, 113–118

differences of opinions: welcoming, 173–174, 179–182

disorders of coercion and subordination of others, 102–105

disorders of conformity and obedience, 102–105

dissent: punishment of, 35–41, 59–60, 97–112; respect for, 97–112, 171–176; within one's mind, 44–48

diversity: processing and containing, 81–86, 161–171

Doherty, William J., 418–419n32

dreams, 158, 266, 297, 298–302

DSM (*Diagnostic and statistical manual of mental disorders*), 99, 390–391n6

Duke, David, 423–424n11

Duriez, Bart, 386–387n4

Dworzecki, Meir, 423–426

dying: accepting fear of, 265–266; and decision to die, 3

Earth: future of, 272–273, 428–429n43

eating disorders, 3. *See also* anorexia

ecocide, 104; definition of, 393n8

educational system: failures of, 24

Efran, Jay S., 418–419n32

Ellis, Albert, 44, 322

emotions: totality of, 292

emotions versus actions. *See* feelings versus actions

empiricism, 91–96

Encyclopedia of genocide, 375, 420–422n2, 426–427n18

Encyclopedia of world problems and human potential, 27, 328, 417n31

energy: full momentum of, 283–285

Enver, 114

epistemology, 6–10

equality: couples and, 323–324; and inequality, 3, 66, 113–124, 176–179, 250, 323–324, 341–351; intrinsic, even in unequal relationships, 347

errors: acknowledging when possible, 347–349

"escape from freedom," 20, 24

ethical values: and mental-health clinical practice, 313–318

ethics: and psychology, 307, 313–318

eugenics, 41–42

Index

Jahoda, Marie, 250
Janis, Irving, 106
Japanese: destructiveness in Manchuria
and denial, 184, 333, 337–378, 420n2;
emperor, 285
Japanese Unit 731: and murderous medi-
cal experiments, 333, 338, 420n2
Jehovah's Witnesses, 349
Jemal, 114
Jewish ethical tradition, 8
John Paul II (pope), 420–422n4
Johnson, Virginia C., 212, 213–214, 233,
404n11
Jones, Reverend Jim, 100–101
Jonestown cult, 99, 100–101, 104
Jourard, Sidney M., 209
joy: in being alive, 3
Jung, Carl G., 115

Kahneman, Daniel: and pessimism about
human decision making, 25–26
Kaplan, Helen S., 404n11
Karzai, Hamid, 305, 415n5
Kaslow, Florence W., 406n16
Kelley, Douglas M., 391–393n7
Kelley, Truman Lee, 42
Kelman, Herbert, 373
Kfar Kassem, 335, 416n19, 423n8
Khan, Ghengis, 114
Khmer Rouge, 62–63, 353
Khomeini, Ayatollah, 18
kibbutz children: Bettleheim's observa-
tions of, 30
killing: as natural imagery, 266; joy of,
399n7
killing fields: in Cambodia, 62
King, Martin Luther, 370, 397n1
Kinzel, Augustus F., 412n4
Kipnis, David, 408–409n23
knowledge: purpose being to promote
life, 304, 415n3, 417–418n31
Koch, Sigmund, 249–250
Koresh, David, 100–101
Kosovo: NATO intervention in, 368
Kottler, Jeffrey, 388n15

Krell, Robert, 374
Kren, George, 39
Kuper, Leo, 368, 394–395n20, 396n1

Laing, Ronald D., 308, 322, 387n12
Langs, Robert, 414n25
Lankton, Carol H., 52
Lankton, Stephen R., 52
Lanzmann, Claude (*Shoah*), 416n19,
423n8
Lasch, Christopher, 379n4
law and genocide, 417n30
leaders, 113–118
"learned helplessness": concept of, 250
learning to care about human life as a
psychological developmental process,
324–327. *See also* life
Leiby, Richard, 17
L'Estrange, R., 413n10
Levinson, Daniel, 306
Levy, David M., 413–414n15
life: and balancing our lives and goals,
208, 331–332; and a "Campaign for
Life," 397n1; and the concept live and
let live, 329; dedication of this book
to, 377; and learning to care for, 324–
327; and losses, 366; overcommitment
to, as a possible basis for fascism,
327–328; respect and caring for, 2–10,
111–112, 115, 126, 136–140, 151, 181, 207–
208, 255, 291–292, 295, 304–329, 396n1,
417n31; ruining, 195–196
Lifton, Robert Jay, 18, 39, 40, 140, 306,
308, 373, 384n41, 397n1, 400n12
losses in life, 366
love and hate: integrating, 84, 94–96, 122,
159, 272, 274, 288, 290–291, 292–295,
389n5
love: demands for, 321
loving: accepting and containing, 270–271
loyalty and criticism, 288
Lynch, Aaron, 35

madness: as a fascist certainty, 295–296;

464